Selected Readings in Speech Communication

D1409475

JANE BLANKENSHIP

UNIVERSITY OF MASSACHUSETTS, AMHERST

First edition entitled:
Selected Readings in Public Speaking,
eds., Jane Blankenship and Robert Wilhoit

Dickenson Publishing Company, Inc.
Encino, California
Belmont, California

ISBN-0-8221-0108-4

Library of Congress Catalog Card Number: 73-76615

Printed in the United States of America

Printing (last digit): 9 8 7 6 5 4 3 2 1

Contents

Preface

This revised collection of readings retains its original twofold purpose: (1) as a core of material around which the teacher can design a course in speech communication, and (2) as a collateral reader to be used in conjunction with textbooks in public speaking and speech communication. The collection attempts to present a consistent point of view—that of speech communication as a dynamic, persuasive and pervasive force in our contemporary society.

The material included in this book has been written by scholars of rhetorical and communication theory, psychology, linguistics, and sociology. From their various orientations, most of these writers view communication as persuasion. Persuasion is, here, broadly conceived to range from unintentional persuasion, through the various forms of identification, to intentional attempts to change the attitudes and opinions of others.

Since we believe the student, even the beginning student, should be exposed to as wide a range of material as possible, we have included various types of readings. Some reveal a humanistic approach to rhetoric and speech communication; others, a behavioral approach. This is done on the assumption that both approaches have much to offer and that each may be better illuminated when juxtaposed with the other.

My thanks go to Robert Wilhoit who edited the original *Readings* with me; to my colleagues at the University of Massachusetts who have offered many suggestions; to Mike Snell of Dickenson who encouraged us to do the second edition; to Linda Malevitz Hashmi, my production editor; and to Barbara Loveland for her help in preparing the manuscript. My thanks also go to Hermann Stelzner, Edward Murphy, and Marie Rosen-wasser, who team teach a freshman criticism class with me, for preparing original articles especially for this book. But, especially, my thanks must go to those who used the first edition and who over the past few years offered suggestions for deletion and inclusion in this second edition. It is my hope that, together, we have made this a useful book.

Jane Blankenship
University of Massachusetts, Amherst

Introduction

This book is concerned largely with that species of speech communication called *a* speech. What is a speech? Very generally, it is a verbal communication shaped by a certain kind of subject matter, a certain kind of intent, and a certain form. Let us discuss the implications of this definition.

Subject Matter

A speech is characterized by a certain kind of subject matter. In casual conversation, clearly we talk about all kinds of topics. These topics may range from the weather, the latest American League standings and the Humphrey Bogart film festival at the Student Union, to troop withdrawls in Indochina, the potentiality for new flare-ups in the Middle East, or the financial plight of the cities.

Let us consider some of these topics briefly. First, most of us talk about the weather in casual conversation. We say such things as: "Do you think it will ever stop raining?" or "This kind of weather makes you want to go fishing." While, in a limited sense, we exchange "information" in such communications, our primary purpose is to establish rapport, to "commune" with one another. Few of us, perhaps with the exception of meteorologists or Mark Twain,[1] would give a formal speech about the weather.

We often talk about baseball (or football, or tennis, or hockey, or lacrosse, etc.) casually. We may say: "Did you hear about the White Sox's trade with the Yankees?" or "Tom Seaver just became the first National League pitcher to win nine games this season." In the Seaver example, the speaker goes beyond "communing" and offers explicit information. There is also implicit information: The maker of such a statement holds winning to be of value.

If we are film buffs, we may like to talk to our fellow addicts about the "oldies but goodies." For example:

"There's never been anybody who can match Bogart."

"Oh, I don't know about that. What about Cagney?"

"You going to see the *Treasure of the Sierra Madre* over at Campus Cinema?"

"No. I'd rather see a new movie."

"Did you see *Casablanca* last night?"

"Only the last part but I didn't think it was as good as *The African Queen*. Did you?"

Here, we have made explicit evaluations (new movies are better; Bogart is the best) and the attitudes revealed by those evaluations suggest one particular *action* rather than another, in this case going to see one movie rather than another.

The kind of communication in which we engage, the information we disclose, the attitudes we express, and the policy we formulate are affected by the *topic* of discussion. The topic "weather" does not lend itself to the same kind of subjective reverie that the topic "movies" does or the careful deliberation required in a discussion of the topic "Vietnamization."

When we discuss topics such as troop withdrawals from Indochina or the financial plight of the cities, we not only exchange information and express opinions, but very often find ourselves discussing explicitly stated programs of action (policies) and the like; e.g.,

> *Should* we withdraw all forces from Indochina?
> How *soon* should we withdraw all troops?
> How shall we *reorder our priorities* in peacetime spending?
> Which of several alternative Model Cities proposals should we undertake?

We prepare to act, do act, and evaluate our actions many times daily.[2] Observe how naturally *action* preoccupies us. For example, consider random TV shows on one day.[3] On NBC, the mayors of Atlanta, Gary, Boston, New Orleans, Wilmington, and Milwaukee talked about: revenue sharing, deterioration of city services, the busing problem, racial problems, and increases in the crime rate. On ABC, Senators Henry Jackson and Charles Percy talked about: the arms limitation pact with the USSR, a peace in Southeast Asia, and ABM. An evening newscaster talks of: political assassinations and assassination attempts, violence in Northern Ireland, and a variety of other topics. At a dinner party later that same night, conversation turned, among other topics to: tenure and promotion policies at the university, specific topics in the news such as recent wiretapping incidents, and attempts to clean up the Great Lakes.

Life Magazine of the same week covered such topics as:[4]

> Hubert Humphrey vs. George Schultz on taxes and government services;
> "An earthy preacher [who] . . . moves among the Ku Klux Klan and Blacks, building bridges";
> The Big Year Off—students taking a break between high school and college to learn about themselves.

Here one may ask: *Why* is it often *valuable* for many students to take a year off from school after high school? *How* can even an "earthy" preacher build bridges between the KKK and Blacks? Whose appraisal of taxes is more persuasive, that of Humphrey or that of Schultz? Once again we see how closely the topics for public discussion help us answer such questions as:

> (1) *Should* I (we) act?
> (2) *How should* I (we) act?
> (3) After I (we) have acted, how may I (we) *evaluate* the action?

Communications function in various ways and we may diagram the functions in a kind of continuum:

COMMUNION–INFORMATION–INTERPRETATION–EVALUATION–ACTION

Note that as the continuum proceeds it takes us from casual conversation to advocation of policies in formal situations. All along the continuum note how *choice* is involved. Communicators (whether speaking or listening) will ask: With whom will I communicate? What information, opinions, "feelings" do I wish to share? What information is relevant to the particular communication situation? Is my information complete enough and recent enough to be accurate? Have I used the best examples possible when I explain something? Is my interpretation valid? Have I checked it against varying interpretations? Have I made a careful evaluation or have I come to a hasty judgment? Have I looked at alternative ways of acting before I advocate one way rather than another? The questions could continue almost ad infinitum.

Communion, information, interpretation, evaluation, action are all inextricably tied to *choice*. Thus, we may observe that the subject matter of speech communication is implicit in choice situations where decisions must be made. That is why some have maintained that the speaker's preeminent concern is the giving of *good reasons:* good reasons for acting or not, good reasons for choosing one way of acting rather than another, and, good reasons for evaluating our actions the way we do.[5]

Today this emphasis on *good reasons* as the substance of oral discourse is perhaps more important than ever before. As a catalytic agent in the nurturing of human values, the speaker activates the "principles we believe in, the substance of things for which we live."[6]

Intent

A speech is characterized not only by a certain kind of subject matter, but by a certain intent as well. Clearly a large part of our speech communication is not aimed directly at attitude change or opinion change; we do not explicitly or even implicitly say to ourselves or to others, "The reason I am saying this is because I want to make you change your mind. . . ." As we observed earlier, much of communication is largely *communal* in intent and effect. We talk to others because through talk we *socialize;* through talk we *share* our thoughts and feelings, we *identify* with one another and that makes *cooperation* possible.

There may be times when we talk without the *conscious intention* of "being persuasive" but our talk has that *effect* anyway. People may be affected by who we are, what we have said in the past, our appearance and clothes, who we "represent," and what role we are playing in a particular situation.

Yet, most formal speeches *are* given to elicit a response. Few people give speeches to empty rooms or for the "sheer joy" of giving them. Even when we describe an event or show somebody how to do something, we likely want them to agree that our description is clear and accurate or that the method we are recommending is efficient. In short, often even in exposition, we are *seeking agreement.* We are attempting, at a very basic level, to persuade—to get the audience to *listen* to what we are saying, to accept us as somebody worth listening to.

In some speeches, the persuasive intent is still more clear. We ask people to vote for a certain candidate and to reject others; we ask people to accept one course of action rather than another. When we ask someone to accept our opinions as valuable, to follow the courses of action we propose, we are consciously trying to persuade them. Thus, speeches are verbal means of inducing cooperation or reconciliation in our society.

"Men want reasons to reconcile their minds to what is done, as well as motives originally to act right," said Edmund Burke. This "reconciling" goes on in our everyday conversation with friends as well as in the Congress and the Supreme Court.

This giving of reasons is, according to Donald C. Bryant, the act of "adjusting ideas to people and . . . people to ideas"[7] But whether it is called adjusting, reconciling, seeking agreement, or persuading, when the speaker gives a speech he is presumably asking his listeners to become somehow different than they were before. They will go away from his speech knowing something new, considering new courses of action, reconsidering old courses of action, and reaffirming old values or developing new ones. They have somehow been moved to action. Boulding discusses what kind(s) of changes in our behavior, our

Image of the world, result from the messages with which we are bombarded.[8] And, Clevenger points out that all messages, even those we dismiss as trivial or insignificant, *have* effects.[9] Contemporary communication theory seem to confirm the old aphorism, "No one steps into the same river twice."

Form

In addition to characteristic subject matter and intent, *a* speech has form. Although it does not have a rigidly prescribed form such as a sonnet, it does have *formal* characteristics. In large measure, speech form is dictated by the fact that it is *addressed* to an audience. Before determining what speech form is, let us explore more fully the concept of speech as *addressed.*[10]

Communication formally requires at least three elements: the speaker, the speech, and the spoken-to (listener). If the speaker is to facilitate cooperation, he has to shape his speech so as to identify with the spoken-to. Unless he does so, communication, whether one sentence or an hour long speech, has little chance of succeeding. "Identification" allows the speaker and the listener to recognize that they are alike in some ways. Through speech, then, the sharing of ideas, attitudes, opinions, and values is possible.

When any verbal communication takes place, it involves two or more separate beings. The speaker and the listener are different people who know different sets of facts, who hold different attitudes and who possess different "property" in the sense of both physical and intellectual goods. But by the very act of *saying* anything we are attempting to overcome these differences. We use words to allow us to coexist, to cooperate in the building of our community.

A speech, as we have noted earlier, derives its special form from the fact that it is *addressed* to someone. A speech therefore, must be designed to gain the attention (from a complex of competing stimuli) of the listener. It must employ "signs" which refer in some way to experiences common to both the speaker and the listener. A speech must be designed to arouse needs in the listener and suggest some ways to meet those needs. And lastly, a speech must be in a form appropriate to the situation and time.

In short, a speech is a response to a given situation, and although a speaker can talk "directly" to an increasingly large number of people via TV and radio, he has a conception of "audience" in his mind as he prepares the speech. Even the political speaker who often gives the same speech over and over generally gives that speech to audiences that share certain characteristics, or he adjusts to the specific characteristics of his audiences.[11]

Often speakers address one audience and are "overheard" by others. The 1972 "Address to the Russian People" by the President is a case in point. Notice some of the particular kinds of adaptation to the Russian people the President used.[12] Some were obvious; e.g., the greeting ("Dobry Vecher") and the closing ("Spasibo y Do Svidaniya"). Some adaptations may have had particular meaning to the Russians but had to be *interpreted* for other audiences:

Shortly after we arrived here on Monday afternoon, a brief rain fell on Moscow, of a kind that I am told is called a mushroom rain, a warm rain, with sunshine breaking through that makes the mushrooms grow and is therefore considered a good omen.

Some were Russian stories which could be enjoyed for their *implications* by the world audience as well:

> Some of you may have heard an old story told in Russia of a traveler who was walking to another village. He knew the way, but not the distance. Finally he came upon a woodsman chopping wood by the side of the road and he asked the woods-man, "How long will it take to reach the village?"
> The woodsman replied, "I don't know."
> The traveler was angry, because he was sure the woodsman was from the village and therefore knew how far it was. And so he started off down the road again. After he had gone a few steps, the woodsman called out, "Stop. It will take you about 15 minutes."
> The traveler turned and demanded, "Why didn't you tell me that in the first place?"
> The woodsman replied, "Because then I didn't know the length of your stride."

Some materials were drawn from the direct experiences of the Russian people but were ones the world audience could identify with because of their *associations* with the losses of any war:

> Yesterday, I laid a wreath at the cemetery which commemorates the brave people who died during the Seige of Leningrad in World War II. At the cemetery, I saw the picture of a 12-year-old girl. She was a beautiful child. Her name was Tanya. The pages of her diary tell the terrible story of war. In the simple words of a child, she wrote of the deaths of the members of her family. "Geine in December, Grannie in January. Lyosha then next. Then Uncle Vafya, then Uncle Lyosha, then Mama and then the Savizhevs." And then finally, these words, the last words in her diary: "All are dead. Only Tanya is left."

Whether the cemeteries are at Leningrad, or Normandy, or Arlington, most would agree with John Donne's comment:

> Each man's death diminishes me for I am a part of mankind.

We grieve also over *universal* bones.

The speeches which endure in our literature do so because they appeal to basic human values to which many generations can respond. Still, all have been shaped by the occasion and audience for which they were first intended. Churchill and Lincoln did not address only later generations, they also spoke to national audiences in their own moments of crisis. For as Nichols observes: "Great speeches reveal man at the intellectual crossroads of his public life. They are responses to situations that man has had to confront rather than to flee."[13]

Conclusion

We have argued here, very generally, that speeches are governed largely by the attempt to elicit responses from those who hear them. They are organized not only according to the logical principles of internal consistency of materials, but also according to psycho-logical principles of audience analysis.

Eternally, people have been concerned with action and with discourse which prompts it, directs it, and evaluates it. Many centuries ago Aristotle noted that people "have a sufficient instinct for what is true, and usually do arrive at the truth."[14] Even the cynic who does *not* believe that people have an "instinct" for the truth or those who would take a more pluralistic view and change the Aristotelian notion of "truth" to "truths," can agree with him that speech communication is a useful subject of inquiry for at least four reasons:

1. Things that are true have a natural tendency to prevail over their opposites, so if decisions are not what they should be, the defeat must be due to the speakers themselves.

2. Audiences, being human beings, do not even when they possess knowledge always feel moved to action, and therefore need to be persuaded by speakers.

3. Speech communication (of the best kind) involves thorough preparation through vigorous search and inquiry into the nature of things. This allows a person to see all sides of a question so that he can more clearly know *why* one side is better than another.

4. A person ought to be able to develop one of the most characteristically human qualities—power of speech—as a means of achieving the best kind of life he can.[15]

Because we view ourselves as free persons making free choices, our public communication (and almost all communication is *public* in character, even our conversations) contributes to the number and quality of decisions society is capable of making.

Notes

1. See, for example, Mark Twain's speech "The Weather," address at the New England Society's Seventy-First Annual Dinner, New York City, in *Mark Twain's Speeches* Albert B. Paine, ed. (New York: Harper, 1923), pp. 53-57.

2. "The Substance of Rhetoric: Good Reasons," *Quarterly Journal of Speech* (October, 1963), p. 241. The article is reprinted in full in this text.

3. June 18, 1972: "Meet the Press"; "Issues and Answers"; Garrick Uttley, NBC, "Sunday Evening News."

4. *Life Magazine* (June 16, 1972).

5. The Substance of Rhetoric," pp. 247-48.

6. Richard Murphy, "Preface to an Ethic of Rhetoric," in *The Rhetorical Idiom,* ed. Donald C. Bryant (Ithaca: Cornell University Press, 1958), p. 141.

7. "Rhetoric: Its Functions and Its Scope," *Quarterly Journal of Speech* (December, 1953), p. 413.

8. Kenneth Boulding, *The Image* (Ann Arbor: University of Michigan Press, 1961), pp. 3-18. The "Introduction" to *The Image* is reprinted in this text.

9. Theodore Clevenger, Jr., *Audience Analysis* (Indianapolis: Bobbs-Merrill Co., 1966), p. 40. See the chapter reprinted from Clevenger in this text.

10. This discussion follows the work of Kenneth Burke. See, for example, *A Rhetoric of Motives* (Englewood Cliffs, N.J.: Prentice-Hall, Inc., 1950).

11. Kurt W. Ritter, "Ronald Reagan and 'The Speech': The Rhetoric of Public Relations Politics," in J. Jeffrey Auer, ed., *The Rhetoric of Our Times,* (New York: Appleton-Century-Crofts, 1969), pp. 400-08.

12. From a mimeographed text of the speech supplied by the White House.

13. Marie Hochmuth Nichols, *Rhetoric and Criticism* (Baton Rouge: Louisiana University Press, 1963), p. 64.

14. *Rhetoric,* 1335a 15-17.

15. Ibid., 1355a 22-1355b 8.

Part One

Communication and Rhetoric

Because of the particular focus of this text, rhetorical communication, two terms may require definition: "communication" and "rhetoric." "Communication" is the broader of the two terms, so the first article in this section has to do with it.

Jurgen Ruesch and Gregory Bateson suggest that a human organism as a whole "can be conceived of as an instrument of communication, equipped with sense organs, the receivers; with effector organs, the senders; with internal transmitters, the humoral and nervous pathways; and with a center, the brain."[1] The anatomical analogy, although not precise, does allow us to compare the individual with a social organization in which messages are transmitted, relayed, and received. As the individual matures, he realizes the need to share and transmit information to obtain the views of others. It is this need for social interaction that is "the moving force" which compels human beings "to master the tools of communication."[2]

No two communication situations are alike, but as David Berlo in "A Model of the Communication Process" points out, "we can attempt to isolate certain elements that all communication situations have in common." We can construct a general communication *model* by ascertaining the *essential ingredients* in communication situations and by detailing their *interrelationships*. First, Professor Berlo asks: "What *is* a process?" Then, he asks: "What are the ingredients of the *communicative* process?" Lastly, he outlines a model of communication which includes message source, message, channel, and receiver. (Even at this early stage you may want to see alternative communication models. We have included sources of them in "A Further Note on Communication Models.")

Rhetorical communication is communication aimed at altering perceptions of reality; that is, rhetorical communication is *influential.* Marie Nichols, in her article, "The Constituents of the Rhetorical Act," defines rhetoric as verbal activity "primarily concerned with effecting persuasion, whether it be done by writing or speaking." She discusses the rhetorical act as a "multicelled organism" whose units consist of speaker, audience, place, purpose, time, content, and form. These units are inextricably associated with one another.

"Persuasion," Professor Nichols stresses, "requires choices among alternatives." The facts and opinions the speaker chooses reveal his "philosophic outlook and commitment." The words he chooses "contain not only rational meanings. They contain experience also and represent attempts to create and release emotional tensions." The speaker's arguments "are directives for action" directed at the motives of people. The speaker, again, chooses the particular motives to which he will appeal.

As she discusses the constituents of the rhetorical act, she tends to reinforce Berlo's comment that every "communication situation differs in some ways from every other one. . . ." Thus, the range of choices is wide, indeed.

In *all* communication situations, however, the speaker (A) is not *identical* with his audience (B). "But insofar as their interests are joined, A is *identified* with B. Or he may *identify himself* with B even when their interests are not joined, if he assumes that they are, or is persuaded to believe so."[3] As Kenneth Burke explains it: "In being identified with B, A is 'substantially one' with a person other than himself. Yet at the same time he remains unique, an individual locus of motives. Thus he is both joined and separate, at once a distinct substance and consubstantial with another."[4]

If people were not *apart* from one another there would be no reason for identification. Yet, precisely because there *is* division, identification is necessary to *compensate* for that division.

The range of ways in which we affect identification is wide. It can be deliberate as when a speaker says: "I was a farmer once myself." Or identification may take place when we identify with people who wear certain types of clothes, belong to the same organizations as we do, etc.

The brief selections from this author's writings, "Rhetoric as Identification" and "Establishing Identification" are meant to be illustrative materials for the fuller work of Kenneth Burke.[5] Basically, they take the position that too much emphasis has been placed on rhetoric as *manipulative* and that the essential talk of the speaker is often, if not always, to evoke in the audience a sense of "communion," a "sense of collaboration" which permits speaker and audience to work together to achieve the goals they commonly come to share.

Identification may be thought of as both means and end—it is the means through which we seek communion. and may also *be* that communion.

Wayne Brockriede in his article, "Dimensions of the Concept of Rhetoric," also conceives of rhetoric broadly. He terms it "the study of how interpersonal relationships and attitudes are influenced within a situational context. . . ." Such a definition, for example, "assumes the presence of the rhetorical impulse in such diverse acts as a speaker addressing an audience face to face or through mass media, a group of people conferring or conversing, a writer creating a drama or a letter to an editor, or a government or some other institution projecting an image."

Professor Brockriede focuses on what he terms the "interpersonal dimensions" of the rhetorical act—Liking, Power, and Distance. These three dimensions may be viewed as functioning both in an *instrumental way* and as *principal goals.* Liking, Power, and Distance function *instrumentally* as they have "some influence on a rhetorical act which aims primarily at attitudinal influence or situational appropriateness." They may often also represent the *principal goals* themselves.

You will note that Professor Brockriede also views the dimensions as "interrelational"; that is, "each dimension bears a relationship to every other dimension."

All of the writers included in this section hold the view that rhetoric operates in the area of the contingent where choice is possible, where decisions are called for. Thus, broadly speaking the rhetorical situation is a choice-making situation.[6]

In the last article in this section, Karl Wallace asks: If rhetoric is to be viewed as the art of adjusting ideas to people and people to ideas,[7] then what *ideas,* what *materials* do speakers adjust and adapt to their hearers? Thus, he turns to a discussion on the *substance* of rhetoric. He argues that the basic materials of discourses are values and information relevant to them. The substance of speeches consists of assertions and statements that concern human behavior and conduct: ". . . the foundation materials of speeches are statements that are evoked by the need to make choices in order that we may act or get ready to act or to appraise our acts after their doing. . . ." As "choosing itself is a substantive act," then, "the statement of a choice is a substantive statement."

Speakers consistently ask several fundamental questions: "What shall I do or believe? What ought I to do?" As they answer these questions they express or imply a series of judgments. "Judgments," as Professor Wallace points out, are "statements having to do with action, motives, feelings, emotions, attitudes, and values." Generally, values appear to fall into three all-embracing categories: the desirable, the obligatory, and the praise-worthy or the admirable. The substance of speeches, then, consists of the "good reasons" the speaker gives his audience as to why they should believe or do as he suggests they ought.

Notes

1. Jurgen Ruesch and Gregory Bateson, *Communication: The Social Matrix of Psychiatry* (New York: W. W. Norton Co., Inc., 1968, 1951), p. 12.
2. Ibid., p. 20.
3. Kenneth Burke, *The Rhetoric of Motives* (Berkeley: University of California Press, 1969), p. 20. Originally published 1950.
4. Ibid., p. 21.
5. Ibid., pp. 19-29; 35-37; 55-59.
6. Lloyd Bitzer, "The Rhetorical Situation," *Philosophy and Rhetoric* (Winter, 1968), pp. 1-14.
7. Donald Bryant, "Rhetoric: Its Function and Scope," *Quarterly Journal of Speech* (December, 1953), pp. 401-24.

A MODEL OF THE COMMUNICATION PROCESS

DAVID K. BERLO

Every communication situation differs in some ways from every other one, yet we can attempt to isolate certain elements that all communication situations have in common. It is these ingredients and their interrelationships that we consider when we try to construct a general model of communication.

We attach the word "process" to our discussion of communication. The concept of process is itself complex. If we begin to discuss a model of the communication process without a common meaning for the word "process," our discussion might result in distorted views about communication.

The Concept of Process

At least one dictionary defines "process" as "any phenomenon which shows a con-tinuous change in time," or "any continuous operation or treatment." Five hundred years before the birth of Christ, Heraclitus pointed out the importance of the concept of process when he stated that a man can never step in the same river twice; the man is different and so is the river. Thomas Wolfe's novel of the 1940's, *You Can't Go Home Again,* makes the same point.

If we accept the concept of process, we view events and relationships as dynamic, ongoing, ever-changing, continuous. When we label something as a process, we also mean that it does not have *a* beginning, *an* end, a fixed sequence of events. It is not static, at rest. It is moving. The ingredients within a process interact; each affects all of the others.

The concept of process is inextricably woven into the contemporary view of science and physical reality. In fact, the development of a process viewpoint in the physical sciences brought about one of the twentieth-century revolutions that we mentioned earlier. If we analyze the work of physical scientists up to and including Isaac Newton, we do not find a comprehensive analysis of process. It was believed that the world could be divided into "things" and "processes." It was believed also that things *existed,* that they were static entities, that their existence was independent of the existence or operations of other "things."

The crisis and revolution in scientific philosophy brought about by the work of Einstein, Russell, Whitehead, and others denied both of these beliefs in two ways. First, the concept of relativity suggested that any given object or event could only be analyzed or described in light of other events that were related to it, other operations involved in observing it. Second, the availability of more powerful observational techniques led to the demonstration that something as static or stable as a table, a chair, could be looked on as a constantly changing phenomenon, acting upon and being acted upon by all other objects in its environment, changing as the person who observed it changes. The traditional division between things was questioned. The traditional distinction between things and processes was broken down. An entirely different way of looking at the world had to be developed—a process view of reality.

Communication theory reflects a process point of view. A communication theorist rejects the possibility that nature consists of events or ingredients that are separable from all other events. He argues that you cannot talk about *the* beginning or *the* end of communication or say that a particular idea came from one specific source, that communication occurs in only one way, and so on.

The basis for the concept of process is the belief that the structure of physical reality cannot be *discovered* by man; it must be *created* by man. In "constructing" reality, the theorist chooses to organize his perceptions in one way or another. He may choose to say that we can call certain things "elements" or "ingredients." In doing this, he realizes that he has not discovered anything, he has created a set of tools which may or may not be useful in analyzing or describing the world. He recognizes that certain things may precede others, but that in many cases the order of precedence will vary from situation to situation. This is not to say that we can place no order on events. The dynamic of process has limitations; nevertheless, there is more than one dynamic that can be developed for nearly any combination of events.

When we try to talk or write about a process, such as communication, we face at least two problems. First, we must arrest the dynamic of the process, in the same way that we arrest motion when we take a still picture with a camera. We can make useful observations from photographs, but we err if we forget that the camera is not a complete reproduction of the objects photographed. The interrelationships among elements are obliterated, the fluidity of motion, the dynamics, are arrested. The picture is a representation of the event, it is not the event. As Hayakawa has put it, the word is not the thing, it is merely a map that we can use to guide us in exploring the territories of the world.

A second problem in describing a process derives from the necessity for the use of language. Language itself, as used by people over time, is a process. It, too, is changing, ongoing; however, the process quality of language is lost when we write it. Marks on paper are a recording of language, a picture of language. They are fixed, permanent, static. Even spoken language, over a short period of time, is relatively static.

In using language to describe a process, we must choose certain words, we must freeze the physical world in a certain way. Furthermore, we must put some words first, others last. Western languages go from left to right, top to bottom. All languages go from front to back, beginning to end—even though we are aware that the process we are describing may not have a left and right, a top and a bottom, a beginning and an end.

We have no alternative if we are to analyze and communicate about a process. The important point is that we must remember that we are not including everything in our discussion. The things we talk about do not have to exist in exactly the ways we talk about them, and they certainly do not have to operate in the order in which we talk about them. Objects which we separate may not always be separable, and they never operate independently—each affects and interacts with the others. This may appear obvious, but it is easy to overlook or forget the limitations that are necessarily placed on any discussion of a process.

To illustrate the point, let us take an example other than communication. Education is a process. In discussing education, we can list certain ingredients. We have students, teachers, books, classroom lectures, libraries, discussion, meditation, thought, etc. We can order the ingredients. We can say that, in education, a teacher lectures to students (50 minutes at a time, three days a week, for x years). We can say that a student reads books (6 books, 119 books, any number of books). We can say that the library has 100,000 volumes, or 1,000,000 volumes, or 6,000,000 volumes. We can say that students will hold x discussion sessions, spend y hours meditating, and write z papers or examinations.

When we put all this together, we can say that if all of these ingredients are available and have been used, the student has received "an education." We *can* say this, but if we do we have forgotten the concept of process, the dynamics of education. As any good cook knows, it is the mixing process, the blending, that makes a good cake; ingredients are necessary, but not sufficient.

For an example in the communication field, take the theatre. What is "theatre"? Again, we can list ingredients: a playwright, a play, directors, actors, stage hands, audiences, scenery, lighting, an auditorium. Add them, and the total is theatre? Definitely not. Again, it is the blending, the dynamic interrelationships among the ingredients developed in the process that determine whether we have what we would call "theatre."

We need to remember that the dynamic of movement which relates the ingredients is vital. The concept of dynamic also implies that factors that we may overlook in any single listing of the ingredients also determine what is produced.

The dynamic of theatre is in part related to whether the play is produced for an audience before or after they have eaten dinner, or whether they had a heavy or a light meal, whether they enjoyed it or disliked it. The dynamic of education is in part determined by whether the student has just come from another situation in which he learned something which still excites him or whether he is fresh and has an "uncluttered" mind, whether he is taking an elective course he chose himself or a required one, whether his classmates make comments which stimulate him, or whether he has only his own thinking to help him, and so on.

Much of the scientific research in communication attempts to isolate factors which do or do not make a difference in the development of the process. Obviously, all the ingredients have not been determined—in fact, there is considerable basis for doubt as to whether they ever will be determined.

In any case, we need constantly to remember that our discussion of a process is incomplete, with a forced order and possibly a distorted perspective. Discussion is useful; it can lead to greater insight about a process. But it is not a complete picture, it can never reproduce the process itself. We cannot list all the ingredients nor talk adequately about how they affect each other. We can provide some suggestions, some hints about both the ingredients and the dynamic of the process.

There have been approaches to analyzing communication that have not been process-oriented. Such approaches might be labeled as "hypodermic needle" concepts of how communication works, or "click-click; push-pull" points of view. Such descriptions of communication are restricted to saying that first the communicator does A, then he does B, then C happens, and so on.

Much of the early discussion of the effects of the mass media of communication were of the "hypodermic needle" variety. Critics as well as advocates of the print or electronic media (radio, TV) talked about how these media would affect the American public. Their concept of effects implied that a radio broadcast or a television program could be viewed as a hypodermic needle. If we would just stick these messages in the minds of the public, learning or entertainment or greater participation in civic affairs would be produced. The research conducted on the effects of the media indicates otherwise; whether or not these sources of communication are effective depends on a complex of factors, some of which the media can control and some of which they cannot.

Much of the debate over the effects of comic books on children, the effects of the movies, advertising, or political campaigns on the public is of this variety. Critics and commentators often overlook the effect of children on the contents of the comics, the effect of the public on movies, etc. It certainly is true that newspapers affect public opinion, but a process point of view argues that it is equally true that public opinion affects the newspapers.

With the concept of process established in our minds, we can profit from an analysis of the ingredients of communication, the elements that seem necessary (if not sufficient) for communication to occur. We want to look at elements such as *who* is communicating, *why* he is communicating, and to *whom* he is communicating. We want to look at communication behaviors: *messages* which are produced, *what* people are trying to communicate. We want to look at style, how people *treat* their messages. We want to examine the means of communication, the *channels* that people use to get their messages to their listeners, their readers. In short, we want to list the elements in the communication process that we must take into account when (a) we initiate communication, (b) we respond to communication, or (c) we serve as communication observers or analysts.

The Ingredients of Communication

The concern with communication has produced many attempts to develop models of the process—descriptions, listing of ingredients. Of course, these models differ. None can be said to be "right," or "true." Some may be more useful than others, some may correspond more than others to the current state of knowledge about communication.

In the *Rhetoric,* Aristotle said that we have to look at three communication ingredients: the speaker, the speech, and the audience. He meant that each of these elements is necessary to communication and that we can organize our study of the process under the three headings of (1) the person who speaks, (2) the speech that he produces, and (3) the person who listens.[1]

Most of our current communication models are similar to Aristotle's, though somewhat more complex. One of the most-used contemporary models was developed in 1947 by Claude Shannon, a mathematician, and explained to the nonmathematician by Warren Weaver.[2] Shannon and Weaver were not even talking about human communication. They were talking about electronic communication. In fact, Shannon worked for the Bell Telephone Laboratory. Yet behavioral scientists have found the Shannon-Weaver model useful in describing human communication.

The Shannon-Weaver model certainly is consistent with Aristotle's position. Shannon and Weaver said that the ingredients in communication include (1) a source, (2) a transmitter, (3) a signal, (4) a receiver, and (5) a destination. If we translate the source into the speaker, the signal into the speech, and the destination into the listener, we have the Aristotelian model, plus two added ingredients, a transmitter which sends out the source's message, and a receiver which catches the message for the destination.

There are other models of the communication process, developed by Schramm,[3] Westley and MacLean,[4] Fearing,[5] Johnson,[6] and others. The suggested readings at the end of the book list several of these. A comparison will indicate the great similarities among them. They differ partly in terminology, partly in the addition or subtraction of one or two elements, partly in the differences in the point of view of the disciplines from which they emerged.

In developing the model presented here, I have tried to be consistent with current theory and research in the behavioral sciences. It has been changed many times in the past few years, as a result of using it with students in the classroom, with adults in extension courses, and with workshops and seminars in industry, agriculture, and government. It is similar to other communication models and is presented only because people have found it a useful scheme for talking about communication in many different communication situations.

A Communication Model

We can say that all human communication has some *source,* some person or group of persons with a purpose, a reason for engaging in communication. Given a source, with ideas, needs, intentions, information, and a purpose for communicating, a second ingredient is necessary. The purpose of the source has to be expressed in the form of a *message.* In human communication, a message is behavior available in physical form—the translation of ideas, purposes, and intentions into a code, a systematic set of symbols.

How do the source's purposes get translated into a code, a language? This requires a third communication ingredient, an *encoder.* The communication encoder is responsible for taking the ideas of the source and putting them in a code, expressing the source's purpose in the form of a message. In person-to-person communication, the encoding function is performed by the motor skills of the source—his vocal mechanisms (which produce the oral word, cries, musical notes, etc.), the muscle systems in the hand (which produce the written word, pictures, etc.), the muscle systems elsewhere in the body (which produce gestures of the face or arms, posture, etc.).

When we talk about more complex communication situations, we often separate the source from the encoder. For example, we can look at a sales manager as a source and his salesmen as encoders: people who produce messages for the consumer which translate the intentions or purposes of the manager.

For the present, we shall restrict our model to the minimum complexity. We have a communication source with purpose and an encoder who translates or expresses this purpose in the form of a message. We are ready for a fourth ingredient, the *channel.*

We can look at channels in several ways. Communication theory presents at least three meanings for the word "channel." For the moment, it is enough to say that a channel is a medium, a carrier of messages. It is correct to say that messages can exist only in *some* channel; however, the *choice* of channels often is an important factor in the effectiveness of communication.

We have introduced a communication *source,* an *encoder,* a *message,* and a *channel.* If we stop here, no communication has taken place. For communication to occur, there must be somebody at the other end of the channel. If we have a purpose, encode a message, and put it into one or another channel, we have done only part of the job. When we talk, somebody must listen; when we write, somebody must read. The person or persons at the other end can be called the communication *receiver,* the target of communication.

Communication sources and receivers must be similar systems. If they are not similar, communication cannot occur. We can go one step further and say that the source and the receiver may be (and often are) the same person; the source may communicate with himself—he listens to what he says, he reads what he writes, he thinks. In psychological terms, the source intends to produce a stimulus. The receiver responds to that stimulus if communication occurs; if he does not respond, communication has not occurred.

We now have all the basic communication ingredients except one. Just as a source needs an encoder to translate his purposes into a message, to express purpose in a code, the receiver needs a *decoder* to retranslate, to decode the message and put it into a form that the receiver can use. We said that in person-to-person communication the encoder would be a set of motor skills of the source. By the same token, we can look at the decoder as the set of sensory skills of the receiver. In one- or two-person communication situations, the decoder can be thought of as the senses.

These, then, are the ingredients that we will include in our discussion of a model of the communication process:

1. the communication source;
2. the encoder;
3. the message;
4. the channel;
5. the decoder;
6. the communication receiver.

We will mention many other communication factors; however, we will return to these six ingredients again and again, as we talk about communication at various levels of complexity.

The Parts of the Model

What do we mean by a source, an encoder, and so on? Our preliminary discussion has given us the beginnings of a meaning for each of these terms—but only the beginnings. At this point, precise definitions of each term might not be as useful as a set of examples which include all the ingredients.

Let us start with a common communication situation: two people talking. Suppose it is Friday morning. We find Joe and Mary in the local coffee shop. There is a picnic scheduled for Sunday afternoon. Suddenly, Joe realizes that Mary is *the* girl to take picnic. Joe decides to ask her for a Sunday afternoon date. Joe is now ready to act as a communication source—he has a purpose: to get Mary to agree to accompany him on Sunday. (He may have other purposes as well, but they are not our concern.)

Joe wants to produce a message. His central nervous system orders his speech mechanism to construct a message to express his purpose. The speech mechanism, serving as an encoder, produces the following message: "Mary, will you go to the picnic with me on Sunday?"

The message is transmitted via sound waves through air, so that Mary can receive it. This is the channel. Mary's hearing mechanism serves as a decoder. She hears Joe's message, decodes the message into a nervous impulse, and sends it to her central nervous system. Mary's central nervous system responds to the message. It decides that Friday is too late to ask for a Sunday date. Mary intends to refuse the date, and sends an order to her speech mechanism. The message is produced: "Thanks, Joe, but no thanks." Or something somewhat more polite.

This is a very elementary and oversimplified treatment of the nature of the communication process, but it includes, at least superficially, all six ingredients we have introduced. Let us try another example.

Take the communication situation in which you are now engaged: reading this chapter. In this communication situation, I served as the writing mechanisms served as an encoder (of course, typewriters, typists, and printing presses also served as encoders). The message includes the words on this page, and the way that the words are arranged. The message is transmitted to you through the medium of a book, by means of light waves. Your eye is the decoder. It receives the message, decodes it, retranslates it into a nervous impulse, and sends it to your central nervous system. Your central nervous system is the receiver. As you read, you will make responses to the book.

Let us take another example, and look at it more closely. Suppose Bill and John are at the dinner table. Bill has a problem. He is ready to eat a sandwich. He likes salt on a sandwich. The salt is at John's end of the table. Bill wants the salt. What does he do? He could reach from his end of the table to John's end and get the salt himself; however, this not only would be rude, it would be work. More likely, Bill asks John to pass the salt. Being a congenial sort of fellow, John passes Bill the salt. Bill puts it on his sandwich. All is well.

Again, what has happened, in terms of our communication model? Bill's central nervous system served as a communication source. He had a need, *salt on sandwich.* He had an intention, a purpose, to get John to pass him the salt. Bill relayed this purpose as a nervous impulse to his encoder, his speech mechanism. His encoder translated and expressed his purpose in code—English—and produced a message. The message: "Pass me the salt, please."

Bill transmitted this message via sound waves, through the air, in such a way that John could receive the message. John's hearing mechanism caught the message, decoded it, and sent it on to John's central nervous system. John had meaning for the message, responded to it, and passed Bill the salt. Mission accomplished.

This is communication. These are elementary examples, but even here communication is quite complex. The process we have just described occurs in only a small fraction of the time it took to talk about it—and we oversimplified our description at that. What were some of the things that could have gone wrong?

Suppose Bill did not have a clear idea of his purpose. He knew he needed something for his sandwich but he did not know what he needed. How could he have instructed his encoder to transmit a message?

Suppose Bill did not like John, or thought that John was inferior to him. This information might get through his encoder, and the message might come out something like "Hey, you, gimme the salt—now." John might pass the salt—or he might say, "Get it yourself."

Suppose Bill was a new clerk in the company, and John was a vice-president. Bill might not feel that he should start any communication with John—and Bill eats a sandwich without salt.

Suppose wires get crossed between Bill's nervous system and his encoder, and he produces an embarrassing message such as "Sass me the palt." Suppose his encoder is deficient, and it substitutes an "m" for an "s"; the message becomes "Pass me the malt." Either John gives Bill something Bill doesn't want or he doesn't give him anything at all.

Suppose the coffee shop is crowded and noisy. John does not hear Bill because the communication channel is overloaded. Result—John does not respond, and Bill never eats with John again. Finally, suppose John and Bill come from different cultures. In John's culture people do not eat salt on meat, or John might even disapprove of anyone using salt on meat. Result—he might not understand Bill, or he might not think as well of him.

These are only a few examples of the kinds of things that can go wrong, even in a simple two-person communication situation. You might like to return to our example of Joe asking Mary for a date or of your reading of this manuscript. What kinds of things could have happened at one or another stage of the process to cause those two communication situations to break down?

Our examples have been confined to relatively uncomplicated communication situations. The model is equally useful in describing the communication behavior of a complex organization. In such a situation, the encoding and decoding functions often are separable from source and receiver functions. Correspondingly, certain people in the organization occupy roles as both sources and receivers.

Take a large-city newspaper as an example. The operation of the newspaper involves a complex network of communication. The newspaper hires people whose prime job is decoding—reporters who observe one or more kinds of events in the world and relay them to the "central nervous system" of the paper, the "desk" or "slot" or central control office.

When the messages are received, some decision is reached by the editorial staff. As a result of these decisions, orders are given from the control desk to produce or not produce a given message in the paper. Again, the encoding function becomes specialized. The paper employs rewrite men, proofreaders, linotype operators, pressmen, delivery boys. They all are responsible for one or another part of the encoding and channeling functions, getting the message out of the control office on to the pages of the newspaper, and thence to a different set of receivers, the reading public.

The communication model can be used to describe the personal behavior of any member of the newspaper staff. At the same time, it can be applied at a different level of analysis, and used to describe the workings of the organization as a communication network.

Within the paper, elaborate subdivisions of communication responsibility are made. Some people decode only certain kinds of messages: police work, society behavior, sports, etc. Others are assigned to a more general beat. Some people do not feed information into the paper, but are responsible solely for encoding messages which get this information back out. Still others neither decode nor encode (at the network analysis level), but are responsible for receiver-source behaviors; in other words, for making decisions about the messages they receive and giving orders about messages they want sent out.

The newspaper is one example of a communication network. Others might include the behaviors of any information organization, the operations of the Department of State, and the structure of a large industrial organization. Communication analysis can be performed on communicative institutions or on a specific person. The model is equally applicable to both. It represents a point of view, a way of looking at behavior, whether the behavior is individual or institutional.

The examples given have several implications for further discussion. One is the varying nature of communication purposes. To a large extent, the modern newspaper is not an "original" source of communication. It specializes in interpreting information it receives from one set of sources and transmitting this information, as interpreted, to another set of receivers. It works as an intermediary in communication.

At the same time, through the editorial page, the newspaper does originate messages, does transmit "original" information to its reading audience. It both originates and interprets. One of the canons of responsible journalism is the requirement that the newspaper keep these two functions separate—that it avoid originating material while pretending to be interpreting material received from outside its own system.

There are other examples of the originator-interpreter distinction. The New York Stock Exchange is a good illustration. The operation of the market can be analyzed as an intricate communication network, in which the behaviors allowed to people performing various roles are explicitly defined and rigorously enforced. Some brokers on the floor are primarily encoders. They transmit the intentions of the main office or of customers who may live far from the exchange itself. Other brokers are both encoders and decoders. They transmit their employer's purposes and decode messages from others about the state of the market, the price of a particular stock. They send these messages to their office, where a decision is made. Still others are allowed to make decisions by themselves. They may buy or sell on their own initiative, for their firms or their personal holdings.

A second implication of the examples given concerns the way in which we should interpret the concepts of source, encoder, decoder, and receiver. These should not be viewed as separate things or entities or people. They are the names of behaviors which have to be performed for communication to occur. More than one person may be involved in the same behavior-form (multiple sources, encoders, etc.). One person may perform more than one set of behaviors. The same person may be both a source and a receiver, even simultaneously. The same person may—and usually does—both encode and decode messages. This illustrates the earlier point that the ingredients of communication, or of any process, are not separable, cannot be divided into independent or nonoverlapping entities.

The examples also can be used to illustrate the principle of relativity referred to earlier. At one level of analysis, we can describe a reporter as a decoder. At another, he is both a source and a receiver and performs both encoding and decoding behaviors. What we call him depends upon our own purposes, how we view him, in what context we place him, and so on.

Finally, the examples demonstrate the meaning of process, the interrelationship of the ingredients of communication. Within the newspaper, we cannot order communication events as (1) reporting, (2) decision-making by the central office on the value of messages received, (3) orders to put certain articles in the paper, and (4) encoding of those articles. It is hard to say which comes first.

Clearly, the reporter is affected by what he believes his editors want him to report, by the deadlines he faces in order to meet the requirements of the encoding process, etc. The central office is limited by what it receives from its reporters. It also is affected by what it believes to be the editorial policy of the publisher, his political beliefs, the space available in the paper, the time and costs of encoding, etc. And, of course, all employees are affected at all times by their assumptions as to the purposes of the reader who eventually will consume the paper. What they believe the reader wants affects what they report, what they interpret, and what they encode.

The communication of news is a process. All the ingredients of the process affect each other. A dynamic peculiar to that specific process is developed. A journalism student can quickly become familiar with the ingredients of journalism: events, typewriters, articles, city desks, printing presses, distribution systems, etc. It is the dynamic which is hard to learn, and which usually has to be experienced before it is understood.

The ingredients discussed are essential to communication. Whether we talk about communication in terms of one person, two persons, or an institutional network, the functions labeled as source, encoder, decoder, and receiver have to be performed. Messages always are involved and must exist in some channel. How they go together, in what order, and with what kinds of interrelationships depend on the situation, the nature of the specific process under study, the dynamic developed.

It is useful to use these ingredients to talk about communication. It is dangerous to assume that one comes first, one last, or that they are independent of each other. This denies the concept of process, and communication is a process. The importance of process might best be typified by the traditional argument of the relative priority of chickens and eggs. One useful deterrent to forgetting about interrelationships within a process is to remember the following defintion: a chicken is what an egg makes in order to reproduce itself.

Notes

1. W. Rhys Roberts, "Rhetorica," in *The Works of Aristotle,* ed. W. D. Ross (New York: Oxford University Press, 1946, Volume XI), p. 14.

2. Claude Shannon and Warren Weaver, *The Mathematical Theory of Communication* (Urbana: University of Illinois Press, 1949), p. 5.

3. Wilbur Schramm, "How Communication Works," in *The Process and Effects of Mass Communication,* ed. Wilbur Schramm (Urbana: University of Illinois Press, 1954), pp. 3-26.

4. Bruce Westley and Malcolm MacLean, Jr., "A Conceptual Model for Communication Research," *Journalism Quarterly,* 34 (1957): 31-38.

5. Franklin Fearing, "Toward a Psychological Theory of Human Communication," *Journal of Personality,* 22 (1953): 71-78.

6. Wendell Johnson, "The Fateful Process of Mister A Talking to Mister B," in *How Successful Executives Handle People,* Harvard Business Review (1953), p. 50.

COMMUNICATION MODELS: A FURTHER NOTE

The Berlo model, just discussed, was intended simply to introduce you to the concept of "model," to point out some of the constituents of the model, and to indicate several of the basic interactions in the communication process. Some of you will want to pursue more complex communication models. There is a wide variety of alternative models to choose from; e.g., a mathematical model,[1] a helical spiral model,[2] a conceptual model,[3] a mosaic model,[4] or a transactional model.[5] All of these would give you additional insights into the process of communication.

At this point in your study of the communication process what is most consequential are certain postulates these models share:[6]

1. *Communication is dynamic.* Recall Berlo's point here: "Communication is not static, at rest. . . . The ingredients within [the] process interact; each affects all of the others." David Mortensen reminds us, however, that although not static, communication, "through all the fluctuations maintains its stability and identity. There is a certain evolving, elastic quality to the experience of communicating with another human being."[7] He continues: "The [communication] act is constantly taking new shape, but only in a state of equilibrium that changes along lines which are consistent with the immediate expectations and past experience of the respective parties. The sequence may change the participants in some discernible way, but never in ways that are completely foreign to what has already taken place."[8]

2. *Communication is continuous.* When are we *not* communicating with the physical world or with other human beings? Even when we are asleep or under conditions of sensory deprivation our brain remains active. As Susanne Langer puts it: "The brain works as naturally as the kidneys and the blood vessels. It is not dormant just because there is no conscious purpose to be served at the moment. If it were, indeed, a vast and intricate telephone exchange, then it should be quiescent when the rest of the organism sleeps. . . . Instead of that, it goes right on manufacturing ideas—streams and deluges of ideas, that the sleeper is not using to *think* with about anything. But the brain is following its own law; it is actively translating experiences into symbols, in the fulfillment of a basic need to do so. It carries on a constant process of ideation."[9]

Kenneth Boulding, whose discussion of the way we are continually developing, reassessing, and modifying our "image" of the world, is printed later in this text, points out that: "The accumulation of knowledge is not merely the difference between messages taken in and messages given out. It is not like a reservoir; it is rather an active internal organizing principle much as the gene is a principle or entity organizing the growth of bodily structure."[10]

3. *Communication is irreversible.* Berlo, in his article, recalls the words of Heraclitus the Pre-Socratic philosopher when he observed that a person "can never step in the same river twice" because the person "is different and so is the river." We emerge from each communicative transaction somehow different than we were before. As Mortensen observes: "Irreversibility assumes that people engaged in communication can only go forward from one state to the next. It also gives importance to the spontaneity of the existing moment of experience to the accumulative significance of what unfolds."[11] Thus, as Gordon Allport observes, we are perpetually in a state of *becoming.*[12]

4. *Communication is interactive and proactive.* Clearly human beings are not self-contained entities; we *interact* with our environment and with each other. The old notion

that we are passive receivers of stimuli has given way to the more accurate view of people; we do not just react, we assign significance, we construct meanings, we rule in or out, we distort or seek to sharpen and clarify, we order the phenomena of our world, we conceive of new relationships as manifested in such "verbal atom cracking" as the pun or metaphor both of which may reveal hitherto unexpected connections between things.

"Stones, old shoes, bars of iron," Allport reminds us, "are purely reactive; they will not move unless they are manipulated. They are incapable of becoming."[13] But people are not "moved" the same way objects are moved. We do not reason with objects; we do not persuade them, cajole them, threaten them (at least with any expectation that the threat will elicit a reply). We *do* reason with people, we cajole them, we persuade them; but we also implicitly know that in a very real sense they are self-moving. Because the persons we are talking to remain the ones who make the decision to *be* cajoled, persuaded, etc. we say that they have a "choice" in the matter. Kenneth Burke aptly summarizes the point: "If one cannot make a choice, one is not acting; one is being moved, like a billard ball tapped with a cue and behaving mechanically in conformity with the resistances it encounters."[14] Thus, action is the essence of human behavior. In order to act we must choose, and it is choosing that makes us essentially self-moving beings.

Moreover we interact with each other and our environment with total involvement; that is, we respond as *total* beings. The article by Kenneth Boulding, reprinted later in this volume, illustrates the full impact of this statement. Here, we will simply observe that people do not function in neat categorical ways; body/mind; reason/emotion; thought/action; verbal/nonverbal.

5. *Communication is contextual.* All communication takes place somewhere; it takes place in a scene.[15] Wayne Brockriede calls this scene in which a communication takes place an "encompassing situation."[16] Nichols, in the next article in this book, explores the influence that both the physical and the metaphysical aspects of place have on communication.

Randall Harrison and Albert Mehrabian, in their articles reprinted later in this text, discusses "context" in yet another sense of the word; that is, the nonverbal context in which messages occur.

Notes

1. Claude Shannon and W. Weaver, *The Mathematical Theory of Communication* (Urbana: University of Illinois Press, 1949).

2. See, for example, Frank E. X. Dance, "A Helical Model of Communication," in Dance, ed., *Human Communication* (New York: Holt, Rinehart and Winston, Inc., 1967), pp. 294-98; and Dance, "The 'Concept' of Communication," *Journal of Communication* (1970), pp. 201-10.

3. B. H. Westley and M. MacLean, Jr., "A Conceptual Model of Communication Research," *Journalism Quarterly* (1957), pp. 31-38.

4. See, for example, Samuel L. Becker, "Toward an Appropriate Theory for Contemporary Speech-Communication," in David H. Smith, ed., *What Rhetoric (Communication Theory) Is Appropriate for Contemporary Speech Communication?* Proceedings of the University of Minnesota Spring Symposium in Speech-Communication (1968), pp. 9-25; and, Becker, "Rhetorical Studies for the Contemporary World," in Lloyd F. Bitzer and Edwin Black, eds., *The Prospects for Rhetoric* (Englewood Cliffs, N.J.: Prentice-Hall, Inc., 1971), pp. 21-43.

5. See, for example, Dean C. Barnlund, "Communication: The Context of Change," in C. E. Larson and Frank E. X. Dance, eds., *Perspectives on Communication* (Milwaukee: The Speech Communication Center, 1968), pp. 24-40; and, Barnlund, "A Transactional Model of Communication," in Kenneth K. Sereno and C. David Mortensen, eds., *Foundations of Communication Theory* (New York: Harper and Row, 1970), pp. 83-102.

6. For further treatment of these points, see particularly Barnlund, "A Transactional Model of Communication," op. cit., pp. 88-94 and C. David Mortensen, *Communication: The Study of Human Interaction* (New York: McGraw-Hill Book Co., 1972), pp. 14-21.

7. Mortensen, op. cit., p. 15.

8. Ibid.

9. Susanne Langer, *Philosophy in a New Key* (New York: Mentor Books, 1942), p. 46.

10. Kenneth Boulding, *The Image* (Ann Arbor: University of Michigan Press, 1956), p. 18.

11. Mortensen, op. cit., p. 16.

12. Gordon W. Allport, *Becoming: Basic Conditions for a Psychology of Personality* (New Haven: Yale University Press, 1955).

13. Ibid., p. 21.

14. Kenneth Burke, *Rhetoric of Religion* (Boston: Beacon Press, 1961), p. 188. See also Burke, *Language as Symbolic Action* (Berkeley: University of California Press, 1966).

15. See, e.g., Kenneth Burke, *Grammar of Motives* (Berkeley: University of California Press, 1969), pp. 3-20.

16. Wayne Brockriede, "Dimensions of the Concept of Rhetoric," *Quarterly Journal of Speech* (February 1968), pp. 1-12. The article is reprinted in full in this text.

THE CONSTITUENTS OF THE RHETORICAL ACT

MARIE HOCHMUTH NICHOLS

Traditionally the speech has functioned both as an end in itself and as a means to other ends. Thus, Greek and Roman orators perfected the speech as a verbal form serving its own ends. On the other hand, the historian Thucydides employed written forms of speeches in recording the political opinions of the day. Homer, Milton, Shakespeare, and numerous others have employed speeches as techniques for achieving particular effects within larger frameworks of verbal activity. Historically, the prose of the public speech was earliest to achieve artistic perfection; hence, the methods of the speech could be and sometimes were carried over into other forms of literary activity. All of this has been a source of confusion among critics who, at times, have mistaken the verbal record of the speaking event for the speech itself, and who just as often have applied the criteria of poetic to the evaluation of verbal activity demanding other criteria.

Two broad questions pertaining to the speech as a form have been traditional: Is the speech an art form? Is the verbal record of a speech to be considered literature? To the first question we may apply the ancient explanation that things come into being by luck, by nature, by spontaneity, or by art.[1] The records of speech-making indicate that principles and practices have entered into the making of speeches; speeches do not come into being by nature, nor are they typically the results of chance. More akin to architecture than to music as an art, the speech is primarily a practical art form. Just as the architect usually has functional ends primarily in mind in the construction of houses, office buildings, and even churches, occasionally he achieves far more than merely functional ends in a Cathedral of Chartres or of Cologne.

From Marie K. Hochmuth, "The Criticism of Rhetoric," in Marie K. Hochmuth, Ed. *A History and Criticism of American Public Address,* Vol. III (Copyright 1954; New York: Russell & Russell, 1965). By permission of Russell & Russell and Marie Hochmuth Nichols.

To the question: Are speeches literature? the answer, of course, depends on the breadth of definition. If we define literature as a "nation's mind in writing," obviously all verbal activity which is recorded is literature. If we define it as a qualitative factor in verbal activity, then the speech may or may not be literature. If we restrict the term to verbal activity whose primary purpose is to induce immediate pleasurable response, then the speech is clearly not primarily a literary form, although as an incidental aspect it may produce pleasurable response. In our age, the committee for awarding the Nobel Prize for literature chose Sir Winston Churchill in preference to Ernest Hemingway, Graham Greene, and other contenders for the award in literature for his "historical and biographical presentations and for the scintillating oratory in which he has stood forth as a defender of eternal human values."[2] Thus, he takes his place beside Kipling, Shaw, Galsworthy, T. S. Eliot, and others as a "literary" figure.

I am concerned here with evaluating that which the Greeks called rhetoric. One need be under no illusion about the difficulties involved in using the term. Modern critics use it in a variety of ways.[3] Some use it to refer only to the "purple patches." Its use often does not reflect any clear effort to come to grips with the term. Thus, the literary historian, Vernon L. Parrington, writes of Lincoln: "Matter he judged to be of greater significance than manner. Few men who have risen to enduring eloquence have been so little indebted to rhetoric. Very likely his plainness of style was the result of deliberate restraint, in keeping with the simplicity of his nature."[4] Here rhetoric seems to be correlated with "manner," particularly with a style which is not plain. It presupposes a clean division between matter and manner, as if thought and the manner of expressing it were completely separate entities. On the other hand, the literary scholar and editor of Lincoln's speeches, Roy Basler, writes of Lincoln: "It would be difficult to find in all history a precise instance in which rhetoric played a more important role in human destiny than it did in Lincoln's speeches of 1858."[5] The meaning of the term here is not clear. It appears to mean something "in" the speeches—but not necessarily the speeches themselves. Such a confusion leads two critics to come to completely opposite conclusions in evaluating Lincoln's indebtedness to rhetoric. At a pole opposite from many attempts to correlate rhetoric with style, lies the recent observation of Duhamel: "Cicero's style was influenced by his rhetoric."[6] Here rhetoric is a cause of style, not correlative with it.

Because of this troublesomeness, I. A. Richards has recommended that we "would do better to dismiss it to Limbo,"[7] unless the term can be revived to mean a "study of verbal understanding and misunderstanding. . . ."[8] Kenneth Burke, on the other hand, recommends that a strong arm be used to reclaim a traditional province, once perfectly clear, but usurped by other disciplines.[9]

Doubtless no contemporary interpretation of the term throws more light on its proper use than that of the classical systematizers of the art. "Rhetoric may be defined as the faculty of observing in any given case the available means of persuasion," observed Aristotle. The ancients included in the terms all the ingredients of persuasion, the impelling fact, the reasoned argument, the strategic ordering of details, no less than the well-wrought phrase. The art of rhetoric was the art of discovering arguments, adapting them, ordering them, expressing them in clear and proper words, and of using one's personal qualities to enhance the whole to the end of achieving persuasion in an audience. It was the whole rationale of persuasive discourse.[10] The term was so used by Cicero, and Quintilian, and by vigorous eighteenth- and nineteenth-century theorists, George Campbell, Richard Whately, and others. It is also used in this way by the contemporary critic, Burke, by the Chicago school of critics, and generally by critics whose writings regularly appear in the *Quarterly Journal of Speech* and in *Speech Monographs*.

I use the term "rhetoric," then, to apply to verbal activity primarily concerned with effecting persuasion, whether it be done by writing or speaking. Rhetoric operates in the area of the contingent, where choice is to be made among alternative courses of action. Its concern is with substance as well as with form, if any arbitrary distinction is to be made. In this essay I am concerned with evaluating persuasive efficacy as it manifests itself in *oral* verbal activity, the speech. "Typically, a speech is an utterance meant to be heard and intended to exert an influence of some kind on those who hear it," remarks Wayland M. Parrish. "Typically, also the kind of influence intended may be described as persuasion."[11]

If we do not press the analogy too far, we may compare the speech with a multicelled organism, whose units consist of speaker, audience, place, purpose, time, content, and form. In order to evaluate the speech, all these elements, verbal and nonverbal, must be examined.

First, consider the position of a speaker in the persuasive situation. In every instance, some specific "I" is doing the speaking. He may be familiar to us or quite unknown. If he is known, he may be known favorably or unfavorably. To the South during the Civil War, Lincoln was a "guerrilla"; to the North, in part, at least, he was "Honest Abe." Let us note for a moment the significance of the specific "I" in the speaking situation by referring to Emerson's characterization of Disraeli:

> Disraeli, the chiffonier, wastes all his talent on the House of Commons, for the want of character. He makes a smart cutting speech, really introduces new and important distinctions. . . . But he makes at last no impression, because the hearer asks, Who are you? What is dear to you? What do you stand for? And the speech and the speaker are silent, and silence is confession. A man who has been a man has foreground and background. His speech, be it never so good, is subordinate and the least part of him, and as this man has no planet under him, but only his shoes, the hearer infers that the ground of the present argument may be no wider.[12]

Whether Emerson's judgment of Disraeli is or is not vindicated by history is not in question. The point is that when one listens to speeches, the individual "I" is an element in the situation. It may matter little in the judgment of "The Last Supper" who painted it, or of the "Moonlight Sonata," who composed it, or of *Pisan Cantos* whether the poet was or was not a traitor, but there is no gainsaying the fact that when speeches are being evaluated the speaker is of paramount importance. One asks the question, then: What are the predispositions, if any, toward the man who is giving the speech? This is a cell in the organism; it may be healthy or in some way defective. Either because of previous acquaintance or because of signs during the speech itself, the audience comes to some conclusion about the speaker, and this plays a part in the judgment. In the political campaign of 1952, Adlai Stevenson, scarcely known at all at the beginning of the campaign, was being compared with a rival candidate whose name was favorably known to millions. This could hardly fail to be a factor in the ultimate decision. Not only the speaking, but the *man* who spoke was a factor. The critic needs to note and assess the persuasive effect of "echoes and values" attaching to the person and character of the speaker. Rarely is this a simple matter, for the man is not always to be seen as a single individual having his own merits only. Men and women derive force from the symbolic relations in which they stand among others. Thus, Eisenhower became the "man of action" speaking for a nation proud of its ability to "get things done"; Clarence Darrow, according to Maloney in a study in this volume, became a champion for the downtrodden, the underdog, and spoke as the representative of a class. Thus, the impetus given to ideas set in motion by the speaker is not merely the impetus deriving from the force of one man's character, but often from the whole class which he images.

Next, let us consider the audience as a cell in this complex organism. Audiences neither come from a vacuum nor assemble in one. They come with pre-established systems of value, conditioning their perceptions. As Susanne Langer has observed, "Every society meets a new idea with its own concepts, its own tacit, fundamental way of seeing things; that is to say, *with its own questions, its peculiar curiosity.*"[13] We are not without knowledge in regard to the role of perception. We know that perception is selective; we both see and hear with a previously established set of values, theoretical, economic, aesthetic, social, political, and religious.[14] Not only do we have general sets of values that predetermine our responses, we often also have specific predispositions regarding the subject being discussed. The rhetorician discovers his potentials for persuasion in a wise regard for the prevailing attitudes in the audience. Although he need neither compromise his integrity, nor bow in subservience to an audience, he does need to understand the operating forces in the audience and select arguments that induce persuasion. He must remember that his choices are conditioned by the audience. The poem may be written with the audience thrice-removed from the creator, for the poet creates from his experience with his subject. But the speech-maker must compose his speech from the available potentials in his audience. He aims to link his propositions to their value systems, and value systems differ with age, sex, educational development, economic class, social strata, political heritage, specialized interest, and so on. The speaker is a selecter. He must exclude certain arguments and include others. He must decide how to order details and the thought patterns into which material is to be cast. All this is determined by the audience for which the speech is designed. The critic who attempts to discriminate among values without reference to the audience is doing what a rhetorical critic really cannot do. Since the audience conditioned the speaker's choices in selecting the arguments, ordering them, and expressing them, the critic must inevitably consider whether the speaker chose wisely or ill in relation to the audience. The critic's necessary tool, then, is not personal whim but clear perception of the role of choice. He must know the mood of the audience. Was it hostile, neutral, or partisan? What tensions, if any, were to be released? Was it keyed up for any particular occasion? Daniel Webster long ago called attention to the significance of occasion and audience-tone in persuasion: "True eloquence, indeed, does not consist in speech. It cannot be brought from far. Labor and learning may toil for it, but they will toil in vain. Words and phrases may be marshalled in every way, but they cannot compass it. It must exist in the man, in the subject, and in the occasion."[15] Let the critic know, then, the audience for which the speech was intended.

Third, we must consider the function of *place.* Place, of course, is not merely a physical condition. It is also a metaphysical condition, an ideological environment. We hear much of the "industrial" East, the "conservative" Midwest, the "progressive" Far West, "rumor-ridden" Washington. Speeches take place in halls, to be sure, but halls are "sacred halls," "smoke-filled rooms," places "hallowed by the memory of the sacred dead." The church is an "atmosphere" as well as a place. Place conditions both the speaker's method and the audience's reaction. People do not react in a smoke-filled room the way they do in the restrained atmosphere of the Senate gallery.

I do not intend to minimize the purely physical aspect of the place, for this is sometimes important, of course. Comfort and discomfort, audibility or inaudibility may take on considerable proportions. Webster, with 100,000 people milling over Bunker Hill, could not have been expected to be talking to all of them, and an inaugural crowd in a chill wind is not likely to be giving itself completely to the speaker no matter how superlative his genius. No one would expect the playing of a concerto to produce the same effect in a run-down basement room of an apartment-hotel as it does in Carnegie Hall. And no one believes that a painting hung on just any wall will look well. In evaluating speeches, the aspect of place must be recognized as a conditioning factor. "The world will little note, nor long remember what we say here, but it can never forget what they did here," Lincoln observed at Gettysburg, and generations have murmured the words as they have explored the grounds.

Fourth, is the consideration of purpose. After examining the debates in the Constitutional Convention of 1787, the historians Samuel Eliot Morison and Henry Steele Commager concluded that "the main, central and determining consideration that appears throughout the debates, is to erect a government that would be neither too strong nor too shocking to popular prejudices for adoption, and yet be sufficiently strong and well-contrived to work."[16] This analysis highlights the significant role that *purpose* plays in evaluating speech-making. At the outset, it indicates that the finished Constitutional product did not represent anyone's notion of the perfect constitution, but what the Constitutional fathers thought they could get accepted. Presumably all language is uttered with some purpose, whether it be the salutation, "Good morning," or the frankly evangelistic sermon on Sunday. These purposes control choices of materials. Whatever the end the speaker has in mind, his specific purpose is to speak with persuasive effect toward that end; his available resources for persuasion are those which can be directed toward fulfillment of purpose.

The consideration of purpose undoubtedly misleads the critics more often than any other aspect of speaking. In an age oriented toward quick and tangible evidences of success, the critic has tended to make the specific accomplishment of ends the test of rhetorical effectiveness. The number of votes in the ballot box, the amount of money collected as a result of a promotion campaign are taken to be the measure of effectiveness. They are taken to represent the fulfillment of purpose. James Hadley noted the trend in the nineteenth century and expressed concern: "Some have a simple test, and that is persuasiveness; the best oration is the most persuasive, and *vice versa,* the most persuasive is the best; for it best fulfils the end of eloquence, which is persuasion." With shrewd good sense and discrimination, Hadley continued: "The eloquence of Mike Walsh has an effect as persuasive on the collective blackguardism of New York as the eloquence of Daniel Webster has on the collective dignity and learning of the Senate or the Supreme Court. Should we therefore decide that one is no higher than the other? Now persuasiveness . . . is indeed an indispensable element in true eloquence. But there is another element . . . and that is artistic perfection. . . ."[17] In other words, the purpose of the speaker is to discover the available means of persuasion and the appropriate questions are: Did he discover them? What is their quality?

The critic who makes the fulfillment of specific purpose the only test of eloquence is not merely misguided, he is indeed attempting the impossible. As Leonard Bloomfield has observed, "persuasive and . . . powerful [as] . . . effect may be, it is nearly always uncertain."[18] He further observes: "In the long run, anything which adds to the viability of language has also an indirect but more pervasive effect. Even acts of speech that do not prompt any particular immediate response, may change the predisposition of the hearer for further responses: a beautiful poem, for instance, may make the hearer more sensitive to later stimuli. The general refinement and intensification of human response requires a great deal of linguistic interaction. Education or culture, or whatever name we choose to give it, depends upon the repetition and publication of a vast amount of speech."[19]

Clearly, the speaker should not be judged by the fulfillment of specific purpose alone. Who can know how many sinners were "almost" saved as a result of a revival service of Billy Graham? The function of the preacher is to use his talents toward this end, and it is by the talents, not by the accomplishment of the end merely that he should be judged. The odds against the accomplishment of a specific end may be insurmountable. Was Lincoln's First Inaugural rhetorically inferior because it did not prevent the Civil War? The eye of the critic must be focused on the methods used by the speaker and not merely on the ends achieved. It is reason and judgment, not a comptometer, that make a man a critic.

Fifth, is the factor of time and timing. Just as civilizations rise, develop, and decline, so too problems rise, grow in dimension, yield to solution, and eventually give way to other problems. Time represents a stage in the life of problems. It reflects itself in both the proposition of the speaker and in his mode of handling the problem. It likewise represents a stage in the life of feelings toward a proposition. Anyone knows that he is more susceptible to argument and discussion at one time than at another. A man who has just had lunch is not likely to become excited over the promise of release from hunger. A solution presented either prematurely or tardily will be found wanting. The man with an answer at the time when people are searching for an answer is in a much more effective position rhetorically than the man who gives an answer after doubt has already been resolved, or who offers one before the problem has become acute.

But not only are the substance of a speech and the feelings of an audience conditioned by *time,* the mode of handling data is likewise conditioned. Mode of handling is a product of a culture at a given time. The critic who tends to write off the florid style of the nineteenth century is in effect saying that according to his "more enlightened" twentieth-century taste, the nineteenth-century mode of handling was inferior. Not many of us look with undimmed eyes upon the glories of nature and describe what we see. We look with eyes conditioned to see in terms of the language habits we have inherited. The ornate language of the nineteenth century was shared by a multitude of people in the century, and there is little reason to suppose that it was not as persuasive as the language of the twentieth century. Tastes vary with the times. The real question for the critic is: Does the mode of handling represent the tastes of the time? Is it adjusted to the intellectual development and the habits of the hearer? Is it in harmony with aesthetic values of the time? In the poetic age of the translators of the King James Version of the Bible, the translators wrote in God's description of the battle horse to Job:

> Hast thou given the horse strength? Hast thou clothed his neck with thunder? . . .
> The glory of his nostrils is terrible. . . . He saith among the trumpets, Ha, Ha.

Twentieth-century translators, heeding the injunction to produce a Bible "written in language direct and clear and meaningful to people today" write as follows:

> Do you give the horse his might? Do you clothe his neck with strength? . . . His majestic snorting is terrible. . . . When the trumpet sounds, he says, 'Aha![20]

In both cases, presumably, we have the language of the people, designed to have an impact on the readers in their own centuries. Does anyone really believe the new rendering of the passage is superior? A rhetorical critic may note differences in quality, to be sure, but the scale by which one determines persuasive effect must be a scale adjusted to the time in which the product was made.

In our discussion so far we have, in the main, been concerned with a consideration of the extra-verbal aspects of persuasion. We come now to the verbal instrument itself. According to George Campbell, astute eighteenth-century rhetorical theorist and practitioner of the art of rhetoric, "there are two things in every discourse which principally claim our attention, the sense and the expression; or in other words, the thought and the symbol by which it is communicated. These may be said to constitute the soul and the body of an oration. . . ."[21]

Both ancient and contemporary thought might question the dichotomy between "the sense and the expression" as indicated by Campbell. From Aristotle to modern times competent critics have recognized that "there can be no distinction drawn, save in reflection, between form and substance. The work itself *is* matter formed. . . ."[22] The contemporary philosopher, Jordan, notes that "At the point of the abstract ultimate what is said . . . and the way it is said . . . may be the same thing. . . ."[23] Experience, of course, reveals that so united are matter and form that when a speaker struggles to make his thoughts clear but fails, he in fact says something else.

Recognizing the inseparability of matter and form in any art, we may, nevertheless, in "reflection," consider the work in terms of constituents, arguments, broad structural pattern, and particular stylistic features.

Let us first look at the substance of a speech. Persuasion requires choices among alternatives. The speech presumably will consist of persuasions to induce acceptance of the speaker's point of view. Presumably this point of view is directed toward some ultimate Good. Hence, the speaker's persuasions represent directly or by implication his philosophic outlook and commitment. These persuasions will be revealed verbally in statements of fact and of opinion. "Facts cannot be selected without some personal conviction as to what is truth,"[24] observes the historian, Allan Nevins. Likewise, Karl Wallace notes: "Truth is a word I shall use to describe the moment of certainty, or commitment, or decision which signals the resolution of doubt. The decision is revealed verbally as a statement of opinion or value, or as a statement of fact."[25] Accordingly, Richard Weaver remarks: "there is no honest rhetoric without a preceding dialectic."[26] that is, without an attempt to discover truth. Thus, the critic is brought face to face with the necessity of understanding and discriminating among the ideas or the truths to which the speaker has committed himself. But to evaluate the speaker's philosophy involves the critic in a discrimination of ethical values. The warning of Baskerville is well taken: ". . . today's critic often side-steps inquiry into the basic soundness of the speaker's position, offering the excuse that truth is relative, that everyone is entitled to his own opinion, and that the rhetorical critic's task is to describe and evaluate the orator's skill in his craft and not to become entangled in complex ethical considerations."[27]

The simple fact is that audiences do not respond alike to any and every opinion, that whereas the critic may think it not his function to tangle with the problem of truth and the weight of ideas, audiences which determine the degree of persuasion do so involve themselves with these matters. Ideas are a means of persuasion. Emerson responding to Webster's 7th of March speech was keenly aware of Webster's philosophic position: "Nobody doubts that there were good and plausible things to be said on the part of the South. But this is not a question of ingenuity, not a question of syllogisms, but of sides."[28] For Emerson there was always "the previous question: How came you on that side? Your argument is ingenious, your language copious, your illustrations brilliant, but your major proposition palpably absurd. Will you establish a lie?"[29] In evaluating a sermon of an American churchman, a critic recently observed: "His arguments were specious, but his rhetoric was good." That rhetoric can consist of specious arguments as well as sound ones no one will question. But that the validity and the truth of the argument has nothing to do with pronouncing the rhetoric "good" is, indeed, dubious.

The critic's function is to examine the speaker's premises, stated or implied, and to examine the truth of those premises. Inevitably he must ask such questions as: Does the orator argue from an abiding concept of the "nature of things"? from a conception of expediency? from the authority of history? from similitude? from transcendental grounds?

There are conventional means for evaluating the quality of premises. Does the premise presented "correspond" to data which may be revealed to the senses of observers? Does the truth of a premise yield to a pragmatic test? Is the truth of a premise "believed" by the many? Is the truth of a premise "self-evident"?[30] However much the critic may wish to escape discriminating among values, as an effective rhetorical critic he cannot do so.

This may not be the place to argue for any of the particular criteria of truth used through the ages. One may say that great and good men have from time to time used all of these tests, depending upon their general philosophic position. We do not ask too much when we ask a critic to reveal his philosophic position by his choice of criteria for evaluating premises. In fact, we may be paving the way for critical commentary vastly richer and more cogent than if the bases of evaluation were ignored.

Nor is the argumentative substance of the speech the critic's only concern. Persuasion represents deliberate manipulation of symbols. Symbols contain not only rational meanings. They contain experience also and represent attempts to create and release emotional tensions. Woven into the substance of argument are directives to action, terms of interpretation and valuation. Persuasion recognizes men to be creatures of desire; it also recognizes that desire provides a basis for action. Hence, the speaker's persuasions represent techniques for awakening and satisfying desire. Furthermore, within every culture are values that have authority. Thus, "virtue" was the ultimate Good for the Greeks; "courage," an ultimate Good for the Romans; "duty," an ultimate Good in early American Christian civilization. The critic examines the texture of persuasive compositions for those symbols change from age to age. Whereas an early Christian civilization responded to appeals to action, presented in the name of "duty," a later civilization is activated to a greater degree by the promise of earthly "progress." On an ethical scale, we may find considerable difference between the lowest motive and the highest motive to which men will respond. The discerning critic must not only assess both extremes but he must locate the center of gravity. He need not deny the persuasive value of low motives, but he has no moral obligation to sanction the use of such motives under the label of "good" rhetoric.

"The most minute study, the widest experience in the investigation of human actions and their motives," says Gamaliel Bradford, "only make us feel more and more the shifting, terrible uncertainty of the ground under our feet."[31] The difficulty of the task gives no warrant to the critic to shirk his responsibility. Surveying the rhetoric of Hitler's *Mein Kampf,* Kenneth Burke notes: "Here is the testament of a man who swung a great people into his wake. Let us watch it carefully, and let us watch it, not merely to discover some grounds for prophesying what political move is to follow Munich, and what move to follow that move, etc.; let us try also to discover what kind of 'medicine' this medicine-man has concocted, that we may know, with greater accuracy, exactly what to guard against, if we are to forestall the concocting of similar medicine in America."[32] Such an observation suggests the responsibility of the critic. His place should be in the vanguard, not in the rear—wise after the fact. He should be ready to alert a people, to warn what devices of exploitation are being exercised, by what skillful manipulations of motives men are being directed to or dissuaded from courses of action. James G. Randall asks: Was the willful manipulation of men's minds by the wily a factor in the cause of the Civil War? Is it a factor in most wars?[33] The careful examination of motives must not merely furnish an amusing pastime for the critic; it is his urgent responsibility.

Pursuing our examination of aspects of form, we turn "in reflection" to the aspect of structure. Literary art, like all art, observes Daiches, "communicates significance through patterns."[34] A tragedy unravels through a pattern of exposition, complicating circumstances, climax, and denouement. A detective story lays down premises and takes its deductive course. The speech also is a structured organism and this structure must be a concern of the critic. By structure we mean, as Whitehead has suggested, "that eye for the whole chessboard, for the bearing of one set of ideas on another."[35] In speech-making this has traditionally been called *dispositio*. Aristotle defined it as "the arrangement of that which has parts, in respect of place, or of potency or of kind."[36]

Probably all people need forms, for "We take delight in recognition."[37] Whether we speak a word, a sentence, or a whole speech, intelligibility depends on form. To borrow an ancient illustration, we recognize a bronze pitcher only after it has taken form from a mass of bronze and *become* a bronze pitcher.[38] In the laboratory, speech takes on a visual shape, as is shown by spectograph readings. In ordinary communication, meanings are in part determined by organization. Thus, "an rhetoric art is" yields intelligibility by assembling the elements: Rhetoric is an art.

The critic must observe the contribution made by thought pattern to the effectiveness of the whole. A thought pattern is something more than external manifestation of a beginning, a middle, and an end. It is a functional balancing of parts against each other, a determination of the relative strength of arguments. It is reflected in proportion and placing. The speaker who sandwiches weak arguments between strong arguments has at least considered force as a factor in persuasion. Structure reveals the speaker's assessment of his audience in the placement of parts, whether they are partisans, neutrals, or opponents. or a significant mixture of two or more. To that extent, at least, it represents the psychology of the audience rather than the psychology of the speaker.[39]

We come finally to that most elusive of all aspects of the speaking act—style, still another aspect of form. Thonssen and Baird, referring to a rhetorical critic of the last century, have remarked, "Jebb is more deeply concerned with the orator's style than are most present-day critics. In this regard, he is, perhaps, less the rhetorical and more the literary critic."[40] Rhetorical critics unfortunately tend to be less interested in style than they ought to be, for, as Lasswell has noted, "style is an indispensable feature of every configuration of meaning in any process of communication."[41]

Partly because of the difficulty, and partly because of confusion with the function of literary critics, contemporary rhetorical critics have given the matter little attention. Preoccupation with trying to distinguish written from oral style has often yielded results both fruitless and misleading. "Not only are contemporary critics . . . unable to distinguish oral from written style," observes Schrader, "but they are also confused as to the nature of style itself."[42] "Their statements are often based on untenable assumptions, and their conclusions are even contradictory."[43]

If, as Wichelns has remarked, the problem of the orator is "so to present ideas as to bring them into the consciousness of his hearers,"[44] the neglect of style becomes serious, and mistaken notions about it equally hazardous.

It is significant that the two living orators who have achieved greatest distinction for their oratory are both sensitive stylists. Churchill has a feeling for the nobility of the English sentence, and Stevenson's style became a campaign issue in the election of 1952. In general, the style of our orators has been so undistinguished as to escape the notice of listeners, but this may in part account for the lack of impact that many speakers have had on their age. It does not justify the neglect of style by rhetorical critics. If the testimony of the centuries to the importance of style needed support, we could find it in an unsuspected source—from one of the great atomic scientists of the twentieth century. Said J. Robert Oppenheimer:

> The problem of doing justice to the implicit, the imponderable and the unknown is, of course, not unique to politics. It is always with us in science, it is with us in the most trivial of personal affairs, and it is one of the great problems of writing and of all forms of art. The means by which it is solved is sometimes called style. It is style which complements affirmation with limitation and with humility; it is style which makes it possible to act effectively, but not absolutely; it is style which, in the domain of foreign policy, enables us to find a harmony between the pursuit of ends essential to us, and the regard for the views, the sensibilities, the aspirations of those to whom the problem may appear in another light; it is above all style through which power defers to reason.[45]

Thus, in its simplest manifestation, style is a mode of "ingratiation";[46] in its most complex aspects it is the "ultimate morality of mind."[47] It is an "aesthetic sense" says Whitehead, "based on admiration for the direct attainment of a foreseen end, simply and without waste." It is an index of a preference for "good work."[48]

That audiences have value systems pertaining to style is well known. Two thousand years ago Aristotle called attention to reaction tendencies of listeners in regard to stylistic matters: "The effect which lectures produce on a hearer depends on his habits; for we demand the language we are accustomed to, and that which is different from this seems not in keeping but somewhat unintelligible and foreign because of its unwontedness. . . . Thus some people do not listen to a speaker unless he speaks mathematically, others unless he gives instances, while others expect him to cite a poet as a witness. And some want to have everything done accurately, while others are annoyed with accuracy, either because they cannot follow the connexion of thoughts or because they regard it as pettifoggery."[49]

Aristotle's statement has been proved valid by the test of centuries. The language of persuasion must be conditioned by the needs of the audience, and the needs of the audience differ considerably. As we remarked earlier, th ideals of any age, regarding style, may differ. The late John Livingston Lowes said of the King James Version of the Bible: "Its phraseology has become part and parcel of our common tongue—bone of its bone and flesh of its flesh. Its rhythms and cadences, its turns of speech, its familiar imagery, its very words, are woven into the texture of our literature, prose and poetry alike. . . . The English of the Bible . . . is characterized not merely by a homely vigour and pithiness of phrase, but also by a singular nobility of diction and by a rhythmic quality which is, I think, unrivalled in its beauty."[50] The twentieth-century revisers of the Bible were enjoined to "combine accuracy with the simplicity, directness, and spiritual power" of the King James Version, as well as to make it "more readable for the American public of today."[51]

Style is in no sense magic. It is rather a manifestation of a speaker's or writer's temper and outlook. It has the capacity to name objects, to evaluate them, and to incite feelings toward them. In its objective manifestations it pertains to the selection of words and the ordering of them, and in this a preference for "good work" may be shown.

"Style to be good must be clear," notes Aristotle, "as is proved by the fact that speech which fails to convey a plain meaning will fail to do just what a speech has to do."[52] Beyond clearness, of course, lie other properties: appropriateness, distinctive language constructions, rhythm. All of these have concern for the analyst of rhetorical style, for they are means by which the orator reaches the minds of the listeners. They are means by which he seeks identification and ingratiation.

For want of better methods, the rhetorical critic sometimes satisfies himself with a simple enumeration of stylistic devices of the speaker. Unless the enumerations are particularizations of the pervasive tones and effects sought by the speaker, such enumeration probably serves little purpose. We need to ask: What is language doing to further the end of ingratiation or identification? If, for instance, the prevailing tone of a speech is "humorous," we might expect language to behave in such a way as to produce humor. Hence, the rhetorical critic would look to language constructions, the diction, the characteristics of rhythm which contribute to the prevailing tone. If style is the man himself, then a close scrutiny of the details of style should tell us what manner of man is doing the speaking, and in what relationship he conceives himself to be with his audience. If it is style which "complements affirmation with limitation and with humility"; if it is style which "in the domain of foreign policy, enables us to find a harmony between the pursuit of ends essential to us, and the regard for the views, the sensibilities, the aspirations of those to whom the problem may appear in another light"; if it is style "through which power defers to reason"—then, to look to style for manifestations of the groundswells and tensions of our times, for manifestations of healthy states and unhealthy ones must become the imperative task of the critic concerned with the implications of his art for the nation and the world. May not the simple metaphor be the harbinger of death and destruction, or the cock's crow of an era of good feeling as well as a literary tool in the grammar books?

These are the ingredients of the rhetorical situation which must be examined for their contribution to the persuasive efficacy of the whole. As one may observe, some of them are verbal aspects, others are nonverbal. Just an in drama many elements are harmonized to give delight to an audience, so too in the rhetorical situation many elements contribute to the end of persuasion. The total organism is the concern of the critic.

Notes

1. Aristotle *Metaphysica* in *The Works of Aristotle,* VIII, Λ- 3.1070[a].

2. *The New York Times* (October 16, 1953), p. 25, cols. 2, 3, 4.

3. Donald C. Bryant, "Rhetoric: Its Functions and Its Scope," *Quarterly Journal of Speech, 39* (December 1953), 402-7.

4. Vernon Lee Parrington, *The Romantic Revolution in America,* in *Main Currents in American Thought* (New York: Harcourt, Brace and Co., 1927-30), p. 158.

5. *Abraham Lincoln: His Speeches and His Writings* (Cleveland: World Publishing Co., 1946), p. 28.

6. P. Albert Duhamel, "The Function of Rhetoric as Effective Expression," *Journal of the History of Ideas,* 10 (1949), 346.

7. I. A. Richards, *The Philosophy of Rhetoric* (New York: Oxford University Press, 1936), p. 3.

8. Ibid., p. 23.

9. Kenneth Burke, *A Rhetoric of Motives* (New York: Prentice-Hall, Inc., 1950), Introduction, xiii.

10. See Donald C. Bryant, "Rhetoric: Its Functions and Its Scope," op. cit., 401-24.

11. Wayland M. Parish and Marie Hochmuth, *American Speeches* (New York: Longmans, Green & Co., 1954), p. 3

12. *Journals of Ralph Waldo Emerson,* eds. Edward Waldo Emerson and Waldo Emerson Forbes (Boston: Houghton Mifflin Co., 1912), VII, 503.

13. Susanne K. Langer, *Philosophy in a New Key* (New York: Mentor Books; New American Library, 1948), p. 4.

14. Charles E. Osgood, *Method and Theory in Experimental Psychology* (New York: Oxford University Press, 1953), p. 292ff.

15. *A Discourse in Commemoration of the Lives and Services of John Adams & Thomas Jefferson,* Delivered in Faneuil Hall, Boston, August 2, 1826 (Boston: Cummings, Hilliard & Co., 1826), p. 34.

16. Samuel Eliot Morison and Henry Steele Commager, *The Growth of the American Republic,* third ed. (New York: Oxford University Press, 1942), I, 281.

17. James Hadley, "Is Ancient Eloquence Superior to Modern?" *Essays, Philosophical and Critical* (New York: Holt & Williams, 1873), p. 349.

18. Leonard Bloomfield, "Linguistic Aspects of Science," *International Encyclopedia of Unified Science,* Vol. I (No. 4), pp. 16, 17.

19. Leonard Bloomfield, *Language* (New York: Henry Holt & Co., 1938), p. 41.

20. See Dwight MacDonald, "The Bible in Modern Undress," *The New Yorker* (November 14, 1953), pp. 179, 187.

21. *The Philosophy of Rhetoric* (New ed., with the Author's Last Additions and Corrections; Edinburg: Neill & Co., for Archibald Constable & Co., and John Fairbairn, Edinburg; and T. Cadwell & W. Davies, London, 1816), I, 82, 83.

22. John Dewey, *Art as Experience* (New York: Minton, Balch & Co., © 1934), p. 109.

23. E. Jordan, *Essays in Criticism* (Chicago: University of Chicago Press, 1952), p. 193.

24. Allan Nevins, *The Gateway to History* (Boston: D. C. Heath & Co., 1938), p. 38.

25. Karl R. Wallace, "The Field of Speech, 1953: An Overview" (a speech delivered July 17, 1953, Summer Speech Conference, University of Michigan, Ann Arbor [MS University of Illinois, Department of Speech]), p. 10.

26. Richard M. Weaver, *The Ethics of Rhetoric* (Chicago: Henry Regnery Co., 1953), p. 25.

27. Barnet Baskerville, "Emerson as a Critic of Oratory," *The Southern Speech Journal,* 18 (March 1953), 161.

28. *The Complete Works of Ralph Waldo Emerson,* ed. Edward Waldo Emerson (Centenary ed.; Boston: Houghton Mifflin & Co., 1903), XII, 225.

29. "Eloquence," ibid., VII, 131.

30. See C. J. Ducasse, "Propositions, Truth, and the Ultimate Criterion of Truth," *Philosophy and Phenomenological Research,* 5 (September-June, 1943, 1944), 317-40.

31. Cited in Allan Nevins, op. cit., p. 327.

32. "The Rhetoric of Hitler's 'Battle,' " in his *The Philosophy of Literary Form* (Baton Rouge: Louisiana State University Press, 1941), p. 191.

33. J. G. Randall, "A Blundering Generation," in his *Lincoln, The Liberal Statesman* (New York: Dodd, Mead & Co., 1947), pp. 36-64.

34. David Daiches, *A Study of Literature for Readers and Critics* (Ithaca: Cornell University Press, 1948), p. 77.

35. A. N. Whitehead, *The Aims of Education & Other Essays* (New York: Macmillan Co., 1929), p. 18.

36. Aristotle *Metaphysica,* op. cit., Δ 19. 1022^b.

37. Donald A. Stauffer, "Introduction: The Intent of the Critic," op. cit., p. 24.

38. Aristotle *Metaphysica,* Λ. 3. 1070^a.

39. See Kenneth Burke, "Psychology and Form," in *Counter-Statement,* 2nd ed. (Los Altos, Calif.: Hermes Publication, 1953), p. 31.

40. Lester Thonssen and A. Craig Baird, *Speech Criticism* (New York: Ronald Press, 1948), p. 257.

41. Harold Lasswell, Nathan Leites, and Associates, *Language of Politics* (New York: George W. Stewart, Publishers, Inc., 1949), p. 38.

42. Helen Wheatley Schrader, "A Linguistic Approach to the Study of Rhetorical Style," Ph.D. dissertation (Northwestern University, 1949), p. 17.

43. Ibid., p. 15.

44. Herbert A. Wichelns, "The Literary Criticism of Oratory," in *Studies in Rhetoric and Public Speaking in Honor of James Albert Winans* (New York: Century Company, 1925), p. 190.

45. "The Open Mind," *The Bulletin of the Atomic Scientists,* 5:1 (January 1949), 5.

46. Kenneth Burke, *Permanence and Change* (New York: New Republic, 1935), p. 71.

47. A. N. Whitehead, op. cit., p. 19.

48. Ibid., p. 19.

49. Aristotle *Metaphysica,* a. 3.995[a].

50. "The Noblest Monument of English Prose," in his *Essays in Appreciation* (Boston: Houghton Mifflin Co., 1936), pp. 3-5, passim.

51. Dwight MacDonald, op. cit., p. 175.

52. *Rhetorica,* iii. 2. 1404[b].

RHETORIC AND IDENTIFICATION

JANE BLANKENSHIP

Rhetoric as Identification

Too much emphasis may have been placed in the past on rhetoric as *manipulative.* Communication, or communion, is reached when the speaker and his audience find identification with one another. Persuasion is the means through which identification occurs. The task of the speaker is not to manipulate the audience, but to evoke in them "a sense of collaboration."[1]

Perhaps a useful starting point is rhetoric's chief tool, language. Kenneth Burke suggests that we begin by viewing language as symbolic action, a view that requires us to differentiate between motion and action, for although machines are capable of motion, only humans are capable of action.

Our approach to inanimate things is different from our approach to other human beings. We do not reason with machines, or send petitions to them, or persuade them to act; we move them physically. We switch on a light, turn an ignition key, or throw a baseball. We do this because we have some implicit understanding that men have free will and machines do not, and it is the capacity to make choices that is the essential difference between men and the machines they operate. Burke puts it succinctly. "If one cannot make a choice, one is not acting, one is being moved, like a billiard ball tapped with a cue and behaving mechanically in conformity with the resistances it encounters."[2] Thus, action is the essence of our behavior.[3] In order for us to act we must choose, and it is this ability to choose that makes us self-moving beings.

To understand fully this difference between motion and action, let us consider Patrick Henry's speech, "Liberty or Death," delivered March 23, 1775. He suggests that, in their

Jane Blankenship, *Public Speaking: A Rhetorical Perspective,* Second Edition © 1972. Reprinted by permission of Prentice-Hall, Inc., Englewood Cliffs, New Jersey.

struggle with Great Britain, the colonists had, at one time, many alternatives, many ways of choosing to act. They could "remonstrate," "petition," "supplicate," or even "prostrate" themselves before the ministry and Parliament. But, he says, these alternatives have been exhausted. Their

> petitions have been slighted,
> remonstrances have produced additional violence and insult,
> supplications have been disregarded.

and they

> have been spurned, with contempt, from the foot of the throne.

Therefore, he suggests that only one alternative is left: "We must fight." But notice that Patrick Henry's audience retained the option of acting on two alternatives: they could accept his analysis and take up arms, or they could reject it and refuse to arm themselves. Thus, although Patrick Henry could harangue the audience, it was self-moving. Had he shot an arrow, it would have moved because an arrow cannot act of itself. But he could only try to persuade his audience to accept his suggestion as the best or only alternative. An arrow has no choice—it has to move. But the audience makes a decision to act.

As a result of some mental action man causes himself to do A rather than B, and because he himself makes this choice, he is responsible for its results. The purpose in making choices is to act. Since action is based on purpose, since there must be a reason for choosing A instead of B, action is not merely a means of doing, but rather a way of being. If action were only a means to an end, it would be called instrumental; because it is also the end itself, it is termed substantial.[4]

To illustrate this, again consider Patrick Henry's speech and continue our analogy of the arrow. The colonists had a reason for adopting Patrick Henry's resolution, whereas an arrow would have no reason for moving or not moving. An arrow has to move in a certain direction, at a certain rate of speed, and its course and rate are therefore said to be determined by instrumental means. On the other hand, the course of action and rate at which the colonists moved to implement Patrick Henry's resolution are called substantial. The distinction is that the arrow's motive force comes from outside itself—from the motion of the archer's wrist and arm—whereas the colonists' motive force came primarily from inside themselves. Patrick Henry apparently understood this, for he pointed to the nature of that motivating force:

> If we wish to be free—if we mean to preserve inviolate those inestimable privileges for which we have been so long contending—if we mean not basely to abandon the noble struggle in which we have been so long engaged, and which we have pledged ourselves never to abandon until the glorious object of our contest shall be obtained, we must fight!

Because man has reasons for making choices, his action is *purposive*. What moves a man to act helps shape the nature of his action; for example, according to Patrick Henry, *because the colonists wish to remain free* they must strike off the fetters of British tyranny. There would be no reason for taking up arms if they did not wish to remain free. Just as purpose shapes action, motive shapes purpose. Man has not only a reason but also a need for acting, which may be determined by his *motivation*. Certain needs such as the physiological needs, safety, love, esteem and self-fulfillment are shared by all people, and as each need is fulfilled others emerge. Note how Patrick Henry appealed to at least three of them here.

Safety

"Ask yourselves how this gracious reception of our petition comports with those war-like preparations which cover our waters and darken our land."

"Are fleets and armies necessary to a work of love and reconciliation? Have we shown ourselves so unwilling to be reconciled, that force must be called in to win back our love? . . . These are the implements of war and subjugation."

"They are sent over to bind and rivet upon us those chains which the British ministry have been so long forging."

"Our chains are forged! Their clanking may be heard on the plains of Boston!"

Esteem

"Our brethren are already in the field!"

"The battle . . . is not to the strong alone; it is to the vigilant, the active, the brave."

Self-fulfillment

"Is life so dear, or peace so sweet, as to be purchased at the price of chains and slavery?"

". . . give me liberty or give me death!"

It is clear that man feels obliged to socialize his world view because he does consider, explain, and justify the reasons for his choices. Patrick Henry explains why he feels compelled to speak, though others may call him a traitor for doing so:

> Should I keep back my opinions at such a time, through fear of giving offense, I should consider myself as guilty of treason toward my country, and of an act of disloyalty toward the Majesty of Heaven which I revere above all earthly kings.

Socialization is, as Marie Hochmuth Nichols suggests, an individual's appeal to his group through language.[5] Consider how Henry displays conduct that his audience probably deemed admirable. There are at least five dominant character traits manifested. Henry appears:

1. conciliatory
2. reasonable
3. understanding
4. reassuring
5. courageous

Although we cannot discuss this fully here, we can indicate some of the ways this means of identification appears to be working.

1. The opening of the speech is *conciliatory*. The debate which preceded it was heated and passionate, and Henry's audience clearly was divided. One of his tasks was to bring them together as best he could. Even though they do not all agree with him, he does not doubt their patriotism or their abilities.

2. Henry takes great care to appear *reasonable*. He tells them why he should be allowed to speak as he will; he urges that they consider the lessons of experience, and that they ask themselves the real meaning of "those war-like preparations which cover our waters and darken our land"; he asks further questions ("Are fleets and armies necessary to a work of love and reconciliation?"), letting the audience arrive at answers; he continues to question, suggesting that they have done everything they could: "petitioned," "remonstrated," "supplicated," "prostrated ourselves before the throne," "implored its interposition to arrest the tyrannical hands of the ministry and Parliament"); he posits a chain of "ifs." Only after this does he state explicitly his position that the war has already started, and that the Colonists would therefore be reacting to aggression rather than starting a war.

3. In this trying and inflammatory situation, Henry appears to be *understanding*. He realizes why the audience has not acted before, suggesting that it is "natural" to indulge in "the illusions of hope." He is concerned for their safety and for their esteem.

4. Henry is as *reassuring* as he can be in so tense a situation. "The battle," he suggests, "is not to the strong alone; it is to the vigilant, the active, the brave." Moreover, their fight for liberty is a "holy cause." God is on their side.

5. Even if his audience does not agree with him, there is *courage* in both his final appeal and his personal decision. He asks: "Is life so dear or peace so sweet as to be purchased at the price of chains and slavery?" Here his appeal is to man's fulfillment, not his mere existence. In any event, his personal choice is clear: "I know not what course others may take; but as for me, give me liberty or give me death!"

His interests are clearly joined with those of this audience. They all have a "responsibility" to God and country. They may all be forced into "submission"; they may all wear the chains that Great Britain has sent her armies to "bind and rivet" upon them. They would all be subject to the "next gale that sweeps from the north." Thus, they are interested in the same values and they will, largely, share the same fate.

The speaker aligns himself with what he takes to be recurrent patterns in the experience of his audience:

a. Men of debate rather than violence, they are aware that different men (of equal ability and patriotism) often see the same subject in different lights.

b. Most would acknowledge that in proportion to the magnitude of the subject ought to be the freedom of the debate.

c. Most desire peace; few will rush gleefully into the war. That, after all, is *why* the petitions, remonstrances, and the like.

He "talks their language" largely by the manner in which he conducts himself, sharing their interests in safety, esteem, and self-fulfillment, and by virtue of the fact that he and his audience have shared experiences.

This analysis of how one speaker attempted to socialize his view of the world is by no means exhaustive. You may wish to explore further the question of how Patrick Henry appealed to his particular audience.

Now let us ask where the initial motivation for any action comes from? Burke would say from the nature of man himself; that is, generically, man is a biological organism, an animal with need for property—for food and shelter. But he also uses symbols, and therein lies a trait that distinguishes him from other animals. Man not only uses symbols, he invents them.[6] As symbol-inventing, symbol-using animals, we are concerned not only with survival but with other motives as well; for example, we worry about security. We want the freedom to exist without anxiety and doubt; we worry about the quality of our survival.

As animals, we want to exist; as symbol-users, we want to exist as human beings. We attempt to overcome our generic separateness by communication, for, as Nichols puts it, "communication is compensatory to division."[7] Language promotes socialization and thereby facilitates social cohesion. Without socialization and the sense of order it brings, we would face chaos. As philosopher Suzanne Langer has observed, one "can adapt himself somehow to anything his imagination can cope with; but he cannot deal with chaos."[8]

Because we can identify with others, we are able to transcend our separateness. Our identification with one another or with a group does not eliminate our separateness or difference—rather, it resolves them, allowing us to be joined and separate. Each of us remains unique, yet capable of acting with others, as we seek ways of acting together. Identification and communication demand sharing, participation by both speaker and audience.

Thus, language has its origin in the very essence of human behavior. It is a species of action that depends on choice, purpose, and motive, and that translates man's biological needs into symbols which form an orientation in which we can function as human beings. Socialization provides this orientation. Through language and persuasion, we are able to resolve the generic differences among us, and to cooperate in promoting "the good life."[9]

. . . . .

Establishing Identification

In order to persuade a person, the speaker needs to identify his opinion (or the course of action he is suggesting) with one or more of the opinions or customary courses of action of his audience. Identification, which may be thought of as both ends and means to that end, is, of course, the end of communication. The speaker and his audience establish identification with one another so they can act together to preserve the best of their world, or to bring about whatever changes they believe necessary to make it a better place in which to live.

Identification is also a means to the end cooperation. There are a variety of ways by which the speaker may seek identification with his audience:[10]

1. By "talking their language" through speech, gesture, attitude
2. By sharing some principle in common with them
3. By showing that his conduct or proposed act is like the conduct or actions they admire

4. By participating or appearing to participate in those specialized activities which make one a participant in some group
5. By use of certain stylistic devices
6. By aligning himself with whatever recurrent patterns of experience his audience has experienced.

Richard Murphy describes Theodore Roosevelt's sense of identification in this way:

> Everywhere he went he found things in common with his audience: some of his Rough Riders had come from the district, he had close friends in the area, he had read the history of the locality. He told an audience of Presbyterians that he often attended their services because they were so much like those of his own church, the Dutch Reformed. . . . He reminded the legislature in Texas that he had been a legislator. . . . At the Sorbonne, he interjected extemporaneous sentences in French to make meanings clear.[11]

This is not meant to suggest that the speaker compromise his own integrity, that he be subservient to his audience, but it does mean that people listen more easily when they see the common ground they share with the speaker. An audience needs to feel itself directly involved in the speaker's topic, so he should speak *with* them, not merely before them.

One of the most striking opening statements made by a student in a classroom speech urged the other members of the class to support a volunteer service program at one of the local mental hospitals:

> It has been estimated that one out of every ten people in the United States will, during the course of his lifetime, receive help of some kind for mental illness. If these figures are correct, and we have every reason to believe they are, that means three people in this room may some day suffer from one kind of emotional disturbance or another. So, the problem of caring for the mentally ill is a problem which you and I must face very seriously. It is *our* problem.
>
> Now, the first question which probably comes to your mind is this: How can I help care for the mentally ill? I am not a psychologist or a psychiatrist. I am not a trained orderly. The answer to this question is one which dozens of students answer every Thursday night between the hours of seven-thirty and nine-thirty when they perform volunteer services at one of the local mental hospitals.
>
> Today I'd like to tell you about our volunteer program, some of the things we have accomplished, and some of the things we can accomplish with your help.

This speaker found a very direct and attention-getting link between himself, his topic, and his audience. He established that the problem was not just his problem, or the problem of other people, but "our" problem. Thus, the audience became a direct participant in his speech. He kept the audience participating until the last portion, when he dealt with "some of the things which the volunteer services program can accomplish with *your* help." This speaker knew that the task of identification does not end with the opening remarks, that the common ground between the speaker and the listener must continually be established throughout the speech.

Observe a political speaker, campaigning across the country, establishing three different links with three different audiences:

1. In Minnesota: "I am grateful for the opportunity to talk with you about national farm policies. I won't waste your time this afternoon telling you . . . all

about how I am myself a farmer. I own farm land in Illinois, and I come from a family that has lived in the heart of the Corn Belt for over a hundred years. . . . My first venture into public service was in Washington in the old Agricultural Adjustment Administration. . . ."

2. In Virginia: "Here in Richmond tonight, in Virginia, rich both in history and in the knowledge of its history, I am moved to talk for a few minutes of the past. . . . The South is a good place to take our bearings, because in no part of the country does the past—a past of great nobility and great tragedy—more sharply etch the present than in the South."

3. In Massachusetts: "I don't know why it is that an American, no matter where he was born or where he lives, has a feeling in New England of coming home. Perhaps it is because this country of yours looks so homelike; perhaps it is because the people and their welcome are always friendly; perhaps it is because so much of what we are as Americans came out of these valleys and these hills—our habit, for example, of making up our own minds in our own way, and saying what we think—our habit of respect for each other, and for ourselves—our habit, if you please, of freedom."[12]

Identification can be affected either by the speaker's deliberate design or by unconscious factors of appeal. It is "a way of life," an "acting together," and, in acting together, men have common sensations, concepts, images, ideas, and attitudes. To catch a glimpse of the various levels on which identification operates, let's look briefly at related, but somewhat different, levels of identification used by Richard M. Nixon in his April 30, 1970, speech "On the Cambodian Decision."[13] We can see clearly how President Nixon tries to get his audience to "act together" with him, and that he tries to identify his life style with those he has included in his audience. But it is also clear that, by virtue of advocating one life style rather than another, he has excluded as well as included people from his audience. Thus, in identifying with only a portion of the mass audience, he is likely alienating another portion.

1. Identification with what the speaker presumes to be majority values.
   A. Most don't want to "clearly endanger the lives of Americans. . . ."
   B. Most want to be working for peace, to be "conciliatory at the conference table" but not "humiliated."
   C. Most do not want to "get peace at any price now" because a "peace of humiliation for the United States will lead to a bigger war or surrender later."

2. Identification with commonly held basic assumptions or premise, e.g.:
   A. ". . . only the power of the United States deters aggression."
   B. "If when the chips are down, the world's most powerful nation, the United States of America, acts like a pitiful, helpless giant, the forces of totalitarianism and anarchy will threaten free nations and free institutions throughout the world."
   C. "It is not our power but our will and character that is being tested tonight."

3. Identification with certain types of arguments.

4. Identification of self with past Presidents and their policies; e.g., "In this room, Woodrow Wilson made the great decisions which led to victory in World War I. Franklin Roosevelt made the decisions which led to our victory in World War II. Dwight D. Eisenhower made decisions which ended the war in Korea and avoided war in the Middle East. John F. Kennedy, in his finest hour, made the great decisions which removed Soviet missiles from Cuba and the Western Hemisphere."

5. Identification with certain character traits; e.g.:
   A. One does not "take the *easy* political path" [to "blame this war on previous Administrations and to bring all of our men home immediately regardless of the consequences"].
   B. One puts country above self: "I would rather be a one-term President than to be a two-term President at the cost of seeing America become a second-rate power and to see this nation accept the first defeat in its proud 190-year history."
   C. One is strong but conciliatory.
   D. One is humble: "The decision I have announced tonight is not of the same magnitude [as those of Wilson, Franklin D. Roosevelt, and John F. Kennedy in their decisions announced in the same room]."

6. Identification with the men in the field with whom the President also identifies: "It is customary to conclude a speech from the White House by asking support for the President of the United States. Tonight I depart from that precedent. What I ask for is more important. I ask for your support of our brave men fighting tonight halfway around the world—not for territory—not for glory—but so that their younger brothers and their sons and your sons will be able to live together in peace and freedom and justice."

Whether the speaker has managed to identify his ways with those of his audience is decided in the end by the audience.

Notes

1. Hugh Duncan, *Communication and Social Order* (New York: Oxford University Press, Inc., 1968), p. 170.
2. Kenneth Burke, *Rhetoric of Religion* (Boston: Beacon Press, 1961), p. 188.
3. See Kenneth Burke, *Language as Symbolic Action* (Berkeley: University of California Press, 1966).
4. This treatment of Patrick Henry's speech follows, in part, the one originally proposed in Jane Blankenship, *A Sense of Style* (Belmont, Calif.: Dickenson Publishing Co., 1968), pp. 14-17.
5. Marie Hochmuth Nichols, *Rhetoric and Criticism* (Baton Rouge: Louisiana State University Press, 1963), pp. 82-83.
6. Burke, *Rhetoric of Religion,* p. 42n.
7. Nichols, *Rhetoric and Criticism,* p. 82.
8. Susanne K. Langer, *Philosophy in a New Key* (Cambridge, Mass.: Harvard University Press, 1942), p. 241.
9. Nichols, *Rhetoric and Criticism,* p. 91.
10. All of these are suggested in two of Kenneth Burke's books, *The Rhetoric of Motives* (Englewood Cliffs, N.J.: Prentice-Hall, Inc., 1950) and *Counter-Statement* (Chicago: University of Chicago Press, 1931).
11. Richard Murphy, "Theodore Roosevelt," in *History and Criticism of American Public Address,* Vol. III, pp. 338-39.
12. From *Major Campaign Speeches of Adlai E. Stevenson, 1952* (Copyright 1953 by Random House, Inc.), pp. 64, 149, 140. Reprinted by permission.
13. All quotes are transcribed from a tape of the speech delivered over national television.

DIMENSIONS OF THE CONCEPT OF RHETORIC

WAYNE BROCKRIEDE

During recent years a state of cold war has existed in the field of speech. Humanists who seek to understand rhetoric primarily through the use of historical scholarship and behavioral scientists who seek to develop a communication theory primarily through empirical description and experimental research have tended to see one another as threatening enemies. Yet members of these factions have the common objective of studying similar phenomena. The student of communication who conceives his study as focusing on pragmatic interaction of people and ideas is concerned with the rhetorical impulse within communication events.[1]

The purpose of this essay is to sketch the beginning and to encourage the further development of a system of dimensions for the study of rhetorical communication. Five assumptions implicit in this attempt should be stated explicitly from the outset.

First, the conception of rhetoric broadly as the study of how interpersonal relationships and attitudes are influenced within a situational context assumes the presence of the rhetorical impulse in such diverse acts as a speaker addressing an audience face to face or through mass media, a group of people conferring or conversing, a writer creating a drama or a letter to an editor, or a government or some other institution projecting an image.

Second, the concept of rhetoric must grow empirically from an observation and analysis of contemporary, as well as past, events.[2] The dimensions should be selected, developed, structured, and continuously revised to help explain and evaluate particular rhetorical acts.

Third, although the theorist, critic, or practitioner may focus his attention on a rhetorical act, such an act must be viewed as occurring within a matrix of interrelated contexts, campaigns, and processes.

Fourth, the rubrics of a rhetorical act are best viewed as dimensional, each reflecting a wide range of possible descriptions and not as expressing dichotomies.

Fifth, the dimensions of rhetoric are interrelational: each dimension bears a relationship to every other dimension.

This essay, therefore, represents an attempt to sketch a contemporary concept of interrelated interpersonal, attitudinal, and situational dimensions of a broadly conceived rhetorical act.

1

Traditional rhetoric places much less emphasis on interpersonal relationships than does the model presented in this paper. Even the concept of *ethos* frequently has been conceived as personal proof functioning rationalistically as a message variable.[3]

What are here developed as interpersonal dimensions may indeed function in an instrumental way, having some influence on a rhetorical act which aims primarily at attitudinal influence or situational appropriateness. But interpersonal dimensions themselves often

Wayne Brockriede, "Dimensions of the Concept of Rhetoric," *Quarterly Journal of Speech* (February 1968), pp. 1-12. By permission of the Speech Communication Association and the author.

represent the principal goals; and the establishment, change, or reinforcement of such interpersonal relationships as liking, power, and distance may exercise a controlling influence on the other dimensions.

Liking

This interpersonal dimension poses the question: how attracted to one another are the people who participate in a rhetorical act? Liking differs qualitatively and may refer to such continua as spiritual adoration—hate, sexual attraction—repulsion, friendship—enmity, and compatibility—incompatibility. In a dyadic act the feeling may or may not be mutual. When many people are involved—as in hearing a public address, participating in a discussion, or reading a best-seller, a single relationship may be characteristic—as when an audience becomes polarized, or relationships may vary—as when some discussants feel affection for a leader whereas others are repelled. Liking also differs in degree of intensity and in degree of susceptibility to change.

The change or reinforcement of the liking dimension may function as the primary purpose of a rhetorical act; courtship, for example, aims principally at affecting this relationship. Or increasing, maintaining, or decreasing the degree people like one another may be a by-product of a situation which has other chief aims. Or the liking relationship, though it remains essentially unchanged during a rhetorical act, may have a profound influence on whether other dimensions vary, as well as on how they vary.[4]

Power

Power may be defined as the capacity to exert interpersonal influence. Power may be the ultimate purpose or function, as in a power struggle, or it may be a by-product of or an influence on the controlling dimensions. The power dimension includes two primary variables.

First, what are the kinds of power? One is the influence a person has because others like him. The word *charisma* denotes this kind of power when it reaches a great magnitude. But personal magnetism exists also in lesser degrees. The power of personal attractiveness represents a kind of intersection of liking and power. A second type of power stems from position or role in the social system. By having control over the assignment of sanctions, the allocation of rewards and punishments in a social system, a man merely by virtue of his office or role may be powerful. A third type is the control over the communication channels and other elements of the rhetorical situation. This situational power corresponds to what some people call the gatekeeper function. A fourth kind of power is an influence over the sources of information, the norms and attitudes, and the ideology. Such an influence seems to depend on the extent to which other people trust one's ideational competence generally and his special expertise on matters relevant to the rhetorical act, on their perceptions of his general willingness to express himself honestly and accurately and of his special candor on the particular relevant topics, and on their feelings of confidence in their abilities to predict accurately the meaning and significance attached to his statements and actions.[5] Finally, one exercises indirectly a degree of power by having access to and influence on other people who can exercise the other kinds of power more directly. So a first general variable to the power dimension is the degree with which people participating in a rhetorical act can manifest these kinds of power.

A second variable is power structure. Knowing how much power of what kind each rhetorical participant has may be less immediately relevant than knowing the relationship among the power statuses of the people involved. That is, power is relative rather than absolute. The significance of the power of a writer, for example, regardless of the amount or kind he may possess, depends on how much power he has relative to that of his readers. Two questions especially are important in an analysis of the power structure. How disparate are the power positions of the various participants of an act, and does the act function to increase, maintain, or decrease the disparity? How rigid or flexible is the structure, and does the rhetorical act function to increase, maintain, or decrease the stability?[6]

Distance

The concept of distance is related to the other interpersonal dimensions. One generally feels "closer" to those persons he likes and "farther" from those he dislikes, but the greater the power disparity the greater the distance. Like all other dimensions, the establishment of an appropriate distance (whether decreasing, maintaining, or increasing it) may be a rhetorical act's primary function, an incidental outcome, or an influencing factor.

Two kinds of distance make up this dimension. One is an interpersonal distance between each two participants in a rhetorical act. The other is a social distance which exists within the structure of the group or groups within or related to the rhetorical act—such groups as audiences, committees, organizations, societies, and cultures. Although interpersonal and group distance are related closely and tend generally to covary, they are discrete variables in that two persons in a discussion group, for example, may move more closely together while the group structure is in the process of disintegrating.[7]

Several questions about the role of interpersonal and group distance in rhetorical situations seem important. How much distance (of each type) is optimal in achieving certain kinds of interpersonal, attitudinal, and situational rhetorical functions? What conditions of the other dimensions are most likely to increase, maintain, or decrease the distance (of each type)?

2

Controversial ideas which involve a choice among competing judgments, attitudes, and actions form a necessary part of any rhetorical act. Very often, although not always, such a choice is the primary operation, and the various interpersonal and situational dimensions merely create the environment in which the choice is made and influence how the choice is made. Traditionally, rhetoric seems rather consistently to have made this sort of assumption. The principal function of some rhetorical acts is interpersonal interaction or situational appropriateness, however, and the influence on attitudes in the making of choices is secondary. Attitude may be defined as the predisposition for preferential response to a situation. Two kinds of attitudes have rhetorical significance: attitudes toward the central idea in a choice-making situation and the ideological structure of other related attitudes and beliefs.

Central Idea

Several features of attitudes toward the central idea of a rhetorical situation require study.

First, although attitudes customarily have been considered as a point on a scale, this view is inadequate. As Carolyn Sherif, Muzafer Sherif, and Roger E. Nebergall have pointed out, a person's attitude may be described more accurately by placing various alternative positions on a controversy within three latitudes—of acceptance, of rejection, and of noncommitment.[8]. On the policy of the United States toward Vietnam, for example, a person may have one favored position but place other positions within his latitude of acceptance; such additional positions are tolerable. He may have one position that he rejects more strongly than any other but place other positions within his latitude of rejection. Finally, because he lacks information, interest, or decisiveness, he may place other positions within his latitude of noncommitment. To understand or predict the attitudinal interaction in a rhetorical situation one must know whether its central idea falls within the participants' latitude of acceptance, rejection, or noncommitment.

Second, the degree of interest and the intensity of feeling with which the central idea confronted in a rhetorical act occupies a place in whatever latitude will influence potentially all other dimensions of that act.

Third, the way the various latitudes are structured is an influential variable. Sherif, Sherif, and Nebergall identify one such structure which they term ego-involvement. A person who is ego-involved in a given attitude tends to perceive relatively few discrete alternative positions, to have a narrow latitude of acceptance—sometimes accepting only one position, to have a broad latitude of rejection—lumping most positions as similarly intolerable, and to have little or no latitude of noncommitment.[9] The ego-involved hawk, for example, may accept only a strong determination to achieve a military victory, assimilating all positions close to that one; and he may reject all other stands, seeing little difference between unilateral withdrawal and attempts to negotiate that necessitate any genuine concessions to the adversary, and labeling anything less than total victory as appeasement.

Fourth, a person's persuasibility on the central idea of a rhetorical act is a relevant variable. How likely is a person to respond positively to attempts to change his attitude? This question suggests the superiority of the Sherif, Sherif, and Nebergall analysis. The question is not the simple one of how likely is a person to move from "yes" to "no" or from favoring a negotiated settlement in Vietnam which does not involve the possibility of a coalition government in South Vietnam to one which does. It is the far more complex question of whether positions which are now assigned to one latitude can be moved to another one. This concept recognizes, for example, that to move a person from a position of rejection to one of noncommitment is significant persuasion. A person's persuasibility is related, of course, to the nature, intensity, and structure of his attitude.[10] An ego-involved person who feels strongly about an idea is less likely to change his attitude than one who is less ego-involved or less intense.

What the preceding discussion suggests is that the nature, intensity, structure, or persuasibility of the attitude of any participant toward the central idea in a rhetorical transaction will influence the other dimensions and be influenced by them. In addition, the relationship of the attitudes of each participant to those of others in the situation will influence their interaction together. The issue here can be focused in a single question: how similar are the people in a rhetorical act with respect to the nature, intensity, structure, and changeability of their attitudes toward the idea under focus in the rhetorical act? Or, to put the question in a slightly different way: to what extent can people identify with the attitudes of one another?[11]

Ideology

An attitude does not exist in a vacuum. One idea does not occur by itself. Rather, attitudes have homes in ideologies. The ideologies evoked in a rhetorical act influence, and may sometimes dominate, the other dimensions.

Several ideological structures may be identified. Attitudes may relate to other attitudes, to systems of values and norms, to ethical codes, and to philosophic presuppositions about the nature of man, the nature of reality, the nature of language, and the nature of knowledge. About each of these contexts two questions may be raised: What is the nature of the ideological structure of each participant in the act? How similar or different are the ideologies of the various participants?

The central idea of any rhetorical transaction evokes not only attitudes toward that idea but attitudes toward related ideas. In recent years several theories and approaches have developed: balance theory, the theory of cognitive dissonance, the congruity hypothesis, and the social judgment approach.[12] Although these formulations differ and the differences are argued heatedly, one principle seems accepted by most attitude theorists: man has an urge to think himself consistent, to try to achieve homeostasis within his system of attitudes.

Although relatively few persons work out a careful formulation of an ideology which consciously monitors various attitudes, each person very likely has an implicit ideology which consciously affects the development of any attitude in the system. Anyone attempting to change one attitude of a person, therefore, will profit from the admittedly difficult task of identifying that person's other attitudes and of considering how they may facilitate or retard such an attempt and how the target-attitude will, if changed, affect other attitudes. In addition, to understand the rhetorical interaction on some central idea one must also consider how similar or different one person's attitudes toward related ideas are to those of other people in the rhetorical act.

A second ideological variable is the system of values and norms subscribed to by the people in a rhetorical act. Just as a person's attitudes relate to his other attitudes, they relate also to more fundamental principles which he values. Whereas the first relationship may be viewed as a sort of part-to-part analogical inference, the second is a part-to-whole (or whole-to-part) inference. General values both evolve from many particular attitudes, and they also structure new experience in the development of new attitudes toward new situations.[13]

One of the most important sources of each person's fundamental values is his membership in small groups, organizations, societies, and cultures. The argument can be made that all values can be traced generally to a social origin, but some values especially can be associated closely with membership in a particular reference group—whether small group, organization, society, or culture. Such shared values are termed norms. When a rhetorical situation involves the actual or implied presence of such groups, the norms of those groups predictably are going to function as an ideology which will tend to set limits for attitudes of group members.[14]

A third kind of ideology is the ethical variable which raises two questions: What personal morality or public ethic guides the interaction of attitudes? Is the code of conduct acceptable to others who participate in the rhetorical act? A transaction of ideas viewed as unethical by someone with whom a person tries to interact will have adverse effects on many of the other dimensions.[15]

A fourth ideological variable consists of a person's philosophic presuppositions about the nature of man, the nature of reality, the nature of language, and the nature of knowledge. This variable probably functions relatively rarely as the primary goal of a rhetorical act, perhaps only when philosophers engage in dialogue, but it establishes a frame of reference within which attitudes interact. Is a man an object to be manipulated or a decision-maker in the process of making radical choices? To what extent does he behave rationally? To what extent is his rhetorical behavior determined for him and to what extent does he exercise free will? Does one take an Aristotelian, a Platonic, or a phenomenalistic stance on the question of the nature of reality? How does man acquire knowledge? To what extent does he come to know through a priori intellection, through revelation, through existential experience, or through scientific analysis?[16] How each person in a rhetorical act answers these questions, and the degree to which the various answers are similar, will influence how attitudes interact.

3

A rhetorical act occurs only within a situation, and the nature of that act is influenced profoundly by the nature of the encompassing situation. Furthermore, on certain ceremonial occasions situational dimensions dominate the act. A speaker's function in a funeral oration, for example, may be merely to meet the expectations of the occasion. Six situational dimensions form a part of the conceptual framework advanced in this essay: format, channels, people, functions, method, and contexts.

Format

The essential concern of this dimension is how procedures, norms, and conventions operate to determine who speaks and who listens.

Formats fall into two general types which anchor the ends of the dimension. At one extreme is a polarized situation in which one person functions as speaker or writer and others function as listeners or readers. At the other extreme is a type of conference situation in which the functions of the various participants rotate freely between speaking and listening.

Formats vary with respect to the degree of flexibility permitted rhetorical participants. In some situations, for example in written and electronic discourse, a rhetorician has little opportunity to revise his original plans within the act, although he may utilize feedback in designing subsequent acts in a campaign. In other situations a rhetorician has maximum opportunity to observe the reactions of others and to make appropriate decisions accordingly.[17]

Channels

The role of channels in a rhetorical act is manifested in three variables. First, is the communication conveyed verbally, nonverbally, or through a mixture of the two modes?

Radio speaking and written messages are instances of the verbal channel; a silent vigil and pictures employ the nonverbal channel; and face-to-face speaking, television, and books which feature graphic materials illustrate the mixed mode.[18]

Second, if language is employed, is it in oral or written form? Although the distinction between these two channels needs no clarification,[19] their modes of transmission require analysis. Traditional rhetoric has long studied delivery as one of the canons. Although students of written composition have paid far less attention to the study of transmitting messages, such features as the selection of paper, binding, cryptology, and the like may influence the interaction between writer and reader more than the persons playing either role recognize. Delivery, whether in oral or written channel, illustrates well the primary idea of this essay: that each dimension relates to every other dimension. Delivery will influence and be influenced by the interpersonal dimensions of liking, power, and distance; by the attitudes toward the central idea and toward those related to it; and by the other situational dimensions of format, people, functions, method, and contexts.

Third, is the rhetoric transmitted directly or indirectly? A direct channel is a system of communication in which one person relates to someone else without the interference or aid of a third person or a mechanical device. The oral interpretation act, the speaker who reaches the newspaper reader via a reporter, the tape recording, television, and the two-step flow of communication all illustrate the indirect channel.[20] But indirectness admits of degrees. Messages may be transmitted through only one intermediary person or agency, or they may follow a circuitous track, as in a typical rumor, between its originator and its ultimate, and perhaps indefinite, destination.[21]

People

How rhetorical situations are populated forms six variables. One concerns the number of interacting people. Are they few or many?[22]

A second variable is the number of groups which function in the situation, whether as audiences or conferences. The range is from one to many. A speaker may address one particular audience or many audiences, either simultaneously or consecutively. A person may participate in a conference which operates virtually as a self-contained unit or in a conference involving multiple groups.

A third variable has to do with the degree to which the people are organized. The range is from a virtual absence of organization to the status of a highly structured and cohesive reference group.

A fourth variable, closely related to the third, involves the degree of homogeneity among the participating people. They may exhibit a high degree of homogeneity, they may be similar on some and different on other properties, or they may differ so much as to constitute essentially different groups even though they participate in the same situation.[23]

Fifth, participants in a rhetorical situation may vary widely in their degree of awareness of their roles and in their degree of involvement in the situation.

Sixth, those who people a rhetorical situation engage in a range of relationships to that situation. One, some, many, or all of the participants may regard themselves or be regarded by others as depersonalized stimulus objects; as members or agents of a culture, institution, or group; as performing a role; as projecting an image; as manifesting a set of properties or as selves with radical choices to make or commitments to uphold.

Functions

The functions of a rhetorical situation may be viewed from a general perspective or along interpersonal and attitudinal dimensions.

Some questions of situational function seem to apply both to the interpersonal and to the attitudinal aspects of a rhetorical act. To what extent are interpersonal relationships and/or attitudes to be reinforced or changed? What degrees of intensity of reinforcement or changes does the situation call for? If change is to function, in what direction?

Other questions relate directly to the interpersonal dimension. Are people trying primarily to relate, identify, disengage, or in other ways to interact with others in the situation, or are they trying to express their "selves" conjointly? Are they trying to court, please, satisfy, tolerate, dissatisfy, or derogate one another? Are they trying to change or reinforce the power disparity or power structure of the situation? Are they trying to increase, maintain, or decrease social or interpersonal distance? Is group maintenance or group cohesiveness a relevant situational function?

Still other questions relate directly to three kinds of attitude influence. First, a person may present a message with a designative function—to present information, describe, define, amplify, clarify, make ambiguous, obfuscate, review, or synthesize ideas. Second, someone may present a message with an evaluative function—to praise, make commentary, hedge, criticize, or blame some person, object, situation, judgment, or policy. Third, someone may present a message with an advocative function—to solve a problem, create indecision, reinforce a present choice, foster delay, choose a change [sic] alternative, resolve a conflict, propose a compromise, or stimulate action.

The functions of rhetorical situations appear far more complex than implied by the traditional categories of inform, entertain, and persuade.

Method

Any situational function is manifested instrumentally through a number of message variables. These constitute the methodological dimension of the rhetorical act. Method is less often than other dimensions the ultimate function of the act; typically it plays the instrumental role of facilitating whatever dimension is primary.

Method includes the materials presented, the form in which they are structured, and the style in which materials and form are communicated.

Three questions about the material to be presented seem important. How much data should be presented? What kinds of data should be employed? From what sources should they be derived? These questions, of course, have no simple answers universally applicable.

The form variable may be analyzed in two ways. A distinction can be made between a sort of form-in-the-large which permeates the rhetorical method and a more microscopic set of structures which develops. The rhetorical act may be transacted through some conventional medium like an essay, a play, or a speech. A rhetorician may fulfill expectations by using identifiable forms in typical ways, or he may create new forms or employ old forms in new ways. Whether forms are appropriately new or old and whether their development is appropriately conventional or eccentric, of course, depends on the experience and expectations of the other people in the rhetorical act. The method may represent a straightforward management of materials to develop a central idea directly, or reflect an indirect ordering—for example, through the use of irony.[24] How prominent the form-in-the-large is to be is an important issue. Should the form become clearly evident in the discourse, or should it fulfill its function unobtrusively and not call any special attention to itself?

The form variable may also be viewed microscopically. This level of analysis includes a consideration of the logical connection between the material presented and the ideas advanced—which calls for the student of rhetoric to understand the logic of rhetorical interaction and the modes of reasoning appropriate to such interaction.[25] It includes a recognition of the structure which joins the ideas advanced into a pattern which amplifies or supports the central idea—which calls for an understanding of the patterns of expository and argumentative discourse, the analysis of a controversy into its issues, and the methods of problem-solving and negotiation.[26]

Specific formal structures may be recognizable immediately to others in the act and utilized in predictable ways, or they may be new and less obvious. Furthermore, the two levels of form in a discourse, the macroscopic and the microscopic, may function harmoniously toward the same end or constitute incongruity. Form, whether large or small, may de designed to facilitate information transfer or to disrupt it; to create a relatively narrow range of meanings and attitudinal responses or to maximize ambiguity; to present an optimal amount of material efficiently or to aim at redundancy; to achieve identification or alienation; to reinforce meanings and attitudes or to change them; and to increase or decrease the intensity of feelings toward the ideas.

Style, like form, may be viewed macroscopically or microscopically. Rhetorical style may be looked at from the point of view of broad symbolic strategy, a style-in-the-large. I take this concern to be behind much of the writing of Kenneth Burke.[27] Or it may be analyzed by looking at smaller units of analysis—at the level of the phoneme, word, sentence, or paragraph. Perhaps the writing of modern linguists may provide better ways of analyzing style microscopically than rhetoricians have followed traditionally.[28]

Many of the questions raised about form appear to apply also to style. Whether looked at large or small, style, too, provides such issues as efficiency of information transfer, clarity *vs.* ambiguity, conciseness *vs.* redundancy, confidence *vs.* uncertainty, and identification *vs.* alienation. The issues can be resolved only by studying the particular interaction of the other dimensions in each unique rhetorical act.

Contexts

The contexts of time and place may alter in various ways how other dimensions function in the act. In this regard context is typical of situational dimensions. The substance of a rhetorical act is rarely located in the situation: It more characteristically focuses on the interpersonal and attitudinal categories. Aspects of the situation, including context, although not fundamental or ultimate, however, can alter decisively the other categories and hence change the substance of the act.

In addition, time functions in another way. Each rhetorical act has some larger setting and fits into one or more ongoing processes.[29] For example, a novel may be a part of a movement or of several movements, a representation of an ideology or several ideologies, a moment in the career of the writer, a specimen of some formal or stylistic tendency, a phase in some long-term interpersonal relationship with a set of readers, et cetera. Several questions may suggest some of the ways a rhetorical act may relate to its contexts. Does an act occur relatively early or relatively late in one or more processes? To what extent is the act congruous with its larger framework? Does the act play one role in one context and a different, and perhaps conflicting, role in another?

4

Important to the student of rhetoric is the question of points of view. A rhetorical act will be perceived quite differently by each person who participates in it, and still differently by each person who observes and criticizes it from "the outside." Here, as elsewhere, "meanings are in people," not in discourses. Students of rhetoric must try to determine how the various participants and observers have perceived the dimensions of the act and to discover the extent to which such perceptions differ. The points of view of the relevant people become part of an important dimension of the act.

The consideration of point of view may have different implications for theorists, as compared with participants and critics. The theorist tends to be interested in generalizations at the highest level of abstraction he can achieve, whereas participants and critics tend to be interested in making decisions or judgments about one very particular and unique act.

Perhaps the most important single characteristic of rhetoric is that it is a matrix of complex and interrelated variables of the kind discussed in this paper. The theorist cannot meaningfully pluck from the system any single variable and hope to understand it apart from the others. How can one understand style, for example, without knowing how it interrelates with power structure, with distance, with attitudes and ideologies, with the demands of format and context—in short, with every other dimension of the act? Gross generalizations about stylistic characteristics which ignore the assumption that style functions very differently when placed in different combinations with the other variables simply will not do. Unfortunately for the prognosis of theoretical advances in rhetoric, the combinations and permutations of the alternatives afforded by the various dimensions are so many as to approach infinity. But methods will have to be developed to pursue the sort of interrelational kind of analysis which an adequate theory of rhetoric requires.[30]

The practitioner may use such an interrelational analysis before, during, and after a transaction as a guide to the decisions he must make to give himself the best chance of interacting with others as he wishes.

The critic may profitably identify the single most compelling dimension of a rhetorical act under consideration and then investigate how that dimension interrelates with others which appear to be relevant. For example, a critic studying Nikita Khrushchev's interaction with the American public during his 1959 visit to this country might focus primary attention on Khrushchev's reduction of interpersonal distance between himself and his hosts in order to see how his distance-reducing rhetoric related to new American images of Khrushchev personally along liking and power dimensions; to his attempts to make attitudes and ideologies consubstantial; and to his use of various rhetorical situations for these functions. If a critic accepts the fundamental premise that each rhetorical act or process is unique, that dimensions interrelate in a way to create a unity never achieved in the past or in the future, then he commits himself to a search for a new way to select, structure, and weigh dimensions for each new act he criticizes.

My hope is that the dimensions described in this essay may provide a framework for theoretical development, practical decision making, and critical analysis.

Notes

1. Although my treatment differs from Dean C. Barnlund's excellent analysis in his "Toward a Meaning-Centered Philosophy of Communication," *Journal of Communication,* XII (December 1962), 197-211, the scope of my conception of rhetoric seems similar to the scope of his conception of

communication. Gerald R. Miller in his *Speech Communication: A Behavioral Approach* (Indianapolis: 1966), makes explicit (p. 12) his synonymous usage of the terms rhetoric and speech communication.

2. An argument which supports this claim is developed in my essay "Toward a Contemporary Aristotelian Theory of Rhetoric," *Quarterly Journal of Speech,* LII (February 1966), 35-37.

3. For example, in Lester Thonssen and A. Craig Baird's *Speech Criticism* (New York, 1948), the chapter on Ethos (pp. 383-91) is subtitled "Ethical Proof in Discourse."

4. Hugh D. Duncan stresses this dimension in his *Communication and Social Order* (New York, 1962) when he says (p. 170) that "the study of how men court each other . . . will tell us much about the function of rhetoric in society." See also Kenneth Burke, "Rhetoric of Motives" in *A Grammar of Motives* and a *Rhetoric of Motives* (Cleveland, 1962), pp. 732-36. I make no attempt in this essay to catalogue the status of knowledge or to supply bibliographies concerning each of the dimensions discussed. I shall suggest, however, a source or two which will develop further each of the dimensions considered in this essay.

5. Kenneth Andersen and Theodore Clevenger, Jr., provide an excellent synthesis of information on this kind of power in "A Summary of Experimental Research in Ethos," *Speech Monographs,* XXX (June 1963), 59-78.

6. This dimension seems to have been ignored in the study of many rhetorical situations. It is only implied, partially, for example, in the public address doctrine of ethos. During recent years, however, under the headings of leadership and power structure, many small group specialists have emphasized it. See, for example, Dorwin Cartwright and Alvin Zander, *Group Dynamics: Research and Theory,* 2nd ed. (Evanston, Ill., 1960), pp. 487-809. Among a number of useful works in the field of political sociology which are relevant to an understanding of the function of power in rhetorical acts, see *Class, Status, and Power,* eds. Reinhard Bendix and Seymour Martin Lipset, 2nd ed. (New York, 1966), pp. 201-352.

7. One of the shortcomings of the concept of interpersonal distance is that the term is not readily operationalized into specifiable behaviors. Consciously or unconsciously, however, people seem to have a sense of closeness or distance from others; such a feeling can influence rhetorical interaction. The philosophical basis for Kenneth Burke's rhetoric is the view that men are fundamentally divided. His concepts of identification and consubstantiality suggest that one of rhetoric's functions is to reduce man's interpersonal distance from man. See, for example, Burke, pp. 543-51. Edward T. Hall treats distance literally as a variable in communication situations in his *Silent Language* (Garden City, N.Y., 1959), pp. 187-209. The concept of social distance is implied in such terms in small group research as group cohesiveness, primary groups, and reference groups.

8. *Attitude and Attitude Change: The Social Judgment-Ego Involvement Approach* (Philadelphia, 1965), pp. 18-26.

9. Ibid., p. 233.

10. In addition, an individual's personality may be one of the determinants of his persuasibility on controversial propositions. See Irving L. Janis, Carl I. Hovland, et al., *Personality and Persuasibility* (New Haven, Conn., 1959), and Milton Rokeach, *The Open and Closed Mind* (New York, 1960).

11. Kenneth Burke's concept of identification seems to relate to the attitude dimension as well as to the dimension of interpersonal distance.

12. See Fritz Heider, "Attitudes and Cognitive Organizations," *Journal of Psychology,* XVL (April 1946), 107-14; Leon Festinger, *A Theory of Cognitive Dissonance* (Evanston, Ill., 1958); Charles E. Osgood, Percy Tannenbaum, and George Suci, *The Measurement of Meaning* (Urbana, Ill., 1957); and Sherif, Sherif, and Nebergall.

13. In their essay "The American Value System: Premises for Persuasion," *Western Speech,* XXVI (Spring 1962), 83-91, Edward D. Steele and W. Charles Redding state, "Values, as they exist psychologically in the mind of the audience, have been generalized from the total experience of the culture and 'internalized' into the individual personalties of the listeners as guides to the right way to believe or act" (p. 84). Karl R. Wallace argues that general value premises function as the substance of rhetoric—as good reasons which support propositions or value jugments. See "The Substance of Rhetoric: Good Reasons," *Quarterly Journal of Speech,* XLIX (October 1963), 239-49.

14. See A. Paul Hare, *Handbook for Small Group Research* (New York, 1962), pp. 23-61.

15. Edward Rogge, in his "Evaluating the Ethics of a Speaker in a Democracy," *Quarterly Journal of Speech,* XLV (December 1959), 419-25, suggests that the standards used to evaluate a speaker's ethics be those established by the audience and the society of which it is a part.

16. The importance of the philosophic dimension of rhetoric is well argued by Otis M. Walter in "On Views of Rhetoric, Whether Conservative or Progressive," *Quarterly Journal of Speech,* XLIX (December 1963), 367-82.

17. See David K. Berlo, *The Process of Communication* (New York, 1960), pp. 111-16. Ironically,

in public address, a format which offers considerable opportunity for communicative flexibility, the role of feedback has been analyzed very little.

18. Marshall McLuhan's *The Medium Is the Massage* (New York, 1967) is a notable attempt to make the nonverbal code as important in a book as the verbal.

19. Joseph A. DeVito's study of "Comprehension Factors in Oral and Written Discourse of Skilled Communicators," *Speech Monographs,* XXXII (June 1965), 124-28, concluded that written discourse involved a more difficult vocabulary, simpler sentences, and a greater density of ideas than did oral discourse.

20. The two-step flow of communication and the concept of opinion leadership has considerable applicability to rhetoric. See Elihu Katz and Paul F. Lazarsfeld, *Personal Influence* (Glencoe, Ill., 1955), and Elihu Katz, "The Two-Step Flow of Communication: An Up-to-Date Report on an Hypothesis," *Public Opinion Quarterly,* XXI (Spring 1957), 61-78.

21. The classic study of rumor is Gordon W. Allport and Leo Postman, *Psychology of Rumor* (New York, 1947).

22. I am inclined to include the intrapersonal communication of self-address within the scope of rhetoric. An individual's roles may interact intrapersonally and attitudinally in a variety of situational contexts in ways closely analogous to the interpersonal and attitudinal interaction of two or more persons. For support of this position, see Barnlund, 199-201, and Burke, pp. 561-63.

23. The effect of a group's homogeneity and receptivity on the integration and polarization of an audience is admirably discussed in Charles H. Woolbert's pioneer monograph "The Audience," *Psychologial Monographs,* XXI, No. 92 (June 1916), 37-54.

24. For an excellent analysis of rhetorical irony, see Allan B. Karstetter, "Toward a Theory of Rhetorical Irony," *Speech Monographs,* XXXI (June 1964), 162-78.

25. If one accepts the central idea of this essay that rhetoric is a system of interrelated dimensions, he must conclude that a rhetorical logic must accommodate the function of dimensions other than the one concerned with formal relationships among propositions. Irrelevant to rhetorical analysis is any local system which assumes that man is only rational and that men do not vary, that ideas can be divorced from their affective content and from their ideological contexts, and that the only situation is that of the logician talking to the logician.

26. Rhetoricians have tended to treat these various organizational patterns, like logic, as invariant structures, without due regard for the totality of the rhetorical situation—its people, its functions, and its contexts.

27. Burke, for example, says (p. 567) that rhetoric "is rooted in an essential function of language itself, . . . the use of language as a symbolic means of inducing cooperation in beings that by nature respond to symbols." For Burke, rhetorical analysis is an attempt to unearth the essential linguistic strategies of the rhetorical agent.

28. In "A Linguistic Analysis of Oral and Written Style," *Quarterly Journal of Speech,* XLVIII (December 1962), 419-22, Jane Blankenship applied the system of analysis which Charles C. Fries described in his book *The Structure of English* (New York, 1952).

29. Two recent books which display a contextual orientation to rhetoric are Wallace Fotheringham, *Perspectives on Persuasion* (Boston, 1966), and Huber W. Ellingsworth and Theodore Clevenger, Jr., *Speech and Social Action* (Englewood Cliffs, N.J., 1967).

30. Warren Weaver has argued that science must "make a third great advance which must be even greater than the nineteenth-century conquest of problems of simplicity or the twentieth-century victory over problems of disorganized complexity. Science must, over the next fifty years, learn to deal with these problems of organized complexity." See "Science and Complexity," in *The Scientist Speaks,* ed. Warren Weaver (New York, 1945), p. 7. Implicit in my essay is the belief that rhetoric represents a problem of "organized complexity."

THE SUBSTANCE OF RHETORIC: GOOD REASONS

KARL R. WALLACE

Rhetorical theorists have always recognized that speeches have content and substance, and that the content of a particular speech is derived from the setting and occasion. Yet unlike classical rheticians who presented systems of invention, modern writers who offer theories of rhetoric are unclear and uncertain what to say about the materials of discourse. They will include in their theories statements about methods, principles, techniques, and styles of discourse; that is, they talk of the forms and the handling of ideas and are mostly silent about the substance of utterance. Perhaps they are silent for three main reasons. Under the influence of structural linguistics, rheticians may uncritically believe that language is like the symbols of music and mathematics—empty and devoid of substantial meanings. Or they may overlook the full implication of Donald Bryant's reference to rhetoric as an art of adjusting ideas to people and people to ideas.[1] The notion of adjustment—and for that matter, adaptation—directs attention chiefly to acts of manipulation and treatment. It is easy to forget that one cannot engage in manipulation without manipulating something, and that speakers and audiences stand on common ground only through commonalities of meaning and partial identities of experience. If this simple fact is acknowledged, there always bobs up that old, bothersome question: With what ideas, with what materials do speakers adjust and adapt to their hearers? Finally, for the last century or so students of rhetoric seem to have been trapped into accepting a sort of scientific realism, or perhaps I might better say, a naive realism. The argument runs something like this: Since man derives his substantial information and knowledge through his sensory apparatus and since the natural sciences have successfully claimed for themselves both the acquisition and interpretation of sensory materials, discourse is left with nothing to say about the real world that does not properly belong to the sciences. Furthermore, since the behavioral sciences and the disciplines of philosophy and ethics have asserted property rights over the study of human experience and conduct, rhetoric has nothing to say about the behavior of speakers and listeners that these sciences cannot say with greater reliability and authority. Ergo, the substance of discourse comes from finding the right scientific and historical facts and of consulting the right authority. To me this is very much like saying that rhetoric is nothing more than the art of framing information and of translating it into intelligible terms for the popular audience.

1.

My position is this. First, rhetorical theory must deal with the substance of discourse as well as with structure and style. Second, the basic materials of discourse are (1) ethical and moral values and (2) information relevant to these. Third, ethics deal with the theory of goods and values, and from ethics rhetoric can make adaptations that will result in a modern system of topics.

In developing these ideas we must try at the outset to indicate what we mean by *substance*. The concept has carried many meanings, but the ones that are relevant here

Karl R. Wallace, "Substance of Rhetoric: Good Reasons," *Quarterly Journal of Speech* (October 1963), pp. 239-49. By permission of the Speech Communication Association and the author.

may be suggested by calling attention to certain words as correlatives. On one side are *substance, matter, material, content,* and *subject matter.* On the other are *form, structure, order, arrangement, organization, shape,* and *figure.* The words on each side reveal overlapping meanings. This fact must be recognized, of course. But what is important is that the terms on one side are not fully intelligible in the absence of the terms on the other. The notion of form is useless without the notions of matter and material; the notions of order and arrangement are senseless without the notions of matter and substance—of something to be ordered and arranged. In every case we recognize the relationship of figure and shape to that which is figured and shaped, the relationship of form to that which is formed—to that which is material and substantial. In the same sets of words there is also lurking the idea of substratum—of that which stands under, of support. In this sense, form is inconceivable without something as its basis. One does not arrange and order bricks, or think of arranging or ordering them, without having bricks or the idea thereof. One does not build a house without a foundation, nor an oration without spoken or written words and the meanings they carry.

In what sense, then, do we understand substance? An attempt to meet this question requires us to regard an utterance, a linguistic event, a speech, as an object. There are natural objects. These exist, or come into being, without the agency of man. They are the things of land and sea, vegetable and mineral. We say, depending upon our point of view, that natural objects are made by God, by Nature, or by some mysterious force. There are artificial objects, and these are said, in our language, to be man-made. Among these are language itself and whatever one makes with language—novels, poems, commands, instructions, laws, speeches, et cetera. If speeches are objects, rhetoric is related to speeches as theory is related to behavior. Since a theorist tries to explain the particular group of objects, events, and behaviors in which he is interested, a rhetorician endeavors to explain what speeches are, and this task involves his setting forth what speeches are about and how they come about. If speeches exhibit substance and materials—and it is nonsense to say that they do not—the rhetorician must, among other things, characterize the substance of speeches, the materials of which they are made. Theories of rhetoric in the classical tradition, as we know, almost always said a good deal about the substance and materials of speeches. Under the heads Invention and Topics, they described the general materials of speeches and their chief kinds, together with lines of argument that often recurred. Except for Kenneth Burke, the principal writers on modern rhetorical theory— e.g., I. A. Richards—neglect substance and concentrate on processes, methods, techniques, and effects. Most of our textbooks pay little attention to what speeches are about; rather, their point of view is pedagogical. They concentrate on how to make a speech and deliver it. I do not think this condition of affairs could long endure if rhetoric were to rediscover and reassert its concern with subject matter.

Rhetoric, then, ought to deal with the substance, the substratum or foundations of speeches. What is this stuff? In answer to this question, I shall offer three propositions. First, the underlying materials of speeches, and indeed of most human talk and discussion, are assertions and statements that concern human behavior and conduct. The are prompted by situations and contexts that present us with choices and that require us to respond with appropriate decisions and actions. Second, such statements are usually called judgments and appraisals. They reflect human interests and values, and the nature of value-judgments and the ways of justifying them are the special, technical, and expert concern of ethics. Third, the appearance and use of value-judgments in practical discourse are the proper, although not the sole, concern of the theory and practice of rhetoric.

Probably most thoughtful persons will at once agree that the foundation materials of speeches are statements that are evoked by the need to make choices in order that we may act or get ready to act or to appraise our acts after their doing. Furthermore, choosing itself is a substantive act and the statement of a choice is a substantive statement. Rhetoricians will recall that the time-honored classifications of speeches are based upon the typical choice-situations that audiences confront. The deliberative or political kind of speech helps an audience decide what it *ought* to do, and the materials most often appearing are those that bear on the particular audience's ends and purposes and the means to those ends. More specifically, so Aristotle thought, these things give rise to considerations of what is good and evil and what is useful, and these again with respect the problems of war and peace, of national defense, of taxation (or support of the state in relation to the citizen's purse), of the standard of living (or the welfare of the citizen), and of the making of laws and the good that laws can do. The forensic or legal speech helps a jury to decide upon the manner of treating a person who is accused of breaking the moral codes enshrined in law. What is justice in the case at hand? Is the man guilty or innocent? And if guilty, how should he be treated? The epideictic speech helps an audience to assess the ethics and morality of a person's actions. Whether the decision is to praise or blame him will depend upon whether his acts are judged virtuous, noble, right, and good. Evidently, then, large numbers of speeches employ statements whose content is ethical or moral, or they use language in a setting and in ways that logically imply ethical and moral ideas.

Still it may be asked whether there are not speeches in situations that have nothing to do with ethics and morality? What about discourse that is called informative, expository, or scientific?

We consider this question by pointing out that we often label a speech informative when in its proper context it is persuasive. Thomas Huxley's famous lecture, "On a Piece of Chalk," consists predominantly of factual sentences, yet to its English audiences in the 1870's it functioned as a plea for evolution. Much discourse and discussion that is thought of as didactic is probably persuasive in effect if not in intent. The character and bias of the state and nation function to select what is taught in the public schools. The teacher-learner relationship is accordingly less neutral and colorless than we think. Moreover, many teachers employ a method of learning that encourages students to think for themselves, to weigh and consider, to be intelligently appreciative and critical, to select and reject ideas and information that function indirectly, if not directly, to build attitudes and determine preferences. Furthermore, much newspaper discourse is in response to the widespread belief that knowledge is a good thing, and that certain kinds of materials and events are interesting, useful, and satisfying to readers, and other kinds are not. In brief, it would appear that expository speaking and writing recognizes choices and values that differ from those of persuasive discourse principally in that they are more remote and less apparent. So in saying that the materials and the substrata of speeches come about in response to contexts that present alternative possibilities, I want to include what is ordinarily thought of as informative utterance. First, much exposition is functionally persuasive, whether in intent or effect. This fact we have just remarked upon. Second, scientific discourse in itself cannot be utterly devoid of value. It owes its being to two assumptions: (1) knowledge in itself is a good thing, and (2) the information transmitted is accurate, reliable, valid, and true. Furthermore, scientific reporting of observations and experiments—and the criticism thereof—involves *what* a scientist did and did not do, *how* he did it and did not do it, and *why* he did it in one way rather than another.

The scientist cannot escape choices, whether he is addressing other scientists or a popular audience. His decisions are anchored in contexts governed by rules, conventions, and practices, whether they be those of the scientist or those of the nonscientist public.

2.

Although the basic substance of speeches comprises statements that are made when human beings must make choices, the consideration of such statements in their special and technical character in the proper concern of ethics. To support this assertion I must indicate what students of ethics today seem to be focusing on.[2] Despite differences in their special points of view and in the treatment of their material, they see the human being as he uses his reason in practical situations that involve choice and decision. Practical reason is revealed in judgments that guide man's conduct, i.e., judgments are statements having to do with action, motives, feelings, emotions, attitudes, and values. They are responses to one of two fundamental kinds of questions: What shall I do or believe? What ought I to do?[3] Both Toulmin and Baier talk in terms that are familiar to every historian and theorist of rhetoric.[4] Practical reason, for example, appears in three types of behavior: deliberation, justification, and explanation. Deliberation uses reason prior to the act. Justification and explanation use reason after the act. When we justify, we praise or blame; we use terms like right and wrong, good and bad; in general we *appraise*. When we explain, we show what moved the agent and use terms untinctured by praise or censure. Because these three types of rational behavior are carried on almost exclusively in symbolic and linguistic terms, some writers tend to treat ethics as consisting of statements, of kinds of statements, and of the content of statements. Of proper concern are statements in whose predicates are the words, *is a desirable thing, is morally obligatory, is morally admirable or reprehensible, is a good thing, is praiseworthy*, and the like.[5] Included, furthermore, are all statements that imply, though they do not specify, such evaluative words. Edwards achieves considerable simplicity when, following Broad and Findlay, as he says, he presents his theory in terms of two classes of judgments.[6] The first is the value judgment or moral judgment in which key predicate words are *good, desirable, worthwhile*, and their equivalents. The second is the *judgment of obligation*, as signalled by words like *ought, oblige*, and *duty*. We may say, then, that students of ethics are concerned with choice situations that are always signalled by the question, "What ought I to do?" They are concerned, also, with the rational and reasonable responses that human beings make to the question, i.e., with the judgments that we use in making choices and in justifying them.

Since judgments either state values directly or imply them indirectly, ethics as a study examines all values that influence action and are imbedded in judgments. It attempts to explain value-terms and how they are used, to classify them, and to find values that apply widely to our actions. Those of greatest generality are called standards or criteria of conduct. Some of them are compressed in concepts with which all of us are familiar: good and evil, pleasant-unpleasant, duty, obligation, self-interest, altruism, truth telling, promise keeping, honesty, fairness, courage, law-observance, utility, right and wrong, and the like. They appear typically in general statements called rules of conduct, regulations, laws, codes, principles, and moral maxims. With such values in mind, ethics also asks and tries to answer questions like these: Why these values rather than some other ones? And are the methods employed to identify them valid and trustworthy? In a word, modern ethics undertakes to present a theory of values which includes an account of how value-judgments are justified.

It would seem apparent, accordingly, that ethics as a study derives its materials in large measure from men's linguistic behavior when they must choose among alternatives. Their behavior constitutes judgments, and these appear in their reasonings when they deliberate, explain, and justify their choices. It is possible to observe such behavior systematically, to analyze it and theorize about it, and this ethics does. It is also possible to observe such behavior, to note what judgments all men, or most men, or wise men, or the wisest of men in practice accept or reject, and to perceive which of these recur in the materials and premises of men's reasonings. This is what classical rhetorical theory did, and this is what modern rhetorical theory should do. If the modern rhetorical theorist feels that he cannot in his textbook present a workable account of the material basis of speeches, perhaps much as Aristotle did in his *Rhetoric,* at least he can assert that rhetoric is related to ethics as theory is to practice. He can point out that the science of ethics deals with moral principles and standards of conduct as they are abstracted from practice, and that the art of rhetoric encounters moral principles in particular situations, in specific cases in which man in his social and political roles must make up his mind and act in concert, or be ready to act in concert.

If the materials of rhetorical discourse are fundamentally the same as the materials of ethics, it should be possible to derive a scheme of rhetorical topics from the study of ethics. Indeed, this can be done. I shall present now a brief outline of *topoi.* In doing so I am not suggesting that it is a perfect product and ready for incorporation into a textbook on public speaking. I aim only to point the way to a practical instrument.

First I shall sketch the general categories of values that help us to decide whether our decisions and actions are good or bad, right or wrong. There appear to be three, all-embracing classes—the desirable, the obligatory, and the admirable or praiseworthy, and their opposites.[7]

Whether or not something is desirable depends upon one's motives, goals, or ends—upon that for the sake of which we act. We act to reduce certain painful or unpleasant tensions. We rid ourselves of disease and illness to restore health; we banish hunger by seeking and eating food. On the other hand, some tensions produce pleasure, the chief among these being activity associated with sexual behavior, competitive activity in both work and play, and aesthetic excitement. Pleasurable tensions are involved, too, in activity that is venturesome and that involves learning and knowing. We desire things, also, that are in our own interests. Among interests, some are primarily self-centered, such as property and security (although both of these directly depend on social institutions and practices). Some interests are directly social—those for the sake of the general welfare. Other interests are professional, vocational, and recreational in nature. Desirable, furthermore, is personal and group achievement and its attendant pleasure and exhilaration. We derive satisfaction in making and creating something. We take pleasure and pride in achieving the "right" self-image. With this image is associated status—the respect and deference of others to us, and the power and ability to do what we wish. Desirable, moreover, is freedom of choice and action; undesirable are arbitrary restraints. A much-prized good is being loved and liked by others. Finally, there is an overriding, hedonistic desire, that of seeking anything that gives us pleasure and of avoiding acts and states of being that are painful or unpleasant. These, then, are things generally regarded as desirable and good. They are reflected directly or indirectly in the statements through which we make choices and explain or defend them.

Things that are morally obligatory and acts that are praiseworthy seem to acquire their meaning and force in the sort of regard that others have for us. The self-image is built up through the approvals and disapprovals of others, and thus we learn what is "right" and "wrong." Our integrity, our respect for ourselves, is a function of social rewards and sanctions. On the other hand, acts that are desirable and conduct that is goal-directed and that is said to be motivated, all seem to be built around, and come to focus on, the individual organism. The distinction between the desirable and the obligatory appears to be imbedded in our language. It is acceptable to say that playing golf is a good thing to do, but it is odd to say that playing golf is a right thing to do, or that golf playing is a matter of duty.

Within the class of things obligatory are duties. These are acts specified by one's position or role in a group or in a social institution. With respect to the family, a father has duties. With respect to his profession, a physician, a lawyer, a teacher has duties. With respect to the state, a governor has duties, and so does the citizen. There are obligatory actions so deeply woven into the social fabric that, once learned, they are rarely examined. They are truth telling, promise keeping, the paying of debts, and obeying of law. Finally, there are the *mores* of the group, as revealed in codes, customs, commandments, and moral maxims, and enforced by unwritten, social sanctions.

The last class of goods and values is that of the praiseworthy-blameworthy, the admirable-reprehensible. These value-terms are meant to refer to character traits, to behavior classes that have become stable, to what in the older literature of ethics were usually called *virtues*. Among these is conscientiousness, a term that refers not to some mystical, innate sense of the good, but to a concern for living up to one's obligations. There are, too, the familiar virtue names—kindliness, fairness, courage, veracity, honesty, prudence, persistence, tolerance, reliability, and good will (i.e., concern for the welfare of others). Although space does not permit the elaboration of these behavior traits, two or three observations should be made. Some writers call these traits *extrinsic* goods, or instrumental goods, because possession of them leads to the acquisition of other goods and ends. Honesty, for example, leads more often to desirable ends and less often to punishments than stealing and cheating. Although these terms may enter into all kinds of value-judgments, their long usage and genetic development suggest that they typically apply to behavior that is completed and past. Hence, to some writers they are technical terms of appraisal, and we use them most appropriately when we size up conduct that has become history. Yet terms of appraisal often appear in deliberative or policy contexts with persuasive intent. As Aristotle once observed, to praise a man is to hold him up for the imitation of others.

3.

This sketch of value categories has been presented entirely from the point of view of ethics. The categories represent a sort of *topoi* of values. Doubtless it is evident that rhetorical topics can be derived from them. One has only to recall the ordinary ways of analyzing a problem—the Dewey steps in problem-solving, for example, and the surveys for a proposition of fact and a proposition of policy—to perceive that they refer to situations in the present and the past and point to the possible future in terms that are ethical and moral. Such schemata of analytical thought originally had their basis in the logic of choice, decision, and conduct. Their long use and ready application have turned them into formulae whose derivation has been forgotten.

In presenting *topoi* of ethical values, I am not forgetting that the system must also include political values. Although this is not the place to spell out the significant differences between politics and ethics, we do well to remember that politics can be properly included within the scope of ethics, for the art of government is the art of adjusting the desires and values of the individual to the desires and values of others. Accordingly, rhetorical topics derived from ethics will point to political topics in the ways that genus relates to species, in those ways that the general idea suggests the specific idea. So some ethical premises will in use be indistinguishable from political premises. Take, for example, Kant's famous categorical imperative: Do only that thing which you would will all others to do. It appears to apply to political conduct as well as to individual conduct.

Nevertheless, some rhetorical topics will be characteristically political. We all know where to look for them. Government may be viewed as the formal instrument whereby individuals accept a system of law for the benefit of themselves and of each other. Hence from the point of view of politics there is always a triadic relationship of parties: the individual, the political group in which the individual plays the role and goes under the name of *citizen,* and the governor or ruler. With this relationship in mind, one can at once locate the foci of political explanations and arguments. These will center on such concepts as the powers, obligations, and duties of both the ruler and the citizen. These in turn derive much of their meaning from the concepts of liberty, freedom, and justice, and from our ideas about rights, both individual rights and civil rights. From these spring the standards, rules, and maxims of political conduct. Some political theorists, for example, believe that Roman law settled our custom of defining "private affairs in terms of rights, and public affairs in terms of power and responsibilities."[8] Political rules become the substantial bases and premises of appraisals and judgments. They also dictate the method and tone of rational criticism. These, perhaps, are our special heritage from the Greeks.[9] Possibly the deep-rooted, long-unquestioned habit of waiving aside the "consitutionality" of debate propositions has led debaters to ignore the real sources of arguments that are simultaneously material, moving, and interesting.

To see that a *topoi* of values would indeed be possible we need only to glance swiftly at the debater's issues and sources of argument. The debater refers to "evils" and "difficulties" that give rise to "problems." These terms, I suggest, can refer only to situations, persons, groups, or institutions that have experienced unpleasant tensions of one kind or another. They are frustrated because they haven't secured their desires, their goals, their pleasures, and their interests. Somebody is threatening their freedoms, their status, or their power. Somebody is accused of breaking the law, and his character and that of witnesses and of the trial system itself are put to the test. Self-interest, vested interest, or the entrenched power of some group or institution is interfering with the general welfare.

Once the debater has located the evils of the situation, he defines the problem. His explanation of it cannot avoid value-judgments and even his facts that support explanation function in a context of values. If the question be medical care for the aged, the description of the present state of medical care may well support different interpretations of the problem and point to different decisions.

Such, then, are the kinds of materials which, assembled and analyzed, provide the basis of decision. The decision itself—the solution to the problem—emerges either as a proposition in which the words *should* or *ought* appear, or as a proposition in which value-terms are expressed or clearly implied—e.g., the party is innocent (or guilty), the state has an obligation to provide employment opportunities for everyone, this person or this institution is responsible for doing so-and-so. It is well to remark that the *ought* in a proposition of policy means more than a vague pointing to the future. It is a decision in response to the question, What ought we to believe or do? And this question is always, so Baier asserts, an ethical or moral one.[10] Moreover, an *ought* proposition carries a meaning of obligation about it, such that if one accepts the proposition one feels bound to do what is specified or implied.[11] With either individuals or institutions in mind, one can ask sensible questions: Are obligations to be found in the context of the problem? Who is obligated to whom? What is the nature of the obligation? Furthermore, an *ought* seems always to imply that the decision is the best thing to do; it suggests that the speaker has compared all relevant alternatives.[12]

Perhaps enough has been said to show that many rhetorical *topoi* may be readily derived from ethical and moral materials. Indeed, I believe that topics and lines of argument *inevitably*, in the nature of things, lead the investigator to ethical and moral considerations, guide him to decisions and propositions that are ethical and moral, and furnish him with most of the explanations and arguments that support his decision and in whose terms he will recommend it to the consideration of an audience. If modern rhetoricians will face the fact that language symbols are not empty symbols, like those of symbolic logic and mathematics, that the language of practical discourse bears meanings that testify to man's attempt to identify and solve problems of action and conduct, modern rhetoric will formulate a theory of invention and will present a plan of *topoi* in the language of ethics and morals.

4.

If rhetoricians would see the materials of speeches in this light, they would do well, I believe, to take a special term from the field of ethics and employ it, perhaps with minor adjustments. The term is *good reason,* or in the plural form, *good reasons.* What are these? A good reason is a statement offered in support of an *ought* proposition or of a value-judgment. Good reasons are a number of statements, consistent with each other, in support of an *ought* proposition or of a value-judgment. Some examples may prove illuminating.

> The Federal government ought to provide for the medical care of the aged. (Or, more technically: It is desirable that the Federal government . . . .)
> > It will contribute to the security of the aged.
> > It will be in the welfare of everybody.
> > It is in the interest of equity.
> > > The aged spend a disproportionate amount of their income on medical care.
> > > > Their bill for drugs is twice that of persons in age brackets below 60.
> > The government has an obligation to finance medical care for the aged.
> X should not have copied from Y's paper.
> > It was an act of cheating.
> > Cheating is wrong.
> Jones made a good speech.
> > It conformed to most of the principles and rules of speechmaking.
> > Its consequences will be good.
> This man ought not be elected sheriff.
> > He is not qualified to hold the office.
> > He cannot be depended on.

These illustrations serve to point out what good reasons are and what they support. If the rhetorician were to adopt the term, good reasons, he would have a technical label that refers to all the materials of argument and explanation.

There are advantages to the use of the term, good reasons. Both rhetorician and teacher would be ever reminding the speaker, as well as themselves, that the substance of rhetorical proof has to do with values and value-judgments, i.e., with what is held to be good. One can scarcely declare that something is desirable without showing its relevance to values. It may be desirable, for example, to adjust the balance of power between management and labor, on the ground that justice has become too partisan, that basic rights are not being respected, and the like. Moreover, the word *reason* indicates that the process of proof is a rational one and can be used to cover such traditional forms of reasoning as deduction and induction, the syllogism, generalization, analogy, causation, and correlation. Furthermore, the term *good reason* implies the indissoluble relationship between content and form, and keeps attention on what form is saying. If we could become accustomed to the concept, good reasons, we might cease worrying over our failure to find perfect syllogisms in the arguments of everyday life; rather, we would recognize, as the examination of practical reason seems to indicate, that reasons which govern practice are quite different from the syllogism as usually presented. I think that most ethicists would agree that the measurement of validity in practical discourse quite commonly resides in the general principle and its applicability. Brandt has this to say on the point: "Any particular ethical statement that is valid *can be supported by a valid general principle. . . .*"[13] X should not have copied from Y's paper, for in doing so he cheated, and cheating is wrong. In this case, clearly there are facts that could or could not be established. Clearly, the general principle, "cheating is wrong," is relevant and functions as a warrant. The principle is applicable, or is applicable as qualified, if particular circumstances call for qualification. The principle itself is valid to the extent that it corresponds with the beliefs and conduct of the group which gives it sanction. Such statements, Edwards observes, are objective in the sense that they are independent of the speaker's subjective attitudes. It is true, of course, that the speaker's attitude may prompt his giving a general principle as a reason; nevertheless, the general principle can be tested for its truth-value quite apart from his attitude.[14] What a good reason is is to some extent fixed by human nature and to a very large extent by generally accepted principles and practices which make social life, as we understand it, possible. In a word, the concept of good reasons embraces both the substance and the processes of practical reason. One could do worse than characterize rhetoric as the art of finding and effectively presenting good reasons.

If rhetoricians could accept good reasons as the substance of discourse, we would immediately secure additional advantages. Any distinctions that modern rhetoric may be trying to maintain between logical, ethical, and emotional modes of proof would immediately become unreal and useless, except for purposes of historical criticism. For the practitioner, both communicator and respondent, the correct questions would always be: What is my choice? What are the supporting and explanatory statements? What information is trustworthy? It would be absurd to ask: Is my choice a logical one? Shall I support my position by logical, ethical, or emotional means? For the theorist, analyst, and critic of discourse, the disappearance of those weasel concepts, logical proof and emotional proof, would permit a description of the materials of practical discourse in terms of two broad categories: materials deriving from the specific occasion, and materials consisting of general value-judgments. Furthermore, perhaps practitioners would get into the habit of applying first and foremost to any instance of communication, the searching queries: Who or what is the responsible agent? What person or agent is taking the responsibility, or should take it? If the proposition be supported by reasons that immediately or ultimately relate to value-statements whose content reflects the desirable, the obligatory, and the admirable, then for whom is the message desirable and admirable? Upon whom do the obligations and duties rest? Discourse to which such questions are habitually applied cannot long remain abstract, distant, colorless, and unreal. Rather, it could well become personal and direct. The speechmaking of the Greeks, who understood ethos, was eminently personal.

5.

It seems probable that if students of rhetoric looked to the substance as well as to the forms of practical discourse they would discover a set of statements or value-axioms that would constitute a modern system of invention. The axioms would consist of those political and ethical values that apply to public discussion. Derived in theory from politics and ethics and in practice from the rules and conventions that speakers appeal to explicitly and implicitly when they explain, advocate, deliberate upon, and justify their choices, the axioms would serve as a base for finding good reasons and thus for providing fundamental materials in any given case of rhetorical discourse. Eubanks and Baker have recently reminded rhetoricians of Aristotle's position that "If rhetoric has any sort of *special* subject matter province, that substance is constituted in the popular and probable value axioms related to the civil decision making of a free society."[15] The hypothesis should be put to the test.

Notes

1. The point of view is fully expressed in Donald C. Bryant, "Rhetoric: Its Functions and Its Scope," *Quarterly Journal of Speech,* XXXIX (December 1953), 401-24.
2. My chief informants have been Richard B. Brandt, *Ethical Theory: The Problems of Normative and Critical Ethics* (Englewood Cliffs, N.J., 1959); Kurt Baier, *The Moral Point of View: A Rational Basis of Ethics* (Ithaca, N.Y., 1958); Paul Edwards, *The Logic of Moral Discourse* (Glencoe, Ill., 1955); P. H. Nowell-Smith, *Ethics* (Baltimore, Md., 1954 [Penguin Books]); Philip Blair Rice, *On the Knowledge of Good and Evil* (New York, 1955); Charles L. Stevenson, *Ethics and Language* (New Haven, 1944); and Stephen Edelston Toulmin, *An Examination of the Place of Reason in Ethics* (Cambridge, Eng., 1961).
3. Baier, p. 46.
4. For example, see Baier, pp. 148-56.
5. See Brandt, pp. 2-4.
6. Edwards, p. 141.
7. In developing general categories of values, I have been most helped by Brandt.
8. D. G. Hitchner and W. H. Harbold, *Modern Government: A Survey of Political Science* (New York, 1962), p. 175.
9. Ibid., p. 174.
10. Baier, p. 86.
11. Brandt, esp. pp. 353-54.
12. Ibid.
13. Ibid., p. 20.
14. Edwards, pp. 148, 157.
15. Ralph T. Eubanks and Virgil L. Baker, "Toward an Axiology of Rhetoric," *Quarterly Journal of Speech,* XLVIII (April 1962), 162.

Part Two

Audiences: Attitudes, Opinions, Values

Our behavior, Kenneth Boulding contends, largely depends on our Image of the world: on what we "believe to be true." Our Image of the world is made up of all our past experiences and is constantly expanding and changing as we undergo new experiences.

Our Image changes, then, as we receive new "messages"; that is, new information. When a message hits an Image several things can happen to that Image: (1) it may remain *unchanged*; (2) it may simply be *added to* our stock of experience; or (3) it may *change us in revolutionary ways* and cause us to *reorganize* our experience, our Image of the world. As messages alter our Image they alter our behavior. In "Introduction to 'The Image,' " Professor Boulding explores the relationship of messages to behavior.

In this section of the book we will be looking at *attitudes, opinions* and *values*; we will be looking at the "stuff" of audiences and that of which Images are made.

Daniel Katz in "The Functional Approach to the Study of Attitudes" discusses the nature of attitudes. He explores the *dimensions* of an attitude, points out how attitudes *function* for the individual and discusses the *determinants of attitude arousal and attitude change.*

Professor Katz defines an attitude as "the predisposition of the individual to evaluate some symbols or object or aspect of his world in a favorable or unfavorable manner." These evaluations may be expressed in both verbal and nonverbal behavior. All attitudes contain an *affective* and a *cognitive* dimension; they contain *both* a "*feeling core* of liking or disliking" and a *belief element* which "describe the object of the attitude, its characteristics, and its relations to others."

Attitude appears to Katz to perform four major functions: an instrumental, adjusting or utilitarian function; an ego-defensive function; a value-expressive function; and a knowledge function. These functions help us to understand *why* people hold the attitudes they do.

While Katz's theory of attitudes and attitude change may be labeled, as you might suspect, a "functional theory" of attitudes, any phenomenon so complex as attitudes is bound to provoke a variety of way to account for it, to explain it. Thus, there are a number of other theories that you may also want to read.[1]

Opinions were previously viewed by Daniel Katz as the expression of attitudes. In "Processes of Opinion Change," Herbert Kelman discusses three processes of *social influence* which affect opinion change: *compliance, identification,* and *internalization.*

Compliance occurs when "an individual accepts influences from another person or from a group because he hopes to achieve a favorable reaction from the other."

Identification occurs when "an individual adopts behavior derived from another person or a group because this behavior is associated with a satisfying self-defining relationship to this person or group"; that is, with a "role relationship that forms a part of the person's self-image."

Internalization occurs when "an individual accepts influence because the induced behavior is congruent with his value system"; the "content" of the induced behavior is intrinsically rewarding.

Each of these three processes, compliance, identification, and internalization has a different set of antecedents and consequents. They are first summarized by Kelman (see p. 83) and then discussed.

It would be accurate to say that within the body of literature relating to speech communication, more has been written about attitudes and opinions than about values. In his article "The Role of Values in Public Opinion Research," Milton Rokeach provides a clear and useful discussion of the relationship between attitudes, opinions and values.

Rokeach defines attitudes as "an enduring organization of several beliefs focused on a *specific* object (physical or social, concrete or abstract) or situation, predisposing one to respond in some preferential manner." (Here, you may want to pause to consider some of the similarities and dissimilarities in the Rokeach definition and the Katz definition.)

Values, he says, "transcend specific objects and specific situations: values have to do with *modes of conduct* and *end-states of existence.* . . . [To] say that a person 'has a value' is to say that he has an enduring belief that a particular mode of conduct or that a particular end-state of existence is personally and socially preferable to alternative modes of conduct or end-states of existence." Thus, a value serves as a standard or criterion that tells us *"how to act or what to want;* it is a standard that tells us *what attitude we should hold;* it is a standard we employ *to justify behavior, to morally judge,* and *to compare ourselves with others."* (My italics.)

According to Rokeach, we hold two kinds of values: instrumental and terminal. *Instrumental values* "include the beliefs that most of us have that we should behave courageously, responsibly, honestly, and open-mindedly." *Terminal values* include "beliefs in salvation, a world at peace, equality, and inner-harmony as desirable end-states of existence."

Values exist within value hierarchies; we tend to rank order values along a continuum of importance. These value systems function, then, to help us "choose between alternatives and to resolve conflicts between alternatives in everyday life."

In another section of this text, we have included speeches by Spiro Agnew and George Wallace, two speakers who have long claimed the national attention. What values appear to be embraced by Agnew and Wallace in those speeches? What are the value hierarchies expressed within them? Both speeches are rich with potential for study of attitudes, opinions and values—not only those held by the speakers, but yours as well.

Notes

1. Alternative attitude and attitude change theories you may be interested in are: Muzafer Sherif, Carolyn Sherif, and Rober Nebergall, *Attitude and Attitude Change* (Philadelphia: W. B. Saunders Co., 1965); Chester A. Insko, *Theories of Attitude Change* (New York: Appleton-Century-Crofts, 1967); Robert Abelson and Milton Rosenberg, "The Resolution of Belief Dilemmas," *Journal of Conflict Resolution* (1959), pp. 343-52; Milton J. Rosenberg, et al., *Attitude Organization and Change* (New Haven: Yale University Press, 1960); Arthur Cohen, *Attitude Change and Social Influence* (New York: Basic Books, Inc., Publisher, 1964); Martin Fishbein, ed., *Readings in Attitude Theory and Measurement* (New York: John Wiley and Sons, Inc., 1967); William J. McGuire, "Attitudes and Opinions," *Annual Review of Psychology* (1966), pp. 457-514.

INTRODUCTION TO "THE IMAGE"

KENNETH BOULDING

As I sit at my desk, I know where I am. I see before me a window; beyond that some trees; beyond that the red roofs of the campus of Stanford University; beyond them the trees and the roof tops which mark the town of Palo Alto; beyond them the bare golden hills of the Hamilton Range. I know, however, more than I see. Behind me, although I am not looking in that direction, I know there is a window, and beyond that the little campus of the Center for the Advanced Study in the Behavioral Sciences; beyond that the Coast Range; beyond that the Pacific Ocean. Looking ahead of me again, I know that beyond the mountains that close my present horizon, there is a broad valley; beyond that a still higher range of mountains; beyond that other mountains, range upon range, until we come to the Rockies; beyond that the Great Plains and the Mississippi; beyond that the Alleghenies; beyond that the eastern seaboard; beyond that the Atlantic Ocean; beyond that is Europe; beyond that is Asia. I know, furthermore, that if I go far enough I will come back to where I am now. In other words, I have a picture of the earth as round. I visualize it as a globe. I am a little hazy on some of the details. I am not quite sure, for instance, whether Tanganyika is north or south of Nyasaland. I probably could not draw a very good map of Indonesia, but I have a fair idea where everything is located on the face of this globe. Looking further, I visualize the globe as a small speck circling around a bright star which is the sun, in the company of many other similar specks, the planets. Looking still further, I see our star the sun as a member of millions upon millions of others in the Galaxy. Looking still further, I visualize the Galaxy as one of millions upon millions of others in the universe.

I am not only located in space, I am located in time. I know that I came to California about a year ago, and I am leaving it in about three weeks. I know that I have lived in a number of different places at different times. I know that about ten years ago a great war came to an end, that about forty years ago another great war came to an end. Certain dates are meaningful: 1776, 1620, 1066. I have a picture in my mind of the formation of the earth, of the long history of geological time, of the brief history of man. The great civilizations pass before my mental screen. Many of the images are vague, but Greece follows Crete, Rome follows Assyria.

I am not only located in space and time, I am located in a field of personal relations. I not only know where and when I am, I know to some extent who I am. I am a professor at a great state university. This means that in September I shall go into a classroom and expect to find some students in it and begin to talk to them, and nobody will be surprised. I expect, what is perhaps even more agreeable, that regular salary checks will arrive from the university. I expect that when I open my mouth on certain occasions people will listen. I know, furthermore, that I am a husband and a father, that there are people who will respond to me affectionately and to whom I will respond in like manner. I know, also, that I have friends, that there are houses here, there, and everywhere into which I may go and I will be welcomed and recognized and received as a guest. I belong to many societies. There are places into which I go, and it will be recognized that I am expected to behave in a certain manner. I may sit down to worship, I may make a speech, I may listen to a concert, I may do all sorts of things.

I am not only located in space and in time and in personal relationships, I am also located in the world of nature, in a world of how things operate. I know that when I get into my car there are some things I must do to start it; some things I must do to back out of the parking lot; some things I must do to drive home. I know that if I jump off a high place I will probably hurt myself. I know that there are some things that would probably not be good for me to eat or to drink. I know certain precautions that are advisable to take to maintain good health. I know that if I lean too far backward in my chair as I sit here at my desk, I will probably fall over. I live, in other words, in a world of reasonably stable relationships, a world of "ifs" and "thens," of "if I do this, then that will happen."

Finally, I am located in the midst of a world of subtle intimations and emotions. I am sometimes elated, sometimes a little depressed, sometimes happy, sometimes sad, sometimes inspired, sometimes pedantic. I am open to subtle intimations of a presence beyond the world of space and time and sense.

What I have been talking about is knowledge. Knowledge, perhaps, is not a good word for this. Perhaps one would rather say my *Image* of the world. Knowledge has an implication of validity, of truth. What I am talking about is what I believe to be true: my subjective knowledge. It is this Image that largely governs my behavior. In about an hour I shall rise, leave my office, go to a car, drive down to my home, play with the children, have supper, perhaps read a book, go to bed. I can predict this behavior with a fair degree of accuracy because of the knowledge which I have: the knowledge that I have a home not far away, to which I am accustomed to go. The prediction, of course, may not be fulfilled. There may be an earthquake, I may have an accident with the car on the way home, I may get home to find that my family has been suddenly called away. A hundred and one things may happen. As each event occurs, however, it alters my knowledge structure or my image. And as it alters my image, I behave accordingly. *The first proposition of this work, therefore, is that behavior depends on the image.*

What, however, determines the image? This is the central question of this work. It is not a question which can be answered by it. Nevertheless, such answers as I shall give will be quite fundamental to the understanding of how both life and society really operate. One thing is clear. The image is built up as a result of all past experience of the possessor of the image. Part of the image is the history of the image itself. At one stage the image, I suppose, consists of little else than an undifferentiated blur and movement. From the moment of birth if not before, there is a constant stream of messages entering the organism from the senses. At first, these may merely be undifferentiated lights and noises. As the child grows, however, they gradually become distinguished into people and objects. He begins to perceive himself as an object in the midst of a world of objects. The conscious image has begun. In infancy the world is a house and, perhaps, a few streets or a park. As the child grows his image of the world expands. He sees himself in a town, a country, on a planet. He finds himself in an increasingly complex web of personal relationships. Every time a message reaches him his image is likely to be changed in some degree by it, and as his image is changed his behavior patterns will be changed likewise.

We must distinguish carefully between the image and the messages that reach it. The messages consist of *information* in the sense that they are structured experiences. *The meaning of a message is the change which it produces in the image.*

When a message hits an image one of three things can happen. In the first place, the image may remain unaffected. If we think of the image as a rather loose structure, something like a molecule, we may imagine that the message is going straight through without hitting it. The great majority of messages is of this kind. I am receiving messages all the time, for instance, from my eyes and my ears as I sit at my desk, but these messages are ignored by me. There is, for instance, a noise of carpenters working. I know, however, that a building is being built nearby and the fact that I now hear this noise does not add to this image. Indeed, I do not hear the noise at all if I am not listening for it, as I have become so accustomed to it. If the noise stops, however, I notice it. This information changes my image of the universe. I realize that it is now five o'clock, and it is time for me to go home. The message has called my attention, as it were, to my position in time, and I have reevaluated this position. This is the second possible effect or impact of a message on an image. It may change the image in some rather regular and well-defined way that might be described as simple addition. Suppose, for instance, to revert to an earlier illustration, I look at an atlas and find out exactly the relation of Nyasaland to Tanganyika. I will have added to my knowledge, or my image; I will not, however, have very fundamentally revised it. I still picture the world much as I had pictured it before. Something that was a little vague before is now clearer.

There is, however, a third type of change of the image which might be described as a revolutionary change. Sometimes a message hits some sort of nucleus or supporting structure in the image, and the whole thing changes in a quite radical way. A spectacular instance of such a change is conversion. A man, for instance, may think himself a pretty good fellow and then may hear a preacher who convinces him that, in fact, his life is worthless and shallow, as he is at present living it. The words of the preacher cause a radical reformulation of the man's image of himself in the world, and his behavior changes accordingly. The psychologist may say, of course, that these changes are smaller than they appear, that there is a great mass of the unconscious which does not change, and that the relatively small change in behavior which so often follows intellectual conversion is a testimony to this fact. Nevertheless, the phenomenon of reorganization of the image is an important one, and it occurs to all of us and in ways that are much less spectacular than conversion.

The sudden and dramatic nature of these reorganizations is perhaps a result of the fact that our image is in itself resistant to change. When it receives messages which conflict with it, its first impulse is to reject them as in some sense untrue. Suppose, for instance, that somebody tells us something which is inconsistent with our picture of a certain person. Our first impulse is to reject the proffered information as false. As we continue to receive messages which contradict our image, however, we begin to have doubts, and then one day we receive a message which overthrows our previous image and we revise it completely. The person, for instance, whom we saw as a trusted friend is now seen to be a hypocrite and a deceiver.

Occasionally, things that we see, or read, or hear, revise our conceptions of space and time, or of relationships. I have recently read, for instance, Vasiliev's *History of the Byzantine Empire*. As a result of reading this book I have considerably revised my image of at least a thousand years of history. I had not given the matter a great deal of thought before, but I suppose if I had been questioned on my view of the period, I would have said that Rome fell in the fifth century and that it was succeeded by a little-known empire centering in Constantinople and a confused medley of tribes, invasions, and successor states. I now see that Rome did not fall, that in a sense it merely faded away, that the history of the Roman Empire and of Byzantium is continuous, and that from the time of its greatest extent the Roman Empire lost one piece after another until only Constantinople was left; and then in 1453 that went. There are books, some of them rather bad books, after which the world is never quite the same again. Veblen, for instance, was not, I think, a great social scientist, and yet he invented an undying phrase: "conspicuous consumption." After reading Veblen, one can never quite see a university campus or an elaborate house in just the same light as before. In a similar vein, David Riesman's division of humanity into inner-directed and other-directed people is no doubt open to serious criticism by the methodologists. Nevertheless, after reading Riesman one has a rather new view of the universe and one looks in one's friends and acquaintances for signs of inner-direction or other-direction.

One should perhaps add a fourth possible impact of the messages on the image. The image has a certain dimension, or quality, of certainty or uncertainty, probability or improbability, clarity or vagueness. Our image of the world is not uniformly certain, uniformly probable, or uniformly clear. Messages, therefore, may have the effect not only of adding to or of reorganizing the image. They may also have the effect of clarifying it, that is, of making something which previously was regarded as less certain more certain, or something which was previously seen in a vague way, clearer.

Messages may also have the contrary effect. They may introduce doubt or uncertainty into the image. For instance, the noise of carpenters has just stopped, but my watch tells me it is about four-thirty. This has thrown a certain amount of confusion into my mental image. I was under the impression that the carpenters stopped work at five o'clock. Here is a message which contradicts that impression. What am I to believe? Unfortunately, there are two possible ways of integrating the message into my image. I can believe that I was mistaken in thinking that the carpenters left work at five o'clock and that in fact their day ends at four-thirty. Or, I can believe that my watch is wrong. Either of these two modifications of my image gives meaning to the message. I shall not know for certain which is the right one, however, until I have an opportunity of comparing my watch with a timepiece or with some other source of time which I regard as being more reliable.

The impact of messages on the certainty of the image is of great importance in the interpretation of human behavior. Images of the future must be held with a degree of uncertainty, and as time passes and as the images become closer to the present, the messages that we receive inevitably modify them, both as to content and as to certainty.

The subjective knowledge structure or image of any individual or organization consists not only of images of "fact" but also images of "value." We shall subject the concept of a "fact" to severe scrutiny in the course of the discussion. In the meantime, however, it is clear that there is a certain difference between the image which I have of physical objects in space and time and the valuations which I put on these objects or on the events which concern them. It is clear that there is a certain difference between, shall we say, my image of Stanford University existing at a certain point in space and time, and my image of the value of Stanford University. If I say "Stanford University is in California," this is rather different from the statement "Stanford University is a good university, or is a better university than X, or a worse university than Y." The latter statements concern my image of values, and although I shall argue that the process by which we obtain an image of values is not very different from the process whereby we obtain an image of fact, there is clearly a certain difference between them.

The image of value is concerned with the *rating* of the various parts of our image of the world, according to some scale of betterness or worseness. We, all of us, possess one or more of these scales. It is what the economists call a welfare function. It does not extend over the whole universe. We do not now, for instance, generally regard Jupiter as a better planet than Saturn. Over that part of the universe which is closest to ourselves, however, we all erect these scales of valuation. Moreover, we change these scales of valuation in response to messages received much as we change our image of the world around us. It is almost certain that most people possess not merely one scale of valuation but many scales for different purposes. For instance, we may say A is better than B for me but worse for the country, or it is better for the country but worse for the world at large. The notion of a hierarchy of scales is very important in determining the effect of messages on the scales themselves.

One of the most important propositions of this theory is that the value scales of any individual or organization are perhaps the most important elements determining the effect of the messages he receives on his image of the world. If a message is perceived that is neither good nor bad it may have little or no effect on the image. If it is perceived as bad or hostile to the image which is held, there will be resistance to accepting it. This resistance is not usually infinite. An often repeated message or a message which comes with unsual force or authority is able to penetrate the resistance and will be able to alter the image. A devout Moslem, for instance, whose whole life has been built around the observance of the precepts of the Koran will resist vigorously any message which tends to throw doubt on the authority of his sacred work. The resistance may take the form of simply ignoring the message, or it may take the form of emotive response: anger, hostility, indignation. In the same way, a "devout" psychologist will resist strongly any evidence presented in favor of extrasensory perception, because to accept it would overthrow his whole image of the universe. If the resistances are very strong, it may take very strong, or often repeated messages to penetrate them, and when they are penetrated, the effect is a realignment or reorganization of the whole knowledge structure.

On the other hand, messages which are favorable to the existing image of the world are received easily and even though they may make minor modifications of the knowledge structure, there will not be any fundamental reorganization. Such messages either will make no impact on the knowledge structure or their impact will be one of rather simple addition or accretion. Such messages may also have the effect of increasing the stability, that is to say, the resistance to unfavorable messages, which the knowledge structure or image possesses.

The stability or resistance to change of a knowledge structure also depends on its internal consistency and arrangement. There seems to be some kind of principle of minimization of internal strain at work which makes some images stable and others unstable for purely internal reasons. In the same way, some crystals or molecules are more stable than others because of the minimization of internal strain. It must be emphasized that it is not merely logical consistency which gives rise to internal cohesiveness of a knowledge structure, although this is an important element. There are important qualities of a nonlogical nature which also give rise to stability. The structure may, for instance, have certain aesthetic relationships among the parts. It may represent or justify a way of life or have certain consequences which are highly regarded in the value system, and so on. Even in mathematics, which is of all knowledge structures the one whose internal consistency is most due to logic, is not devoid of these nonlogical elements. In the acceptance of mathematical arguments by mathematicians there are important criteria of elegance, beauty, and simplicity which contribute toward the stability of these structures.

Even at the level of simple or supposedly simple sense perception we are increasingly discovering that the message which comes through the senses is itself mediated through a value system. We do not perceive our sense data raw; they are mediated through a highly learned process of interpretation and acceptance. When an object apparently increases in size on the retina of the eye, we interpret this not as an increase in size but as movement.

Indeed, we only get along in the world because we consistently and persistently disbelieve the plain evidence of our senses. The stick in water is not bent; the movie is not a succession of still pictures; and so on.

What this means is that for any individual organism or organization, there are no such things as "facts." There are only messages filtered through a changeable value system. This statement may sound rather startling. It is inherent, however, in the view which I have been propounding. This does not mean, however, that the image of the world possessed by an individual is a purely private matter or that all knowledge is simply subjective knowledge, in the sense in which I have used the word. Part of our image of the world is the belief that this image is shared by other people like ourselves who also are part of our image of the world. In common daily intercourse we all behave as if we possess roughly the same image of the world. If a group of people are in a room together, their behavior clearly shows that they all think they are in the same room. It is this shared image which is "public" knowledge as opposed to "private" knowledge. It follows, however, from the argument above that if a group of people are to share the same image of the world, or to put it more exactly, if the various images of the world which they have are to be roughly identical, and if this group of people are exposed to much the same set of messages in building up images of the world, the value systems of all individuals must be approximately the same.

The problem is made still more complicated by the fact that a group of individuals does not merely share messages which come to them from "nature." They also initiate and receive messages themselves. This is the characteristic which distinguishes man from the lower organisms—the art of conversation or discourse. The human organism is capable not only of having an image of the world, but of talking about it. This is the extraordinary gift of language. A group of dogs in a pack pursuing a stray cat clearly share an image of the world in the sense that each is aware to some degree of the situation which they are all in, and is likewise aware of his neighbors. When the chase is over, however, they do not, as far as we know, sit around and talk about it and say, "Wasn't that a fine chase?" or, "Isn't it too bad the cat got away?" or even, "Next time you ought to go that way and I'll go this way and we can corner it." It is discourse or conversation which makes the human image public in a way that the image of no lower animal can possibly be. The term, "universe of discourse" has been used to describe the growth and development of common images in conversation and linguistic intercourse. There are, of course, many such universes of discourse, and although it is a little awkward to speak of many universes, the term is well enough accepted so that we may let it stay.

Where there is no universe of discourse, where the image possessed by the organism is purely private and cannot be communicated to anyone else, we say that the person is mad (to use a somewhat old-fashioned term). It must not be forgotten, however, that the discourse must be received as well as given, and that whether it is received or not depends upon the value system of the recipient. This means that insanity is defined differently from one culture to another because of these differences in value systems and that the schizophrenic of one culture may well be the shaman or the prophet of another.

Up to now I have sidestepped and I will continue to sidestep the great philosophical arguments of epistemology. I have talked about the image. I have maintained that images can be public as well as private, but I have not discussed the question as to whether images are *true* and how we know whether they are true. Most epistemological systems seek some philosopher's stone by which statements may be tested in order to determine their "truth," that is, their correspondence to outside reality. I do not claim to have any such philosopher's stone, not even the touchstone of science. I have, of course, a great respect for science and scientific method—for careful observation, for planned experience, for the testing of hypotheses and for as much objectivity as semirational beings like ourselves can hope to achieve. In my theoretical system, however, the scientific method merely stands as one among many of the methods whereby images change and develop. The development of images is part of the culture or the subculture in which they are developed, and it depends upon all the elements of that culture or subculture. Science is a subculture among subcultures. It can claim to be useful. It may claim rather more dubiously to be good. It cannot claim to give validity.

In summation, then, my theory might well be called an organic theory of knowledge. Its most fundamental proposition is that knowledge is what somebody or something knows, and that without a knower, knowledge is an absurdity. Moreover, I argue that the growth of knowledge is the growth of an "organic" structure. I am not suggesting here that knowledge is simply an arrangement of neuronal circuits or brain cells, or something of that kind. On the question of the relation between the physical and chemical structure of an organism and its knowledge structure, I am quite prepared to be agnostic. It is, of course, an article of faith among physical scientists that there must be somewhere a one-to-one correspondence between the structures of the physical body and the structures of knowledge. Up to now, there is nothing like empirical proof or even very good evidence for this hypothesis. Indeed, what we know about the brain suggests that it is an extraordinarily unspecialized and, in a sense, unstructured object; and that if there is a physical and chemical structure corresponding to the knowledge structure, it must be of a kind which at present we do not understand. It may be, indeed, that the correspondence between physical structure and mental structure is something that we will never be able to determine because of a sort of "Heisenberg principle" in the investigation of these matters. If the act of observation destroys the thing observed, it is clear that there is a fundamental obstacle to the growth of knowledge in that direction.

All these considerations, however, are not fundamental to my position. We do not have to conceive of the knowledge structure as a physico-chemical structure in order to use it in our theoretical construct. It can be inferred from the behavior of the organism just as we constantly infer the images of the world which are possessed by those around us from the messages which they transmit to us. When I say that knowledge is an organic structure, I mean that it follows principles of growth and development similar to those with which we are familiar in complex organizations and organisms. In every organism or organization there are both internal and external factors affecting growth. Growth takes place through a kind of metabolism. Even in the case of knowledge structures, we have a certain intake and output of messages. In the knowledge structure, however, there are important violations of the laws of conservation. The accumulation of knowledge is not merely the difference between messages taken in and messages given out. It is not like a reservoir; it is rather an organization which grows through an active internal organizing principle much as the gene is a principle or entity organizing the growth of bodily structures. The gene, even in the physico-chemical sense may be thought of as an inward teacher imposing its own form and "will" on the less formed matter around it. In the growth of images, also, we may suppose similiar models. Knowledge grows also because of inward teachers as well as outward messages. As every good teacher knows, the business of teaching is not that of penetrating the student's defenses with the violence or loudness of the teacher's messages. It is, rather, that of cooperating with the student's own inward teacher whereby the student's image may grow in conformity with that of his outward teacher. The existence of public knowledge depends, therefore, on certain basic similarities among men. It is literally because we are of one "blood," that is, genetic constitution, that we are able to communicate with each other. We cannot talk to the ants or bees; we cannot hold conversations with them, although in a very real sense they communicate to us. It is the purpose of this work, therefore, to discuss the growth of images, both private and public, in individuals, in organizations, in society at large, and even with some trepidation, among the lower forms of life. Only thus can we develop a really adequate theory of behavior.

THE FUNCTIONAL APPROACH TO THE STUDY OF ATTITUDES

DANIEL KATZ

Nature of Attitudes: Their Dimensions

Attitude is the predisposition of the individual to evaluate some symbol or object or aspect of his world in a favorable or unfavorable manner. Opinion is the verbal expression of an attitude, but attitudes can also be expressed in nonverbal behavior. Attitudes include both the affective, or feeling core of liking or disliking, and the cognitive, or belief, elements which describe the object of the attitude, its characteristics, and its relations to other objects. All attitudes thus include beliefs, but not all beliefs are attitudes. When specific attitudes are organized into a hierarchical structure, they comprise *value systems.* Thus a person may not only hold specific attitudes against deficit spending and unbalanced budgets but may also have a systematic organization of such beliefs and attitudes in the form of a value system of economic conservatism.

The dimensions of attitudes can be stated more precisely if the above distinctions between beliefs and feelings and attitudes and value systems are kept in mind. The *intensity* of an attitude refers to the strength of the *affective* component. In fact, rating scales and even Thurstone scales deal primarily with the intensity of feeling of the individual for or against some social object. The cognitive, or belief, component suggests two additional dimensions, the *specificity* or *generality* of the attiude and the *degree of differentiation* of the beliefs. Differentiation refers to the number of beliefs or cognitive items contained in the attitude, and the general assumption is that the simpler the attitude in cognitive structure the easier it is to change.[1] For simple structures there is no defense in depth, and once a single item of belief has been changed the attitude will change. A rather different dimension of attitude is the *number and strength of its linkages to a related value system.* If an attitude favoring budget balancing by the Federal government is tied in strongly with a value system of economic conservatism, it will be more difficult to change than if it were a fairly isolated attitude of the person. Finally, the relation of the value system to the personality is a consideration of first importance. If an attitude is tied to a value system which is closely related to, or which consists of, the individual's conception of himself, then the appropriate change procedures become more

Excerpted from Daniel Katz, "The Functional Approach to the Study of Attitudes," *Public Opinion Quarterly* 24 (1960), pp. 163-204. Permission of *Public Opinion Quarterly* and the author.

complex. The *centrality* of an attitude refers to its role as part of a value system which is closely related to the individual's self-concept.

An additional aspect of attitudes is not clearly described in most theories, namely, their relation to action or overt behavior. Though behavior related to the attitude has other determinants than the attitude itself, it is also true that some attitudes in themselves have more of what Cartwright calls an action structure than do others.[2] Brewster Smith refers to this dimension as policy orientation[3] and Katz and Stotland speak of it as the action component.[4] For example, while many people have attitudes of approval toward one or the other of the two political parties, these attitudes will differ in their structure with respect to relevant action. One may be prepared to vote on election day and will know where and when he should vote and will go to the polls no matter what the weather or how great the inconvenience. Another man will only vote if a party worker calls for him in a car. Himmelstrand's work is concerned with all aspects of the relationship between attitude and behavior, but he deals with the action structure of the attitude itself by distinguishing between attitudes where the affect is tied to verbal expression and attitudes where the affect is tied to behavior concerned with more objective referents of the attitude.[5] In the first case an individual derives satisfaction from talking about a problem; in the second case he derives satisfaction from taking some form of concrete action.

Attempts to change attitudes can be directed primarily at the belief component or at the feeling, or affective, component. Rosenberg theorizes that an effective change in one component will result in changes in the other component and presents experimental evidence to confirm this hypothesis.[6] For example, a political candidate will often attempt to win people by making them like him and dislike his opponent, and thus communicate affect rather than ideas. If he is successful, people will not only like him but entertain certain favorable beliefs about him. Another candidate may deal primarily with ideas and hope that, if he can change people's beliefs about an issue, their feelings will also change.

Four Functions which Attitudes Perform for the Individual

The major functions which attitudes perform for the personality can be grouped according to their motivational basis as follows:

1. *The instrumental, adjustive, or utilitarian function* upon which Jeremy Bentham and the utilitarians constructed their model of man. A modern expression of this approach can be found in behavioristic learning theory.
2. *The ego-defensive function* in which the person protects himself from acknowledging the basic truths about himself or the harsh realities in his external world. Freudian psychology and neo-Freudian thinking have been preoccupied with this type of motivation and its outcomes.
3. *The value-expressive function* in which the individual derives satisfactions from expressing attitudes appropriate to his personal values and to his concept of himself. This function is central to doctrines of ego psychology which stress the importance of self-expression, self-development, and self-realization.
4. *The knowledge function* based upon the individual's need to give adequate structure to his universe. The search for meaning, the need to understand, the trend toward better organization of perceptions and beliefs to provide clarity and con-

sistency for the individual, are other descriptions of this function. The development of principles about perceptual and cognitive structure have been the contribution of Gestalt psychology.

Stated simply, the functional approach is the attempt to understand the reasons people hold the attitudes they do. The reasons, however, are at the level of psychological motivations and not of the accidents of external events and circumstances. Unless we know the psychological need which is met by the holding of an attitude we are in a poor position to predict when and how it will change. Moreover, the same attitude expressed toward a political candidate may not perform the same function for all the people who express it. And while many attitudes are predominantly in the service of a single type of motivational process, as described above, other attitudes may serve more than one purpose for the individual. A fuller discussion of how attitudes serve the above four functions is in order.

1. The Adjustment Function

Essentially this function is a recognition of the fact that people strive to maximize the rewards in their external environment and to minimize the penalties. The child develops favorable attitudes toward the objects in his world which are associated with the satisfactions of his needs and unfavorable attitudes toward objects which thwart him or punish him. Attitudes acquired in the service of the adjustment function are either the means for reaching the desired goal or avoiding the undesirable satisfactions.[7] The attitudes of the worker favoring a political party which will advance his economic lot are an example of the first type of utilitarian attitude. The pleasant image one has of one's favorite food is an example of the second type of utilitarian attitude.

In general, then, the dynamics of attitude formation with respect to the adjustment function are dependent upon present or past perceptions of the utility of the attitudinal object for the individual. The clarity, consistency, and nearness of rewards and punishments, as they relate to the individual's activities and goals, are important factors in the acquisition of such attitudes.

·   ·   ·   ·   ·

2. The Ego-Defensive Function

People not only seek to make the most of their external world and what it offers, but they also expend a great deal of their energy on living with themselves. The mechanisms by which the individual protects his ego from his own unacceptable impulses and from the knowledge of threatening forces from without, and the methods by which he reduces his anxieties created by such problems, are known as mechanisms of ego defense. A more complete account of their origin and nature will be found in Sarnoff's article in this issue.[8] They include the devices by which the individual avoids facing either the inner reality of the kind of person he is, or the outer reality of the dangers the world holds for him. They stem basically from internal conflict with its resulting insecurities. In one sense the mechanisms of defense are adaptive in temporarily removing the sharp edges of conflict and in saving the individual from complete disaster. In another sense they are not adaptive in that they handicap the individual in his social adjustments and in obtaining the maximum satisfactions available to him from the world in which he lives. The worker who persistently quarrels with his boss and with his fellow workers, because he is acting out some of his own internal conflicts, may in this manner relieve himself of some of the emotional tensions which beset him. He is not, however, solving his problem of adjusting to his work situation and thus may deprive himself of advancement or even of steady employment.

. . . . .

Many of our attitudes have the function of defending our self-image. When we cannot admit to ourselves that we have deep feelings of inferiority we may project those feelings onto some convenient minority group and bolster our egos by attitudes of superiority toward this underpriviledged group. The formation of such defense attitudes differs in essential ways from the formation of attitudes which serve the adjustment function. They proceed from within the person, and the objects and situation to which they are attached are merely convenient outlets for their expression. Not all targets are equally satisfactory for a given defense mechanism, but the point is that the attitude is not created by the target but by the individual's emotional conflicts. And when no convenient target exists the individual will create one. Utilitarian attitudes, on the other hand, are formed with specific reference to the nature of the attitudinal object. They are thus appropriate to the nature of the social world to which they are geared. The high school student who values high grades because he wants to be admitted to a good college has a utilitarian attitude appropriate to the situation to which it is related.

All people employ defense mechanisms, but they differ with respect to the extent that they use them and some of their attitudes may be more defensive in function than others. It follows that the techniques and conditions for attitude change will not be the same for ego-defensive as for utilitarian attitudes.

. . . . .

3. The Value-Expressive Function

While many attitudes have the function of preventing the individual from revealing to himself and others his true nature, other attitudes have the function of giving positive expression to his central values and to the type of person he conceives himself to be. A man may consider himself to be an enlightened conservative or an internationalist or a liberal, and will hold attitudes which are the appropriate indication of his central values. Thus we need to take account of the fact that not all behavior has the negative function of reducing the tensions of biological drives or of internal conflicts. Satisfactions also accrue to the person from the expression of attitudes which reflect his cherished beliefs and his self-image. The reward of the person in these instances is not so much a matter of gaining social recognition or monetary rewards as of establishing his self-identity and confirming his notion of the sort of person he sees himself to be. The gratifications obtained from value expression may go beyond the confirmation of self-identity. Just as we find satisfaction in the exercise of our talents and abilities, so we find reward in the expression of any attributes associated with our egos.

Value-expressive attitudes not only give clarity to the self-image but also mold that self-image closer to the heart's desire. The teenager who by dress and speech establishes his identity as similar to his own peer group may appear to the outsider a weakling and a craven conformer. To himself he is asserting his independence of the adult world to which he has rendered childlike subservience and conformity all his life. Very early in the development of the personality the need for clarity of self-image is important—the need to know "who I am." Later it may be even more important to know that in some measure I am the type of person I want to be. Even as adults, however, the clarity and stability of the self-image is of primary significance. Just as the kind, considerate person will cover over his acts of selfishness, so too will the ruthless individualist become confused and embarrassed by his acts of sympathetic compassion. One reason it is difficult to change the character of the adult is that he is not comfortable with the new "me." Group support for such personality change is almost a necessity, as in Alcoholics Anonymous, so that the individual is aware of approval of his new self by people who are like him.

•   •   •   •   •

4. The Knowledge Function

Individuals not only acquire beliefs in the interest of satisfying various specific needs, they also seek knowledge to give meaning to what would otherwise be an unorganized chaotic universe. People need standards or frames of reference for understanding their world, and attitudes help to supply such standards. The problem of understanding, as John Dewey made clear years ago, is one "of introducing (1) *definiteness and distinction* and (2) *consistency and stability* of meaning into what is otherwise vague and wavering."[9] The definiteness and stability are provided in good measure by the norms of our culture, which give the otherwise perplexed individual ready-made attitudes for comprehending his universe. Walter Lippmann's classical contribution to the study of opinions and attitudes was his description of stereotypes and the way they provided order and clarity for a bewildering set of complexities.[10] The most interesting finding in Herzog's familiar study of the gratifications obtained by housewives in listening to daytime serials was the unsuspected role of information and advice.[11] The stories were liked "because they explained things to the inarticulate listener."

The need to know does not of course imply that people are driven by a thrist for universal knowledge. The American public's appalling lack of political information has been documented many times. In 1956, for example, only 13 per cent of the people in Detroit could correctly name the two United States Senators from the state of Michigan and only 18 per cent knew the name of their own Congressman.[12] People are not avid seekers after knowledge as judged by what the educator or social reformer would desire. But they do want to understand the events which impinge directly on their own life. Moreover, many of the attitudes they have already acquired give them sufficient basis for interpreting much of what they perceive to be important for them. Our already existing stereotypes, in Lippmann's language, "are an ordered, more or less consistent picture of the world, to which our habits, our tastes, our capacities, our comforts and our hopes have adjusted themselves. They may not be a complete picture of the world, but they are a picture of a possible world to which we are adapted."[13] It follows that new information will not modify old attitudes unless there is some inadequacy or incompleteness or inconsistency in the existing attititudinal structure as it relates to the perceptions of new situations.

•   ◦   •   •   •

Determinants and Attitude Arousal and Attitude Change

The problems of attitude arousal and of attitude change are separate problems. The first has to do with the fact that the individual has many predispositions to act and many influences playing upon him. Hence we need a more precise description of the appropriate conditions which will evoke a given attitude. The second problem is that of specifying the factors which will help to predict the modification of different types of attitude.

The most general statement that can be made concerning attitude arousal is that it is dependent upon the excitation of some need in the individual, or some relevant cue in the environment. When a man grows hungry, he talks of food. Even when not hungry he may express favorable attitudes toward a preferred food if an external stimulus cues him. The ego-defensive person who hates foreigners will express such attitudes under conditions of increased anxiety or threat or when a foreigner is perceived to be getting out of place.

The most general statement that can be made about the conditions conducive to attitude change is that the expression of the old attitude or its anticipated expression no longer gives satisfaction to its related need state. In other words, it no longer serves its function and the individual feels blocked or frustrated. Modifying an old attitude or replacing it with a new one is a process of learning, and learning always starts with a problem, or being thwarted in coping with a situation. Being blocked is a necessary, but not a sufficient, condition for attitude change. Other factors must be operative and will vary in effectiveness depending upon the function involved.

Arousing and Changing Utilitarian Attitudes

Political parties have both the problem of converting people with antagonistic attitudes (attitude change) and the problem of mobilizing the support of their own followers (attitude arousal). To accomplish the latter they attempt to revive the need basic to old attitudes. For example, the Democrats still utilize the appeals of the New Deal and the Republicans still talk of the balanced budget. The assumption is that many people still hold attitudes acquired in earlier circumstances and that appropriate communication can reinstate the old needs. For most people, however, utilitarian needs are reinforced by experience and not by verbal appeals. Hence invoking the symbols of the New Deal will be relatively ineffective with respect to adjustive attitudes unless there are corresponding experiences with unemployment, decreased income, and so forth. Though the need state may not be under the control of the propagandist, he can exaggerate or minimize its importance. In addition to playing upon states of need, the propagandist can make perceptible the old cues associated with the attitude he is trying to elicit. These cues may have associated with them favorable affect, or feeling, though the related needs are inactive. For example, the fighters for old causes can be paraded across the political platform in an attempt to arouse the attitudes of the past.

The two basic conditions, then, for the arousal of existing attitudes are the activation of their relevant need states and the perception of the appropriate cues associated with the content of the attitude.

To change attitudes which serve a utilitarian function, one of two conditions must prevail: (1) the attitude and the activities related to it no longer provide the satisfactions they once did, or (2) the individual's level of aspiration has been raised. The Chevrolet owner who had positive attitudes toward his old car may now want a more expensive car commensurate with his new status.

·   ·   ·   ·   ·

The area of freedom for changing utilitarian attitudes is of course much greater in dealing with methods of satisfying needs than with needs themselves. Needs change more slowly than the means for gratifying them, even though one role of the advertiser is to create new needs. Change in attitudes occurs more readily when people perceive that they can accomplish their objectives through revising existing attitudes. Integration of white and Negro personnel in the armed forces came to pass partly because political leaders and military leaders perceived that such a move would strengthen our fighting forces. And one of the powerful arguments for changing our attitudes toward Negroes is that in the struggle for world democracy we need to put our own house in order to present a more convincing picture of our own society to other countries. Carlson has experimentally demonstrated that discriminatory attitudes toward minority groups can be altered by showing the relevance of more positive beliefs to such individual goals and values as American international prestige and democratic equalitarianism.[14]

·　·　·　·

The use of negative sanctions and of punishment to change utilitarian attitudes is more complex than the use of rewards. To be successful in changing attitudes and behavior, punishment should be used only when there is clearly available a course of action that will save the individual from the undesirable consequences. To arouse fear among the enemy in time of war does not necessarily result in desertion, surrender, or a disruption of the enemy war effort. Such channels of action may not be available to the people whose fears are aroused. The experiment of Janis and Feshbach in using fear appeals to coerce children into good habits of dental hygiene had the interesting outcome of a negative relationship between the amount of fear and the degree of change. Lurid pictures of gangrene jaws of old people who had not observed good dental habits were not effective.[15] Moreover, the group exposed to the strongest fear appeal was the most susceptible to counterpropaganda. One factor which helps to account for the results of this investigation was the lack of a clear-cut relation in the minds of the children between failure to brush their teeth in the prescribed manner and the pictures of gangrene jaws of the aged.

·　·　·　·　·

Arousal and Change of Ego-Defensive Attitudes

Attitudes which help to protect the individual from internally induced anxieties or from facing up to external dangers are readily elicited by any form of threat to the ego. The threat may be external, as in the case of a highly competitive situation, or a failure experience, or a derogatory remark. It is the stock in trade of demagogues to exaggerate the dangers confronting the people, for instance, Joe McCarthy's tactics with respect to Communists in the State Department. Many people have existing attitudes of withdrawal or of aggression toward deviants or out-groups based upon their ego-defensive needs. When threatened, these attitudes come into play, and defensive people either avoid the unpleasant situation entirely, as is common in the desegregation controversy, or exhibit hostility.

Another condition for eliciting the ego-defensive attitude is the encouragement given to its expression by some form of social support. The agitator may appeal to repressed hatred by providing moral justification for its expression. A mob leader before an audience with emotionally held attitudes toward Negroes may call out these attitudes in the most violent form by invoking the good of the community or the honor of white womanhood.

A third condition for the arousal of ego-defensive attitudes is the appeal to authority. The insecurity of the defensive person makes him particularly susceptible to authoritarian suggestion. When this type of authoritarian command is in the direction already indicated by his attitudes of antipathy toward other people, he responds quickly and joyously. It is no accident that movements of hate and aggression such as the Ku Klux Klan or the Nazi Party are authoritarian in their organized structure. Wagman, in an experimental investigation of the uses of authoritarian suggestion, found that students high in ego-defensiveness as measured by the F-scale were much more responsive to directives from military leaders than were less defensive students.[16] In fact, the subjects low in defensiveness were not affected at all by authoritarian suggestion when this influence ran counter to their own attitudes. The subjects high in F-scores could be moved in either direction, although they moved more readily in the direction of their own beliefs.

A fourth condition for defensive arousal is the building up over time of inhibited drives in the individual, for example, repressed sex impulses. As the drive strength of forbidden impulses increases, anxiety mounts and release from tension is found in the expression of defensive attitudes. The deprivations of prison life, for example, build up tensions which can find expression in riots against the hated prison officials.

In other words, the drive strength for defensive reactions can be increased by situation frustration. Though the basic source is the long-standing internal conflict of the person, he can encounter additional frustration in immediate circumstances.

. . . . .

The usual procedures for changing attitudes and behavior have little positive effect upon attitudes geared into our ego defenses. In fact they may have a boomerang effect of making the individual cling more tenaciously to his emotionally held beliefs. In the category of usual procedures should be included increasing the flow of information, promising and bestowing rewards, and invoking penalties.

. . . . .

Three basic factors, however, can help change ego-defensive attitudes. In the first place, the removal of threat is a necessary though not a sufficient condition. The permissive and even supportive atmosphere which the therapist attempts to create for his patients is a special instance of the removal of threat . . . .

In the second place, catharsis or the ventilation of feelings can help to set the stage for attitude change. Mention has already been made of the building up of tension owing to the lack of discharge of inhibited impulses. When emotional tension is at a high level the individual will respond defensively and resist attempts to change him. Hence, providing him with the opportunities to blow off steam may often be necessary before attempting a serious discussion of new possibilities of behavior. Again, humor can serve this purpose.

. . . . .

In the third place, ego-defensive behavior can be altered as the individual acquires insight into his own mechanisms of defense. Information about the nature of the problem in the external world will not affect him. Information about his own functioning may have an influence, if presented without threat, and if the defenses do not go too deep into the personality . . . .

Conditions for Arousing and Changing Value-Expressive Attitudes

Two conditions for the arousal of value-expressive attitudes can be specified. The first is the occurrence of the cue in the stimulus situation which has been associated with the attitude. The liberal Democrat, as a liberal Democrat, has always believed in principle that an income tax is more just than a sales tax. Now the issue has arisen in his state, and the group in which he happens to be at the moment are discussing an increase in sales tax.

This will be sufficient to cue off his proposition to the proposal without consideration of the specific local aspects of the tax problem. The second condition for the arousal of this type of attitude is some degree of thwarting of the individual's expressive behavior in the immediate past. The housewife occupied with the routine care of the home and the children during the day may seek opportunities to express her views to other women at the first social gathering she attends.

We have referred to voters backing their party for bread and butter reasons. Perhaps the bulk of voting behavior, however, is the elicitation of value-expressive attitudes. Voting is a symbolic expression of being a Republican or a Democrat. Party identification accounts for more variance in voting behavior than any other single factor.[17] Though there is a minority who consider themselves independent and though there are minor shifts in political allegiance, the great majority of the people identify themselves as the supporters of a political party. Their voting behavior is an expression of this self-concept, and it takes a major event such as a depression to affect their voting habits seriously.

Identification with party is in good measure a function of the political socialization of the child, as Hyman has shown.[18] An analysis of a national sample of the electorate in 1952 by Campbell, Gurin, and Miller revealed that of voters both of whose parents were Democrats, 76 per cent identified themselves as Democrats, another 10 per cent as independent Democrats, and 12 per cent as Republicans.[19] Similarly, of those with Republican parents 63 per cent considered themselves Republican and another 10 percent as independent Republicans. Attachment to party, Hyman suggests, furnishes an organizing principle for the individual and gives stability to his political orientation in the confusion of changing issues.

.   .   .   .   .

Again, two conditions are relevant in changing value-expressive attitudes:

1. Some degree of dissatisfaction with one's self-concept or its associated values is the opening wedge for fundamental change. The complacent person, smugly satisfied with all aspects of himself, is immune to attempts to change his values. Dissatisfaction with the self can result from failures or from the inadequacy of one's values in preserving a favorable image of oneself in a changing world. The man with pacifist values may have become dissatisfied with himself during a period of fascist expansion and terror. Once there is a crack in the individual's central belief systems, it can be exploited by appropriately directed influences. The techniques of brainwashing employed by the Chinese Communists both on prisoners of war in Korea and in the thought reform of Chinese intellectuals were essentially procedures for changing value systems.

.   .   .   .   .

2. Dissatisfaction with old attitudes as inappropriate to one's values can also lead to change. In fact, people are much less likely to find their values uncongenial than they are to find some of their attitudes inappropriate to their values. The discomfort with one's old attitudes may stem from new experiences or from the suggestions of other people. Senator Vandenburg, as an enlightened conservative, changed his attitudes on foreign relations from an isolationist to an internationalist position when critical events in our history suggested change.

.   .   .   .   .

Arousing and Changing Attitudes which Serve the Knowledge Function

Attitudes acquired in the interests of the need to know are elicited by a stimulus associated with the attitude. The child who learns from his reading and from his parents that Orientals are treacherous will not have the attitude aroused unless some appropriate cue concerning the cognitive object is presented. He may even meet and interact with Orientals without identifying them as such and with no corresponding arousal of his attitude. Considerable prejudice in this sense is race-name prejudice and is only aroused when a premium is placed upon social identification. Since members of a minority group have many other memberships in common with a majority group, the latent prejudiced attitude may not necessarily be activated. Prejudice based upon ego-defensiveness, however, will result in ready identification of the disliked group.

The factors which are productive of change of attitudes of this character are inadequacies of the existing attitudes to deal with new and changing situations. The person who has been taught that Orientals are treacherous may read extended accounts of the honesty of the Chinese or may have favorable interactions with Japanese. He finds his old attitudes in conflict with new information and new experience, and proceeds to modify his beliefs. In this instance we are dealing with fictitious stereotypes which never correspond to reality. In other cases the beliefs may have been adequate to the situation but the world has changed. Thus, some British military men formerly in favor of armaments have changed their attitude toward disarmament because of the character of nuclear weapons. The theory of cognitive consistency later elaborated in this issue [*Public Opinion Quarterly,* 24 (1960)] can draw its best examples from attitudes related to the knowledge function.

Any situation, then, which is ambiguous for the individual is likely to produce attitude change. His need for cognitive structure is such that he will either modify his beliefs to impose structure or accept some new formula presented by others. He seeks a meaningful picture of his universe, and when there is ambiguity he will reach for a ready solution. Rumors abound when information is unavailable.

Global Influences and Attitude Change

In the foregoing analysis we have attempted to clarify the functions which attitudes perform and to give some psychological specifications of the conditions under which they are formed, elicited, and changed. This material is summarized in the table. We must recognize, however, that the influences in the real world are not as a rule directed toward a single type of motivation. Contact with other peoples, experience in foreign cultures, group pressures, group discussion and decision, the impact of legislation, and the techniques of brainwashing are all global variables. They represent combinations of forces. To predict their effectiveness in any given situation it is necessary to analyze their components in relation to the conditions of administration and the type of population toward which they are directed.

Summary

The purpose of this paper was to provide a psychological framework for the systematic consideration of the dynamics of public and private attitudes. Four functions which attitudes perform for the personality were identified: the *adjustive function* of satisfying utilitarian needs, the *ego-defensive function* of handling internal conflicts, the *value-expressive function* of maintaining self-identify and of enhancing the self-image, and the *knowledge function* of giving understanding and meaning to the ambiguities of the world about us. The role of these functions in attitude formation was described. Their relevance for the conditions determining attitude arousal and attitude change were analyzed. Finally, constellations of variables such as group contact and legislative control of behavior were considered in terms of their motivational impact.

**Determinants of Attitude Formation, Arousal, and Change
in Relation to Type of Function**

Function	Origin and Dynamics	Arousal Conditions	Change Conditions
Adjustment	Utility of attitudinal object in need satisfaction. Maximizing external rewards and minimizing punishments	1. Activation of needs 2. Salience of cues associated with need satisfaction	1. Need deprivation 2. Creation of new needs and new levels of aspiration 3. Shifting rewards and punishments 4. Emphasis on new and better paths for need satisfaction
Ego defense	Protecting against internal conflicts and external dangers	1. Posing of threats 2. Appeals to hatred and repressed impulses 3. Rise in frustrations 4. Use of authoritarian suggestion	1. Removal of threats 2. Catharsis 3. Development of self-insight
Value expression	Maintaining self identity; enhancing favorable self-image; self-expression and self-determination	1. Salience of cues associated with values 2. Appeals to individual to reassert self-image 3. Ambiguities which threaten self-concept	1. Some degree of dissatisfaction with self 2. Greater appropriateness of new attitude for the self 3. Control of all environmental supports to undermine old values
Knowledge	Need for understanding, for meaningful cognitive organization, for consistency and clarity	1. Reinstatement of cues associated with old problem or of old problem itself	1. Ambiguity created by new information or change in environment 2. More meaningful information about problems

Notes

1. David Krech and Richard S. Crutchfield, *Theory and Problems of Social Psychology* (New York: McGraw-Hill, 1948), pp. 160-63.

2. Dorwin Cartwright, "Some Principles of Mass Persuasion," *Human Relations,* Vol. 2 (1949), pp. 253-67.

3. M. Brewster Smith, "The Personal Setting of Public Opinions: A Study of Attitudes toward Russia," *Public Opinion Quarterly,* Vol. 11 (1947), pp. 507-23.

4. Daniel Katz and Ezra Stotland, "A Preliminary Statement to a Theory of Attitude Structure and Change," in *Psychology: A Study of a Science,* Vol. 3, ed. Sigmund Koch (New York: McGraw-Hill, 1959), pp. 423-75.

5. See Ulf Himmelstrand, "Verbal Attitudes and Behavior: A Paradigm for the Study of Message Transmission and Transformation," *Public Opinion Quarterly,* Vol. 24 (1960), pp. 224-50.

6. Milton J. Rosenberg, "A Structural Theory of Attitude Dynamics," *Public Opinion Quarterly,* Vol. 24 (1960), pp. 319-40.

7. Katz and Stotland, op. cit., pp. 434-43.

8. Irving Sarnoff, "Psychoanalytic Theory and Social Attitudes," *Public Opinion Quarterly,* Vol. 24 (1960), pp. 251-79.

9. John Dewey, *How We Think* (New York: Macmillan Company, 1910).

10. Walter Lippmann, *Public Opinion* (New York: Macmillan Company, 1922).

11. Herta Herzog, "What Do We Really Know about Daytime Serial Listeners?" in *Radio Research* 1942-43, Paul F. Lazarsfeld and Frank N. Stanton, eds. (New York: Duell, Sloan & Pearce, 1944), pp. 3-33.

12. From a study of the impact of party organization on political behavior in the Detroit area, by Daniel Katz and Samuel Eldersveld, in manuscript.

13. Lippmann, op. cit., p. 95.

14. Earl R. Carlson, "Attitude Change through Modification of Attitude Structure," *Journal of Abnormal and Social Psychology,* Vol. 52 (1956), pp. 256-61.

15. Irving L. Janis and Seymour Feshbach, "Effects of Fear-arousing Communications," *Journal of Abnormal and Social Psychology,* Vol. 48 (1953), pp. 78-92.

16. Morton Wagman, "Attitude Change and the Authoritirian Personality," *Journal of Psychology,* 40 (1955), pp. 3-24. The F-scale is a measure of authoritarianism comprising items indicative of both defensiveness and ideology.

17. Angus A. Campbell, Philip Converse, Warren Miller, and Donald Stokes, *The American Voter* (New York: Wiley, 1960).

18. Herbert H. Hyman, *Political Socialization* (Glencoe, Ill.: Free Press, 1959).

19. Angus A. Campbell, Gerald Gurin, and Warren Miller, *The Voter Decides* (Evanston, Ill.: Row, Peterson, 1954).

PROCESS OF OPINION CHANGE

HERBERT C. KELMAN

The Study of Social Influence

Social influence has been a central area of concern for experimental social psychology almost since its beginnings. Three general research traditions in this area can be distinguished: (1) the study of social influences on judgments, stemming from the earlier work on prestige suggestion;[1] (2) the study of social influences arising from small-group interaction;[2] and (3) the study of social influences arising from persuasive communications.[3] In recent years, there has been a considerable convergence between these three traditions, going hand in hand with an increased interest in developing general principles of social influence and socially induced behavior change.

One result of these developments has been that many investigators found it necessary to make qualitative distinctions between different types of influence. In some cases, these distinctions arose primarily out of the observation that social influence may have qualita-

Excerpted from Herbert C. Kelman, "Process of Opinion Change," *Public Opinion Quarterly,* 25 (1961), pp. 58-78. Permission by *Public Opinion Quarterly* and the author.

tively different effects, that it may produce different kinds of change. For example, under some conditions it may result in mere public conformity—in superficial changes on a verbal or overt level without accompanying changes in belief; in other situations it may result in private acceptance—in a change that is more general, more durable, more integrated with the person's own values.[4] Other investigators found it necessary to make distinctions because they observed that influence may occur for different reasons, that it may arise out of different motivations and orientations. For example, under some conditions influence may be primarily informational—the subject may conform to the influencing person or group because he views him as a source of valid information; in other situations influence may be primarily normative—the subject may conform in order to meet the positive expectations of the influencing person or group.[5]

My own work can be viewed in the general context that I have outlined here. I started out with the distinction between public conformity and private acceptance, and tried to establish some of the distinct determinants of each. I became dissatisfied with this dichotomy as I began to look at important examples of social influence that could not be encompassed by it. I was especially impressed with the accounts of ideological conversion of the "true believer" variety, and with the recent accounts of "brainwashing," particularly the Chinese Communist methods of "thought reform."[6] It is apparent that these experiences do not simply involve public conformity, but that indeed they produce a change in underlying beliefs. But it is equally apparent that they do not produce what we would usually consider private acceptance—changes that are in some sense integrated with the person's own value system and that have become independent of the external source. Rather, they seem to produce new beliefs that are isolated from the rest of the person's values and that are highly dependent on external support.

These considerations eventually led me to distinguish three processes of social influence, each characterized by a distinct set of antecedent and a distinct set of consequent conditions. I have called these processes *compliance, identification,* and *internalization.*[7]

Three Processes of Social Influence

Compliance can be said to occur when an individual accepts influence from another person or from a group because he hopes to achieve a favorable reaction from the other. He may be interested in attaining certain specific rewards or in avoiding certain specific punishments that the influencing agent controls. For example, an individual may make a special effort to express only "correct" opinions in order to gain admission into a particular group or social set, or in order to avoid being fired from his government job. Or, the individual may be concerned with gaining approval or avoiding disapproval from the influencing agent in a more general way. For example, some individuals may compulsively try to say the expected thing in all situations and please everyone with whom they come in contact, out of a disproportionate need for favorable responses from others of a direct and immediate kind. In any event, when the individual complies, he does what the agent wants him to do—or what he thinks the agent wants him to do—because he sees this as a way of achieving a desired response from him. He does not adopt the induced behavior—for example, a particular opinion response—because he believes in its content, but because it is instrumental in the production of a satisfying social effect. What the individual learns, essentially, is to say or do the expected thing in special situations, regardless of what his private beliefs may be. Opinions adopted through compliance should be expressed only when the person's behavior is observable by the influencing agent.

Identification can be said to occur when an individual adopts behavior derived from another person or a group because this behavior is associated with a satisfying self-defining relationship to this person or group. By a self-defining relationship I mean a role relationship that forms a part of the person's self-image. Accepting influence through identification, then, is a way of establishing or maintaining the desired relationship to the other, and the self-definition that is anchored in this relationship.

The relationship that an individual tries to establish or maintain through identification may take different forms. It may take the form of classical identification, that is, of a relationship in which the individual takes over all or part of the role of the influencing agent. To the extent to which such a relationship exists, the individual defines his own role in terms of the role of the other. He attempts to be like or actually to *be* the other person. By saying what the other says, doing what he does, believing what he believes, the individual maintains this relationship and the satisfying self-definition that it provides him. An influencing agent who is likely to be an attractive object for such a relationship is one who occupies a role desired by the individual—who possesses those characteristics that the individual himself lacks—such as control in a situation in which the individual is helpless, direction in a situation in which he is disoriented, or belongingness in a situation in which he is isolated.

The behavior of the brainwashed prisoner in Communist China provides one example of this type of identification. By adopting the attitudes and beliefs of the prison authorities —including *their* evaluation of *him*—he attempts to regain his identity, which has been subjected to severe threats. But this kind of identification does not occur only in such severe crisis situations. It can also be observed, for example, in the context of socialization of children, where the taking over of parental attitudes and actions is a normal, and probably essential, part of personality development. The more or less conscious efforts involved when an individual learns to play a desired occupational role and imitates an appropriate role model would also exemplify this process. Here, of course, the individual is much more selective in the attitudes and actions he takes over from the other person. What is at stake is not his basic sense of identity or the stability of his self-concept, but rather his more limited "professional identity."

The self-defining relationship that an individual tries to establish or maintain through identification may also take the form of a reciprocal role relationship—that is, of a relationship in which the roles of the two parties are defined with reference to one another. An individual may be involved in a reciprocal relationship with another specific individual, as in a friendship relationship between two people. Or he may enact a social role which is defined with reference to another (reciprocal) role, as in the relationship between patient and doctor. A reciprocal-role relationship can be maintained only if the participants have mutually shared expectations of one another's behavior. Thus, if an individual finds a particular relationship satisfying, he will tend to behave in such a way as to meet the expectations of the other. In other words, he will tend to behave in line with the requirements of this particular relationship. This should be true regardless of whether the other is watching or not: quite apart from the reactions of the other, it is important to the individual's own self-concept to meet the expectations of his friendship role, for example, or those of his occupational role.

Thus, the acceptance of influence through identification should take place when the person sees the induced behavior as relevant to and required by a reciprocal-role relationship in which he is a participant. Acceptance of influence based on a reciprocal-role relationship is similar to that involved in classical identification in that it is a way of establishing or maintaining a satisfying self-defining relationship to another. The nature of the relationship differs, of course. In one case it is a relationship of identity; in the other, one of reciprocity. In the case of reciprocal-role relationships, the individual is not identifying with the other in the sense of taking over *his* identity, but in the sense of empathically reacting in terms of the other person's expectations, feelings, or needs.

Identification may also serve to maintain an individual's relationship to a group in which his self-definition is anchored. Such a relationship may have elements of classical identification as well as of reciprocal roles: To maintain his self-definition as a group member an individual, typically, has to model his behavior along particular lines and has to meet the expectations of his fellow members. An example of identification with a group would be the member of the Communist Party who derives strength and a sense of identity from his self-definition as part of the vanguard of the proletarian revolution and as an agent of historical destiny. A similar process, but at a low degree of intensity, is probably involved in many of the conventions that people acquire as part of their socialization into a particular group.

Identification is similar to compliance in that the individual does not adopt the induced behavior because its content per se is intrinsically satisfying. Identification differs from compliance, however, in that the individual actually believes in the opinions and actions that he adopts. The behavior is accepted both publicly and privately, and its manifestation does not depend on observability by the influencing agent. It does depend, however, on the role that an individual takes at any given moment in time. Only when the appropriate role is activated—only when the individual is acting within the relationship upon which the identification is based—will the induced opinions be expressed. The individual is not primarily concerned with pleasing the other, with giving him what he wants (as in compliance), but he is concerned with meeting the other's expectations for his own role performance. Thus, opinions adopted through identification do remain tied to the external source and dependent on social support. They are not integrated with the individual's value system, but rather tend to be isolated from the rest of his values—to remain encapsulated.

Finally, *internalization* can be said to occur when an individual accepts influence because the induced behavior is congruent with his value system. It is the content of the induced behavior that is intrinsically rewarding here. The individual adopts it because he finds it useful for the solution of a problem, or because it is congenial to his own orientation, or because it is demanded by his own values—in short, because he perceives it as inherently conducive to the maximization of his values. The characteristics of the influencing agent do play an important role in internalization, but the crucial dimension here—as we shall see below—is the agent's credibility, that is, his relation to the content.

The most obvious examples of internalization are those that involve the evaluation and acceptance of induced behavior on rational grounds. A person may adopt the recommendations of an expert, for example, because he finds them relevant to his own problems and congruent with his own values. Typically, when internalization is involved, he will not accept these recommendation *in toto* but modify them to some degree so that they will fit his own unique situation. Or a visitor to a foreign country may be challenged by the different patterns of behavior to which he is exposed, and he may decide to adopt them (again, selectively and in modified form) because he finds them more in keeping with his own values than the patterns in his home country. I am not implying, of course, that internalization is always involved in the situations mentioned. One would speak of internalization only if acceptance of influence took the particular form that I described.

Internalization, however, does not necessarily involve the adoption of induced behavior on rational grounds. I would not want to equate internalization with rationality, even though the description of the process has decidedly rationalist overtones. For example, I would characterize as internalization the adoption of beliefs because of their congruence with a value system that is basically *irrational.* Thus, an authoritarian individual may adopt certain racist attitudes because they fit into his paranoid, irrational view of the world. Presumably, what is involved here is internalization, since it is the content of the induced behavior and its relation to the person's value system that is satisfying. Similarly, it should be noted that congruence with a person's value system does not necessarily imply logical consistency. Behavior would be congruent if, in some way or other, it fit into the person's value system, if it seemed to belong there and be demanded by it.

It follows from this conception that behavior adopted through internalization is in some way—rational or otherwise—integrated with the individual's existing values. It becomes part of a personal system, as distinguished from a system of social-role expectations. Such behavior gradually becomes independent of the external source. Its manifestation depends neither on observability by the influencing agent nor on the activation of the relevant role, but on the extent to which the underlying values have been made relevant by the issues under consideration. This does not mean that the individual will invariably express internalized opinions, regardless of the social situation. In any specific situation, he has to choose among competing values in the face of a variety of situational requirements. It does mean, however, that these opinions will at least enter into competition with other alternatives whenever they are relevant in content.

It should be stressed that the three processes are not mutually exclusive. While they have been defined in terms of pure cases, they do not generally occur in pure form in real-life situations. The examples that have been given are, at best, situations in which a particular process predominates and determines the central features of the interaction.

Antecedents and Consequents of the Three Processes

For each of the three processes, a distinct set of antecedents and a distinct set of consequents have been proposed. These are summarized in the table below. First, with respect to the antecedents of the three processes, it should be noted that no systematic quantitative differences between them are hypothesized. The probability of each process is presented as a function of the same three determinants: the importance of the induction for the individual's goal achievement, the power of the influencing agent, and the prepotency of the induced response. For each process, the magnitude of these determinants may vary over the entire range: Each may be based on an induction with varying degrees of importance, on an influencing agent with varying degrees of power, and so on. The processes differ only in terms of the *qualitative* form that these determinants take. They differ, as can be seen in the table, in terms of the *basis* for the importance of the induction, the *source* of the influencing agent's power, and the *manner* of achieving prepotency of the induced response.

Summary of the Distinctions Between the Three Process

	Compliance	Identification	Internalization
Antecedents:			
1. Basis for the *importance of the induction*	Concern with social effect of behavior	Concern with social anchorage of behavior	Concern with value congruence of behavior
2. Source of *power of the influencing agent*	Means control	Attractiveness	Credibility
3. Manner of achieving *prepotency of the induced response*	Limitation of choice behavior	Delineation of role requirements	Reorganization of means-ends framework
Consequents:			
1. Conditions of performance of induced response	Surveillance by influencing agent	Salience of relationship to agent	Relevance of values to issue
2. Conditions of change and extinction of induced response	Changed perception of conditions for social rewards	Changed perception of conditions for satisfying self-defining relationships	Changed perception of conditions for value maximization
3. Type of behavior system in which induced response is embedded	External demands of a specific setting	Expectations defining a specific role	Person's value system

1. The processes can be distinguished in terms of the basis for the importance of the induction, that is, in terms of the nature of the motivational system that is activated in the influence situation. What is it about the influence situation that makes it important, that makes it relevant to the individual's goals? What are the primary concerns that the individual brings to the situation or that are aroused by it? The differences between the three processes in this respect are implicit in the descriptions of the processes given above: (a) To the extent that the individual is concerned—for whatever reason—with the *social effect* of his behavior, influence will tend to take the form of compliance. (b) To the extent that he is concerned with the *social anchorage* of his behavior, influence will tend to take the form of identification. (c) To the extent that he is concerned with the *value congruence* of his behavior (rational or otherwise), influence will tend to take the form of internalization.

2. A difference between the three processes in terms of the source of the influencing agent's power is hypothesized. (a) To the extent that the agent's power is based on his *means control,* influence will tend to take the form of compliance. An agent possesses means control if he is in a position to supply or withhold means needed by the individual for the achievement of his goals. The perception of means control may depend on the agent's *actual* control over specific rewards and punishments, or on his *potential* control, which would be related to his position in the social structure (his status, authority, or general prestige). (b) To the extent that the agent's power is based on his *attractiveness,* influence will tend to take the form of identification. An agent is attractive if he occupies

a role which the individual himself desires[8] or if he occupies a role reciprocal to one the individual wants to establish or maintain. The term "attractiveness," as used here, does not refer to the possession of qualities that make a person likable, but rather to the possession of qualities on the part of the agent that make a continued relationship to him particularly desirable. In other words, an agent is attractive when the individual is able to derive satisfaction from a self-definition with reference to him. (c) To the extent that the agent's power is based on his *credibility,* influence will tend to take the form of internalization. An agent possesses credibility if his statements are considered truthful and valid, and hence worthy of serious consideration. Hovland, Janis, and Kelley[9] distinguish two bases for credibility: expertness and trustworthiness. In other words, an agent may be perceived as possessing credibility because he is likely to *know* the truth, or because he is likely to *tell* the truth. Trustworthiness, in turn, may be related to overall respect, likemindedness, and lack of vested interest.

3. It is proposed that the three processes differ in terms of the way in which prepotency is achieved. (a) To the extent that the induced response becomes prepotent—that is, becomes a "distinguished path" relative to alternative response possibilities—because the individual's choice behavior is limited, influence will tend to take the form of compliance. This may happen if the individual is pressured into the induced response, or if alternative responses are blocked. The induced response thus becomes prepotent because it is, essentially, the only response permitted: the individual sees himself as having no choice and as being restricted to this particular alternative. (b) To the extent that the induced response becomes prepotent because the requirements of a particular role are delineated, influence will tend to take the form of identification. This may happen if the situation is defined in terms of a particular role relationship and the demands of that role are more or less clearly specified; for instance, if this role is made especially salient and the expectations deriving from it dominate the field. Or it may happen if alternative roles are made ineffective because the situation is ambiguous and consensual validation is lacking. The induced response thus becomes prepotent because it is one of the few alternatives available to the individual: his choice behavior may be unrestricted, but his opportunity for selecting alternative responses is limited by the fact that he is operating exclusively from the point of view of a particular role system. (c) Finally, to the extent that the induced response becomes prepotent because there has been a reorganization in the individual's conception of means-ends relationships, influence will tend to take the form of internalization. This may happen if the implications of the induced response for certain important values—implications of which the individual had been unaware heretofore—are brought out, or if the advantages of the induced response as a path to the individual's goals, compared to the various alternatives that are available, are made apparent. The induced response thus becomes prepotent because it has taken on a new meaning: as the relationships between various means and ends become restructured, it emerges as the preferred course of action in terms of the person's own values.

Depending, then, on the nature of these three antecedents, the influence process will take the form of compliance, identification, or internalization. Each of these corresponds to a characteristic pattern of internal responses—thoughts and feelings—in which the individual engages as he accepts influence. The resulting changes will, in turn, be different for the three processes, as indicated in the second half of the table. Here, again, it is assumed that there are no systematic quantitative differences between the processes, but rather qualitative variations in the subsequent histories of behavior adopted through each process.

1. It is proposed the the processes differ in terms of the subsequent conditions under which the induced response will be performed or expressed. (a) When an individual adopts an induced response through compliance, he tends to perform it only under conditions of *surveillance* by the influencing agent. These conditions are met if the agent is physically present, or if he is likely to find out about the individual's actions. (b) When an individual adopts an induced response through identification, he tends to perform it only under conditions of *salience* of his relationship to the agent. That is, the occurrence of the behavior will depend on the extent to which the person's relationship to the agent has been engaged in the situation. Somehow this relationship has to be brought into focus and the individual has to be acting within the particular role that is involved in the identification. This does not necessarily mean, however, that he is consciously aware of the relationship; the role can be activated without much awareness. (c) When an individual adopts an induced response through internalization, he tends to perform it under conditions of *relevance of the values* that were initially involved in the influence situation. The behavior will tend to occur whenever these values are activated by the issues under consideration in a given situation, quite regardless of surveillance or salience of the influencing agent. This does not mean, of course, that the behavior will occur every time it becomes relevant. It may be out-competed by other responses in certain situations. The probability of occurrence with a given degree of issue relevance will depend on the strength of the internalized behavior.

2. It is hypothesized that responses adopted through the three processes will differ in terms of the conditions under which they will subsequently be abandoned or changed. (a) A response adopted through compliance will be abandoned if it is no longer perceived as the best path toward the attainment of social rewards. (b) A response adopted through identification will be abandoned if it is no longer perceived as the best path toward the maintenance or establishment of satisfying self-defining relationships. (c) A response adopted through internalization will be abandoned if it is no longer perceived as the best path toward the maximization of the individual's values.

3. Finally, it is hypothesized that responses adopted through the three processes will differ from each other along certain qualitative dimensions. These can best be summarized, perhaps, by referring to the type of behavior system in which the induced response is embedded. (a) Behavior adopted through compliance is part of a system of external demands that characterize a specific setting. In other words, it is part of the rules of conduct that an individual learns in order to get along in a particular situation or series of situations. The behavior tends to be related to the person's values only in an instrumental rather than an intrinsic way. As long as opinions, for example, remain at that level, the individual will tend to regard them as not really representative of his true beliefs. (b) Behavior adopted through identification is part of a system of expectations defining a particular role—whether this is the role of the other which he is taking over, or a role reciprocal to the other's. This behavior will be regarded by the person as representing himself, and may in fact form an important aspect of himself. It will tend to be isolated, however, from the rest of the person's values—to have little interplay with them. In extreme cases, the system in which the induced response is embedded may be encapsulated and function almost like a foreign body within the person. The induced responses here will be relatively inflexible and stereotyped. (c) Behavior adopted through internalization is part of an internal system. It is fitted into the person's basic framework of values and is congruent with it. This does not imply complete consistency: The degree of consistency can vary for different individuals and different areas of behavior. It does

mean, however, that there is some interplay between the new beliefs and the rest of the person's values. The new behavior can serve to modify existing beliefs and can in turn be modified by them. As a result of this interaction, behavior adopted through internalization will tend to be relatively idiosyncratic, flexible, complex, and differentiated.

Notes

1. See, for example, S. E. Asch, *Social Psychology* (New York: Prentice-Hall, 1952).

2. See, for example, D. Cartwright and A. Zander, eds., *Group Dynamics* (Evanston, Ill.: Row, Peterson, 1953).

3. See, for example, C. I. Hovland, I. L. Janis, and H. H. Kelley, *Communication and Persuasion* (New Haven: Yale University Press, 1953).

4. See, for example, L. Festinger, "An Analysis of Compliant Behavior," in M. Sherif and M. O. Wilson, eds., *Group Relations at the Crossroads* (New York: Harper, 1953), pp. 232-56; H. C. Kelman, "Attitude Change as a Function of Response Restriction," *Human Relations,* Vol. 6 (1953), pp. 185-214; J. R. P. French, Jr., and B. Raven, "The Bases of Social Power," in D. Cartwright, ed., *Studies in Social Power* (Ann Arbor: Institute for Social Research, 1959), pp. 150-67; and Marie Jahoda, "Conformity and Independence," *Human Relations,* Vol. 12 (1959), pp. 99-120.

5. See, for example, M. Deutsch and H. B. Gerard, "A Study of Normative and Informational Social Influence upon Individual Judgment," *Journal of Abnormal and Social Psychology,* Vol. 51 (1955), pp. 629-36; J. W. Thibaut and L. Strickland, "Psychological Set and Social Conformity," *Journal of Personality,* Vol. 25 (1956), pp. 115-29; and J. M. Jackson and H. D. Saltzstein, "The Effect of Person-Group Relationships on Conformity Precesses," *Journal of Abnormal and Social Psychology,* Vol. 57 (1958), pp. 17-24.

6. For instance, R. J. Lifton, " 'Thought Reform' of Western Civilians in Chinese Communist Prisons," *Psychiatry,* Vol. 19 (1956), pp. 173-95.

7. A detailed description of these processes and the experimental work based on them will be contained in a forthcoming book, *Social Influence and Personal Belief: A Theoretical and Experimental Approach to the Study of Behavior Change,* to be published by John Wiley and Sons.

8. This is similar to John Whiting's conception of "Status Envy" as a basis for identification. See J. W. M. Whiting, "Sorcery, Sin, and the Superego," in M. R. Jones, ed., *Nebraska Symposium on Motivation* (Lincoln: University of Nebraska Press, 1959), pp. 174-95.

9. Op. cit., p. 21.

THE ROLE OF VALUES IN PUBLIC OPINION RESEARCH

MILTON ROKEACH

Despite the fact that public opinion research seeks to understand better the determinants of public opinion, it has thus far paid remarkably little attention to the *values* underlying public opinion. This neglect is not so much a matter of choice as it is a matter of necessity. Given the present state of employment of the social science it is not yet conceptually meaningful or technologically feasible to assess routinely the values underlying public opinion. We do not as yet have a clear enough consensus about the con-

Milton Rokeach, "The Role of Values in Public Opinion Research," *Public Opinion Quarterly* (Winter, 1968-69), pp. 547-559. Permission by *Public Opinion Quarterly* and the author.

The work reported herein was supported by a grant from the National Science Foundation and is part of an ongoing research program on organization and change in values, attitudes, and behavior.

ceptual differences between values and attitudes, or about the relation between them. We do not as yet have methods for assessing values in a manner that would be distinct from the assessment of attitudes. One major aim of the research program to be described here is to provide the necessary concepts and methods.

Over and above the need to understand better the values underlying public opinion, I believe that our approach can also help to remove or to alleviate two major weaknesses in contemporary public opinion research. The first weakness pertains to what might be called its "race-horse philosophy." The kinds of data obtained by public opinion research and disseminated in the mass media seem designed more to entertain than to inform. The quality of the information conveyed seems not much different from that conveyed in the sports pages or, better yet, the daily racing form. This "race-horse philosophy" is apparent during an election year, especially in the mass media. On April 1, 1968 CBS televised a "Special" immediately following President Johnson's dual announcement that he had decided to call a partial halt to the bombing in North Vietnam and that he had decided to withdraw from the presidential race. CBS's "Special" did not concern itself with the presidential race. CBS's "Special" did not concern itself with reactions to Johnson's speech in New York, or Saigon, or Moscow, or London, or with a discussion of its implications for ending the war, or with its implications for strengthening or weakening the student protest movement at home or abroad, or for halting nuclear proliferation, or for winning the civil war now raging between our inner and outer cities. Rather, the "Special" restricted itself to speculations about the possible effects of Johnson's speech on the fortunes and misfortunes that might befall approximately half a dozen individuals aspiring to the presidency. The CBS "Special" deepened my understanding of the implication of LBJ's statement at about the same intellectual level as midseason speculations about possible Rose Bowl contenders deepened my understanding about who will end up playing in the Rose Bowl.

A second weakness of contemporary public opinion research is its at least occasional insensitivity to its own value preferences, or perhaps the value preferences of its major clients, the mass media. Dr. Herbert Krugman recently had occasion to draw my attention to a Gallup poll reported in the *New York Times* on February 28, 1969. It carried the headline "Poll Finds Crime Top Fear at Home," and it described public responses to the question "What is the most important problem facing this community today?" The report came up with the somewhat extraordinary finding that "crime and lawlessness" is the major domestic problem seen by the American public and that "racial problems" was only eighth in importance as a domestic problem. However, "crime and lawlessness" turned out to be the most frequent domestic problem because Gallup lumped together under this category "crime," "lawlessness," "riots," "looting," and "juvenile delinquency." The results would have been dramatically different had the Gallup organization kept these categories separate and instead had lumped together with "racial problems" such other categories as "poor quality of education," "unemployment," "slums," "overcrowded housing" and "lack of cultural and recreational facilities." The implication of the Gallup report as it now stands is that we need better police protection against "crime and lawlessness" but that we do not need to do much about "racial problems" because it is, after all, only eighth in importance and there are seven other problems more deserving of immediate attention.

Translating all this into the language of values, let me suggest that both the Gallup report and the *New York Times'* failure to exercise its journalistic conscience in its uncritical reporting of this report reflect the hidden value system of a white society which traditionally places a high value on freedom and a low value on equality, a white society which in the year 1968, fearing yet more encroachments on freedom for whites and yet more extensions of equality for blacks, translates the secret values, to which it cannot openly confess, into conscious preoccupations with "crime and lawlessness." This sort of Aesopian language places both pollster and journalist in the position of bedfellows trying to defend or to reinforce the values of the *status quo* under the guise of publishing objective reports designed to "inform the public." Were public opinion research more explicitly concerned with the problem of values it would not only lead to a generally better understanding of the determinants of public opinion and to a more truly informed public, but it would also help avoid the kinds of embarrassments just discussed.

Few will dispute the proposition that it is the attitude concept which has occupied a central position in the social psychological sciences. The late Gordon Allport remarked as long ago as 1935: "The concept of attitude is probably the most distinctive and indispensable concept in contemporary social psychology. No other term appears more frequently in the experimental and theoretical literature."[1] McGuire has observed only within this past year: "The last five social psychology textbooks which have appeared devoted an average of 25 per cent of the space to attitude work, far more than any of the other topics, such as group process and socialization."[2] McGuire goes on to observe, "Between the 1961 and 1965 volumes of the *Psychological Abstracts* the number of studies on attitudes has not only increased continuously, but had increased faster than did social psychology as a whole."[3] During this same period, I would like to add, the ratio of attitude studies to value studies cited in the *Psychological Abstracts* was more or less constant: about 5 or 6 attitude studies for every value study.

Relationship between Attitudes and Values

A look at the literature provides some clues to the reasons for the discrepancy. Half a century after Thomas and Znaniecki first introduced the attitude concept into social psychology there is still very little consensus about the exact conceptual difference between an attitude and a value; we sometimes employ these two concepts interchangeably and sometimes differentially. We sometimes employ them in the singular and sometimes in the plural, as if we have not yet learned how to count them. Most of the literature on attitudes does not concern itself with values, and most of the literature on values does not concern itself with attitudes. And most of the methodological advances concern the measurement of attitudes and not the measurement of values and value systems.

What exactly is the conceptual difference between an attitude and a value, and what is the relation between them? How should we proceed empirically in order to assess a person's values and attitudes without confusing one with the other? If a person's values form a value system, in what sense do they constitute a system and by what operations can such a system be revealed? If you somehow change a man's values do you necessarily change his attitudes, and if you somehow change a man's attitudes do you necessarily change his values?

I will define an attitude as an enduring organization of several beliefs focused on a specific object (physical or social, concrete or abstract) or situation, predisposing one to respond in some preferential manner.

Values, on the other hand, transcend specific objects and specific situations: values have to do with *modes of conduct* and *end-states of existence.* More formally, to say that a person "has a value" is to say that he has an enduring belief that a particular mode of conduct or that a particular end-state of existence is personally and socially preferable to alternative modes of conduct or end-states of existence. This formal definition of value accomplishes two things: it distinguishes value from attitude, and it avoids at the same time such difficult terms as "ought," "should," or "desirable," terms I would be obliged to define were I to use them, a task I would rather avoid.

So defined, a value is a standard or criterion that serves a number of important purposes in our daily lives: it is a standard that tells us how to act or what to want; it is a standard that tells us what attitudes we should hold; it is a standard we employ to justify behavior, to morally judge, and to compare ourselves with others. Finally, a value is a standard we employ to tell us which values, attitudes, and actions of others are worth or not worth trying to influence. If you claim to have a "value" and you do not want to influence anyone else under the sun to have it too, the chances are it is not a value.

Defined in this way, attitudes and values differ from one another in three important respects. First, a value transcends specific objects and situations, while an attitude focuses directly on specific objects and situations; second, a value, unlike an attitude, is a standard or yardstick guiding not only attitudes, but also actions, comparisons, evaluations, and justifications of self and others; third, a value, unlike an attitude, is a distinct preference for a specified mode of behavior or for a specified end-state of existence.

Modes of conduct and end-states of existence point to two different kinds of values, what I will henceforth call *instrumental* and *terminal* values. Examples of instrumental values include the beliefs that most of us have that we should behave courageously, responsibly, honestly, and open-mindedly. Examples of terminal values, on the other hand, are beliefs in salvation, a world at peace, equality, and inner harmony as desirable end-states of existence.

A final concept I would like to define is the concept of value system. A value system, as I will employ it, signifies nothing more than a hierarchical arrangement of values, a rank-ordering of values along a continuum of importance. And given the distinction just made between instrumental and terminal values, all men can be said to have two kinds of value systems—an instrumental value system and a terminal value system.

Over and above the functions served by each value considered alone as a separate standard, the function of a person's value system is to help him choose between alternatives and to resolve conflicts between alternatives in everyday life. Given any situation a person may find himself in, it is all but impossible for him to behave in a manner that is equally congruent with all of his values. The situation may activate two or more values in conflict with one another, or it may activate one value more strongly than another. A person may, for example, sometimes have to choose between behaving truthfully or behaving kindly, but not both, or between behaving courageously or behaving patriotically, but not both. Similarly, a given situation may activate two or more terminal values in conflict with one another; for example, an exciting life versus inner harmony, mature love versus a comfortable life, self-fulfillment versus social recognition, salvation versus a life of pleasure. A person's value system may thus be said to represent a learned organization of rules for making choices and for resolving conflicts—between two or more modes of behavior or between two or more end-states of existence.

Given a reasonably sizable number of values to be arranged in a hierarchy, a large number of variations is theoretically possible, but it is extremely unlikely that all such value patterns will actually be found. Many social factors can confidently be expected to restrict sharply the number of variations obtained. Similarities of culture, social system, caste and class, sex, occupation, education, religion, and political identification are some of the major variables that are likely to shape in more or less similar ways the value systems' of large numbers of people. We may thus expect that while personality factors will give rise to variations in individual value systems, cultural, institutional, and social factors will nevertheless restrict such variations to a reasonably small number, perhaps a few million.

The conceptual distinctions just drawn between attitudes and values, between instrumental and terminal values, and between values and value systems now permit us to make at least a rough count of the numbers of attitudes, instrumental values, and terminal values which a person may be said to have. A grown person possesses many thousands of attitudes—as many attitudes as he has had encounters with specific objects and specific situations—but he possesses far fewer instrumental values, say, five or six dozen, and he possesses an even fewer number of terminal values, perhaps a dozen and a half, give or take a few. Let us assume that all these thousands of attitudes are in the service of and related to these five or six dozen instrumental values and that these are, in turn, in the service of and related to the dozen and a half terminal values. This interconnected value-attitude system, as I shall call it, forms a hierarchical mental organization which is in some psychological sense internally consistent. Any change in any part of the value-attitude system will affect other parts; also, any change in the value-attitude system should lead to behavioral change.

This theory describes the organization of value-attitude systems. With a few additional elaborations the theory can also describe how value-attitude systems may undergo change. Let us assume that every person has a need to maintain consistency, or the illusion of consistency, between all the elements that I have represented within the person's value-attitude system. Let us assume further that day-to-day reality and experience continually conspire to bring various elements of the value-atttitude system into a dissonant relation with one another. A person may, for example, be confronted with the realization that two beliefs he has about an attitude object are contradictory, or he may be confronted with a contradiction between a terminal and an instrumental value, or he may be confronted with a contradiction between a value and an attitude. For lack of space I will not here go into a more extended discussion of all the different kinds of dissonant experiences which a person may experience or may be experimentally induced to experience. A fuller discussion is presented elsewhere (Rokeach, 1968).[4] For present purposes it is perhaps sufficient to suggest that given the central role that values play within the value-attitude system, especially terminal values, the most enduring and the most far-reaching changes within a person's value-attitude system would be brought about by bringing one or more of the terminal values into a dissonant relation with other elements in the system. For example, a particular terminal value may be brought into a dissonant relation with another terminal value, or with an instrumental value, or with an attitude. Such experienced dissonant relations should give rise to motivational forces leading an individual to change his values and attitudes in such a way that they would become more pyschologically consistent with one another.

Research Method and Illustrative Findings

These, then, are some of our theoretical formulations. Our first empirical efforts were, of course, directed toward finding some method for measuring values and value systems, and we tried to keep in mind the following ideal characteristics in developing our method: it should be reasonably reliable; it should be simple and economical to administer; it should enable us to speak meaningfully and quantitatively about single values as well as about systems of values; it should enable us to measure change in single values as well as change systems of values; it should not be susceptible to response sets or to social desirability factors; it should be readily adaptable to cross-cultural settings; it should contain a reasonably comprehensive list of the most important values; and, finally, it should be intrinsically interesting.

Over the past two years we have expended considerable effort to develop a method for measuring values which would have as many as possible of the ideal characteristics mentioned. Our most satisfactory version to date consists of 18 alphabetically arranged terminal values presented on one page and 18 alphabetically arranged instrumental values presented on a second page. The two sets of values are shown in Table 1.

Table 1   The Terminal and Instrumental Value Scales

Terminal Values	Instrumental Values
A Comfortable Life (a prosperous life)	Ambitious (hard-working, aspiring)
An Exciting Life (a stimulating, active life)	Broadminded (open-minded)
A Sense of Accomplishment (lasting contribution)	Capable (competent, effective)
A World at Peace (free of war and conflict)	Cheerful (lighthearted, joyful)
A World of Beauty (beauty of nature and the arts)	Clean (neat, tidy)
Equality (brotherhood, equal opportunity for all)	Courageous (standing up for your beliefs)
Family Security (taking care of loved ones)	Forgiving (willing to pardon others)
Freedom (independence, free choice)	Helpful (working for the welfare of others)
Happiness (contentedness)	Honest (sincere, truthful)
Inner Harmony (freedom from inner conflict)	Imaginative (daring, creative)
Mature Love (sexual and spiritual intimacy)	Independent (self-reliant, self-sufficient)
National Security (protection from attack)	Intellectual (intelligent, reflective)
Pleasure (an enjoyable leisurely life)	Logical (consistent, rational)
Salvation (saved, eternal life)	Loving (affectionate, tender)
Self-Respect (self-esteem)	Obedient (dutiful, respectful)
Social Recognition (respect, admiration)	Polite (courteous, well-mannered)
True Friendship (close companionship)	Responsible (dependable, reliable)
Wisdom (a mature understanding of life)	Self-Controlled (restrained, self-disciplined)

The method we are using takes advantage of recent technological advances in the manufacture of glue. Each value is printed on a gummed label with a short definition in parentheses. The subject's task is to find the most important value, peel it off, and paste it in Box 1, then to find the next most important value, peel it off and paste it in Box 2, and so on, until he has pasted all 18 values in Boxes 1 to 18. The gummed labels are easily movable, and, should the subject change his mind, they are easily removable and re-arrangeable.

You will notice that all the values we employ are socially desirable ones and one may well wonder whether it is at all possible for a person to rank-order such highly important values with any degree of consistency. We find that our subjects can indeed rank-order the values in a reasonably reliable manner. With three to seven weeks intervening between test and retest, the median reliability for the terminal value is .78 to .80, and for the instrumental values it is .70 to .72. The reliabilities obtained with the gummed labels are better than those obtained by the traditional method of rank-ordering, and they are about as good as those obtained with the method of paired comparison.

I should like to stress that these results concern the stability of value systems considered as a whole. But the logic of our method also enables us to determine stability and change in each value considered separately. The test-retest reliabilities of the individual terminal values range from .51 to .88; for the individual instrumental values, from .45 to .70.

We find that various combinations of these terminal and instrumental values significantly differentiate men from women, hippies from nonhippies, hawks from doves, policemen from unemployed Negroes, good students from poor students, fifth-graders from seventh-, ninth-, and eleventh-graders, retail merchants from sales clerks, Jews from Catholics, Democrats from Republicans, and so forth.

We find significant relationships between values and behavior, and between values and attitudes. In Table 2, I show all the values which differentiate significantly between churchgoing and nonchurchgoing college students. You will notice that of the 36 terminal and instrumental values, 18 differentiate significantly. Of all the values that significantly differentiate frequent churchgoers from all others, the one which differentiates most sharply is *salvation*. Subjects who report that they go to church "once a week or more" on the average rank *salvation* first among 18 terminal values, but those who report that they go to church "monthly" rank it seventeenth, and those who report that they "rarely" or "never" go to church rank it last. The frequent churchgoers also value significantly more than the other groups *family security,* and behavior which is *forgiving, helpful,* and *loving.* Nonchurchgowers, on the other hand, care significantly more for a *world of beauty* and *freedom,* and they care more for behavior which is *imaginative, independent,* and *intellectual.*

We have found that Michigan State University students who differ in their attitudes toward civil rights demonstrations exhibit statistically significant value differences. This time the value that differentiates best is *equality,* those participating in civil rights demonstrations ranking it fifth and those unsympathetic toward civil rights demonstrations ranking it seventeenth in importance.

Going beyond the value differences associated with variations in a single attitude, we also find significant differences in values for college students who think of themselves as liberals, middle-of-the-roaders, and conservatives. Table 3 shows that the liberals value significantly more than do the conservatives *a world at peace, a world of beauty, equality,* and *wisdom;* conservatives, on the other hand, value *social recognition* significantly more. As for the instrumental values, the liberals care significantly less than do the conservatives about being *ambitious* and *logical* and they care significantly more about being *helpful, independent,* and *intellectual.* Note especially the differential preferences for behavior which is *intellectual* and *logical.* Liberals seem to care more about being *intellectual,* while conservatives seem to care more about being *logical.*

Table 2 Significant Value Differences for Churchgoers*
and Nonchurchgoers

	Never	Rarely	Monthly	Weekly
Terminal Values				
A comfortable life	14	12	8	14
An exciting life	12	11	11	15
A world of beauty	11	17	16	17
Family security	13	9	10	7
Freedom	1	1	1	3
Pleasure	15	16	15	18
Salvation	18	18	17	1
Social recognition	16	15	14	16
Instrumental Values				
Capable	7	7	10	12
Forgiving	13	13	12	7
Helpful	14	15	15	8
Honest	2	2	2	1
Imaginative	8	12	13	16
Independent	3	5	4	11
Intellectual	4	11	11	10
Logical	11	6	9	14
Loving	12	10	6	2
Obedient	18	18	18	18

*Figures shown are composite rank-orders, 18 values. Significance was determined by Kruskal-Wallis one-way analysis of variance.

Table 3 Significant Value Differences for
Liberals, Middle-of-the-Roaders, and Conservatives*

	Liberals N = 54	Middle N = 216	Conservatives N = 27
Terminal Values			
A world at peace	6	9	11
A world of beauty	13	18	18
Equality	7	11	15
Social recognition	17	15	13
Wisdom	1	3	6
Instrumental Values			
Ambitious	12	3	3
Helpful	13	12	16
Imaginative	11	15	11
Independent	3	9	9
Intellectual	4	11	12
Logical	10	13	4

*Figures shown are composite rank-orders, 18 values. Significance was determined by Kruskal-Wallas one-way analysis of variance.

Further results of our research to date, including some studies of value change, are reported in the references cited in footnote 4.

Some Specific Implications for Public Opinion Research

I began this paper with some general implications for public opinion research that are suggested by our work on values. I would now like to conclude with a set of more specific implications:

1. Public opinion research can become routinely depth-oriented when the value scales become available which are reasonably reliable, valid, and easy to administer. This is a report of the progress we have made so far in achieving this objective. The National Opinion Research Center has recently carried out a first study on a national sample with our value scales, and I hope to be able to report soon the results obtained on American value systems, on the value systems of various subgroups of Americans, on the relation between value systems and expressed opinions, and on the underlying factorial structure of American value systems.

2. Raymond Bauer's book[5] on social indicators has recently attracted widespread attention in social science circles as well as in the Congress. Bauer and his colleagues, especially Bertram M. Gross, have already emphasized the importance of values as social indicators, and, needless to say, I strongly agree with this emphasis. When feasible and inexpensive methods for measuring values become available, I believe that a strong argument can be made for the periodic assessment of value systems. Knowledge of their value systems, and the changes in these value systems, would serve as important social indicators on the welfare and state of health of the American people.

3. As value-system data on representative samples of Americans become available it will only be a matter of time before we will want to ask about the value systems of other national and cultural groups. If we assume, as I do, that the number of human values is limited and universal, and if we further assume that cultural variations are primarily variations of the same limited, universal set of values, then a cross-cultural and comparative public opinion research becomes conceivable, organized around an assessment of value systems in various cultures, a study of their underlying structure by multivariate procedures, and a study of their antecedents and consequents.

4. Consider next our findings concerning *freedom* and *equality*.[6] These findings suggest that it would be especially helpful for the understanding of public opinion on political issues if we were regularly to assess the relative importance of *freedom* and *equality* in our respondents and to relate these to whatever political opinions are under consideration.

5. It is reasonable to assume that political candidates running for public office have differing value systems and that their appeal to the voter will depend on the degree of congruence between candidate and voter value systems. I believe that public opinion research in a democratic society should not only study the public's value systems but should also report those of candidates running for political office (by methods similar to those we have used, for example, in analyzing Barry Goldwater's *Conscience of a Conservative*), and study and report the degree of congruence between candidate and voter value systems.

6. Finally, I believe that our research findings have important implications for the changing of values, attitudes, and behavior through public opinion research. Imagine the possible cumulative effects upon millions of individuals who are continually exposed to

information through the mass media which would draw attention to the values of the various groups and subgroups they identify (and do not identify) with, which would draw attention to the relationships between selected instrumental and terminal values, between values and attitudes, between values and behavior, and which, moreover, would draw attention to the inconsistencies found in this or that group between and within specific values, attitudes, and behaviors.

I believe there is a paradox inherent in the oft-heard claim that public opinion research seeks to create a more informed public yet does not seek to influence this public. I believe that public opinion research should not only try to report accurately the state of public opinion but should also try to awaken it and to change it. I believe that a more truly informed public opinion would be created if the public were encouraged to look more closely at its own values and attitudes, more closely at the various inconsistencies observed within its own value-attitude systems, and more closely at the inconsistencies observed within the value-attitude systems of its public figures. It would lead to a public opinion that, by virtue of becoming better informed, would be influenced to change its values and attitudes in the direction of becoming more internally consistent and, consequently, more mature, more self-aware, and more enlightened. And, finally, I believe that it is possible for the field of public opinion research to candidly seek to influence public opinion without at the same time opening itself to the charge of political partisanship.

Notes

1. Gordon W. Allport, "Attitudes," *A Handbook of Social Psychology* (Worcester, Mass: Clark University Press, 1935), p. 798.

2. William McGuire, from a preliminary draft entitled "Nature of Attitudes and Attitude Change," in Gardner Lindzey and Elliot Aronson, eds., *Handbook of Social Psychology* (Cambridge, Mass.: Addison-Wesley, 2nd ed. [in press]).

3. Ibid.

4. M. Rokeach, *Beliefs, Attitudes, and Values* (San Francisco: Jossey-Bass, 1968); M. Rokeach, "A Theory of Organization and Change within Value-Attitude Systems," *Journal of Social Issues,* Vol. 24 (1968). pp. 13-33.

5. Raymond A. Bauer, ed., *Social Indicators* (Cambridge, Mass.: MIT Press, 1965).

6. These are reported in detail in Rokeach, "A Theory of Organization and Change within Value-Attitude Systems." Briefly, these two values vary strikingly in importance between different groups, as is indicated in the table below:

Composite Rank-Order for Freedom and Equality
for Four Samples (12 Values)

	50 Policemen	141 Unemployed Whites	28 Unemployed Negroes	75 Calvinist Students
Freedom	1	3	10	8
Equality	12	9	1	9

Part Three

Message Planning: Evidence and Arguments

In the first section of this book, Karl Wallace points out that speeches are usually given by people who are: getting ready to act, acting, or evaluating their actions.

After the speaker has defined the nature of his particular speech situation, and thus begins to limit his topic, he may also want to begin to limit and direct the main thrust of his speech because of the particular audience he is addressing. As Theodore Clevenger, Jr. observes in "The Function of Audience Analysis," the analysis of an audience enters into the speaker's planning at several stages—audience selection, message planning, message pretesting, and monitoring effects. In this section, we focus mainly on message planning. Information about his audience suggests alternative courses of action (possible topics, purposes, illustrations) and may suggest "choices among alternatives."

Further, Clevenger points out some general relationships between messages and effects:

(1) Messages, even those we are inclined to dismiss as relatively trivial and insignificant, have effects.

(2) The same message may have different effects upon different auditors, or on the same auditor at different times.

(3) Even a short message is likely to have more than a single effect upon any given auditor.

(4) Some of the effects of a message are unlikely to have been anticipated by the message source.

Knowing as much relevant information as possible about his audience allows the speaker to make some tentative predictions about effects. Regardless of topic, the speaker has at his disposal three general ways of "asking" the audience to "believe" in him:

(1) Listen to me because of who I am; because I have a certain reputation, character, "image."

(2) Listen to me because of the evidence and arguments I use in my speech.

(3) Listen to me because as a human being I share certain motives, certain emotions, certain goals with you.[1]

Theorists from the time of Aristotle have labeled these three types of rhetorical proofs as ethical proof, logical proof, and emotional proof. Probably listeners do not categorize them quite so neatly. Thus, they are useful merely as shorthand labels for the kinds of "materials" the speaker offers as proof. Aristotle's definition of rhetoric is: "the faculty of observing in any given case the available means of persuasion."[2] In "any given case" reinforces a central point we have been trying to make, that rhetoric is *situational.* Some situations call forth the rhetorical act; the act itself becomes a situation.

Aristotle observed that of the means of persuasion, ethos is probably the most potent. He described three dimensions of ethos: intelligence, character, good will. Rhetorical theorists have continued to raise the questions: "Of what is ethos or source credibility made?" "How precisely does it affect the impact of the message?"

A variety of studies review the experimental findings on both the impact of ethos on the effect of communication and the techniques for developing ethos.[3] Andersen and Clevenger, for example, define ethos as "the image held of a communicator at a given time by a receiver."[4] Note that although the speaker may attempt to "generate" an ethos, it is the *audience's image of the speaker,* what *they* perceive about him, that effects persuasion.

Generally, studies relating to ethos may be classified into two categories: (a) those having to do with fixed or variable ethos and (b) those having to do with extrinsic or intrinsic ethos. Those who view ethos as "fixed" hold that during a particular speech act, the ethos of the speaker remains constant. Those who view ethos as variable suggest that even during a particular communicative event the audience's perception of the speaker may change.

Extrinsic factors consist of features of the communicative event exclusive of or outside the content of the message itself. Intrinsic factors refer to actual message content; they may range from the use of expert testimony supporting the speaker's own judgment to references about his own past record.

Most conclude that source credibility *is* related in some way to message impact. This generalization appears to apply not only to political, economic, social and religious issues but also to matters of personal taste and aesthetic judgment as well.

Intelligence is often cited as a dimension of ethos. One major way the speaker manifests an intelligence is through the judicious selection of evidence and arguments to support his point of view, the proposition he would have his audience accept. As Gerald Miller suggests, when a speaker uses evidence and argument, he is establishing his reason for believing the assertions that he has made, and even more important, he is attempting to induce belief in a skeptical listener. In his article "Evidence and Argument," he defines evidence as "*those data that are intended to induce a sense of belief in the proposition which the data purportedly support.*" As you review the types and tests of evidence with Miller, certain implications of his definition will become clear. First, "belief" refers to a *psychological* condition, and secondly, the logical factors involved in evidence and argument provide only a means to that psychological end.

There are a variety of different ways of talking about the anatomy of an argument. Wayne Brockriede and Douglas Ehninger in "Toulmin on Argument: An Interpretation and Application" describe and discuss the approach of Stephen Toulmin in his work *The Uses of Argument.* Taking as his model the discipline of jurisprudence, Toulmin claims: "Logic is concerned with the soundness of the claims we make—with the solidity of the grounds we produce to support them, the firmness of the backing we provide for them— or, to change the metaphor, with the sort of *case* we present in defense of our claims."[5] He suggests that any person who "makes an assertion puts forward a claim—a claim on our attention and to our belief."[6] Brockriede and Ehninger define argument as "a *movement* from accepted data, through a *warrant,* to a *claim.*" Three parts appear to be essential to an argument: data or evidence, claim or conclusion, and, warrant or the authorization for the leap from the data to the claim. What is perhaps most important about this view is that argument is *dynamic*; it moves from the known to the unknown. Note how even our simplest "arguments" involve this "leap" from known to unknown; they involve an "inference."

ARGUMENT A: Those are storm clouds so you had better wear a raincoat today.

ARGUMENT B: Don't buy brand X tires. My last one began to show tread wear at only 10,000 miles.

In both cases, the speaker offered evidence (the type of cloud, past experience in observing rate of wear of brand X tire) to support his claim about the way his listener(s) should act (wearing a raincoat, buying a tire).

There is an implicit warrant in both of these arguments: past experience as a predictor of future experience; e.g., both speaker and listener would probably both agree on the known (rain is usually associated with certain types of clouds). A good argument, however, often contains other elements: *backing* (that which certifies the warrant), *rebuttal* (the safety valve that takes possible exceptional circumstances into consideration), and the *qualifier* (a statement which suggests the *degree* of probability the claim has of being accurate). The backing of the first argument might be meteorological findings. But even with an abundance of scientific findings there is still the possibility of intervening factors such as wind currents that would blow the clouds away before it rains in a given area. Thus, the speaker is likely even in casual conversation to use a qualifier, "It looks like rain so you probably ought to wear a raincoat today."

Toulmin's system for classifying proof is in some ways related to that of Aristotle. The nature of the relationship might be schematized as follows:

Aristotle	*Toulmin*
logical	substantive
ethical	authoritative
emotional	motivational

On the whole, the kinds of claims are different because the leaps from data to claim are based on different kinds of warrants. The warrant of a *substantive proof* "reflects an assumption concerning the way in which things are related in the world about us." These essential relationships may be viewed as being arguments from cause, sign, generalization, parallel case, analogy and classification. The warrant of an *authoritative proof* "affirms the reliability of the source from which these (the data) are denied"; that is, it reaffirms that the source is credible. The warrant of a *motivational proof* "provides a motive for accepting the claim by associating it with some inner drive, value, desire, emotion, or aspiration, or with some combination of such factors."

Data and warrants help to support four different *kinds of claims:*

Types of Claims	*Question Answered*
designative	whether something is?
definitive	what is it?
evaluative	of what worth is it?
advocative	what course of action should be pursued?

The parts of an argument correspond to the *types of questions an audience might raise when hearing a claim:* What is it based on (data)? How does the speaker get from the data to the claim (warrant)? Is that leap really warranted (backing)? But are there not some exceptions to what the speaker says (rebuttal)? If there are some possible exceptions, then does the speaker qualify the claim (qualifier)? These questions remain fairly constant regardless of the *kind* of claim advanced.

In the end, it is the *audience* who determines what it will accept as "proof." As the speaker selects evidence and designs arguments, he "tests" them not only for their intrinsic worth (their accuracy, recency, relevancy) but he also raises such questions as: "Will they likely get and maintain the attention and interest of my audience?" "Will they be understood by my audience?" "Will my audience 'accept' them?" That is not to say that these questions *replace* questions of intrinsic validity. It is to say, however, that the communicative act calls for the participation of both speaker and listener.

Notes

1. Jane Blankenship, *Public Speaking: A Rhetorical Perspective,* 2nd ed. (Englewood Cliffs, N.J.: Prentice-Hall, Inc., 1972). See Chapter Three. This, as you may know, is a contemporary modification of the Aristotelian modes of proof.
2. Aristotle, *Rhetoric,* trans. W. Rhys Roberts (New York: Random House, 1954), p. 24.
3. Kenneth Andersen and Theodore Clevenger, Jr., "A Summary of Experimental Research in Ethos," *Speech Monographs* (June 1963), pp. 59-78.
4. Ibid., p. 59.
5. Stephen Toulmin, *The Use of Argument* (Cambridge, Mass.: Cambridge University Press, paperback edition, 1964), p. 7.
6. Ibid., p. 11.

THE FUNCTIONS OF AUDIENCE ANALYSIS

THEODORE CLEVENGER, JR.

[It is possible to speak] of communication strategy largely in terms of planning a single speech, but it is also possible to consider more elaborate strategies. These may involve several audiences, numerous speakers, several levels of purpose, many speeches, and several stages of development. In order to allow for both simple and complex planning, we shall discuss both preanalysis of audiences and posttesting for the effect of a particular speech.

Preanalysis of Audiences

Audience analysis enters into strategy most directly at four points: audience selection, message planning, message pretesting, and monitoring of effects.

Audience Selection

Frequently a speaker is not at liberty to select the groups before which he will appear. Anyone who accepts an invitation to deliver a commencement address or to speak to a businessmen's luncheon or to participate in a TV debate, must work with whatever audience will attend the commencement or the luncheon or will tune in the debate. In these situations the audience (or their representative) has selected the speaker; the speaker may try to find out as much as possible about his audience in order to adapt to their idiosyncrasies, but he must accept them as they are.

To be sure, the speaker may decide that not all of the audience before which he will speak is of interest to him, and that he is concerned only with communicating something of importance to a certain set of auditors within the larger group. At commencement, for example, he may choose to tailor his speech to the graduates; others (parents, teachers, friends) will be present in the audience and will also hear the speech, but the speaker may virtually ignore them and speak to the graduates alone. Or, as important statesmen often do, the speaker may ignore everyone in the immediate audience and tailor his speech for a nationwide audience that will hear, see, or read the speech through the mass media. In either case, the speaker is in effect selecting an audience in the sense that he is tailoring the speech for its impact on some target group, and is treating other groups of auditors as essentially irrelevant eavesdroppers.

Sometimes, though, a speaker is able to select the group or groups that will hear him speak. If his object is to spread information about a particular idea, event, or program, he may consider who would be in the most strategic position to pass the information on to others. By tailoring a message for key groups he may be able to multiply his own efforts through the amplifying effects of these secondary communicators. For this reason, writers, newsmen, and community leaders are considered prime audiences; a word to them under the right circumstances will be enormously amplified through retransmission.

If the speaker's object is to foster adoption of a new idea (whether it be a new variety of seed corn, a new hairdo, or a new program for social welfare) he may find it possible to economize his efforts and reduce the likelihood of mobilizing an opposition by speaking first to people who are more likely to be favorable or open-minded toward changes of the sort he wishes to propose. Depending upon the idea, he may consider it wise to address his initial efforts to the young, the rich, the well-educated, the cosmopolitan, the aspiring, the disenchanted, the desperate, or whatever other group he judges most likely to offer fertile ground for his idea. Of course, if the speaker wishes to address himself to an audience having certain attitudes or characteristics, then it becomes a part of his communication strategy either to find such an audience or to create one. This is not always easy to do, but, where possible, it does increase the likelihood that the idea, when it comes to the attention of a more general public, will bring with it some degree of public support.

The decision to tailor his speech to part of the whole audience or the decision to seek out a particular audience to address cannot be made without considering differences between audiences or groups of auditors. Nor can such decisions be made without considering the relationships between these audience differences and the speaker's topic and purpose. Thus, where choice of audience is a factor in planning a communication strategy, audience analysis plays a vital role.

Message Planning

The planning of a long verbal message, such as a newspaper story, a television commercial, or a public speech involves hundreds of choices. Some of these are made unconsciously and automatically, like certain choices of word order that are dictated by the syntactic rules of language, or choices determined by the speaker's own idiosyncratic thought and language habits. Such choices cannot really be called "decisions" because the speaker is not conscious of making them. However, at least some of the choices that a speaker makes in planning any speech are consciously made and are decisions in the full sense of the word. In broadest terms message planning involves five major decision areas: (1) topic selection, (2) specific purpose formulation, (3) laying out major lines of development, (4) selecting supporting details, and (5) choice of language.

The occasions that call forth public speaking vary greatly with respect to the degree of freedom they offer the speaker to choose his topic. At one extreme are situations which give him no freedom at all. For example, an audience may invite a speaker because of his special knowledge of a certain subject, in which case they will expect him to speak on that subject and no other, or a speaker may participate in public debate on a controversial issue, in which case only speeches on that issue will be tolerated. At the other extreme are many situations that place no restrictions at all upon what the speaker may talk about. For instance, provided he gives it proper treatment, a speaker is free to talk about anything at all in most public-speaking classrooms, most entertainment situations such as after-dinner speeches, and certain purely ceremonial occasions such as commencements. Between these two extremes lie a variety of situations that offer the speaker varying degrees of choice concerning what he will talk about.

Often the speaker is restricted to a broad subject but is free within its limits to choose any specific topic on which to speak. For instance, submarine explorer Jacques-Yves Cousteau might choose to discuss quite different aspects of the broad topic of undersea exploration for different audiences. He might focus on undersea adventure, on aquatic life, submarine technology, his descents into the Mariannas Trench, the high cost of submarine exporation, safety in skin diving, or the feasibility of ocean farming. Though more or less restricted to a single broad topic, Cousteau often has considerable latitude in choosing a specific topic within the broader one. Among other factors that may contribute to the selection of the specific topic, information concerning the knowledge, attitudes, interests, and potential influence of the auditors will play a large part.

Just as knowledge about the audience may contribute to selecting a specific topic, so may it contribute to the selection of a specific purpose within the context of some long-range goal. A speaker whose ultimate goal is to build public support for a relaxation of laws concerning birth control will find many audiences so unaccustomed to the idea, so firmly opposed to it, or so ill-informed about the subject as to be unaffected or even outraged by a speech presenting direct appeals for support. Under these circumstances, the speaker may decide that his best strategy lies in adopting a more limited purpose; for example, to acquaint the audience with population statistics and predictions. For a different audience (better informed, more thoroughly acquainted with the issue, or more open-minded toward the proposed change) a speech on population statistics would at best be inefficient and at worst it might offend the audience by suggesting that the speaker had underestimated their sophistication or employed a devious approach. A specific purpose appropriate for either audience might be utterly inappropriate for the other.

The examples we have given concerning the role of audience analysis in topic selection and specific-purpose formulation have their counterparts in the finer details of message construction. As in the foregoing examples, each of these decisions (laying out major lines of development, choosing supporting details, selecting appropriate language) is involved when we become concerned with making choices among alternative ways of putting a message together. Although any given speech will not necessarily allow or require decisions in all five areas, most of the conscious choices that speakers confront in message planning fall into one of the five. In making these decisions, the speaker often must balance many factors; questions of coherence and elegance, of personal standards and taste, of economies of time and energy. Among the other considerations, factors in the audience often play a significant part.

Regardless of which message-decision area is involved, knowledge gained from audience analysis will contribute in two ways. First, information about the audience will suggest alternative courses of action; that is, considering auditors leads a speaker to think of possible topics, purposes, illustrations, and so on. Second, information about the audience will suggest choices among alternatives. For example, given two authorities to quote on wages and prices, or two ways of saying that wage increases lead to price increases, a speaker's choice between them will be influenced by the knowledge that he is addressing the CIO rather than the National Association of Manufacturers. In other words, with respect to message planning, audience analysis serves both a creative and a critical function.

Message Pretesting

When a message is particularly important, and especially when it is to be presented many times to different audiences, it is sometimes possible to pretest it—that is, to present it to a small sample of the audience (or to a similar audience) and to observe their reactions to it. If several pretests are made, it may be possible to determine whether the message has different effects for different types of listeners or listener groups, to observe whether the predicted and desired effects of the message do in fact occur, and to note the presence of unanticipated side effects. On the basis of these findings, the message may be altered, its exposure may be limited to certain types of audiences, or it may be discarded as unsuitable.

The most widely-publicized use of message pretesting is in the preparation of commercial advertisements. A commercial is prepared that is expected to have an effect upon viewers of a certain type. It may be tailored to increase product appeal, to promote a favorable image of the advertiser, to facilitate brand loyalty, or to accomplish some other objective with a particular audience such as identity-seeking teenagers (the Pepsi Generation), status-striving suburbanites (Volkswagen) or adolescent males of all ages (Brylcreem. Are you man enough to try it?). The pretest is then run on a sample audience that usually includes some persons from the target audience and from other potential audiences as well. Responses in the various groups are recorded and compared, and auditors may be interviewed concerning such matters as their impressions of the advertiser, the product, and its competitors. Sometimes this procedure merely confirms the ad writer's prediction that the commercial would have its intended effect. However, the results of the pretest may suggest changes in the commercial or alternative ways of advertising the product or of preparing advertisements for the target audience in the future.

The message pretest has become more or less routine for nationwide advertising; however, it is also useful in any other form of communication. For instance, most self-instructional materials such as programmed textbooks and teaching machines have been pretested for effectiveness. After some unit of material (say a fifty-minute recorded lecture) has been prepared, but before it is put into widespread use, it is presented to a group of students of the age and background level for which it was intended. After exposure to the lecture, the students are tested for their retention of its content and their evaluation of interest value and general effectiveness. If pretest results are unsatisfactory, the lecture may be revised or discarded. If they are encouraging, the instructional unit may be put into use with greater confidence and with fuller knowledge of its probable effects.

A modification of this pretesting procedure is often followed in preparing for public speaking. Proposed basic points, supporting details, turns of phrase, or even the complete speech, may be tried out on family or friends and their reactions used as a basis for retaining, modifying, or eliminating the tested material. To the student or the individual speaker who does not have access to market research agencies or educational testing services, such informal pretesting can be of material value. By selecting pretest listeners carefully and asking them the right questions, the speaker may be able to improve his effectiveness materially.

Monitoring Effects

So far we have discussed those uses of audience analysis concerned with activities and decisions taken before the message is presented to its target audience. However, audience analysis is also used during the presentation of the speech and after it is over, for the speaker may wish to know how the audience responded during the speech and what they were left with when it was finished.

Situations vary greatly with respect to the importance of knowing how the audience responded to a speech. In general, the more a speaker's course of future action will be determined by the response an audience gives to a speech, the more important it is to observe just what effect the communication has upon the audience, rather than assuming that the speech has those effects (and only those effects) that the speaker intended.

Most of us are inclined to think about the outcome of a speech in terms of whether the speaker produced the effect that he intended throughout the whole audience or in some major or important part of the audience. When listing the effects of a speech, we are likely to restrict our attention to anticipated effects only. If the speaker says that he intended to inform the audience about some object or event, we think of the effects of the speech in terms of whether the majority of the audience did in fact acquire that information. We are not likely to consider how many in the audience developed favorable or unfavorable attitudes toward the topic or the speaker, how many learned from the speech something other than what was intended, how much misinformation was read into the speech along with the facts presented, or what various auditors did with the new information after they got it.

By focusing on the audience, however, rather than on the speaker or the speech, we see quite clearly that every communication event is attended by its own particular set of consequences, and that these consequences are richly varied. Although this variety of response is present in virtually every communication situation, we may enhance our appreciation for its richness if we observe it first in some communication other than a public speech.

Multiple Effects

Consider the case of a television commercial for a popular brand of cigarettes that portrays an attractive young couple in swim suits listening to a portable radio aboard a sailboat skimming along the shoreline against a backdrop of tree-lined beach on a sunny day. The commercial lasts sixty seconds, but during that brief interval a viewer may experience a number of effects, some of which remain with him long after the commercial has been forgotten.

As I watch the commercial, the accented rhythms of the background music may be pleasantly stimulating, and so may the behavior or the appearance of the actors. A word or phrase in the narration may strike a sympathetic note. The narrator's voice may inspire my trust, or his dialect may raise my hackles. For these and other reasons, I may attend to the commercial or largely ignore it. If I pay attention, my levels of interest and satisfaction will probably vary substantially during the sixty-second interval. At some points my blood pressure may actually increase, my pupils dilate, or my palms sweat. My eyelids may droop, or I may sit up straighter in my chair.

Watching the commercial, I may feel an urge to smoke, or make a mental note to try (or to avoid) the brand advertised, or feel better or worse disposed toward television advertising, or wonder what the world is coming to. I may recall that once I decided to take up sailing but got too busy to do it, and wonder where I can find a good used sailboat; or I may reflect that I ought to get out more often to the beach. The appearance of the actors may arouse faint guilt feelings; I may decide that now is the time for that diet, or resolve to get into the sun tomorrow, or remember that it has been a long time since I had a haircut. My desire for a transistor radio may increase. I may reinforce my image of a society filled with beautiful, affluent, fun-loving people, or be depressed by the spectacle of waste and frivolity in a world torn by unsolved problems and filled with starving millions.

From watching the commercial, I may have learned some things to look for in a cigarette (charcoal filter, light tobacco), a vocabulary for describing cigarette qualities (mildness, full-bodied flavor), a company slogan, some odds and ends about sailing, and the fact that there is a town in Rhode Island named Newport. In addition to this information, I may have changed my attitudes in subtle ways. I may be more inclined to perceive Brand X as a sophisticated cigarette, two-piece swim suits as interesting apparel, or sailing as a worthwhile leisure-time activity. In some instances my behavior may change as well. I may start (or stop) smoking, switch to (or from) Brand X, whistle the tune to the commercial, talk more about outdoor sports, plan a picnic, or write a letter to the Federal Communications Commission complaining of the deteriorating taste displayed on TV commercials. All of these things and more are possible effects depending upon my experiences, prior knowledge and attitudes, and my psychological set at the time of listening.

The list of possible effects might be extended indefinitely, but even these few possibilities suggest four points worth remembering:

(1) Messages, even those we are inclined to dismiss as relatively trival and insignificant, have effects.

(2) The same message may have different effects upon different auditors, or on the same auditor at different times.

(3) Even a short message is likely to have more than a single effect upon any given auditor.

(4) Some of the effects of a message are unlikely to have been anticipated by the message source.

Types of Effects

Both in monitoring effects and in message pretesting, it is important to make several distinctions among types of effects. The first of these, which is implied in the preceding example, is a distinction between dominant and idiosyncratic message effects. In one sense, of course, all message effects are idiosyncratic because all message effects occur within individuals; however, some effects are much more likely to occur among individuals in a given audience than are others. An effect that we have reason to believe will occur or that we have observed to occur among a significant fraction of a given audience may be called a *dominant effect*. This terminology does not imply that dominant effects control the behavior of the individual auditor to a greater extent than other effects, but simply that, when we look at the responses of all of the auditors, the dominant effects occur very frequently.

An effect that we have reason to believe will occur or that we have observed to occur among only a few auditors may be called an *idiosyncratic effect*. For many auditors the strongest effect of the speech will be the idiosyncratic effects that the message has upon them. Generally we use the dominant reactions of an audience to generalize about how the audience as a whole responded to the speech, but these dominant responses usually leave out of consideration a wealth of qualitatively different individual responses.

A second important distinction among message effects, also suggested by the TV commercial example, is a distinction between anticipated effects and surprise effects. An *anticipated effect* is either one that the speaker deliberately set out to achieve or it is a side-effect that he recognized probably would occur and that he was prepared to accept. Of course, an anticipated effect may not occur in any sizeable fraction of an audience, but if the speaker is looking for it, then either its occurrence or its nonoccurrence will be noted. One of the purposes of audience analysis is to eliminate *surprise effects,* so if audience analysis has been effective, then most surprise effects will be idiosyncratic. When a dominant effect is unanticipated, the surprise may be a happy one or it may be disastrous.

A third and final distinction among message effects is the distinction between process and product effects. A *process effect* is one that occurs during the speech and is subject to modification by subsequent portions of the message; it is what goes on in the listener as he listens to the speech. A *product effect* is one that is left as a residue after the message has concluded. I may or may not thrill to the language of a brilliant orator (process), but whether I do or not, I may remember his words and quote them later (product).

Strictly speaking, of course, this distinction between process and product is invalid because every response of an audience is an effect of whatever stimuli produced it, and there are no "process effects" but only "processes." Effect follows effect in the speech until the speaker stops talking, and what have here been called "product effects" are simply the difference between the listener's states at the beginning and at the end of the speech. On the other hand, to talk conveniently about the effects of speeches, which are really not single stimuli but are complicated sequences of stimuli, we need some verbal shorthand for distinguishing between what happens from moment to moment during the speech, on the one hand, and what change has been produced by the whole sequence, on the other; and we shall therefore find it convenient to distinguish as we have here between process and product effects.

In discussing certain types of public speaking, we often devote all of our attention to product effects—to "what comes of the speech"—and tend to overlook process effects—the brief, subtle changes in the auditor from moment to moment during the speech. But process effects are of great interest in communication for two reasons.

First, it is through process effects that product effects come about. If a listener is somehow different after the speech than he was beforehand, it is extremely unlikely that he changed all at once at some critical point in the speech. On the contrary, he was probably led to his new position through a series of minute steps, each almost imperceptible yet each contributing to their combined effect.

Second, communication often is presented and received largely for the sake of the process effects themselves, though our customary way of talking about communication tends to prevent us from recognizing this fact. When a person has seen a good play or heard a powerful eulogy, or watched an exciting TV drama, or laughed at a fine after-dinner speech, he is likely to say that he has been entertained or moved or inspired or amused. But the primary objective of such communications as these is not to produce some terminal state of entertainment or emotion after the message is over; it is to evoke a changing pattern of reaction and response while the communication is in process, while it is still going on. To be sure, we may be "left with a message" or feel "transformed" afterward, but the participation in such communication events is rewarding even when we do not feel much differently afterward than we did beforehand, for the primary value of such messages is realized during, not after, their presentation.

We need to remember that the effects of communication are important to the communicator for three main reasons. First, as implied earlier in discussing communication strategy, the speaker's purpose in speaking is generally phrased in terms of the effects that he hopes to produce in the audience, so that settling upon a purpose involves specifying desired effects. Second, it is with an eye to effects that other elements in the communication strategy are most evaluated and chosen. Finally, when the consequences of a given message will be used as a basis for deciding future plans, some method of detecting relevant effects is essential.

Two Modes of Audience Analysis

In the foregoing discussion of the role of audience analysis in communication strategy we have not touched upon either of two important questions: (1) What is it useful to know about an audience? (2) How do you use the information once it is in hand? In one sense, most of the remainder of this book is devoted to answering these questions, but in another sense, both questions are unanswerable. Before going further it is essential to understand what sort of answers can be given to those two vital questions and to understand the extent to which it is impossible to provide complete answers, for it is only through such an understanding that we can avoid being misled by our own efforts to think systematically about the analysis of audiences. We can approach this understanding most conveniently by contrasting two forms of audience analysis: demographic and purpose-oriented.

Demographic Analysis

The first mode of audience analysis was proposed by the ancient Greek philosopher-scientist Aristotle. He advised the speaker to consider such characteristics of his audience as age and wealth, because these tend to make an individual more susceptible to some arguments and ideas and less responsive to others. He even sketched out a sort of crude audience typology: Old Men are prone to be deliberate, are less moved by passions, are cautious, and the like; Young Men are self-confident, venturesome, inclined to action more than words, and so forth.

The general properties of a group, such as age, sex, income, place of residence, occupation, marital status, size of household, political party preference, years of schooling, religion, and other such characteristics are called its *demographic characteristics.* An audience analysis based upon them may be called a *demographic audience analysis.* It is this approach to audience analysis that first comes to mind, to begin by recording certain standard information about an audience and then, on the basis of experience and research, to infer about the audience such matters as knowledge, temperament, attitudes, habits of thought, language preferences, or other matters that will enter into their responses to communication. The demographic characteristics are *observed;* they are then used as a basis for *inferences* concerning matters related to the speaker, speech, and occasion.

When demographic information about the audience is available, it almost invariably proves valuable to the speaker to examine it and reflect upon it. The phrase "reflect upon it" is deliberately chosen in this instance, for it suggests a ruminative, creative, relatively unsystematic sort of mental activity rather than a rigorous application of principle. The demographic information about an audience often will *suggest* specific content, treatment, or approach, but there is no standard formula for extracting speech ideas from demographic audience analysis. A moment's reflection will show why this is so.

To begin with, there is no way of knowing what demographic characteristics will be most useful in a given case because *any* property of the audience might be useful in some cases, but *no* property of the audience is invariably useful. For example, in discussing water fluoridation a speaker would find it helpful to know how many Christian Scientists are in the audience, although ordinarily the knowledge that he is addressing a group composed mostly of Christian Scientists would at most suggest an example or a comparison but certainly have a very small effect, if any, on the speech. On political topics it is important to know how many members of the John Birch Society or Americans for Democratic Action are in the audience, but on nonpolitical topics this information usually will be of very limited use.

Consequently, though persuaders and rhetoricians throughout history have wished for an ideal list of audience characteristics that could be used as a basis for audience analysis in every situation, all efforts to find such a list have ended in frustration. People and communication are too variable.

This is not to say that a given speaker might not devise a list of audience characteristics important to his own particular communication problems. On the contrary, because a given speaker is likely to operate within a relatively limited range with respect to purpose, audience, topic, and occasion, such a list of important audience characteristics might be extremely useful to him. But such a list must grow out of his own experience and include only those questions about audience characteristics that he has found important for his purposes. The same list would be of far less value to another speaker.

Purpose-Oriented Analysis

A second mode of audience analysis begins from an entirely different point of view. Instead of initiating the analysis by asking some standard set of questions about audience characteristics, this approach begins by asking what about the audience is most likely to be important in light of the speaker's purposes. The search for information about the audience is then governed by what it is that the speaker needs to know about his audience in the context of a given communication situation.

To see how the purpose-oriented approach might work in a specific case, let us suppose that you are to make a speech on the structure of the United Nations, the major purpose of which is to improve your audience's grasp of how that organization works. If you were following a purpose-oriented approach, you would begin the analysis by asking yourself just what you needed to know about the audience in order to enhance their knowledge of the UN as far as possible. Some of your information requirements would be clear at the outset; however, in order to determine your needs fully, you would have to work out a preliminary plan for the speech. This preliminary speech plan would tell you about additional information that you might like to have, and on the basis of that additional information the preliminary plan might be revised. It is even possible that this revised speech plan might suggest needs for still further information about the audience, which might lead to still further revisions in the speech plan. Working back and forth between speech plan and audience analysis, your speech would gradually take on the shape which was, in your judgment, best suited to accomplish your purpose with the particular audience. The following considerations are a sample of the issues you might confront.

To begin with, you would want to know how much information your audience already had about the UN. Without this information you might very well waste your entire effort by "informing" your audience mostly about things they already knew or by assuming that they had background for your speech which in fact they did not have. In either case you would add little to their knowledge.

We may pause for a moment to consider how you might get such information. In very rare cases, you might be able to pretest a representative sample of the audience in order to determine how much they knew about the UN but ordinarily you would at best be able to talk informally with one or two representative audience members. By establishing their general level of knowledge and asking them questions about other audience members they know, you may be able to get a fair idea of the average level of audience knowledge about the topic. This approach will be especially useful if the audience is composed of members of a well-defined group such as a civic club, professional or business organization, fraternal or other society with regular meetings and frequent interpersonal contact, for the members of such natural groups have much in common and often know a good deal about one another.

At worst, you may have to try to infer knowledge of the UN from general audience characteristics. Based on your own previous experiences with the topic, you may have some idea concerning how much the average listener knows about the UN; you may then ask whether this audience has any special characteristics that would cause it to know less or more about the topic than the average audience. For instance, if they were a high school group, you might want to check whether they had recently studied the UN. If they were predominantly over fifty and without more than average education for persons of that age, you might infer that they would know relatively little about the structure of the organization, although they might have general information about its more publicized activities.

With a general picture of audience knowledge in mind, you could now begin to plan a speech designed to build upon what they already knew. As you added each new thread to the fabric of your message, you would test it against your knowledge of, or inferences about, the audience. For instance, suppose you consider the possibility of illustrating the UN's lack of sovereignty by comparing it with the American confederation of pre-Constitutional times. As American citizens, your audience will amost certainly know of the confederation, but how much about it will they know? In order for the comparison to be really effective, will you have to tell them as much about the confederation as you would have to tell them about the UN to make the same point? With some auditors, such as college sophomores who have been exposed recently to American history, the comparison might work rather well; but for other auditors, such as middle-aged members of an Indiana Grange, the comparison would probably take more explaining than it would be worth.

The judgment of what it is worth, of course, has to be made within the context of a speaker's particular purpose(s). The limited value of the confederation comparison in this case extends only to its information value. As you reflect upon the example, it may seem very appropriate to you in the context of your total purpose, and you may feel strongly disposed to use it even though it adds no information. If this happens, you may pause a moment to consider whether information really is your only purpose. Is it possible that in the back of your mind, all along, you have been hoping to show your audience that the UN is a workable idea that deserves our increased support and needs more power to operate effectively? If so, then the confederation example is entirely appropriate whether it informs or not, for it will serve to associate the UN (something your audience may feel uneasy or mildly distrustful about) with the growth of the American government. Whether they recall, or have ever been exposed to, the full details of the post-Revolutionary era, they certainly will have been told at some time about the difficulties experienced by the confederation and will have learned to regard the Constitutional Convention as necessary and desirable. The comparison of the confederation with the UN will then tend to establish in their minds an image of the world organization that is consistent with your subsidiary purpose.

With this secondary purpose in mind, it becomes important to accumulate some additional information about the audience: Do they display any special characteristics that might predispose them for or against the UN? Many people who were of literate age during the early years of the League of Nations, for instance, will tend to associate the UN with the League, which failed in its purpose to preserve world peace. How many of your auditors fall into that age group? Would it be better to ignore the League altogether, hoping that your audience will do so too, or would it be better to compare the League with the UN to show the differences between them? Is your subsidiary purpose important enough to warrant your spending much preparation or speaking time on such a comparison? Or, having thought of the comparison originally as a persuasive device, can you use it, nevertheless, for informational purposes? Would such a comparison add a dimension of understanding to the speech for auditors of the type to whom you will speak? And if so, is it possible, in light of their special characteristics, to combine the informational and the persuasive purpose in the single comparison so as to contribute toward both effects with a single unit of content?

We have only sampled here some of the kinds of issues that arise during the course of purpose-oriented audience analysis. To begin with, we have observed that this form of audience analysis is not limited to a single information-gathering stage before the speech is planned. On the contrary, this form of audience analysis continues throughout the entire message preparation. Second, we have observed that the information about the audience is not gathered according to some predetermined formula but is determined by the needs of the speaker as he makes decisions concerning the content and desired effects of his message. Third, we have noted that there is a complex set of relations among audience, purpose, and content: (1) It is not possible to know in advance just what or how much information about the audience will be required in a given case. (2) Special characteristics of an audience may suggest including or excluding certain content. (3) During the analysis the speaker may discover previously hidden purposes of his own. (4) The newly-revealed purposes may lead to needs for additional knowledge about the audience. All of these must be worked out through various stages of development and may lead the speaker in somewhat unpredictable directions.

Audience analysis which is purpose-oriented, then, is not a stage of speech preparation; it is a dynamic and integral part of every stage of speech preparation.

Technology and Art in Audience Analysis

Having contrasted the two dominant modes of audience analysis, we now are in a position to consider what sort of answers may be given to the two questions: (1) What is it useful to know about an audience? (2) How do you use the information once it is in hand? We must interpret these questions in light of the fact that in most instances audience analysis is not so much a technology as it is an art.

In a well-developed technology, such as automotive engineering, bridge design, steel-making, or electronics, decision rules covering most of the relevant possibilities are already worked out or may be constructed from comprehensive theories. Establishing rules is possible because the number of factors that must be taken into account is predictable and the range of possible desirable outcomes is relatively restricted.

In the case of an art, however, the exact factors that must be taken into account in solving a particular problem are unpredictable, and the range of desired outcomes is either infinite or else so large as to be virtually so. Under these circumstances, decision rules may be formulated to cover a few recurring problems, but most problems must be approached individually. In music, psychiatry, teaching, and architecture, for example, practice may be influenced by general principles but cannot be dictated by decision rules.

As we noted earlier, something like a limited technology of audience analysis is possible for a single speaker operating in a limited range of communication situations and pursuing a limited set of goals. Under these circumstances the possibilities are sufficiently reduced in number that the communicator may hope eventually to formulate decision rules covering most or all of them. But in the general case no such analysis is possible. Ignoring speaker and media for a moment, the communication formula provides us with three other factors—the topic, the context, and the desired effects that must be taken into account in determining what we may need to know about a particular audience. For each combination of a certain type of topic, context, and effect, we should require a particular type of information about the audience. Given no more than one hundred varieties of topic, context, and effect, we would have one million combinations of the three to be taken into account in specifying the type of audience information required. If we now add considerations of speaker and media, this number is multiplied many times over, and the number of different patterns of demand for audience information reaches into the billions.

To understand how it is possible to operate in a universe of so many possibilities, we need to appreciate the difference between two kinds of decision principles: the algorithmic and the heuristic. The difference between them can be illustrated by comparing the way we learn to play chess and tic-tac-toe. It is possible to formulate a set of decision rules for tic-tac-toe that are essentially infallible; they guarantee the player who uses them that he will at worst play to a draw and that he will never lose. The rules specify all of the possible situations in the game and provide a rule to follow in every situation. Chess, on the other hand, cannot be played in this fashion; to be sure, it is possible to formulate rules that work most of the time, but a good chess player can always win against an opponent who is following a rigid system of rules. The number of possible positions on the chess board is so vast that there is no single move that is always best. Good chess players operate with certain very general principles in mind, several of which may apply to the decision concerning a single move. The player uses these general principles as a basis for analyzing any given board situation, but his specific decision is governed by the particular situation in which he finds himself. The principles of tic-tac-toe are algorithmic; the principles of chess are heuristic. Chess principles give the player some help in analyzing the situation, but they do not lead him through to a foregone conclusion in the same way that the tic-tac-toe principles do.

When we say that audience analysis principles are heuristic, we do not mean that they are vague or indefinite but only that they must be used in a certain way. They must be understood as a means of getting into the analysis, as tools for thinking about the audience situation, as suggestive principles only. If we try to develop algorithms for audience analysis—rules that are capable of carrying us rigorously through a complete analysis to communication decisions—or if we try to treat whatever principles are developed as if they could be made to work in this way, then valid and effective analysis will always be beyond our reach. It is only when we understand audience analytic techniques as beginning points for analysis that we can use them effectively.

What this means is that the communicator must, at some point in his analysis of the audience, formulate his own analytic principles to cover the specific situation in which he finds himself. General principles may get him started and set the direction of his analysis, but when he gets into the details of the problem, he will usually find himself on his own without specific recommendations to follow and with only general principles to guide him.

At this point education and experience become especially important in communication. One reason why educated and experienced individuals almost invariably communicate more effectively than uneducated and inexperienced ones is that they know more about people, and consequently they are able to determine more readily than others just what it would be useful to know about their auditors and how to interpret the information once they have it. If I do not know that most Southern Baptists are opposed to dancing for religious reasons, then I will not be alert to the presence of Baptists in making my speech on recreational opportunities in the campus area; and even if I should by accident come across the fact that there were Baptists in my audience, I would not know how to put this information to use.

That is why neither this book nor any other treatment of audience analysis can substitute for education and experience in analyzing audiences and formulating strategies of communication. Anything at all about an auditor may be useful on some occasion for predicting how he will respond to communication, regardless of whether we are using a demographic or a purpose-oriented mode of analysis, and the more a speaker knows about people and their society, the greater will be the variety of different ways in which he may understand and respond to his auditors.

But heuristic principles may get an analysis started, and our purpose here will be to suggest beginning points and general frameworks for audience analysis in a variety of communication situations. They will be useful to the communicator in proportion to his knowledge and experience; the more he knows and has experienced, the more these suggestive principles will suggest to him.

EVIDENCE AND ARGUMENT

GERALD MILLER

This chapter deals with the role of evidence in argument. Although the term *evidence* smacks of the courtroom, it should be obvious that its scope is much wider; in fact, we usually demand that most statements or propositions be supported by some form of evidence. You may, for example, assert to a friend (let us call this friend "Skeptic") that you expect to receive an A in argumentation class. Skeptic, being a questioning soul, inquires about the reasons for this claim, whereupon you enumerate the facts that you received A's on all the speeches you have presented, that you received an A on the midterm examination, that you have participated freely in classroom discussion, and that you have missed no classes or assignments. In enumerating these facts to Skeptic, you are presenting evidence for your claim that you will receive a grade of A in the course. Or, on another occasion, you may remark to Skeptic that college professors are rather peculiar people. When Skeptic asks you the basis for such a statement, you are likely to respond somewhat as follows: "I know Professor X, and he is peculiar; I know Professor Y, and he is peculiar; and I know Professor Z, and he is peculiar; therefore, I have concluded that college professors are rather peculiar people." Your mention of particular professors to Skeptic is an attempt to provide evidence for the generalization that college professors are rather peculiar people.

In the above examples, what is it that you are attempting to accomplish by your enumeration of particulars? I would hold that you are establishing your reasons for believing the assertions that you have made, and even more important, you are attempting to induce in Skeptic a sense of belief in these same assertions. Insofar as Skeptic responds favorably to your evidence, you will be successful in convincing him; insofar as Skeptic, for any number of reasons, views your evidence with distrust, you will be unsuccessful.

If I am correct in my assumption that your primary objective was the development in Skeptic of a sense of belief, and if this assumption holds for most of the communication that occurs among the "Skeptics" of the world, the following may be offered as a useful,

From *Perspectives on Argumentation* by Gerald R. Miller and Thomas R. Nilsen. Copyright © 1966 by Scott, Foresman and Company. Reprinted by permission of the publisher.

tentative definition for the term *evidence: Evidence consists of those data that are intended to induce a sense of belief in the proposition which the data purportedly support.* Thus, the term *evidence* embraces a large body of diverse and varied materials; the common defining characteristic of these materials is to be found in the function they perform.

Several implications of this definition should be explored more fully. First, this definition implies that questions regarding the nature and uses of evidence are essentially psychological and involve considerations of the bases for people's beliefs and of the kinds of materials most likely to induce in a particular person or persons a sense of belief. This approach to the study of evidence is somewhat different from the one most commonly encountered in books on debate and argumentation. Generally, these works have dealt with criteria for evaluating sources of evidence and rules for valid inductive inferences.[1] Although these matters will be considered in this chapter, I believe that such a viewpoint embraces only a part of the general problem of evidence. Specifically, this approach emphasizes the ways in which evidence *ought* to affect people and the ways in which evidence *ought* to be used; to a large extent, it ignores the ways in which evidence often *does* affect people and the ways in which evidence often *is* used. In other words, it minimizes *description* to concentrate on *prescription,* an approach that no doubt stems from a view of argumentation as rational, reasoned discourse, rather than a view which emphasizes the behavior effects of argumentative discourse on audiences. In treating evidence, I shall try to combine the salient elements of both approaches.

The decision to divide discussion between the psychological and logical aspects of evidence stems from the assumption, considered earlier and explicit in the definition of evidence adopted here, that one's primary purpose in employing evidence is to induce a sense of belief. To illustrate, let us return to the example in which you are detailing to Skeptic your evidence for the assertion that college professors are rather peculiar people. The evidence consists of examples of particular professors of your acquaintance who also qualify for the label "rather peculiar people." In using such evidence—often referred to as *examples* or *specific instances*—you may ask yourself several questions: Have I mentioned a sufficient number of professors who fit the appellation "rather peculiar people"? Are these professors typical? Have I been accurate and truthful in my enumeration of examples? Such questions deal with the logical characteristics of the evidence employed; specifically, they involve considerations of whether one is justified in performing the inductive leap. Probably, however, the paramount question you will consider can be phrased in the following manner: Will the examples I have employed produce in Skeptic a sense of belief in my assertion that college professors are rather peculiar people? This crucial question deals with the psychological characteristics of the evidence employed.

Many times, of course, attention to logical characteristics of the evidence serves to enhance its psychological impact. If Skeptic is a trained logician or a professor of argumentation, he is likely to be quite sensitive to violation of the rules of evidence and inference. Even so, logical factors provide only a means to the psychological end. If both you and Skeptic are acquainted with a single professor of marked idiosyncratic tendencies, you may find it more advantageous, in terms of inducing belief, to allude to this single example and to ignore all others, even though such a decision violates the accepted standards of inductive inference.

A second implication of the above stipulated definition of evidence, and one that is closely related to the preceding point, has to do with the use of the term *belief* in the definition. After Bertrand Russell, I will define a belief as "a certain kind of state of body or mind or both."[2] This definition emphasizes that the term *belief* refers to a psychological condition of the individual. On the other hand, I will use terms such as *fact* and *truth* to refer to empirically ascertainable phenomena that exist as part of the physical world. Thus, to say that one holds a particular belief is or is not a true statement of fact; but the psychological state of the belief and the factual assertion of the belief's existence are not identical, or even roughly synonymous.

Perhaps an example will best serve to illustrate this point. Our friend Skeptic asserts, "I believe in the existence of Centaurs." Being sophisticated and intelligent individuals, we know that the statement "There exist on this earth creatures known as Centaurs," is a false statement of fact. Consequently, we attempt to induce in Skeptic a new belief, specifically, a belief in the assertion, "Centaurs do not exist." In order to support this latter assertion, we cite evidence, consisting of copious testimony by noted scientists, which asserts the impossibility of the existence of Centaurs. Skeptic responds to our efforts by asserting, "I believe in the existence of Centaurs." We have failed to change Skeptic's belief, even though both our evidence and the proposition it supports are factually true.

The point to be emphasized is that the function of evidence in argument is to induce belief, not necessarily to aid in communicating truth or establishing fact. Granted, fact and truth may sometimes be consistent with the belief that an arguer hopes to induce; many times, however, this is simply not the case. Almost all of the evidence utilized by the Nazi Party to induce a sense of belief in certain propositions dealing with the superiority of the German people was factually false; even so, the evidence was effective in its function of inducing such a sense of belief. While we can, and should, condemn attempts to induce belief in such ethically repugnant propositions, we should remain aware that our objection involves values; that is, it concerns the way evidence *ought* to be used, not the way that evidence frequently *is* used.

Still another implication of the definition of evidence given above concerns the phrase, "that the data *purportedly* support." What conclusions may be validly drawn from certain items of evidence is a question associated with the logical rules of inference and with the emprical status of certain related propositions. In some cases, this question may be of crucial significance in inducing a sense of belief in the proposition; in other cases, it may be of little import. To illustrate, we will return to Skeptic and his Centaurs and ask how he has come to hold the strange belief that Centaurs exist. Let us assume that Skeptic gained his belief in Centaurs in the following manner: A friend, given to levity, once remarked, "Skeptic, Writer A has written about Centaurs; Writer B has written about Centaurs; and Writer C has written about Centaurs; therefore, I conclude that there exist on this earth creatures known as Centaurs." Henceforth, Skeptic's belief in the existence of Centaurs has been unshakeable.

What may we conclude concerning the role played by evidence in this whimsical example? The data utilized consist of statements of particular writers who have mentioned creatures known as Centaurs; these data are then used to support the proposition that Centaur-objects exist. You and I are aware that no such statement is logically or empirically warranted by this evidence. We know that authors have also mentioned Unicorns, Slithy Toves, Three-Winged Jabberwockies, and a host of other strange creatures, but we also know that inventing a name and stipulating a verbal definition for an animal do not constitute proof of the creature's physical existence. As a result, we would hold that the evidence more logically supports statements such as "Many authors have written about imaginary creatures known as Centaurs" or "The Centaur is a popular figure in mythological literature."

But our rationality may have little effect on Skeptic's belief. If his own psychological posture is such that he is willing to accept these instances as proof for the existence of Centaur-objects, then the evidence has been effective only in inducing belief in the existence of Centaurs. Although the example we have used may seem farfetched, it is obvious that considerations dealing with the question of what sorts of statements may be inferred from certain data are often significant. We can, for example, collect mountains of evidence demonstrating that a large number of individuals withdrew great amounts of money from the banks during the depression days of the 1930's. Does this evidence support the proposition that our economy was suffering from dire problems, or does it support the proposition that if enough people *believe* the economy is suffering from dire problems, they will, by their behavior, create such problems, i.e., they will engage in behavior calculated to result in what Robert Merton has labeled the "self-fulfilling prophecy"?[3] In other words, were the instances of withdrawal of money a *symptom* of a problem that already existed or a *cause* that contributed to the development of a problem? Among economists, each interpretation has its defenders; the significant point here is that the same evidence may be used to induce belief in two or more greatly disparate propositions.

The above discussion has focused on some of the implications of the definition of evidence offered in this chapter. True, matters have been somewhat exaggerated; after all, how many noninstitutionalized people entertain a serious belief in the existence of Centaur-objects? It may have occurred to you that if Skeptic were a sensible man, he would have sought further evidence to support his belief in Centaurs, once he had been exposed to the negative testimony of eminent and respected scientists. The present discussion, however, has been an attempt to emphasize the psychological complexities associated with any consideration of evidence and its role in argument. Men often do operate from extra-rational considerations, and evidence is frequently employed in a post hoc manner to buttress beliefs that have been derived entirely apart from some ideal, rational model of man. After all, Freud might suggest that Skeptic's belief in Centaurs resulted from a traumatic childhood experience, not from testimony gleaned from any reliable authority nor for instances in literature in which authors referred to Centaur-objects.

Fortunately, however, there is also evidence to indicate that man frequently seeks rationality and that a sense of belief may be induced by employing evidence that appeals to his rational side.[4] We may say, then, that some concern for the logical aspects of evidence may, on numerous occasions, lead the arguer to choose data that are maximally suited to the function of inducing belief. Thus, the logical and the psychological aspects of evidence cannot be separated into discrete categories.

Two major considerations remain to be dealt with in succeeding sections of this chapter. In the second section, I will examine the kinds of propositions in which men often profess belief and discuss the kinds of evidence likely to engender belief in these propositions. In the third section, I will consider how the attitudes and knowledge of others may affect men's responses to various kinds of evidential data and examine some of the questions and tests that may be used to choose and evaluate evidence in terms of its primary function of inducing belief.

One other preliminary remark is in order. Some may feel that the preceding discussion has strayed from matters involving evidence and has dealt with questions more traditionally covered in discussions of logic and inference. Let me clarify my position by stating that I recognize two modes of inference, deduction and induction. Problems regarding particular *genres* of these two general species are, to me, problems that deal primarily with evidence, not with inference. Thus, the rules of inference for the two inductive forms commonly labeled *argument from authority* and *argument from example* are the same; differences in the analysis of the two forms result from the sorts of evidence employed, not from variations in the inferential format. Although some may disagree with this proposition, it is a distinction that I shall maintain throughout the entire chapter; consequently, the reader will be aided if he keeps it in mind.

Propositions and Evidence

Having examined some of the implications of the definition of evidence stipulated in the preceding section, let us examine various types of propositions in which men commonly profess belief and discuss the kinds of evidential data that have led to these beliefs. An analysis of some sample propositions should aid in accomplishing this objective.

"The sun rises in the east" and "Columbus discovered America in 1492" are two propositions that all of us believe. You may justifiably say that you no longer demand evidence to sustain your belief in the truth of these assertions; however, as we analyze the statements more fully, it will become apparent that you were led to your belief in these propositions by evidence to which you were exposed, and that for at least one of the propositions you are constantly encountering further evidence which buttresses your belief in its truth.

As a beginning step in our analysis, let us attach the label *statement of fact* to these two propositions and to others like them. After Gustav Bergmann, we may define a statement of fact as one that "says something about the object or objects it mentions; and depending only on the properties of these objects, . . . is either true or false."[5] Thus, the first proposition above says something about the sun, i.e., that it consistently rises at a point in space designated as *east,* while the second proposition says something about Columbus, i.e., that he was the man who discovered the geographical area designated as *America.*

Bergmann's definition emphasizes that a statement of fact may be either true or false. Thus, if the first proposition above read, "The sun rises in the west," we would regard the assertion as a false statement to fact, since the sun does not have a property of rising in the west. Consistent with the distinction drawn earlier between *fact* or *truth* as opposed to *belief,* it should be apparent that one can be induced to believe a false statement of fact. Before Columbus discovered America, many people believed the false statement of fact, "The earth is flat." Each time a religious sect predicts the world will end on a certain date, only to have the prediction disconfirmed, we witness another instance of a group of individuals who have professed belief in what has proven to be a false statement of fact.[6]

Before examining the kinds of evidential data that have engendered our belief in the sample propositions given above, it would be well to make one further point about statements of fact. You may be thinking that propositions such as "Columbus discovered America in 1492" are not the stuff of which argument is made. If so, you are unquestionably correct; we usually spend little time disputing such assertions. There are, however, a host of statements of fact that are not amenable to immediate verification; i.e., they cannot be labeled as *true* or *false* at the time they are uttered. Statements such as "The United States is leading the Soviet Union in the missile race," "Cigarette smoking causes lung cancer," and "We can change an individual's intelligence quotient by changing his environment" are examples of statements of fact that have been hotly disputed. . . .

For now, however, we can return to the propositions "The sun rises in the east" and "Columbus discovered America in 1492." We know that we have labeled these propositions *statements of fact,* and we know that we believe they are true. But why do we believe in the truth of these assertions? What kinds of evidential data have induced this sense of belief? Is our basis of belief the same for both propositions? It is to these questions that we will now turn.

Suppose your imaginary friend Skeptic remarks, "The sun rises in the east," and you respond with the question, "How do you know?" The intent of this question may be more fully stated as follows: "What evidence has led you to profess belief in the proposition, 'The sun rises in the east'?"

Let us ignore the problems of induction associated with the statement, "The sun rises in the east," and focus on Skeptic's probable response to your query. Although he may conceivably answer that he read this statement in a science or logic text, his most probable response will be of the order, "Why, I saw it rise in the east this morning," or, "Haven't you ever seen the sunrise?" By means of such statements, Skeptic is asserting that his belief in the proposition, "The sun rises in the east," has been induced by a number of observations of the occurrence of this event; i.e., that he believes the statement because he has directly experienced the physical event labeled "sun rising in the east."

As was implied earlier, there was a time in Skeptic's life when this proposition would have induced no sense of belief. Only after a number of occurrences of the evidential datum, "experiencing the physical event labeled, 'sun rising in the east,' " does Skeptic profess belief in the proposition. Furthermore, each additional instance of experiencing this event provides further assurance that his belief is well founded. In fact, it is interesting, albeit somewhat frightening, to speculate about the way Skeptic would react should he ever experience an instance of a physical event labled, "sun rising in the west."[7]

Thus, we see that one sort of evidential datum which may induce belief in propositions involving statements of fact is the direct experiencing of the event or events mentioned in the proposition. This is the type of datum employed in science. When scientists wish to test the truth or falsity of a proposition, they establish a set of conditions for observing the event mentioned in the proposition. The results of their observations serve as evidence to induce a sense of belief in the proposition, or to induce a sense of belief in some alternative statement of fact, e.g., the statement, "Our proposition is false."

Sometimes, however, the observations necessary to determine the truth or falsity of a factual proposition are more complex and involved than is the case in the sunrise example discussed above. This occurs when the event or situation mentioned in the proposition is complex and its truth or falsity is dependent upon a number of related observations. What observations must be made to verify the factual proposition, "The United States is leading the Soviet Union in the missile race"? It is possible to conceive of a horrible experiment in which we place a group of observers in space and then have the United States and the Soviet Union fire all of their missiles at each other. Assuming that we could arrive at an objective measure of destruction, our observers could then determine its extent in each nation; and, on the basis of their findings, we could label the original proposition as either true or false. All of us fervently hope, however, that no such experiment will ever take place. In its absence, the missile race proposition will continue to be an argumentative one, and it will be possible to utilize various kinds of evidential data in attempting to induce belief in its truth or falsity.

We are now ready to examine our second sample proposition of fact, "Columbus discovered America in 1492." Suppose Skeptic has expressed a belief in this statement, and you have again inquired as to his reasons for believing it. Will he respond differently than in the case of the proposition, "The sun rises in the east"?

Obviously, the answer to this question is affirmative. It is difficult to conceive of Skeptic replying, "Why, I saw Columbus discover America," or, "Didn't you see Columbus discover America?" Rather, he is likely to respond, "I learned that from my first-grade teacher," or, "I read about Columbus' discovery in the encyclopedia." In other words, Skeptic will never have directly experienced the physical event labeled "Columbus discovering America"; rather, his belief in the truth of the proposition that asserts the occurrence of this event is occasioned by the evidential data consisting of testimony.

It is obvious that using testimonial data to induce Skeptic to believe in the truth of a proposition involves something more than when the data consist of Skeptic's direct experiences. When the evidence consists of testimony, Skeptic must first believe, or be induced to believe, the statement, "X testifies truthfully"; from this will stem his belief in the particular proposition that X has uttered. We might, in fact, suggest that Skeptic's psychological state as expressed in the assertion, "I believe that Columbus discovered America," might be more accurately portrayed by the statement, "I believe that X (and Y, and Z, etc.) consistently utter true propositions."[8]

You may say that, as evidential data, direct experience and testimony differ only in degree, not in kind, and that implicit in the acceptance of evidence based on direct experience is the belief that our senses do not lie.[9] To this I can only reply that the difference, whether of degree or kind, is sufficiently great to be of practical significance. While I seldom have occasion to consciously question the reliability of my senses—unless in the presence of a magician or a perceptual illusion—I frequently have reason to entertain consciously the belief, "X does not testify truthfully." Thus, I would hold that for the purpose of analyzing their effects and functions in argumentation, direct experience and testimony differ as evidential data.

We can see, therefore, that for the purpose of inducing belief in propositions involving statements of fact, there are two broad categories of evidential data, direct experience and testimony. It sould be obvious, however, that in most instances to which we assign the label *argumentation,* the evidential data consist of some form of testimony. Although it may, on occasion, be possible to arrange an actual demonstration of the physical event, the vast majority of cases require that the disputant rely on testimony about the event as a means of inducing belief.

There is, however, a second kind of proposition in which men often profess belief. Let us take as samples of this type of proposition the statements "Capital punishment is morally reprehensible" and "Communism is the worst form of government." Even before we discuss these propositions, you are intuitively aware that they differ from such statements as "The sun rises in the east" or "The United States is leading the Soviet Union in the missile race." Why is this the case?

Let us attach the label *value judgment* to the first two propositions above, and to others like them. Turning again to Bergmann, we find the following definition for a value judgment:

> A value judgment is misunderstood if it is taken to ascribe a property to the object, act, or situation it mentions in the same sense in which a statement of fact is such

an ascription; it is, therefore, *literally neither true nor false.* [Italics mine.] What it involves and misleadingly states as the property of an object, act, or situation alone is the fact that this object, act, or situation causes in the one who makes the judgment a certain state of mind, say, for instance, of positive aesthetic appreciation or of moral approval.[10]

The above definition sets forth the common sense core of ethical relativism, a position to which I shall subscribe in the following discussion. Succinctly put, this position holds that the statement, "The United States is leading the Soviet Union in missile development," differs from the proposition,. "Capital punishment is morally reprehensible," primarily because the former says something about the properties of the act mentioned (missile race), while the latter says nothing about the properties of the act (capital punishment); rather, it provides information only about the state of mind of the individual making the assertion.

An example will best serve to illustrate this point. Both you and Skeptic have accepted jobs as newspaper reporters, and you have both been assigned to cover the execution of a convicted murderer. As the switch is thrown, Skeptic turns to you and remarks, "Justice has been served." You respond, "Society is once again guilty of a heinous crime."

Have Skeptic and you literally experienced a different event? Common sense suggests that you have not. Each of you has witnessed the execution of the same murderer, in the same electric chair, by the same executioner. Could the two of you, as a result of evidential data resulting from direct experience, agree on your belief in the truth or falsity of such factual assertions as, "The convicted murderer was pronounced dead at approximately 12:05 A.M.," "The convicted murderer was wearing a blue suit," or, "The warden had brown hair"? Undoubtedly you could. Why, then, do you find it impossible to agree on your beliefs regarding the goodness or badness of the act itself?

The reason is not to be found in any objective properties of the act, but rather in the different predispositions and attitudes that you and Skeptic hold regarding the act. Whereas the locus of disagreement concerning propositions of fact lies "out there" in the objects, acts, and situations themselves, the locus of disagreement concerning value judgments lies in the minds of the disputants, i.e., in the different attitudes that they bring to the dispute. Given this distinction, it becomes readily apparent that value judgments are literally *neither* true nor false, in the sense that statements of fact are *either* true or false.[11]

Several implications of the nature of value judgments should be considered. First, it is apparent that almost any value judgment can provide a basis for argument. Suppose, for example, that Skeptic and you attend a movie at the Campus Theater entitled, *Long Is the Night.* Is it likely that the two of you will argue about the title of the movie or about the name of the theater that you attended. Such factual quibbles exemplify the ultimate in triviality. On the other hand, if Skeptic states that *Long Is the Night* is the finest movie he has ever seen and you respond that it was a deplorable picture, a lively and interesting argument is likely to ensue. This is because—contrary to what is implied in the language Skeptic and you have used in making your assertions—you are not arguing about any properties of the film itself, but rather about the esthetic contents of your minds, i.e., your beliefs and attitudes about what constitutes a pleasing movie.

The use of the term *beliefs* in the preceding sentence calls to mind once again our earlier distinction between *truth* or *fact* as opposed to *belief.* The position outlined above denies the possibility of ascertaining the truth or falsity of a value judgment; certainly, however, it does not deny that people can be induced to profess strong beliefs in value propositions. Skeptic is quite confident of his beliefs in the moral desirability of capital punishment and the esthetic perfection of *Long Is the Night,* even though you may be able to demonstrate cogently to him that he can never verify the truth or falsity of such moral and esthetic assertions. In fact, the history of mankind is replete with instances of violent argument about value propositions.

At this point, let us turn to a consideration of the kinds of evidential data that can be used to induce belief in value propositions. Once again, our two broad categories of direct experience and testimony may seem appropriate. Concerning the former category, however, some qualifications and reservations are in order.

While most of us have directly experienced the event designated in the proposition, "The sun rises in the east," I would hold that no one has directly experienced an event corresponding to what is contained in the proposition, "Communism is the worst form of government." In the latter case, what one has experienced is a series of related events (imprisonment for six months, deprivation of property, assertions by one's father that the communists are tyrants, etc.) that have led to a belief in the value implied by the proposition, "Communism is the worst form of government." A second individual, however, may experience a series of related events (twenty years of education, appointment to a prosperous governmental position, high office in the party, etc.) that have led him to a belief in the value implied in the proposition, "Communism is the best form of government." While we would be willing to grant the rationality of both of these individuals (after all, few of us would question that Brezhnev's belief in the latter proposition is rational), we would, on the other hand, have serious doubts about an individual who asserted that his experiences had led him to doubt the truth of the factual proposition, "The sun rises in the east." Thus, while direct experiences may serve as evidential data calculated to induce belief in both factual and value propositions, the nature of these experiences and, even more important, what the experiences themselves imply will differ for factual and value propositions.

Although we could examine the preceding point at greater length, I will dispense with further discussion, since most instances of argumentation concerning value judgments involve evidential data of the kind we have labeled *testimony*. Think, for example, of most of the values you now hold. Are your religious values, for example, a function of direct experiences you have had with the major religions of the world, or are they largely a result of testimony by X, Y, and Z which has induced you to believe the value proposition, "This religion is the best"? For most of you, I am certain that the latter case prevails. The same could probably be said for most of the political and social values you hold and, though perhaps to a lesser extent, for your current tastes in the arts.

It should be apparent that the mechanism for inducing belief by means of testimony is similar for both factual and value propositions; i.e., an individual must first believe the proposition, "X testifies truthfully," after which he is more likely to be induced to believe in the proposition about which X is testifying. Given the fact that testimony embraces similar psychological processes for both factual and value propositions and granted the assumption that most instances of argumentation involve testimony as the sole evidential datum, you may feel that I have been unnecessarily laborious in distinguishing between factual and value propositions. Actually, however, the distinction is a crucial one, since the category *testimony* is a broad one that embraces a number of different kinds of materials. In the next section of this chapter, I hope to show that all kinds of testimonial data are not equally effective for both factual and value propositions;

rather, it should become apparent that some kinds of testimonial data are more suited to factual than to value propositions, while for others the converse is true. For this reason, the distinction between the two types of propositions is important.

One final remark is in order. I have made no mention of the type of proposition commonly labeled *policy,* a type frequently discussed in texts on argumentation and debate. This is because I hold that a policy proposition has no distinguishing characteristics which set it apart from fact and value propositions; that is, I believe that if any meaningful argument is to occur, a policy proposition must be disputed as either a proposition of fact or a proposition of value. The key to the choice of a factual or value orientation lies in the definition of the term *should*—a term which occurs in most policy propositions. If *should* is defined in terms of means-ends interests (we would increase our gross national product, we would win the war, etc.), then the issue becomes one of fact, revolving around considerations of whether or not the stipulated ends would occur. If *should* is defined in terms of intrinsic ethical considerations (it would be morally good to do this, men of good will ought to behave this way, etc.), then the issue becomes one of value, revolving around the goodness or badness of these moral precepts. Although the two may overlap, it should be apparent that all parties to the dispute must first agree on where the emphasis should be placed; otherwise, the argument will proceed from different premises, and no clash of ideas can occur. Also, the choice of a factual or value orientation will determine which kinds of evidential data will be maximally effective in inducing a sense of belief on the part of the particular audience involved. It is to this matter that we now turn.

Types and Tests of Evidence

In this section, we turn to an examination of specific kinds of testimony in their evidential role of inducing belief in the various types of propositions. The decision to discuss only testimony is based on the earlier assertion that direct experience is seldom involved in instances that we would consider argumentation. Two specific kinds of testimony will be considered. Although it would be convenient to find neat one- or two-word labels for the two categories, I have, after some thought, deserted the search; I choose to call them *testimony composed of statistical data* and *testimony composed of authority-based assertion.* Although no claim is made for either the exhaustiveness or the exclusiveness of the two categories, I believe they will enable us to consider the kinds of evidential data most frequently employed to induce belief in argumentative propositions.

A brief outline of the organizational format of this section may be of assistance to the reader. I shall first discuss the use of testimony composed of statistical data as a means of inducing belief in propositions of fact and propositions of value, and I shall then follow the same procedure in discussing testimony composed of authority-based assertion. The examination of each kind of testimony will consist of two major phases: first, a consideration of some general psychological facts related to the evidential effectiveness of the particular form of testimony; and, second, a discussion of some of the questions and tests that may be used to choose and evaluate the particular form of testimony in terms of its primary function of inducing belief.

Testimony Composed of Statistical Data

As a beginning step, it would be well to stipulate how the term *statistical data* will be used. Simply, the term is used to designate testimony that asserts any fact about a sample drawn from a population or, in some cases, testimony that asserts a fact about an entire population. The samples and populations involved may consist of people, bushels of corn, or any other physical phenomenon.

Perhaps an example will best serve to distinguish that which is testimony composed of statistical data from that which is not. Suppose that our imaginary friend Skeptic asserts, with a crestfallen smile, that his group had an average of 3.3 cavities after brushing one year with Brand A, while a similar group had an average of 1.1 cavities after brushing one year with Brand B. This is testimony composed of statistical data; i.e., it asserts a fact about each of two samples randomly drawn from a larger population, specifically, a population composed of all those individuals who have brushed, or will brush, their teeth. Ordinarily, we would use the testimony of Skeptic to induce belief in factual propositions such as "Brand B offers greater protection against cavities than does Brand A."

Let us now suppose, however, that we hear Skeptic make only the statement, "Brand B is three times as good a toothpaste as Brand A." If this is all we know about the situation, we would not classify Skeptic's remark as testimony composed of statistical data, even though it contains the number *three*. The basis for Skeptic's assertion may be that he prefers the taste of Brand B to Brand A, that he managed to obtain a long desired date shortly after switching to Brand B, or any of a number of personal factors such as these. Actually, the statement may be a proposition inferred from Skeptic's participation in the above mentioned scientific test; however, in its bare essentials, it more closely resembles our second kind of testimony, authority-based assertion, than testimony composed of statistical data.

I would hold that the major distinction between statistical data and other forms of evidence is to be found in the alleged precision with which the former is collected and the "typicalness" that results from such precise collection. Thus, if our friend Skeptic states that he has owned and driven a Whizzo automobile for a year and has discovered that Whizzo is the best on the market, we may, by virtue of this testimony, be induced to believe the proposition, "Whizzo is the best auto that can be purchased." This belief, however, does not result from precision in the manner of collecting the evidential data. On the other hand, if a leading research firm samples the attitudes of a population composed of all individuals owning Whizzo automobiles and discovers that 89 per cent of this group judges Whizzo to be the best automobile they have ever owned, there is at least the implication that these evidential data were precisely collected and are typical of all Whizzo owners.

Having examined some defining characteristics of testimony composed of statistical data, let us turn to a consideration of some of the psychological factors related to its effectiveness as evidence. P. Albert Duhamel has asserted that rhetoric (which, consistent with our present concern, Aristotle has defined as discovery of the available means of persuasion[12]) is dependent upon the prevailing psychology, metaphysic, and epistemology of the age.[13] Nowhere is the truth of this assertion more apparent than in the current concern for the use of statistical data as evidence. Turn on the television set and you are barraged with statements concerning the performance characteristics of various automobiles, the relative percentage of cavities incurred by groups brushing with two different toothpaste formulas, etc. Nor is this interest in numbers limited to advertising: insurance premiums are fixed by referring to actuarial tables; academic success is at least tentatively predicted by examining scores on several paper-and-pencil tests; and many industries hire and fire partially on the basis of test scores. Statistical data provide the basis for many policy decisions and serve to induce belief in a host of factual propositions.

The frequent evidential use of testimony composed of statistical data is undoubtedly related to the rapid ascendency of science in the last several centuries. At least one writer has suggested that *science* is one of the ultimate rhetorical god-words of our contemporary society.[14] Perhaps you would not wish to be this extreme; even so, it should be apparent that science is an integral part of our daily lives. As a result, it is not surprising that statistical data—a kind of evidence that is replete with scientific trappings and carries with it the aura of precision and objectivity associated with science—has come into vogue.

The preceding remarks are in no way meant to ridicule or condemn the strategic employment of testimony composed of statistical data; in fact, they are meant to suggest that in its evidential function of inducing belief such testimony has, with many audiences, psychological advantages which maximize its probable effectiveness. It should also be apparent, however, that for certain kinds of audiences testimony based on statistical data is likely to be an unpalatable form of evidence. Some individuals in our society, particularly those who identify with the humanities and with the arts, feel that science has been emphasized beyond all reasonable proportion. Given this attitude, an attempt to induce belief in certain propositions by use of statistical data may well be met with psychological resistance. Thus, although the general tenor of contemporary society may be said to psychologically favor testimony composed of statistical data, a careful analysis of the particular audience involved will aid in deciding whether such evidence is likely to induce belief.

Let us now assume for a moment that we are attempting to induce belief in an audience by means of testimony based on statistical data. If we wish to accomplish this objective, what are some of the tests that we should apply for intelligent usage of such testimony? I shall consider this question as it applies to both propositions of fact and propositions of value.

Again, let us begin with an example, Skeptic and you have been discussing the merits of a program of federal medical insurance. In the course of the discussion, Skeptic introduces the results of a recent survey which indicate that only 2 per cent of the citizens of the United States cannot afford adequate medical care, a finding which he uses in an attempt to induce your belief in the proposition, "Adequate medical care can be provided without a program of federal medical insurance."

At this juncture of the argument you feel disillusioned, since, although you and Skeptic have disagreed in the past, you have never previously had reason to doubt his veracity. Yet you have before you the results of a survey, conducted by a reputable research agency, which show that 27 per cent of the citizens of the United States cannot afford adequate medical care. You are forced to believe either that Skeptic is deliberately misleading you or that he has been taken in by inaccurate evidential testimony.

The circumstance described above occurs quite frequently in argumentative situations in which the disputing parties utilize evidence consisting of testimony composed of statistical data. Before forming any premature conclusions, the reader should understand that the results of both the surveys cited are probably accurate, and that the integrity of all parties involved is probably unquestionable. Even so, the existence of an apparent discrepancy suggests the first test for intelligent usage of testimony composed of statistical data.

It is obvious that both teams of researchers had to stipulate a definition of the phrase "those who can afford adequate medical care" before they could conduct their surveys. Generally, the method they would employ is one that has been labeled *operational definition*. Simply stated, the essence of operationism is that the meaning of a concept consists of the things one does (i.e., *operations*) to derive it.[15] In the case of the survey quoted by Skeptic, the operational definition for "those who can afford adequate medical care" may have been stipulated as follows: Go out and ask each individual if he could afford to spend $100 a year for medical expenses; each person who responds affirmatively falls into the class of "those who can afford adequate medical care." Conversely, in the case of the survey you have examined, the operational definition may have been stipulated identically, *with the single exception* that the figure "$750," rather than "$100," was utilized.

Unless there is knowledge of the different amounts employed in the two operational definitions, the argument is at an impasse. Once the difference is established, however, it is possible to proceed by questioning the relative usefulness of the two definitions. The answer to this question may be complex and may require the use of further evidence, some of which may itself be testimony composed of statistical data. In fact, it is conceivable that $100 may be judged too conservative, while $750 may be considered too extravagant. Hence, Skeptic and you may agree that the operational definitions employed negate the value of both surveys, and you may decide to seek a survey in which $425 is the figure used. Whether or not this is the case, the important point is that one test for intelligent use of testimony composed of statistical data is whether or not the operational definitions of the key concepts in the problem are supplied. If such definitions are not stipulated, it becomes difficult to interpret the evidence in relation to the proposition it is intended to support.

If we carry our hypothetical example a bit further, we encounter a second test for intelligent use of testimony composed of statistical data. Let us assume that Skeptic has provided you with the $100 figure upon which his quoted survey is based and you have asked his reasons for assuming that this is a useful figure. Skeptic replies that the amount seems sensible to him, since he has evidence which indicates that the average amount spent on medical care per family in the previous year was $75.[16] This being the case, Skeptic asserts that he believes $100 is a perfectly reasonable figure to use in defining "those who can afford adequate medical care."

Skeptic has used a statistic—the average or mean—that all of us frequently encounter. It is one of several statistics referred to as *measures of central tendency,* i.e., measures used to describe certain general characteristics about a group of scores. Other such measures include the median (i.e., that point at which 50 per cent of the group of scores fall) and the mode (i.e., the single point on the distribution at which the greatest number of scores fall). Actually, these measures—along with other statistics that tell us about the variability of the scores in the distribution—give us a convenient shorthand for condensing a great deal of information into capsule form.

Unfortunately, however, these measures can be quite misleading to someone who does not understand *what* information such measures are intended to convey; in fact, they have provided the impetus for such amusing and informative books as *How to Lie with Statistics.*[17] Although I would disagree with the position that statistics lie, I would certainly accept the contention that people do an excellent job of using them to lie. This is particularly true with such measures as the average quoted by Skeptic.

Perhaps this can be demonstrated more effectively by examination of Table 1, which contains a distribution of the scores on which Skeptic based his quoted average. For purposes of illustration, the distribution has been exaggerated to demonstrate the marked effect of extreme values on the average of the scores. Certainly, few people would accept Skeptic's quoted average as descriptive of the economic expenditures of the six families involved. Although the $75 figure may imply to some that all families spend about this much yearly for medical care, examination of the sample indicates that this is not true, rather, what is involved is a situation in which one family spends much more than $75, while the other five families spend nothing. In order to describe this particular distribution accurately, then it would have been more appropriate to use the median or mode measure.[18]

Table 1   Figures from which Skeptic's quoted average was derived

Family	Amount Spent of Medical Care	
1	$450.00	
2	0.00	Average or Mean $75.00
3	0.00	
4	0.00	Median $ 0.00
5	0.00	
6	0.00	Mode $ 0.00

This brief discussion suggests that the second test for intelligent use of testimony composed of statistical data has to do with the accuracy with which the particular data describe the existing empirical state of affairs. Generally speaking, every effort should be made to choose statistical measures that describe the situation accurately and to provide enough information for the audience to see that such a selection has been made.

The tests for use of testimony composed of statistical data discussed above are equally appropriate when such testimony is used as evidence to induce belief in either propositions of fact or propositions of value. For the latter propositions, however, certain additional considerations involving the limitations of testimony composed of statistical data are of significance.

As we established earlier, propositions of value cannot be labeled *true* or *false,* because such propositions deal with ethical and esthetic problems. As a result, one sometimes encounters an argumentative situation in which one of the parties commits the error of attempting to induce belief in qualitative propositions entirely by the use of quantitative data. Again, an example may best serve to illustrate this situation.

Let us assume that Skeptic and you have managed to find a survey you are both willing to accept, which indicates that only 3 per cent of the citizens of the United States cannot afford adequate medical care. Armed with this evidence, Skeptic elatedly asserts that you must now surely accept his proposition that a program of federal medical care is unnecessary. After all, 97 per cent of the population can afford adequate medical care without any federal assistance.

Rather than accepting Skeptic's proposition, you should be quick to point out that his evidence is not sufficient to induce belief. After all, respect for the dignity and value of the individual is an integral aspect of the democratic ideology. Perhaps some countries whose political and social philosophy is based on a collective ethic are willing to sacrifice 3 per cent of the population; however, you quickly point out to Skeptic that you, for one, are quite concerned about this minority's welfare. Once you have pressed Skeptic on this point, he will find it exceedingly difficult to maintain his position without marshaling new evidence or invoking some added tertiary propositions. This is because one of the major issues of the dispute revolves around a qualitative question; it cannot be resolved by recourse to testimony involving quantitative data alone.

The above discussion does not imply that testimony composed of statistical data cannot be effectively used to induce belief in value propositions; rather, it indicates that such evidence has greater limitations when utilized to induce belief in value propositions than when employed to induce belief in propositions of fact. While one may be induced to believe the proposition, "The Moslem religion is the largest in the world," on the basis of testimony composed of statistical data, it is doubtful that a member of the Christian faith is likely to believe the proposition, "The Moslem religion is the best religion in the world," on the basis of the same evidence. This is because the latter proposition involves moral and ethical matters that cannot be entirely resolved by resort to numbers, even if the numbers are an accurate reflection of the physical state of the world.

Testimony Composed of Authority-Based Assertion

We turn now to a consideration of the second kind of testimony to be discussed, testimony composed of authority-based assertion. Certainly, this kind of testimony is widely used in argumentative situations. From whence does its psychological effectiveness stem, and what are some of the tests for intelligent use of such evidence?

As a beginning step, a definition of the term *authority-based assertion* is appropriate. The term is here used to designate testimony presented by one whom the audience is likely to think of as an honest and dependable source. The content of the testimony is phrased in the form of an assertion or opinion, with little or no indication of the basis for the assertion; however, the individual using such testimony always hopes the source's reputation will be sufficient to induce audience belief that the testimony is well grounded. Thus, even more than testimony composed of statistical data (which often is not attributed to any single source), testimony composed of authority-based assertion is largely dependent upon *who* made the assertion rather than upon the apparent basis for *what* was asserted.[19]

For example, let us assume that Skeptic and you are still engaged in a discussion of the pros and cons of federal medical insurance. Skeptic, tiring in his efforts to induce belief by means of testimony composed of statistical data, brings to your attention a quotation by Mr. X, President of the Iowa Medical Association, which asserts that federal medical insurance would be harmful to the American system of medicine. Skeptic also points out that Mr. Y, Mr. Z, and Mr. A. have all made similar statements; therefore, you should accept the proposition, "A program of federal medical insurance is undesirable."

It can be seen that the bases for Messrs. X, Y, Z, and A's assertions are not at all clear. The grounds for testimony composed of statistical data are usually apparent if one understands the meanings associated with the terms, but in the above example there is no way of determining what led the individuals quoted to make their assertions. Of course, Skeptic is hopeful that you will assume the assertion is well founded on the basis of your respect for the sources.

History provides ample evidence that testimony composed of authority-based assertion is highly effective in inducing belief in numerous propositions. Obviously, as was mentioned earlier, many of the propositions in which we profess belief are buttressed by our acceptance of the proposition, "X testifies truthfully." Bertrand Russell asserts, "When we are told anything emphatically or authoritatively, it is an effort not to believe it, as anyone can experience on April Fools' Day."[20] Ample precedence for the psychological effectiveness of testimony composed of authority-based assertion can be found in the learning experiences to which most people are exposed. Sociologists and psychologists have commented extensively on the role of the primary family group in shaping an individual's social and political beliefs. Since much of early childhood consists of the development of a belief system based on assertion by authority, the process of child development produces adults who rely heavily on such testimony. It is not surprising that vestiges of this early training survive, to a greater or lesser extent, throughout the individual's entire life.

Also, the vast scope of contemporary knowledge dictates the acceptance of testimony composed of authority-based assertion. All of us soon realize the complete impossibility of being adequately informed about the many complex problems and fields of knowledge that exist today. As a result, we find it imperative to develop a sense of faith in the statements of others whom we know to be informed about particular areas of concern. We assume that assertions such as "This proposal would be desirable," "That proposal would be harmful," etc., are based on intelligent consideration of the issues involved. Although the ideal of the Renaissance man is an inviting one, we realize that it is an ideal impossible to achieve in the twentieth century.

Thus, there are several psychological factors that account for the evidential effectiveness of testimony composed of authority-based assertion. It should be pointed out, however, that the weight of authority bears much more heavily on some individuals than on others. Extensive research by psychologists such as Adorno and Rokeach has led to the differentiation of two broad categories of people—identified by such labels as "High Authoritarian" and "Low Authoritarian" or "Open-Minded" and "Closed-Minded."[21] The Low Authoritarian or Open-Minded person is far less dependent on authority as a means of supporting and formulating his beliefs than is the High Authoritarian or Closed-Minded individual. This does not imply that the former places no reliance on authority; rather, it suggests that his use of authority conforms more closely to the accepted model of the rational man.[22] The point to be emphasized is that no generalizations can be made about the probable psychological effectiveness of testimony composed of authority-based assertion; rather, one must consider the particular audience in which he hopes to induce belief.

As we did when discussing testimony composed of statistical data, let us now examine some of the tests for intelligent use of testimony composed of authority-based assertion. Again, as was the case in dealing with testimony composed of statistical data, no attempt is made to suggest that one must always meet these tests in order for the testimony to serve its evidential function of inducing belief in the proposition being disputed; rather, these considerations relate to a set of value judgments regarding the way argument ought to be conducted.

Let me begin by suggesting that many of the authority-based assertions used as evidence in argumentation are obviously trivial. Again, an example will best serve to illustrate. Your friend, Skeptic, is still struggling to gain your acceptance of his position regarding the federal medical insurance controversy. In desperation he reaches into his figurative card file and pulls out a quotation by the president of a large voluntary health association which asserts that private insurance plans are superior to governmental medical plans. Surely, says Skeptic, you will accept the assertion of this intelligent and respected executive.

Of course you will not. Rather than composing an elaborate category system for testing authorities (i.e., honesty, knowledge, lack of bias, etc.), I suggest that a whole host of statements may best be disposed of by the question: What else would you expect him to say? In other words, I prefer to dispense with elaborate discussions of motives and substitute the general, common sense observation that people utter many statements which are entirely consistent with what everything we know about them would lead us to expect them to say; in fact, we would be shocked if they violated these expectations.

All of us have witnessed lengthy arguments consisting largely of a laborious exchange of such banalities. How much more profitable it would be if the disputants could present testimony containing assertions that one would *not* expect the particular source to make. Thus, in our hypothetical dispute about federal medical insurance, Skeptic would do well to seek out assertions regarding the good aspects of voluntary medical plans that have been set forth by authorities who are not so likely to make such statements, e.g., a member of Congress who is known to be in favor of a bill establishing federal medical insurance. Or, conversely, if you wish to argue in favor of such a plan, you should seek statements by executives of voluntary insurance companies in which they admit to some advantages for federal programs. Granted, this kind of testimony is more difficult to discover; in fact, it may sometimes be nonexistent, but on those occasions when it is discovered, it should have a powerful psychological impact. As a beginning step, then, one should seek testimony composed of authority-based assertion in which the assertions made are not what would be routinely expected.

A second test for intelligent use of such testimony is the extent to which authorities agree on the assertion being made. It should go without saying that assertions upon which there is general agreement (or, at least, some degree of consensus) by authorities will carry greater weight than assertions upon which there is wide variance in opinion. For example, if five reputable authorities assert that the only way to combat the increasing cost of medical care is through a program of federal medical insurance, the probability of inducing belief in propositions such as "The economic costs of medical care can best be met by federal medical insurance" is much greater than if Authority 1 states that the only way to meet costs is through a program of federal medical insurance; Authority 2 suggests that we can meet the costs by supplementing voluntary plans with federal insurance; and so on to the point that Authority 5 asserts that the costs can be entirely borne by voluntary programs. Thus, unanimity, or, at least, a clear majority, is another test for intelligent use of testimony composed of authority-based assertion.

One further point should be made regarding the use of testimony composed of authority-based assertion. From our previous discussion of the nature of value propositions, it should be apparent that authority-based assertion is frequently invoked in disputes over value questions. Indeed, most of the major tenets of the world's religions are at least partially based on testimony composed of authority-based assertion, as is a good deal of the content of the major political ideologies. This fact suggests that testimony composed of authority-based assertion—although certainly useful as evidence in matters involving propositions of fact—often has its greatest psychological impact in the realm of value disputes.

Although this chapter has focused on selected psychological aspects of evidence, there are, as was mentioned earlier, numerous other vantage points from which an observer might view the role of evidence in argumentation. My decision to emphasize psychological considerations should not be interpreted to imply that there is no value in adopting an alternative approach; rather, it reflects my commitment to the belief that argumentation has as its primary end the inducement of behavioral change on the part of individuals comprising some immediate or ultimate audience. Given this frame of reference, the decision to hew to a psychological orientation toward evidence follows naturally.

These qualifying statements conclude our brief consideration of the role of evidence in argumentation. Without in any sense apologizing, I feel I should at least "regularize" by asserting that such a brief examination can hardly do more than scratch the surface of such a complex topic. Even so, it is hoped that this chapter will encourage further thought about, and exploration of, the problem of evidence and its argumentative role in inducing belief. Perhaps some reader may wish to prepare a rejoinder in Skeptic's behalf.

Notes

1. See, for example, A. Craig Baird, *Argumentation, Discussion, and Debate* (New York: McGraw-Hill, 1950), pp. 90-115. A recent work by Douglas Ehninger and Wayne Brockriede, *Decision by Debate* (New York: Dodd, Mead & Company, 1963), pp. 110-25, places some emphasis on the psychological nature of evidence; even so, the primary focus still appears to be on the value aspects of its use.

2. Bertrand Russell, *Human Knowledge: Its Scope and Limits* (New York: Simon and Schuster, Inc., 1962), p. 145.

3. Robert K. Merton, *Social Theory and Social Structure,* rev. ed. (New York: Free Press of Glencoe, Inc., 1957), pp. 421-39. It should be added that if the evidence more logically supports the latter proposition, it again emphasizes the distinction between *fact* and *belief* outlined above, since the beliefs of these depositors are contrary to the factual state of the economy.

4. Recently, one of the more interesting areas dealing with man's desire for rationality and order has been that of balance theory in psychology. Basically, theorists of this school argue that man cannot tolerate two inconsistent cognitions and that he must strive to regain balance by eliminating inconsistency. Although such behavior seems reasoned and rational, these same theorists also recognize that the *means* an individual adopts to achieve the *end* of cognitive consistency may be quite irrational in nature. For a discussion of the problem see Leon Festinger, *A Theory of Cognitive Dissonance* Stanford: Stanford University Press, 1962), and Milton J. Rosenberg and others, *Attitude Organization and Change: An Analysis of Consistency Among Attitude Components* (New Haven: Yale University Press, 1960).

5. Gustav Bergmann, "Ideology," *Ethics,* LXI (1951), 206.

6. The effects of such a disconfirmation on the attitudes and beliefs of group members have been studied, and the findings make for interesting and informative reading. See Leon Festinger, Henry W. Riecken, Jr., and Stanley Schachter, *When Prophecy Fails* (Minneapolis: University of Minnesota Press, 1956).

7. The problem of induction mentioned above has to do with the impossibility of observing all of the possible instances of the physical event labeled "sun rising in the east." Thus, though one may have psychological certainty that the sun has risen, and will continue to rise, in the east, he can never have logical certainty that such will be the case. Obviously, this unverifiable assumption of continuity in the physical world underlies all scientific enterprise and should be called to the attention of those individuals who assert naïvely that science is completely objective in nature.

8. This consideration provides one good reason for the claim that primary source material (i.e., material taken from the source himself) is superior to secondary source material (i.e., material in which a second party relates what the original source had stated). In the case for the former, one has only to induce the belief, "X testifies truthfully about the event in question," while with the latter, one must induce the twin beliefs that "(1) Y testifies truthfully about what X has stated, and (2) X testifies truthfully about the event in question." Thus, when secondary source material is utilized the problem of inducing belief becomes psychologically more complex and difficult.

9. Here, we have touched upon a number of complex philosophical problems having to do with the relative merits of realism and idealism as theories of knowledge. For a discussion of these problems see, for example, A. J. Ayer, *The Problem of Knowledge* (Baltimore: Penguin Books, Inc., 1962).

10. Bergmann, 206.

11. I am grateful to the editor of *Southern Speech Journal* for permission to quote parts of the above from an article appearing in that journal. See Gerald R. Miller, "Questions of Fact and Value: Another Look," *Southern Speech Journal*, XXVIII (1962), 116-23.

12. Aristotle, *Rhetoric*, trans. W. Rhys Roberts (New York: Random House, Inc., 1954), 1355^b 26.

13. P. Albert Duhamel, "The Function of Rhetoric as Effective Expression," *Journal of the History of Ideas*, X (1949), 344-56.

14. Richard M. Weaver, *The Ethics of Rhetoric* (Chicago: Henry Regnery Company, 1953), pp. 215-16.

15. The concept of operationism was first introduced by Percy W. Bridgman in *The Logic of Modern Physics* (New York: Macmillan Company, 1927). Since its introduction, operationism has been heartily embraced by the social sciences. For an excellent discussion of its limitations and uses see Gustav Bergmann, "Sense and Nonsense in Operationsim," in *The Validation of Scientific Theories*, ed. Phillipp J. Frank (Boston: Beacon Press, 1956), pp. 41-52.

16. Let us, for the sake of this illustration, ignore the obvious circularity of defining "those who can afford adequate medical care" in terms of the average amount spent on medical care per family. Such an approach obviously begs the question.

17. Darrell Huff, *How to Lie with Statistics* (New York: W. W. Norton & Company, Inc., 1954).

18. Ideally, we would also like to have a descriptive statistic that indicates the variability of the scores. Such a statistic is the standard deviation. Unfortunately, this statistic is often not readily available.

19. As one would suspect, there is a good deal of experimental evidence which indicates that *who* the source is makes a difference apart from what is said. See, for example, Carl I. Hovland and Walter Weiss, "The Influence of Source Credibility on Communication Effectiveness," *Public Opinion Quarterly*, XV (1952), 635-50, and Herbert C. Kelman, "Process of Opinion Change," *Public Opinion Quarterly*, XXV (1961), 57-79.

20. Russell, p. 166.

21. T. W. Adorno and others, *The Authoritarian Personality* (New York: Harper & Row, Publishers, Inc., 1950), and Milton Rokeach, *The Open and Closed Mind* (New York: Basic Books, Inc., Publishers, 1960).

22. For example, Powell found that Open-Minded individuals were more capable than Closed-Minded individuals of differentiating the source of a message and the message content. See Fredric A. Powell, "Open- and Closed-Mindedness and the Ability to Differentiate Source and Message," *Journal of Abnormal and Social Psychology*, LXV (1962), 61-65.

TOULMIN ON ARGUMENT: AN INTERPRETATION AND APPLICATION

WAYNE BROCKRIEDE and DOUGLAS EHNINGER

During the period 1917-1932 several books, a series of articles, and many Letters to the Editor of *Quarterly Journal of Speech* gave serious attention to exploring the nature of argument as it is characteristically employed in rhetorical proofs.[1] Since that time, however, students of public address have shown comparatively little interest in the subject, leaving to philosophers, psychologists, and sociologists the principal contributions which have more recently been made toward an improved understanding of argument.[2]

Among the contributions offered by "outsiders" to our field, one in particular deserves more attention than it has so far received from rhetoricians. We refer to some of the formulations of the English logician Stephen Toulmin in his *The Uses of Argument*, published in 1958.[3]

Wayne Brockriede and Douglas Ehninger, "Toulmin on Argument: An Interpretation and Application," *Quarterly Journal of Speech* (February, 1960), pp. 44-53. By permission of the Speech Communication Association and the authors.

Toulmin's analysis and terminology are important to the rhetorician for two different but related reasons. First, they provide an appropriate structural model by means of which rhetorical arguments may be laid out for analysis and criticism; and, second, they suggest a system for classifying artistic proofs which employs argument as a central and unifying construct. Let us consider these propositions in order.

1.

As described by Toulmin, an argument is *movement* from accepted *data*, through a *warrant,* to a *claim.*

Data (D) answers the question, "What have you got to go on?" Thus *data* correspond to materials of fact or opinion which in our textbooks are commonly called *evidence.* Data may report historical or contemporary events, take the form of a statistical compilation or of citations from authority, or they may consist of one or more general declarative sentences established by a prior proof of an artistic nature. Without data clearly present or strongly implied, an argument has no informative or substantive component, no factual point of departure.

Claim (C) is the term Toulmin applies to what we normally speak of as a *conclusion.* It is the explicit appeal produced by the argument, and is always of a potentially controversial nature. A claim may stand as the final proposition in an argument, or it may be an intermediate statement which serves as data for a subsequent inference.

Data and claim taken together represent the specific contention advanced by an argument, and therefore constitute what may be regarded as its *main proof line.* The usual order is *data* first, and then *claim.* In this sequence the *claim* contains or implies "therefore." When the order is reversed, the *claim* contains or implies "because."

Warrant (W) is the operational name Toulmin gives to that part of an argument which authorizes the mental "leap" involved in advancing from data to claim. As distinguished from data which answer the question "What have you got to go on," the warrant answers the question "How do you get there." Its function is to *carry* the accepted data to the doubted or disbelieved proposition which constitutes the claim, thereby certifying this claim as true or acceptable.

The relations existing among these three basic components of an argument, Toulmin suggests, may be represented diagrammatically:

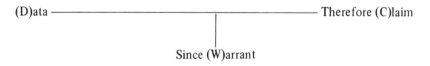

(D)ata ———————————————————————— Therefore (C)laim

Since (W)arrant

Here is an application of the method:

Therefore
(D) ———————————————————————— (C)
Russia has violated 50   Russia would violate the
of 52 international   proposed ban on nuclear
agreements   weapons testing

Since
(W)
Past violations are symptomatic of probable future violations

In addition to the three indispensable elements of *data, claim,* and *warrant,* Toulmin recognizes a second triad of components, any or all of which may, but need not necessarily, be present in an argument. These he calls (1) *backing,* (2) *rebuttal,* and (3) *qualifier.*

Backing (B) consists of credentials designed to certify the assumption expressed in the warrant. Such credentials may consist of a single item, or of an entire argument in itself complete with data and claim. Backing must be introduced when readers or listeners are not willing to accept a warrant at its face value.

The rebuttal (R) performs the function of a safety valve or escape hatch, and is, as a rule, appended to the claim statement. It recognizes certain conditions under which the claim will not hold good or will hold good only in a qualified and restricted way. By limiting the area to which the claim may legitimately be applied, the rebuttal anticipates certain objections which might otherwise be advanced against the argument.

The function of the qualifier (Q) is to register the degree of force which the maker believes his claim to possess. The qualification may be expressed by a quantifying term such as "possibly," "probably," "to the five per cent level of confidence," etc., or it may make specific reference to an anticipated refutation. When the author of a claim regards it as incontrovertible no qualifier is appended.

These additional elements may be superimposed on the first diagram:

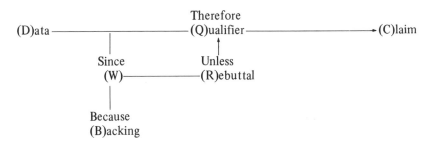

We may illustrate the model as follows:

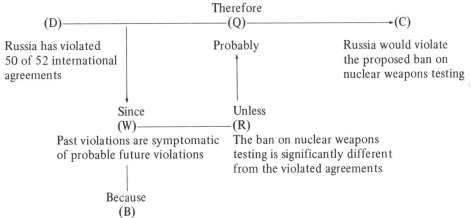

Other nations which had such a record of violations continued such action/Expert X states that nations which have been chronic violators nearly always continued such acts/etc.

2.

With Toulmin's structural model now set forth, let us inquire into its suitability as a means of describing and testing arguments. Let us compare Toulmin's method with the analysis offered in traditional logic, the logic commonly used as a basic theory of argumentation in current textbooks. We conceive of arguments in the customary fashion as (1) deriving from probable causes and signs, (2) proceeding more often by relational than implicative principles, (3) emphasizing material as well as formal validity, (4) employing premises which are often contestable, and (5) eventuating in claims which are by nature contingent and variable.

The superiority of the Toulmin model in describing and testing arguments may be claimed for seven reasons:

1. Whereas traditional logic is characteristically concerned with *warrant-using* arguments (i.e., arguments in which the validity of the assumption underlying the inference "leap" is uncontested), Toulmin's model specifically provides for *warrant-establishing* arguments (i.e., arguments in which the validity of the assumption underlying the inference must be established—through backing—as part of the proof pattern itself).[4]

2. Whereas traditional logic, based as it is upon the general principle of implication, always treats proof more or less as a matter of classification of compartmentalization, Toulmin's analysis stresses the inferential and relational nature of argument, providing a context within which all factors—both formal and material—bearing upon a disputed claim may be organized into a series of discrete steps.

3. Whereas in traditional logic arguments are specifically designed to produce universal propositions, Toulmin's second triad of backing, rebuttal, and qualifier provide, within the framework of his basic structural model, for the establishment of claims which are no more than probable. The model directs attention to the ways in which each of these additional elements may operate to limit or condition a claim.

4. Whereas traditional logic, with its governing principle of implication, necessarily results in an essentially static conception of argument, Toulmin by emphasizing *movement* from data, through warrant, to claim produces a conception of argument as dynamic. From his structural model we derive a picture of arguments "working" to establish and certify claims, and as a result of his functional terminology we are able to understand the role each part of an argument plays in this process.

5. Whereas the modes based on the traditional analysis—enthymeme, example, and the like—often suppress a step in proof, Toulmin's model lays an argument out in such a way that each step may be examined critically.

6. Whereas in the traditional analysis the division of arguments into premises and conclusions (as in the syllogism, for example) often tends to obscure deficiencies in proof, Toulmin's model assigns each part of an argument a specific geographical or spatial position in relation to the others, thus rendering it more likely that weak points will be detected.

7. Whereas traditional logic is imperfectly equipped to deal with the problem of material validity, Toulmin makes such validity an integral part of his system, indicating clearly the role which factual elements play in producing acceptable claims.

In short, without denying that Toulmin's formulations are open to serious criticism at several points[5]—and allowing for any peculiarities in our interpretations of the character of traditional logic—one conclusion emerges. Toulmin has provided a structural model which promises to be of greater use in laying out rhetorical arguments for dissection and testing than the methods of traditional logic. For although most teachers and writers in the field of argumentation have discussed the syllogism in general terms, they have made no serious attempt to explore the complexities of the moods and figures of the syllogism, nor have they been very successful in applying the terms and principles of traditional logic to the arguments of real controversies. Toulmin's model provides a practical replacement.

3.

Our second proposition is that Toulmin's structural model and the vocabulary he has developed to describe it are suggestive of a system for classifying artistic proofs, using argument (defined as *movement* from data, through warrant, to claim) as a unifying construct.[6]

In extending Toulmin's analysis to develop a simplified classification of arguments, we may begin by restating in Toulmin's terms the traditional difference between *inartistic* and *artistic* proof. Thus, conceiving of an argument as a movement by means of which accepted data are carried through a certifying warrant to a controversial claim, we may say that in some cases the data themselves are conclusive. They approach the claim without aid from a warrant—are tantamount to the claim in the sense that to accept them is automatically to endorse the claim they are designed to support. In such cases the proof may be regarded as *inartistic.* In another class of arguments, however, the situation is quite different. Here the data are not immediately conclusive, so that the role of the warrant in carrying them to the claim becomes of crucial importance. In this sort of argument the proof is directly dependent upon the inventive powers of the arguer and may be regarded as *artistic.*

If, then, the warrant is the crucial element in an artistic proof, and if its function is to carry the data to the claim, we may classify artistic arguments by recognizing the possible routes which the warrant may travel in performing its function.

So far as rhetorical proofs are concerned, as men have for centuries recognized, these routes are three in number: (1) an arguer may carry data to claim by means of an assumption concerning the relationship existing among phenomena in the external world; (2) by means of an assumption concerning the quality of the source from which the data is derived; and (3) by means of an assumption concerning the inner drives, values, or aspirations which impel the behavior of those persons to whom that argument is addressed.

Arguments of the first sort (traditionally called *logical*) may be called *substantive;* those of the second sort (traditionally called *ethical*) may be described as *authoritative;* and those of the third sort (traditionally called *pathetic*) as *motivational.*

Substantive Arguments

The warrant of a substantive argument reflects an assumption concerning the way in which things are related in the world about us. Although other orderings are possible, one commonly recognized, and the one used here, is sixfold. Phenomena may be related as cause to effect (or as effect to cause), as attribute to substance, as some to more, as intrinsically similar, as bearing common relations, or as more to some. Upon the first of these relationships is based what is commonly called argument from *cause;* on the second, argument from *sign;* on the third, argument from *generalization;* on the fourth, argument from *parallel case;* on the fifth, argument from *analogy;* and on the sixth, argument from *classification.*

Cause

In argument from cause the data consist of one or more accepted facts about a person, object, event, or condition. The warrant attributes to these facts a creative or generative power and specifies the nature of the effect they will produce. The claim relates these results to the person, object, event, or condition named in the data. Here is an illustration, from cause to effect:

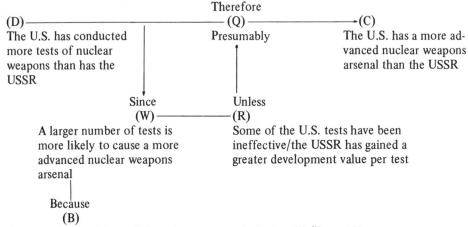

When the reasoning process is reversed and the argument is from effect to cause, the data again consist of one or more facts about a person, object, event, or condition; the warrant asserts that a particular causal force is sufficient to have accounted for these facts; and the claim relates this cause to the person, object, event, or condition named in the data.

Sign

In argument from sign the data consist of clues or symptoms. The warrant interprets the meaning or significance of these symptoms. The claim affirms that some person, object, event, or condition possesses the attributes of which the clues have been declared symptomatic. Our first example concerning Russia's violation of international agreements illustrates the argument from sign.

Generalization

In argument from generalization the data consist of information about a number of persons, objects, events, or conditions, taken as constituting a representative and adequate sample of a given class of phenomena. The warrant assumes that what is true of the items constituting the sample will also be true of additional members of the class not represented in the sample. The claim makes explicit the assumption embodied in the warrant. The form can be diagrammed so:

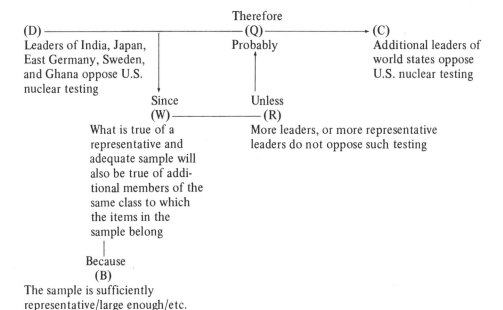

Therefore
(D) ─────────────────────────────(Q)──────────────▶(C)
Leaders of India, Japan,   Probably   Additional leaders of
East Germany, Sweden,   ▲   world states oppose
and Ghana oppose U.S.   │   U.S. nuclear testing
nuclear testing   │
                    Since   Unless
                    (W)─────────────── (R)
          What is true of a   More leaders, or more representative
          representative and   leaders do not oppose such testing
          adequate sample will
          also be true of addi-
          tional members of the
          same class to which
          the items in the
          sample belong

          │
          Because
          (B)
The sample is sufficiently
representative/large enough/etc.

Parallel Case

In argument from parallel case the data consist of one or more statements about a single object, event, or condition. The warrant asserts that the instance reported in the data bears an essential similiarity to a second instance in the same category. The claim affirms about the new instance what has already been accepted concerning the first. Here is an illustration:

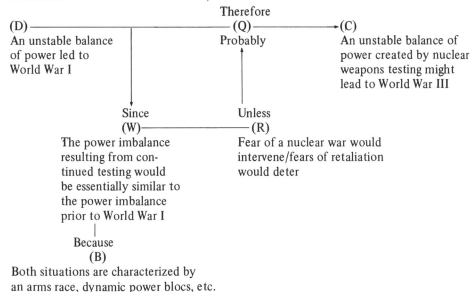

Therefore
(D) ─────────────────────────────(Q)──────────────▶(C)
An unstable balance   Probably   An unstable balance of
of power led to   ▲   power created by nuclear
World War I   │   weapons testing might
                                               │   lead to World War III
                    Since   Unless
                    (W)─────────────── (R)
          The power imbalance   Fear of a nuclear war would
          resulting from con-   intervene/fears of retaliation
          tinued testing would   would deter
          be essentially similar to
          the power imbalance
          prior to World War I

          │
          Because
          (B)
Both situations are characterized by
an arms race, dynamic power blocs, etc.

In argument from parallel cases a rebuttal will be required in either of two situations: (1) if another parallel case bears a stronger similarity to the case under consideration; or (2) if in spite of some essential similarities an essential dissimilarity negates or reduces the force of the warrant. The example illustrates the second of these possibilities.

Analogy

In argument from analogy the data report that a relationship of a certain nature exists between two items. The warrant assumes that a similar relationship exists between a second pair of items. The claim makes explicit the relationship assumed in the warrant. Whereas the argument from parallel case assumes a resemblance between two *cases*, the analogy assumes only a similarity of *relationship*. Analogy may be illustrated so:

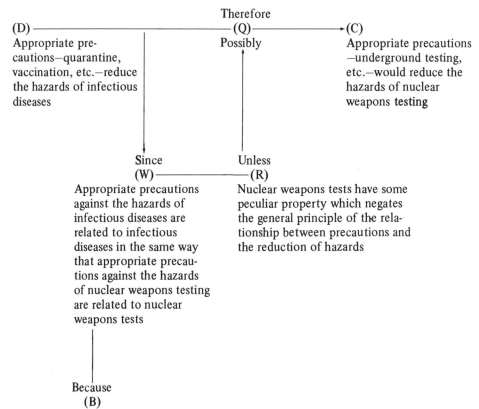

                                        Therefore
(D) ————————————————————— (Q) ——————————————►(C)
Appropriate pre-   Possibly   Appropriate precautions
cautions—quarantine,   —underground testing,
vaccination, etc.—reduce   etc.—would reduce the
the hazards of infectious   hazards of nuclear
diseases   weapons testing

                    Since   Unless
                    (W) ——————————— (R)
              Appropriate precautions   Nuclear weapons tests have some
              against the hazards of   peculiar property which negates
              infectious diseases are   the general principle of the rela-
              related to infectious   tionship between precautions and
              diseases in the same way   the reduction of hazards
              that appropriate precau-
              tions against the hazards
              of nuclear weapons testing
              are related to nuclear
              weapons tests

              Because
                (B)
Both participate in the general relationship between precautions and the reduction of hazards

In most cases the analogical relation expressed in an argument from analogy will require a strongly qualifying "possibly."

Classification

In argument from classification the statement of the data is a generalized conclusion about known members of a class of persons, objects, events, or conditions. The warrant assumes that what is true of the items reported in the data will also be true of a hitherto unexamined item which is known (or thought) to fall within the class there described. The claim then transfers the general statement which has been made in the data to the particular item under consideration. As illustrated, the form would appear:

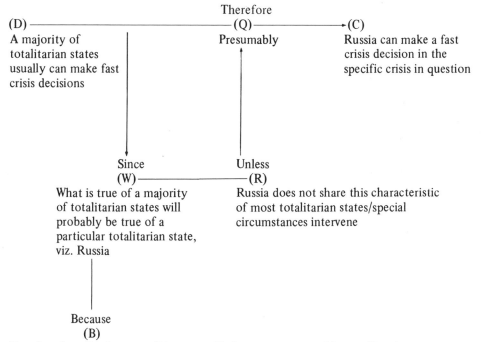

Two kinds of reservations may be applicable in an argument from classification: (1) a class member may not share the particular attribute cited in the data, although it does share enough other attributes to deserve delineation as a member of the class; and (2) special circumstances may prevent a specific class member from sharing at some particular time or place the attributes general to the class.

Authoritative Arguments

In authoritative arguments the data consist of one or more factual reports or statements of opinion. The warrant affirms the reliability of the source from which these are derived.

The claim reiterates the statement which appeared in the data, as now certified by the warrant. An illustration follows:

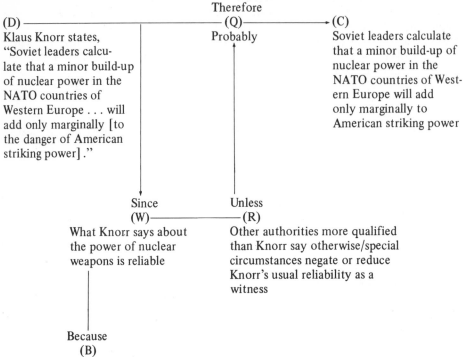

The structure and function of an authoritative argument remains basically the same when the source of the data is the speaker or writer himself. The data is carried to claim status by the same sort of assumption embodied in the warrant. We may infer a claim from what Knorr says about nuclear weapons whether he is himself the speaker, or whether another speaker is quoting what Knorr has said. Thus the *ethos* of a speaker may be studied by means of the Toulmin structure under the heading of authoritative argument.

Motivational Arguments

In motivational arguments the data consist of one or more statements which may have been established as claims in a previous argument or series of arguments. The warrant provides a motive for accepting the claim by associating it with some inner drive, value, desire, emotion, or aspiration, or with a combination of such forces. The claim as so warranted is that the person, object, event, or condition referred to in the data should be accepted as valuable or rejected as worthless, or that the policy there described should or should not be adopted, or the action there named should or should not be performed. Illustrated the form would appear:

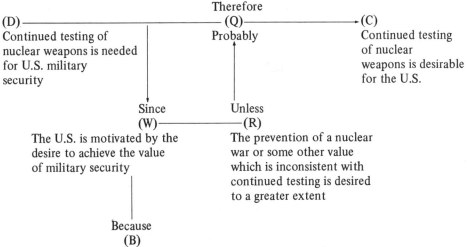

Military security is related to self-preservation, the maintenance of our high standard of living, patriotism, the preservation of democracy, etc.

4.

We have exhibited the structural unity of the three modes of artistic proof by showing how they may be reduced to a single invariant pattern using argument as a unifying construct. Let us as a final step explore this unity further by inquiring how artistic proofs, so reduced, may conveniently be correlated with the various types of disputable questions and the claims appropriate to each.

Let us begin by recognizing the four categories into which disputable questions have customarily been classified: (1) Whether something is? (2) What it is? (3) Of what worth it is? (4) What course of action should be pursued? The first of these queries gives rise to a question of *fact,* and is to be answered by what can be called a *designative claim;* the second, to a question of *definition,* to be answered by a *definitive claim;* the third, to a question of *value,* to be answered by an *evaluative claim;* and the fourth, to a question of *policy,* to be answered by an *advocative claim.*

Supposing, then, that an arguer is confronted with a question of fact, calling for a designative claim; or a question of policy, calling for an advocative claim, etc., what types of argument would be available to him as means of substantiating his claim statement? Upon the basis of the formulations developed in earlier sections of this paper, it is possible to supply rather precise answers.

Designative Claims

A designative claim, appropriate to answering a question of fact, will be found supportable by any of the six forms of substantive argument, or by authoritative argument, but not by motivational argument. That is, whether something exists or is so may be determined: (1) by isolating its cause or its effect (argument from cause); (2) by reasoning from the presence of symptoms to the claim that a substance exists or is so (argument from sign); (3) by inferring that because some members of a given class exist or are so, more members of the same class also exist or are so (argument from generalization); (4) by inferring because one item exists or is so, that a closely similar item exists or is so (argument from parallel case); (5) by reasoning that D exists or is so because it stands in the same relation to C that B does to A, when C, B, and A are known to exist or to be so (argument from analogy); and (6) by concluding that an unexamined item known or thought to fall within a given class exists or is so because all known members of the class exist or are so (argument from classification). Moreover, we may argue that something exists or is so because a reputable authority declares this to be the case. Motivational argument, on the other hand, may not be critically employed in designative claims, because values, desires, and feelings are irrelevant where questions of fact are concerned.

Definitive Claims

The possibilities for establishing definitive claims are more limited. Only two of the forms of substantive argument and authoritative argument are applicable. We may support a claim as to what something is: (1) by comparing it with a closely similar phenomenon (argument from parallel case); or (2) by reasoning that because it stands in the same relation to C as B does to A it will be analogous to C, where the nature of C, B, and A are known (argument from analogy). In addition, we may support a definition or interpretation by citing an acceptable authority. Among the substantive arguments, cause, sign, generalization, and classification are inapplicable; and once again motivational argument is irrelevant since emotions, wishes, and values cannot legitimately determine the nature of phenomena.

Evaluative Claims

Evaluative claims may be supported by generalization, parallel case, analogy, and classification, and by authoritative and motivational arguments. By generalization a class of phenomena may be declared valuable or worthless on the ground that a typical and adequate sample of the members of that class is so. By classification, in contrast, we infer from the worth of known members of a class the probable worth of some previously unexamined item known or thought to belong to that class. By parallel case, we infer goodness or badness from the quality of an item closely similar. By analogy, however, we infer value on the basis of a ratio of resemblances rather than a direct parallel. In authoritative argument our qualitative judgment is authorized by a recognized expert. In motivational argument, however, an item is assigned a value in accordance with its usefulness in satisfying human drives, needs, and aspirations. Arguments from cause and sign, on the other hand, are inapplicable.

Advocative Claims

Advocative claims may legitimately be established in only four ways. We may argue that some policy should be adopted or some action undertaken because a closely similar policy or action has brought desirable results in the past (argument from parallel case). We may support a proposed policy or action because it bears the same relation to C that B does to A, where B is known to have brought desirable results (argument from analogy). Or, of course, we may support our claim by testimony (authoritative argument), or by associating it with men's wishes, values, and aspirations (motivational argument).

This analysis concerning the types of arguments applicable to various sorts of claims may be summarized in tabular form:

	Designative	Definitive	Evaluative	Advocative
Substantive				
A. Cause	x			
B. Sign	x			
C. Generalization	x		x	
D. Parallel Case	x	x	x	x
E. Analogy	x	x	x	x
F. Classification	x		x	
Authoritative	x	x	x	x
Motivational			x	x

The world of argument is vast, one seemingly without end. Arguments arise in one realm, are resolved, and appear and reappear in others; and new arguments appear. If one assumes some rationality among men, a system of logical treatment of argument is imperative. The traditional logical system of syllogisms, of enthymemes, of middles distributed and undistributed, may have had its attraction in medieval times. The inadequacies of such a logic, however, have been described by experts; for example, see J. S. Mill on the syllogism and *petitio principii*.[7] The modern search has been for a method which would have some application in the dynamics of contemporary affairs.

Toulmin has supplied us with a contemporary methodology, which in many respects makes the traditional unnecessary. The basic theory has herein been amplified, some extensions have been made, and illustrations of workability have been supplied. All this is not meant to be the end, but rather the beginning of an inquiry into a new, contemporary, dynamic, and usable logic for argument.

Notes

1. E.g., such books as James M. O'Neill, Craven Laycock, and Robert L. Scales, *Argumentation and Debate* (New York, 1917); William T. Foster, *Argumentation and Debating* (Boston, 1917); and A.Craig Baird, *Public Discussion and Debate* (Boston, 1928); such articles as Mary Yost, "Argument from the Point of View of Sociology," *Quarterly Journal of Speech,* III (1917), 109-24; Charles H. Woolbert, "The Place of Logic in a System of Persuasion," *Quarterly Journal of Speech,* IV (1918), 19-39; Gladys Murphy Graham, "Logic and Argumentation," *Quarterly Journal of Speech,* X (1924), 350-63; William E. Utterback, "Aristotle's Contribution to the Psychology of Argument," *Quarterly Journal of Speech,* XI (1925), 218-25; Herbert A. Wichelns, "Analysis and Synthesis in Argumentation," *Quarterly Journal of Speech,* XI (1925), 266-72; and Edward Z. Rowell, "Prolegomena to Argumentation," *Quarterly Journal of Speech,* XVIII (1932), 1-13, 224-48, 381-405, 585-606; such Letters to the Editor as those by Utterback, XI (1925), 175-177; Wichelns, XI (1925), 286-88; Ralph C. Ringwalt, XII (1926), 66-68; and Graham, XII (1925), 196-97.

2. See, for example, Mortimer Adler, *Dialectic* (New York, 1927); Paul Edwards, *The Logic of Moral Discourse* (Glencoe, Ill., 1955); Carl I. Hovland, Irving L. Janis, and Harold W. Kelley, *Communication and Persuasion* (New Haven, 1953); Charles Perelman, *Traité de l'argumentation,* 2 vols. (Paris, 1958), and *La nouvelle rhétorique* (Paris, 1952); and John Cohen, "Subjective Probability," *Scientific American,* MCMVII (1957), 128-38.

3. (Cambridge: Cambridge University Press). See especially the third of the five essays in the book. Cf. J. C. Cooley, "On Mr. Toulmin's Revolution in Logic," *Journal of Philosophy,* LVI (1959), 297-319.

4. In traditional logic only the epicheirema provides comparable backing for premises.

5. It may be charged that his structural model is merely "a syllogism lying on its side," that it makes little or no provision to insure the formal validity of claims, etc.

6. Our suggestion as to the structural unity of artistic proofs is by no means novel. The ancients regularly spoke of *pathetic* and *ethical* enthymemes, and envisioned the *topoi* as applicable beyond the *pistis.* (See in this connection James H. McBurney, "The Place of the Enthymeme in Rhetorical Theory, *Speech Monograph,* III [1936], 63.) At the same time, however, it must be recognized that especially since the advent of the faculty psychology of the seventeenth and eighteenth centuries, rhetorical thought has been profoundly and persistently influenced by the doctrine of a dichotomy between little or no pathetic and logic appeals. (For significant efforts to combat this doctrine see Charles H. Woolbert, "Conviction and Persuasion: Some Considerations of Theory," *Quarterly Journal of Speech,* III [1917], 249-64; Mary Yost, "Arguments from the Point of View of Sociology," *Quarterly Journal of Speech,* III [1917], 109-24; and W. Norwood Brigance, "Can We Redefine the James-Winans Theory of Persuasion?" *Quarterly Journal of Speech,* XXI [1935], 19-26.)

7. *A System of Logic,* I, Chapter 3, Section 2.

Part Four

Language and Style

In "Toward a Definition of Style," the first article in this section, an individual's style is defined as "his *characteristic way of using the resources of the English language.*" This definition follows the novelist Flaubert's definition of style as a "way of looking at things." Our way of looking at things is in part determined by the nature of language itself, the media we choose for our expression (oral or written discourse), our relationship with others sharing the communicative event, and our unique psychological makeup as it combines with content, purpose and situation.

In "The Encoding of Speech and Writing," Joseph DeVito explores some of the causitive factors for the differences between the styles of oral and written discourse. They are largely: capacities for review and limitations of feedback, differences in the nature of media used, degrees of permanency, strains of constructing sentences, and pressures to avoid redundancy.

Clearly, however, oral and written dimensions are not the only dimensions relevant to a discussion of stylistic differences—"levels of usage" also help to account for the fact that one speaker speaks in a different style from another. To some extent this has basically to do with the personal relationship between the speaker and listener or the writer and reader. Martin Joos, for example, suggests that there are five styles of English ranging from the very formal to the very informal: frozen, formal, consultative, casual, and intimate.[1] A person using each of these five styles might sound like this as he says essentially the same thing to different listeners:

> Frozen: In my opinion he is not the man whom we want.
> Formal: I believe he is not the man we are looking for.
> Consultative: I don't believe he's the man we're looking for.
> Casual: I don't think he's our man.
> Intimate: 'Fraid you've picked a lemon.[2]

In the next article in this section, "A Language Within a Language," Professor Albert Mehrabian discusses the subtleties of language itself "that are a part of the expression of feelings, evaluations, and preferences." He attempts to demonstrate how "stylistic differences of the sentences selected to express a certain idea can be used to infer (1) feelings toward the thing being described, (2) feelings toward the listener, or (3) feelings about the act of saying certain things to a certain listener."

Holding to the assumption that "people seek out and get involved with things they like and they try to minimize their relationship, or if possible, entirely avoid contact with things they dislike or fear," Mehrabian explores the several features (which he labels "nonimmediacy" forms) that are available in language to reflect a speaker's negative feelings.

Emphasizing the concept of *context,* he draws some analogies between the non-immediacy forms of verbal and nonverbal messages. He argues that the listener can make "accurate estimates of the speaker's feelings" if he has accurate knowledge of the context in which the speaker makes those statements.

Even oral-written dimensions, interpersonal relationships and situational dimensions will not account for uniqueness of a given individual's style. J. Middleton Murry in *The Problem of Style* suggests some of what would account for this uniqueness. He defines style as: ". . . a quality of language which communicates precisely emotions or thoughts, or a system of emotions of thoughts, peculiar to the author."[3] Charles Osgood, in exploring some effects of motivation on style of encoding, comments: Style *"is defined as an individual's deviations from norms for the situations in which he is encoding, these deviations being in the statistical properties of those structural features for which there exists some degree of choice in his code."*[4] Hugh Blair aptly puts it: Style "is the peculiar manner in which a man expresses his conceptions by means of language. . . . Style has always some reference to an author's manner of thinking. It is a picture of ideas which arise in his mind, and of the manner in which they rise there."[5] All of these writers would, thus, agree that style reflects not only matter and purpose but also the psychological makeup of the speaker/writer. There is no small measure of truth to J. A. K. Thomson's comment that to write like Caesar, one must be Caesar.[6]

"You persuade a man only insofar as you speak his language . . . ," writes Kenneth Burke.[7] The speaker talks the audience's "language" through the evidence and arguments he uses, through his large-scale linguistic strategies (for example, the pervasive metaphor of birth and rebirth in the "Gettysburg Address"), through his specific language choices, and through the nonverbal cues he presents. Style, thus viewed, is intimately associated with content and operates as a means of persuasion as surely as does content.

Notes

1. Martin Joos, *The Five Clocks: A Linguistic Excursion into the Five Styles of English Usage* (New York: Harcourt, Brace & World, Inc., paperback edition, 1967).

2. Albert Marckwardt, *Linguistics and the Teaching of English* (Bloomington: University of Indiana Press, 1966), p. 40.

3. J. Middleton Murry, *The Problem of Style* (London: Oxford University Press, 1961), p. 65.

4. Charles E. Osgood, "Some Effects of Motivation on Style of Encoding," in Thomas Seboek, ed., *Style in Language* (Cambridge, Mass.: MIT Press, 1960), p. 293.

5. Hugh Blair, *Lectures on Rhetoric and Belles Lettres* (London, 1783), pp. 101-2.

6. J. A. K. Thomson, *Classical Influences on English Prose* (London: Allen & Unwin, 1956).

7. Kenneth Burke, *A Rhetoric of Motives* (Berkeley: University of California Press), p. 55.

TOWARD A DEFINITION OF STYLE

JANE BLANKENSHIP

Style is not an easy concept to discuss. We hear of "good" and "bad" prose style, of expository and narrative style, of "the eighteenth-century style," and of styles in architecture and clothing. One of novelist Ayn Rand's characters even speaks of "the style of a soul."

This book is concerned with style *in language,* but even limited in this way the concept remains elusive. Thus, the first problem is of definition: What *is* style?

The usual Greek word for style, *lexis,* carried with it the three connotations of thought, word (*logos*), and speaking (*legein*). This original meaning, encompassing thought, word, and the expression of word, is a useful one to remember.

Since the ancient Greeks hundreds of definitions have been offered for the term "style," from that of Jonathan Swift—"proper words in proper places"—to that of the French naturalist, Georges Buffon—"Style is the man himself." The first definition perhaps tells us what is good (proper) style but not what style itself is. The second, though more interesting, is so broad it provides no real starting place. The equation *style equals individual man* suggests that if we know the nature of the individual we will know how he uses language, that we gain insight into the man by paying careful attention to the language he uses. These stimulating suggestions, however, also provide no real starting point.

Stephen Ullmann, in *Language and Style,* gives us a beginning when he says that style is "primarily a personal and idiosyncratic mode of vision"[1]—*what* a man "sees," his vision, and *how* he sees, his mode of vision. That is why the French novelist Gustave Flaubert could say that style is a "way of looking at things."[2] In this book we are concerned with how one characteristically communicates his vision of things.

How different is the concept of style as the "garment" of thought,[3] that after one has decided what to say he then decides how to say it. Flaubert once retorted: "These fellows stick to an old comparison: form is a cloak. No indeed! form is the very flesh of thought...."[4] Thus, language and thought are inextricably associated. As Richard Ohmann says, in *Shaw: The Style and the Man:*

> The very many decisions that add up to a style are decisions about what to say, as well as how to say it. They reflect the [speaker's] organization of experience, his sense of life, so that the most general of his attitudes and ideas find expression just as characteristically in his style as in his matter....[5]

Style, then, is not just peripheral ornament added to a speech already thought through; style and content are organically related.

An individual's style is his *characteristic way of using the resources of the English language.* The style of the language consists of all the *regular* features of the language. For example, in English we say "the red rose" but in French *la rose rouge* [the rose red]. The style of the English language is for adjectival modifiers to precede the noun they modify, whereas in French they often follow the noun.[6] One cannot really manipulate that feature of either language and still be said to be speaking English or French.

Yet, although a speaker is restricted by the fact of conforming to the style of English, there are many variations from any given stylistic norm. In his *De duplici copia verborum ac rerum,* Erasmus lists 150 ways of phrasing the Latin sentence *Tuae literae me magnopere delectarunt* [Your letters have delighted me very much]; for example, "On reading your letters, I was filled with joy," and "Your letters provided me with no little pleasure." Notice the slight differences not only in word choice but also in syntax.

When describing a person going down the street, Speaker A might say, "Jack hurried down the street an hour ago and waved as he passed by." Speaker B might say, "Jack, hurrying down the street an hour ago, waved as he passed." Speaker C: "Hurrying down the street an hour ago, Jack waved as he passed by." All three speakers have stayed within the style of the language, but each has manipulated that style to suit his own way of speaking. That the three speakers use different syntax once, or even occasionally, does not mean those syntactical possibilities are distinctive styles, but when one speaker habitually uses a particular syntactical possibility it becomes a part of his *own* style. Dr. Samuel Johnson, for instance, habitually used parallel and antithetical clauses, according to W. K. Wimsatt, and these devices reflected a persistent habit of mind. As Wimsatt says, "Johnson's prose style is a formal exaggeration—in places a caricature—of a certain pair of complementary drives, the drive to assimilate ideas, and the drive to distinguish them—to collect and to separate."[7]

Whether used in the style of the language or of an individual, language categorizes and organizes experience. That language "categorizes experience" means simply that a word acts much like a picture of an object in a mail-order catalog; both word and picture "catalog" or "represent" objects.

We should note here the relationship between the word and the thing—object, event, or process—it "represents." Words represnt things because they produce some replica of the way we have felt, thought, or acted toward the things they refer to. Thus, in talking about things, we have conceptions of them but not the things themselves. And it is the *conceptions,* not the things, *that words directly "mean."*[8] Notice in the Erasmus example above that one reaction to receiving the letters was joy and the other was pleasure. Although *joy* and *pleasure* are sometimes synonymous, one may experience pleasure without at the same time experiencing joy; joy categorizes (or names) one feeling and pleasure another.

Style is not only the *selection* of words but also their combination.[9] It has to do not only with categorizing experience (word choice) but also with organizing it (syntax). Consider these four possible variations of Thomas Paine's "These are the times that try men's souls":

Times like these try men's souls.
How trying it is to live in times like these!
These are trying times for men's souls.
Soulwise, these are trying times.[10]

Although there are slight differences of word choice, the emphasis shifts mainly because the *order* of words changes.

To illustrate more fully the definition of style we began with—style as a personal and idiosyncratic mode of vision—let us look at two versions of the Gettysburg Address, the first as delivered by Abraham Lincoln, the second as another speaker might have given it.[11] We shall try to determine *what* each speaker "saw" and *how* he "saw" it, in short, at the manner in which people express their way of "looking at" things.

THE GETTYSBURG ADDRESS

Version One:
Delivered by
Abraham Lincoln,
November 19, 1863

Version Two:
As It Might Have
Been Delivered by
Another Speaker

Four score and seven years ago our fathers brought forth on this continent, a new nation, conceived in liberty, and dedicated to the proposition that all men are created equal. Now we are engaged in a great civil war, testing whether that nation, or any nation so conceived and so dedicated, can long endure. We are met on a great battlefield of that war. We have come to dedicate a portion of that field, as a final resting place for those who here gave their lives, that that nation might live. It is altogether fitting and proper that we should do this. But, in a larger sense, we can not dedicate—we can not consecrate—we can not hallow—this ground. The brave men, living and dead, who struggled here have consecrated it, far above our poor power to add or detract. The world will little note, nor long remember what we say here, but it can never forget what they did here. It is for us the living, rather, to be dedicated here to the unfinished work which they who fought here have thus far so nobly advanced. It is rather for us to be here dedicated to the great task remaining before us—that from these honored dead we take increased devotion to that cause for which they gave the last full measure of devotion—that we here highly resolve that these dead shall not have died in vain—that this nation, under God, shall have a new birth of freedom—and that government of the people, by the people, for the people, shall not perish from the earth.

Eighty-seven years ago those who came before us established in this country a system of government originated in freedom and based on the idea of the equality of all people. Now there is a battle being waged to decide whether a governmental setup originated and based in such a way can last very long. We are here at one of the scenes of that conflict. We have gathered together to pay tribute to those loved ones who made the supreme sacrifice on this spot to support this government. It is absolutely right for us to do this. But, if you look at the overall picture, we can't pay any tribute, we can't sanctify, we can't hallow this particular area. It was those courageous men, both those who lived and those who died here, who have lent this religious character to this field. The rest of the world will not remember any statements we issue here, but it will never forget their brave deeds here. Our job, the living individuals' job, here is to continue to bear the burden which they made such a big initial effort for. Instead we should decide right here and now to carry out the remainder of the job, and from these deceased, fine individuals to take extra inspiration from those theories to which they were so dedicated, that we make up our minds right here and now that they didn't die without cause, that this government, with the help of God, shall experience a renewed spirit of freedom and that the government of all individuals, by all individuals, and for all individuals, shall not vanish from the world scene.

Listed below are some student responses to the two versions. You might like to add some of your own.

1. *"Fourscore and seven years ago our fathers . . ."*
    "Eighty-seven years ago those who came before us . . ."

    The first has a biblical sound, as illustrated by both "fourscore and seven" and "fathers" rather than "forefathers."
    Both "our" and "fathers" are personal. They both point to a link between past-present.
    The second passage is matter of fact; it is not personal. There is no particular link between past-present indicated.

2. *". . . brought forth on this continent a new nation . . ."*
    ". . . established in this country a system of government . . ."

    The first passage contains a metaphor of birth; no such metaphor is suggested by "establish."
    Passage one stresses "newness." "Nation" carries (at least for some) an emotional connotation.
    "System of government" is only part of a nation. There is little emotional attachment to "government."

3. *". . . conceived in liberty and dedicated to the proposition that all men are created equal."*
    ". . . originated in freedom and based on the idea of the equality of all people."

    The first passage continues the metaphor of birth.
    "Proposition" implies both a sense of resolution and something to be tested.
    "Based on" is not the same thing as "dedicated to."
    ". . . that all men are created equal" does not say the same thing as "the equality of all people."
    "Men" is more personal than "people."

4. *"Now we are engaged in a great civil war, testing whether that nation, . . . so conceived and so dedicated can long endure."*
    "Now there is a battle being waged to decide whether a governmental setup originated and based in such a way can last very long."

    The first passage employs the personal "we."
    The speaker is talking about a "civil war" and not just "a battle."
    "Engaged" is a word referring to personal participation. "Waged" merely says that it is taking place, without any connotation of personal participation.
    Again "nation" versus "governmental setup."

The metaphor of birth versus "originated."

"Dedicated" is repeated in the first.

Notice that the first speaker does not say "can endure long" but rather "can long endure," emphasizing length of endurance, not the endurance itself (as implied in version two).

5. *"We are met on a great battlefield of that war."*
   "We are here at one of the scenes of that conflict."

   "Great" is repeated by the first speaker. Thus, there is a sense of importance attached to the battlefield being dedicated which is not afforded by the second speaker's "one of the scenes."

   It is a "war." "Conflict" lessens the importance of what is occurring.

6. *"We have come to dedicate a portion of that field, as a final resting place for those who here gave their lives, that that nation might live."*
   "We have gathered together to pay tribute to those loved ones who made the supreme sacrifice on this spot to support this government."

   Passage one again utilizes "dedicate." One can "pay tribute" without a sense of dedication.

   "Gave their lives" is direct and implicit, "made the supreme sacrifice" is not. They *did* die.

   Again, the choice of "nation" versus "government."

7. *"It is altogether fitting and proper that we should do this."*
   "It is absolutely right for us to do this."

   "Fitting and proper" is not the same as "right."

   "We" makes the dedication more personal.

8. *"But, in a larger sense, we can not dedicate—we can not consecrate—we can not hallow—this ground."*
   "But, if you look at the overall picture, we can't pay any tribute, we can't santify, we can't hallow this particular area."

   "Overall picture" is a colloquial expression not suited to the seriousness and theme of the occasion. "Can not" is less colloquial than "can't."

   "Dedicate" and "consecrate" are repeated again in the first passage.

   "Ground" is more definite and concrete than "area." Further, there is a tradition of devotion to particular bits of "ground" that the word "area" lacks.

9. *"The brave men, living and dead, who struggled here have consecrated it, far above our poor power to add or detract."*
   "It was those courageous men, both those who lived and those who died here, who have lent this religious character to this field."

Contrast·here the compactness of the first passage with the diffuseness of the second passage; for example, "living and dead" with "both those who lived and those who died."

Passage one is much more definitely rhythmic than passage two.

Passage one says *more* than passage two.

To "consecrate" is not necessarily the same as to give a "religious character" to the battlefield.

"Lent" suggests that the consecration is a temporary thing.

A sense of humility is suggested ("our poor power") in the first passage; it is lacking in the second passage.

10. *"The world will little note, nor long remember what we say here, but it can never forget what they did here."*
    "The rest of the world will not remember any statements we issue here, but it will never forget their brave deeds here."

"World" is still more all-inclusive than "rest of the world."

Orders are "issued."

Emphasis in version one is on the audience receiving the message.

Emphasis in version two is on the people "issuing" statements.

"Can" is stronger than "will." It suggests that, whether people want to forget or not, they will be unable to.

"What they did" is simpler and therefore more impressive than the more grandiose "brave deeds."

11. *"It is for the living, rather, to be dedicated here to the unfinished work which they who fought here have thus far so nobly advanced."*
    "Our job, the living individuals' job, here is to continue to bear the burden which they made such a big initial effort for."

"It is for us, rather, to be dedicated" emphasizes the "us," that is, the people involved. (Note the different emphasis which would have been attached to this passage had the speaker said: "It is rather for us . . . .")

The first speaker does not suggest that the work is a "burden" as the second speaker does.

The second passage leaves out the fighting.

"Big efforts" may or may not be "noble."

"Have thus far . . . advanced" implies something already begun. "Unfinished" explicitly suggests that it is not completed. A sense of continuity is stressed in the first version. It is not particularly evident in the second.

12. *"It is rather for us to be here dedicated to the great task remaining before us . . ."*
    "Instead we should decide right here and now to carry out the remainder of the job . . ."

Dedication is more than simple decision.

"Great task" attaches greater significance to the action than "job."

"Decide right here and now" is too colloquial for such a formal occasion.

13. *". . . that from these honored dead we take increased devotion to that cause for which they gave the last full measure of devotion . . ."*

". . . and from these deceased, fine individuals to take extra inspiration from those same theories to which they were so dedicated . . ."

"Dead" is simpler than "deceased, fine individuals." Further, to be worthy of honor is more than being merely "fine."

"We" makes the first passage more personal.

"Cause" is more than mere "theories."

"These honored dead" has a more collective connotation than "these deceased, fine individuals."

People can be "inspired" without being devoted.

"Last full measure of devotion" is rather poetic.

14. *". . . that we here highly resolve that these dead shall not have died in vain . . ."*

". . . that we make up our minds right here and now that they didn't die without cause. . . ."

"Resolve" is much stronger than "make up our minds."

15. *". . . that this nation, under God, shall have a new birth of freedom . . ."*

". . . that this government, with the help of God, shall experience a renewed spirit of freedom . . ."

"Nation" versus "government."

The birth metaphor appears again in the first version of the speech.

"Under God" is not precisely the same as "with the help of God."

16. *". . . and that government of the people, by the people, for the people, shall not perish from the earth."*

". . . and that the government of all individuals, by all individuals, and for all individuals shall not vanish from the world scene."

Something which "perishes" ceases to exist completely; that which "vanishes" disappears but not necessarily ceases to exist.

"Earth" is simple, direct, and meaningful. "World scene" is not as clear or as meaningful.

"The people" is unifying; "all individuals" is not.

Let us summarize the major features of the first version that are missing, and significantly so, from the second version.

1. The metaphor of birth and rebirth, around which the speech is built, is missing in the second version.
2. The first version is infinitely more personal than the second.
3. *Dedication* appears six times and *nation* five times in the first version; neither appears in the second.
4. The unifying threads, the sense of continuity between generations, living and dead, are more explicit, more clear in the first version.
5. The first version is a resolution, and all that goes before the actual statement of the resolution is by way of preamble.
6. The first version shows much more definite rhythm than does the second.
7. The first version is a highly sophisticated example of the reiterative pattern—alliteration, assonance, repetition of key words, and parallel structure. The second version is much more loosely constructed.

What we have tried to demonstrate in analyzing these two versions of the Gettysburg Address is that two men, asked to give the same speech, reveal, *by their word choice and their syntactic patterns,* two entirely different views of the same moment. Both draw from the same pool of resources; that is, both speak the same language. However, their different ways of using that language reveal not merely a different set of techniques, but a different *mode of vision.* This inquiry, then, tends to substantiate Cardinal Newman's definition of style as "a thinking out into language."[12] which necessarily reveals what we see of the world and how we see it. Because the speaker's style reflects his unique way of responding to the world, it is, like that of the painter, "a question not of technique, but of vision."[13]

Summary

Despite the difficulty of defining the concept, our definition of style—as one's characteristic way of using the resources of the English language—is useful when we consider the question: How may we make our own style more *effective*?

Style involves *selection* and *combination* of words, and because they are organically related to content, a speaker's choice and arrangement of words reveal something about his view of the world. Seneca's comment—"Language most shews a man. Speak that I may know thee"—is therefore important to remember.

Notes

1. Stephen Ullmann, *Language and Style* (New York: Barnes & Noble, Inc., 1964), p. 201.

2. As quoted by Walther von Wartburg, *Evolution et structure de la langue française,* 4th ed. (Berne: A. Franche, 1949), p. 226.

3. For example, Samuel Johnson: "Language is the dress of thought." Also see Lord Chesterfield's consideration of style as the "dress of thoughts."

4. As quoted in Ullmann, op. cit., p. 151. Also, Carlyle wrote in *Sartor Resartus:* "Language is called the garment of thought; however, it should rather be, language is the flesh-garment, the body of thought."

5. Richard Ohmann, *Shaw: The Style and the Man* (Middletown, Conn.: Wesleyan University Press, 1962), p. xii.

6. Occasionally, in these instances if the modifier is placed *before* the word, it changes the meaning of it.

7. W. K. Wimsatt, Jr., *The Prose Style of Samuel Johnson* (New Haven: Yale University Press, 1941), p. viii.

8. Charles E. Osgood, *Method and Theory in Experimental Psychology* (New York: Oxford University Press, 1953).

9. Roman Jakobson and Morris Halle, *Fundamental of Language* (The Hague: Mouton & Co., 1956), p. 60.

10. William Strunk, Jr., and E. B. White, *The Elements of Style* (New York: Macmillan Company, 1962), p. 53.

11. This author composed the second version, occasionally borrowing phrases from the version written by Oliver Jensen. For Jensen's version, see Jane Blankenship, *Public Speaking: A Rhetorical Perspective* (Englewood Cliffs, N.J.: Prentice-Hall, Inc., 1966), pp. 101-102.

12. John Henry Newman, "Literature," in *Representative Essays in the Theory of Style,* ed. William T. Brewster (New York: Macmillan Company, 1921). First published 1905.

13. Marcel Proust, as quoted in Ullmann, *Language and Style,* op. cit., p. 121.

THE ENCODING OF SPEECH AND WRITING

JOSEPH A. DeVITO

Almost 2300 years ago, Aristotle wrote that "each kind of rhetoric has its own appropriate style. The style of written prose is not that of spoken oratory."[1] Today, speech textbooks, such as those by Bryant and Wallace[2] and Brigance,[3] continue to emphasize this distinction. A knowledge of the differences between oral and written language is regarded as a fundamental objective of speech instruction.[4]

In the recent past, a number of articles concerned with these differences in style have appeared and seem to be of two general types. The first type is that of *prescription.* These articles, much like modern textbooks, present analyses of differences between listening and reading and, on these bases, prescribe rules which a speaker must follow if his message is to be understood. Because "there is little opportunity for the listener to ponder over a word or phrase," as Mahaffey[5] put it, the speaker is advised to make his message instantly intelligible—a notion which can be found in Campbell,[6] Blair,[7] Genung,[8] and Phillips[9] as well as in more recent texts.[10] In a more recent article, Burnshaw[11] approached this question in essentially the same way as did Mahaffey and the various textbook writers.

The second type of articles is that of *description.* The often cited study by Borchers[12] and the more recent one by Blankenship[13] have been of this general type. These writers sought to describe the differences that do in fact exist. Dissertations by Bushnell,[14] Kaump,[15] Sterrett,[16] and Green[17] were likewise concerned with a description of the differences between oral and written language.

A teacher of speech, however, encounters some difficulty in his attempt to apply the results of such studies to classroom teaching. Since he knows what differences *do* exist as well as what differences *should* exist, he is generally able to evaluate and criticize the

Joseph A. DeVito, "The Encoding of Speech and Writing," *Speech Teacher* (January 1966), pp. 55-60. By permission of Speech Communication Association and the author.

communicator's product, whether it be his speech or his written composition. Since a teacher seldom knows why such differences between oral and written language occur, he is somewhat at a loss in guiding the actual process of communication. It is, of course, always easier to provide direction and guidance for a process when we know the course it normally and perhaps unconsciously follows and why it follows one course rather than another.

In a study designed to determine the differences between oral and written language, I found the following to be statistically significant:[18]

1. Written language contained more different words.[19]
2. Written language contained more difficult words.[20]
3. Written language contained more simple sentences.[21]
4. Written language contained greater idea density.[22]

In this essay, I shall attempt to postulate possible causative factors for these differences. Since rigorous analysis often consists in a restatement and systematization of more-or-less random observations, no apology is offered for the thoughts which may appear to be obvious and intuitive.

I

The reasons for greater verbal diversity in written language do not seem difficult to find. One of the most obvious distinctions between the encoding processes of speaking and writing is that of time. Speaking is at least five times faster than writing. The writer has time to choose his words; he may merely pause for a moment to think of an appropriate word or he may consult a dictionary, a thesaurus, or perhaps a colleague. The speaker does not have this option. He must find the appropriate word almost immediately or use a less appropriate but more readily available one. While he may pause for a moment or two, the time during which he may remain silent is severely limited by the nature of the speaking situation. This pressure on the time the speaker may take to compose his communication forces him to repeat words. He may also repeat various phrases in order to fill in the silence while he is thinking of the next idea or perhaps while he is searching for a particular word.

Closely related to this is the fact that a writer may review the entire text of what he has already written; the speaker may review only what he can recall from memory. Hence, his span as well as his accuracy of recall is much less than the writer's. Also, the time available for review is severely limited for the speaker while it is almost without limit for the writer. A speaker may not only be unable to recall the specific words he used but he may also fail to recall, for example, the number of the subject or the tense of the verb with which he started. This, it would seem, is one of the reasons why grammatical errors are more common in oral discourse. Bushnell, for instance, found that an average of 6.6 errors per 100 words were made in oral composition and only 2.7 in written composition.[23]

In other words, because of the difference in the encoding process, the writer is afforded a choice, either to repeat the same words or to choose different ones; the speaker, by virtue of the time factor and the limitations of feedback, has less choice.

The direction in which we might expect the differences in speaking and writing to manifest themselves is only partially dependent on the nature of the encoding processes involved; social factors or conventions also exert an influence on the way in which such choices are made. In English, variety rather than sameness seems to be esteemed. In this regard, Jespersen's observation is noted:

> Even where there is no real difference in the value of two words or whether the difference is momentarily disregarded, their existence may not be entirely worthless, as it enables an author to avoid a trivial repetition of the same word, and variety of expression is generally considered one of the felicities of style.[24]

Although variety is also a quality of good speech, even though it is not esteemed as much as in writing, there seems to be greater verbal diversity in writing, partly because the writer has the opportunity for greater verbal diversity and, in conformity to accepted standards, chooses to vary his expression.

Still another important reason why verbal diversity is greater in written discourse is found in the nature of the media utilized in speaking and in writing. Speech, as is obvious, utilizes sound and sound waves as its medium while writing utilizes printed symbols and light waves as its medium. As Francis pointed out, communication depends on the various types of contrasts afforded by the media for its effect.[25] These sets of contrasts are, of course, different for speech and writing.[26] In speech, the most obvious and probably the most important is the contrast between sound and silence. Other contrasts which are employed are those between noise and musical sound, between the varied and numerous tonal colors, between high and low and rising and falling pitch, and between loud and soft volume. In writing, on the other hand, the most fundamental contrast is between a visible shape, i.e., letters or characters, and a plain surface, i.e., a blank space. Other contrasts which may be employed are those in shape, size, intensity, color, and position.

Although the fundamental contrast in speech, between sound and silence, seems to correspond most accurately to the basic contrast in writing, between visible shape and plain surface, even it is not completely faithful. The other contrasts in speech have even less accurate counterparts in the contrasts in writing.

If information is communicated, at least in part, by utilizing the various contrasts offered in the different media and since these contrasts are not directly comparable, it seems logical to assume that additional compensatory factors are introduced. And these additional factors would influence style, particularly verbal diversity.

In most traditional systems of writing, there is no machinery for indicating various relevant features of speech. English, for example, has no convention for indicating intonation. The information which is carried by stress and intonation is either lost in writing or it is carried by certain morphemes of other kinds.

Gleason provided an excellent example which illustrates this loss and the subsequent compensation. A reporting of a dialogue may take the form of "so he said . . . so he said. . . ." The utterances intervening will carry intonation which will approximate those appearing in the original dialogue and will thereby convey the emotional tone. But in a literary report "said" would have to be replaced by such verbs as "shouted," "exclaimed," "snapped," "growled," and various others. "Each of these, in effect," said Gleason, "can be analyzed as carrying two functions: One (the denotation) is to replace "said," the other (the connotation) is to portray the emotional tone of the utterance reported."[27]

Daniel Jones, the British phonetician, expressed essentially the same notion:

> Most of the shades of meaning that speech is capable of conveying by the above means [stress, intonation, *et cetera*] are either incapable of expression in writing or can be expressed only by added words or by alterations of wording.[28]

This phenomenon, of course, occurs with great frequency in everyday speech and writing. In reporting to someone that an individual is extremely sick, we might say: "He is sick," with primary emphasis on the verb *is*. In writing, however, "He is sick" is extremely inadequate because he is sicker than just "sick." So in writing, it might appear as "He sure is sick," or "He is deathly sick." Here the adverb compensates for the loss of the emphasis used in speaking. Although there are various devices which may be employed in print (capitals, italics, et cetera) in order to have the written version correspond more closely to the oral form, there is no one-to-one correspondence.

Changes in emotional tone, while capable of expression in speech by stress and intonation, can be expressed in writing through using words of varying connotations or by using additional words, each of which will lead to greater verbal diversity.

It appears, then, that verbal diversity is greater in written language than in oral because of the differences in the encoding processes involved, principally the temporal difference, and because of differences in the media and the sets of contrasts which they may make available.

II

As verbal diversity seems to be determined by the nature of the encoding process as well as by various external factors so, it appears, is vocabulary difficulty. In the discussion of diversity, it was pointed out that the speaker is under greater pressures of time than is the writer. In addition to repeating various words, the speaker is forced to rely on the words he uses most frequently since these are the ones which will come to mind most readily. Zipf has shown that frequency of usage bears an inverse relationship to the length of words. "The magnitude of words tends, on the whole," said Zipf, "to stand in an inverse (not necessarily proportionate) relationship to the number of occurrences."[29] The relationship of length to difficulty has, of course, been demonstrated in the numerous studies conducted by readability researchers. And the more direct relationship between frequency and difficulty has also been demonstrated by researchers in readability and has been the principal assumption in the construction of word lists such as that by Thorndike and Lorge.[30]

But again, external factors also exert an influence. One of the most obvious differences between speech and writing is that writing is permanent, whereas, unless recorded, speech fades rapidly. This quality of permanence enables written language to be read and reread any number of times by any number of people; consequently, it provides a convenient and readily accessible indication of an individual's knowledge or ability. In fact, according to André Martinet, this is the principal reason for differences between oral and written style:

> The chief reason why people do not write as they speak is probably that since writing leaves permanent traces, whereas speech unless recorded is lost forever, writers are far more careful than speakers. . . . Consequently, written style is not spoken style.[31]

The particular end to which this extra effort is directed is probably a function of a number of factors. One of the principal ones is obviously the type of publication in which the written discourse is to appear. In academic and scholarly journals, for example, simplicity of vocabulary is not regarded as the highest virtue.

This tendency toward vocabulary difficulty in written discourse is well summarized in an anecdote supplied by Phelps:

> An eminent German philosopher is said to have rewritten some pages of his manuscript in the revision of it for the press, because, upon reading them to a company of friends, he found them intelligible at a single hearing. He recast those pages into a more recondite diction on the grounds that, if his meaning were so obvious as to be understood by a hearer, the class of readers whom he aimed to reach would not deem his work worthy of their notice.[32]

III

The postulation of probable causes for the significantly greater number of simple sentences in written language is difficult since sentence structure appears to be a function of so many variables. There seems, however, to be a tendency in speaking to amplify and qualify various phrases and assertions whereas in writing such added verbiage is eliminated in revising the copy. As Blair said, "in books, we look for . . . all redundancies pruned, all repetitions avoided. . . ."[33]

In speaking, such phrases as "I think" or "it seems to me" are frequent and, of course, add to sentence complexity. In writing for publication, such self-references are generally avoided. Frye vividly illustrated this tendency to use "filler phrases":

> The strain of constructing prose sentences is clearly marked even in the speech of the most articulate people. That is to say, the point I want to make is, all of us use, sort of, filler phrases to conceal our nervousness, or something, in working out our, you know, sentence structure.[34]

While there has been some experimental research on sentence construction and the way in which the context of the speaking event influences the types of sentences used,[35] there seems to be no evidence concerning the ways in which sentences are constructed in oral as opposed to written discourse. This is an area which obviously requires a great deal more study.[36]

IV

The reasons for greater density of ideas in written language appear to be due to the fact that there is a certain pressure on the writer to avoid redundancies and repetitions and to incorporate as many ideas as possible into the fewest possible words. This task of the writer, who to Joos is really a "rewriter," is interestingly explained in the following analogy:

> The rewriter is as one who packs his thought for a long journey. Having packed the garment, he does not merely straighten out the folds and close the paragraph. Instead, he unpacks completely and repacks again. And again; and again and again. Each time, he tucks just one more thought into this or that pocket. When he quits, there are more of them than of words. So many labors of love on a single sentence, that many rewards for the rereader. On the surface, one teasing half-reward; others at successively greater and greater depths, so that each reading finds one more.[37]

But even if the speaker attempted to pack more thoughts than words into his discourse, he could not possibly succeed to the degree that the writer might. And this is so because it takes time to pack so many thoughts—time which is unavailable to the speaker. As Joos explained it: "The rewards will lie at successive depths only if they were packed into the text in successive repackings. That is simply the kind of wits we have."[38]

The reasons for differences in vocabulary diversity and difficulty, sentence complexity, and idea density in oral and written language which were discussed here are obviously not the only possible or plausible ones which might be advanced. They do, however, seem reasonable and it is likely that they play at least some part in the resulting stylistic differences.

Researchers and teachers of speech appear to have focused too long solely on the product of communication. Although such an orientation has obvious heuristic as well as practical values, I suggest that greater energy directed to the analysis and description of the process of communication would yield more and significant insights into our principal concern—teaching speech.

Notes

1. Aristotle, *Rhetoric,* trans. W. Rhys Roberts, 1403[b] 15-17, *The Rhetoric and Poetics of Aristotle,* ed. Friedrich Solmsen (New York: Modern Library, 1954).

2. Donald C. Bryant and Karl R. Wallace, *Fundamentals of Public Speaking,* 3rd ed. (New York: Appleton-Century-Crofts, 1960), pp. 264-67.

3. William Norwood Brigance, *Speech: Its Techniques and Disciplines in a Free Society* (New York: Appleton-Century-Crofts, 1952), p. 307.

4. Speech Association of America, Interest Group: Speech in the Secondary School, "Fundamentals of Speech: A Basic Course for High Schools," *Speech Teacher,* 8:2 (March 1959), p. 103.

5. Joseph H. Mahaffey, "The Oral Mode," *Speech Teacher,* 5:3 (September 1956), p. 196.

6. George Campbell, *The Philosophy of Rhetoric,* ed. Lloyd F. Bitzer (Carbondale: Southern Illinois University Press, 1963), bk. III, ch. 2, p. 338.

7. Hugh Blair, *Lectures on Rhetoric and Belles Lettres,* 6th ed. (London: A. Strahan, 1796), vol. 2, pp. 437-38.

8. John F. Genung, *The Practical Elements of Rhetoric* (Boston: Ginn and Company, 1896), p. 77.

9. Arthur Edward Phillips, *Effective Speaking* (Chicago: Newton, 1908), p. 181.

10. Cf., e.g., Eugene E. White and Clair R. Henderlider, *Practical Public Speaking: A Guide to Effective Communication* (New York: Macmillan Company, 1954), p. 262; Brigance, p. 307.

11. Stanley Burnshaw, "Speaking Versus Writing," *Today's Speech,* 6:3 (September 1958), p. 18.

12. Gladys Borchers, "An Approach to the Problem of Oral Style," *Quarterly Journal of Speech,* 22:1 (February 1936), pp. 114-17; see also Gladys Borchers, "A Study of Oral Style," unpublished Ph.D. dissertation (University of Wisconsin, 1927).

13. Jane Blankenship, "A Linguistic Analysis of Oral and Written Style," *Quarterly Journal of Speech,* 48:4 (December 1962), pp. 419-22; see also Fanny Jane Blankenship, "A Linguistic Analysis of Selected Samples of Spoken and Written Discourse," unpublished Ph.D. dissertation (University of Illinois, 1961).

14. Paul P. Bushnell, *An Analytical Contrast of Oral with Written English* (New York: Bureau of Publications, Teachers College, Columbia University, 1930).

15. Ethel Amelia Kaump, "An Analysis of the Structural Differences between Oral and Written Language of One Hundred Secondary School Students," unpublished Ph.D. dissertation (University of Wisconsin, 1940).

16. James Reid Sterrett, "A Comparative Analysis of Certain Language Elements Used by Speakers and Writers," unpublished Ph.D. dissertation (University of Wisconsin, 1941).

17. James Green, "A Comparison of Oral and Written Language," unpublished Ph.D. dissertation (New York University, 1958).

18. Joseph A. DeVito, "Comprehension Factors in Oral and Written Discourse of Skilled Communicators," *Speech Monographs,* 32:2 (June 1965), pp. 124-28; see also, Joseph Anthony DeVito, "A Quantitative Analysis of Comprehension Factors in Samples of Oral and Written Technical Discourse of Skilled Communicators," unpublished Ph.D. dissertation (University of Illinois, 1964).

19. Diversity was measured by means of the type token ratio, the number of different words (types) over the total number of words (tokens).

20. Difficulty was measured by means of the Thorndike-Lorge word list, a word being considered "difficult" if it did not appear on this list. See Edward L. Thorndike and Irving Lorge, *The Teacher's Word Book of 30,000 Words* (New York: Bureau of Publications, Teachers College, Columbia University, 1944). Difficulty was also measured in terms of word length. Both measures yielded statistically significant results (beyond .01).

21. Basically, a simple sentence was regarded as one which contains only one subject-predicate combination. See Reinard Willem Zandvoort, *A Handbook of English Grammar* (London: Longmans, Green and Company, 1957), p. 211.

22. Idea Density was measured in terms of the percentage of content words (generally any noun; verb, except copulatives and auxiliaries; descriptive adjectives; or descriptive adverbs). Cf. Edith Rickert, *New Methods for the Study of Literature* (Chicago: University of Chicago Press, 1929), pp. 74-79.

23. Bushnell, p. 61.

24. Otto Jespersen, *Growth and Structure of the English Language,* 9th ed. (Garden City, N.Y.: Doubleday Anchor, 1956), p. 141.

25. W. Nelson Francis, *The Structure of English* (New York: Ronald Press, 1958), p. 339.

26. The contrasts identified here follow Francis, pp. 339-40.

27. Henry A. Gleason, Jr., *An Introduction to Descriptive Linguistics,* rev. ed. (New York: Holt, Rinehart and Winston, Inc., 1961), p. 437.

28. Daniel Jones, "Differences between Spoken and Written Language," *Journal of Education* (London), 70:5 (May 1943), p. 207

29. George Kingsley Zipf, *The Psycho-Biology of Language* (Boston: Houghton Mifflin Company, 1935), p. 25.

30. Thorndike and Lorge, pp. ix-xii.

31. André Martinet, *A Functional View of Language* (Oxford: Clarendon Press, 1962), pp. 122-23.

32. Austin Phelps, *English Style in Public Discourse with Special Reference to the Usages of the Pulpit* (New York: Charles Scribner's Sons, 1883), p. 341.

33. Blair, Lecture 34, p. 383.

34. Northrop Frye, *The Well-Tempered Critic* (Bloomington: Indiana University Press, 1963), p. 32.

35. Cf., e.g., John B. Carroll, "Process and Content in Psycholinguistics," in *Current Trends in the Description and Analysis of Behavior* (Pittsburgh: University of Pittsburgh Press, 1958), pp. 175-200; Howard Maclay and Stanley Newman, "Two Variables Affecting the Message in Communications," in *Decisions, Values and Groups,* ed. D. K. Wilmer (New York: Pergamon Press, 1960), pp. 218-28.

36. See, e.g., Charles E. Osgood, "On Understanding and Creating Sentences," *American Psychologist,* 18:12 (December 1963), pp. 735-51.

37. Martin Joos, *The Five Clocks* (Bloomington: Indiana University Research Center in Anthropology, Folklore, and Linguistics, 1962), p. 29.

38. Ibid., p. 29.

A LANGUAGE WITHIN LANGUAGE

ALBERT MEHRABIAN

In describing what his girl friend did, John could say, "Mike was dancing with her," "She was dancing with Mike," or "They were dancing together." These three statements show increasing degrees of John's acceptance of what his girl friend did.

Bob could describe his activity to his wife as follows: "Alice and I danced," "She and I danced," "I danced with her," "She danced with me," or "I had to dance with her," depending, perhaps, on his feelings about liking Alice or about his wife's reaction—the last statement being, of course, the most cautious.

Talking about a party you attended, you say, "The food was pretty good," "They had a good time," "They were having a good time," "We had a good time," or "I had a good time." All these are different ways of making a positive statement about the party; however, when analyzed in some detail, they show interesting differences in feeling. . . .

In cultures like our own, these constant companions of what we say constitute an important way of conveying feelings and evaluations, the expression of which would otherwise sometimes be unacceptable. Increased focus on the nonverbal modes may help to overcome the handicapping reliance on words in communication, at least as communication skills are formally taught, and may contribute to a better understanding of the significance of various gestures, postures, and expressions. Let us now note the numerous and frequently overlooked subtleties of speech itself that are part of the expression of feelings, evaluations, and preferences.

Distance in Time and Place

The stylistic differences of the sentences selected to express a certain idea can be used to infer (1) feelings toward the thing being described, (2) feelings toward the listener, or (3) feelings about the act of saying certain things to a certain listener. Here again, we shall use the important concept of immediacy in making inferences about positive-negative feelings revealed in any of these three cases. Notice the difference in each of the following pairs: "Here they are," "There they are"; "These people need help," "Those people need help"; "I can't understand this man," "I can't understand that man"; "I am showing Liz my collection of etchings," "I have been showing Liz my collection of etchings." In each example, the first sentence of the pair is the more immediate one. This is due to the particular use of demonstrative pronouns ("this" or "these" versus "that" or "those"), adjectives ("here," "there"), or verb tense (present versus past).

There are many situations in which either an immediate or nonimmediate form can effectively be used to communicate the verbal message, and thus the particular usage becomes significant. For instance, in talking about a minority group, the speaker who says, "Those people need help" is putting the group further away from himself in this very subtle verbal form than when he says, "These people need help." Consider another example: As a woman enters a crowded room, two men exclaim simultaneously. One says, "Here's Kathy"; the other says, "There's Kathy." It turns out that the first is her current favored escort; the second used to be.

When the form of demonstrative pronoun or tense used is incongruous with the time or place of the actual event, it suggests some special feelings of the speaker. For example, a person says, "I don't understand those people," about some people in the room with him. His demonstrative "those" is incongruous for the situation, which is here and now. In another example, John is showing Mary his cherished collection of plants when his wife, Tina, joins them. When he says, "I am showing Mary the plants," he places the entire activity in the present tense and doubtless is easy in his own mind about the activity. This is closer in time to the actual activity than if he were to say, "I have been showing Mary the plants" or "I showed Mary the plants." If John uses one of the less immediate forms, he may be revealing his awareness of Tina's jealousy of Mary's attentiveness to him or, even though Tina does not mind what she considers to be an innocent relationship, he may feel some edge of uneasiness about his own interest in Mary.

These kinds of nonimmediacy involve putting something at a physical distance through the use of demonstrative pronouns or at a temporal distance through the use of past tenses. But nonimmediacy can be indicated in other ways, one of which is mention of the more unpleasant, or less pleasant, things later in a sequence. Such ordering can occur when we describe different parts of an event or situation. We might refer to a couple we know as "John and Marge," to another couple as "Jane and Jack" and yet another couple as "the Browns." In the first case, chances are that John is the more important, better-known, or better-liked member of the pair. In the second case, Jane may be the more important or better-liked member. In the last case, perhaps neither one of the pair is well known to the speaker, or there is a certain formality and social distance in the relationship with these people.

In describing a day's activities I could say, "We went to the bank, shopped, and visited some friends"; or I could say, "We visited some friends, shopped, and also went to the bank." Assuming that neither one of these orders corresponds to the actual sequence of events, it is safe to infer that the first item mentioned is probably the more important or the more preferred part of the day's activities. In some situations, we may have the necessary information to be able to consider the actual sequence of events and the way in which it is recited in a description. If an event that actually occurred first in the sequence is mentioned last, perhaps the speaker does not like it as well as he does the other items or has delayed mentioning it quite unintentionally. Even stronger negative feelings are implied when he leaves out an item entirely.

If you've had psychotherapy, remember the order in which you described your problems to the therapist in the initial interview.

In the psychotherapy situation, when we mention something first it is not because we like it more but rather because it is easiest for us to mention that particular problem to a stranger. Thus, another value of the order in which things are mentioned is that it shows how easily certain things can be described to someone else. The general rule for making such interpretations is that nonimmediacy can be due to discomfort about saying a particular thing to a particular listener.

There is a related way in which nonimmediacy comes into play in speech. Hesitant and halting speech with errors, incomplete sentences, and repetition of words indicates anxiety and negative feelings. One would tend to make more errors when talking about a distressing subject than a pleasant one. *Note:* "How did it go at the dentist's?" "Well, uh (pause) it went fine"; "Did you cook dinner?" "I, I thought . . . uh, we could go out tonight." This is reminiscent of Freud's discussion of slips of the tongue—a special kind of error, which, in his view, reveals conflicts in the speaker and negative feelings to aspects of the current situation. What, indeed, is the function of halting and faltering speech?

Halting speech delays the completion of a statement. Errors associated with such speech make the descriptions less effective, more difficult to understand, and generally inhibit the communication process. In this sense, the errors serve to delay what a person has to say and lead us to infer that he has at least some reservations about saying it.

The Form of Reference

We can show a less positive feeling toward something by putting it at a distance; by avoiding any mention of it; or, as in the following examples, by referring to it in ambiguous ways. This ambiguity makes it more difficult for our listeners to understand what exactly our statement refers to and reflects our unwillingness to express a certain idea in a certain situation.

One important source of ambiguity of reference is the *overinclusive* statement. Let us say that a friend has recommended a certain restaurant; and, to your chagrin, you have tried it. You have put off mentioning anything about it to him (already, one kind of nonimmediacy), but he asks you, "How did you like your dinner at One-Eyed Joe's?" You say, "It was a pleasant evening" instead of "It was a pleasant dinner." You use the more inclusive term "evening" which involves a broader set of events, thus making an ambiguous positive remark. With this kind of overinclusive statement the involvement with a particular event is minimized since the stated relation includes many parts in addition to the specific referent in question (for example, "evening" includes other events apart from "dinner").

There are two ways of making such overinclusive statements: (1) placing the referent within a more comprehensive category and (2) including oneself within a larger group of people. If I am asked, "How do you like Wanda?" and answer, "I like the Smiths," I have not specifically referred to Wanda in my answer but rather have referred to her and her husband, the Smiths, thereby minimizing involvement. It could be that I have reservations about Wanda or that I am unwilling to say what I feel about her to the person who asked me the question. On the other hand, I could have answered, "We like Wanda," implying that my friends and I like her. Using an inclusive "we" instead of "I" in the statement dilutes the relation with Wanda, which is again indicative of less positive feelings.

The use of "we" instead of "I" is a familiar rhetorical device. If a speaker uses both "I" and "we," we can infer which of his statements he feels more strongly about and which are token statements to placate or gratify his listeners. When a speaker feels strongly about the accuracy of some statement or wishes to be identified with a certain proposition, he is more likely to start that sentence with "I." But when he feels less confident about something and does not want to be held responsible for it, he may use the pronoun "we." *Note:* "I believe that the national economy will respond favorably to increase in money supply" versus "We believe . . ." The "we" may refer to the speaker and his wife, to many Americans, or to some economists; it is not altogether clear to the listeners that this is the speaker's particular stand on the issue.

Euphemisms provide a rich source of overinclusive references and their use is motivated by the desire to diminish the negative or distasteful quality of the expression that they replace "Tickets are available at . . ." instead of "Tickets are sold at . . ." may be popular in advertisements that seek to minimize the implied exchange of money. Familiar examples of such expressions are "passed away" instead of "died"; "exceptional child" instead of "retarded child"; "donation" instead of "price"; "to wash hands" instead of "to go to the bathroom"; and "detention center" instead of "prison."

Many people make up their own euphemisms to refer to disliked persons or events. Can you think of any expressions of this kind that you use only with persons who share the particular negative feeling?

Another way, perhaps more extreme, of diluting the relationship between self and the referent is to make a statement that touches only tangentially on the person or the issue being considered. A question like "What do you think of their marriage?" may be answered with remarks such as "My wife thinks it's great" or "Don't you think it's great?" rather than "I think it's great." In the first two instances, the speaker is implying that not he but someone else thinks the marriage is exceptionally suitable. We may infer that he has some reservations about the soundness of this marriage—or perhaps is simply not particularly interested. Quite frequently, the negative significance of such answers is overlooked, but experimental findings have consistently shown that this kind of non-immediacy is a powerful indicator of a speaker's negative feelings about what he is discussing. The difference between "I lost control of the car" and the more non-immediate form, "The car went out of control," can be similarly interpreted. It is evident that the person making the latter statement is unwilling to accept responsibility for the accident.

Elaborate and adept applications of such tangential references to oneself are very common in public speeches and debates when the speaker feels that a remark may be controversial or that it is only weakly supported by facts and reasoning. Common examples are "You would expect," "You'd think," "It would seem to be," "It would be expected," all of which serve as substitutes for "I think" or "I expect." Similar hedging also occurs frequently in scientific writings, in which it is especially important to empha-size the tentative quality of one's ideas.

The complement of tangential reference to self occurs when a subject of distaste is described in such a way that it is unclear who or what is being described. A mother, in referring to her son's fiancée, could say, "our daughter-to-be," "our son's fiancée," "his fiancée," "his lady-friend," "his friend," "she," or "that thing"—showing increasing non-immediacy and dislike of the girl. Similarly, across the generation gap, a shaven and shorn solid citizen may refer to his hirsute son as "that hippie," while the youth may recipro-cate with "that reactionary" or "that uptight square" (if he uses printable epithets).

An interesting variant of the overinclusive statement is *negation*. Following a brief encounter with someone whom we do not really care to meet again, we say, "Why don't we get together sometime?" instead of "Let's get together." If we are enthusiastic about meeting this person again, we actually suggest a time and place for the next meeting. Our negative feelings toward a listener or our feeling that the listener will feel negative about complying with a request can also become evident in examples such as this: "Why don't you type this one first and then go back to what you were doing." In this instance, the executive may use this particular form to request his secretary to change her priorities because he is aware that she will be inconvenienced and will have a negative reaction to his request.

More generally, the "why don't you" statement is likely to occur when the speaker doubts that his request or suggestion will be complied with, either because he feels that his request may sound imposing or demanding, as in the case of the employer, or because he shares little mutual feeling of goodwill with the listener, as in our first example.

Another kind of negation that reveals one's reservations is illustrated by "How did you like the movie?" answered with "It wasn't bad." This answer conveys a feeling different from that indicated by "It was fine." We can understand the difference in terms of the overinclusive quality of "not bad" relative to "fine." The former includes "fine" as well as "so-so," and more than likely the feeling was indeed "so-so." Other examples are "We're not exactly buddies" and "The movie is not the best I've seen."

Think back to the times when you have answered a question in just this way or made such a statement. You probably used this kind of negation because you did not really care for the experience you were describing but, as a matter of politeness or caution, preferred not to express your strong feelings to your listener.

The exact opposite of the overinclusive statement is yet another source of information about feelings. "I dig being with her, for an evening" shows how, in addition to using overinclusive reference, a speaker can also minimize his relation to a referent by using *overspecific* statements. In this case, the "digging" is restricted to an evening, rather than left unqualified. Overspecification arises when we refer to a part of the referent in a context that requires a more complete statement: "How did you like my new production?" is answered with "I liked the acting" instead of simply "I liked it." In saying "I liked (or enjoyed) the acting," the speaker has managed to pick out the one part of the production that he liked best or, which is more likely to be the case, disliked least. An astute and straightforward producer at this point might say, "What was the matter with the rest of it?" More than likely, however, he will simply go on with a discussion of the acting and will fail to consider possible weaknesses in his play are implied by the remark.

Someone asks you about the ball game he had suggested you go to: "How was the game?" You say, "It was a nice day, and it was fun to be outdoors." These references to the weather and to the outdoors touch only in part on the game and reveal less positive or possibly negative evaluation of the game by you.

Just as overspecificity shows negative feelings when it involves the referent, the same kind of implication is made when it involves the speaker. After an accident, I could say, "My car slid out of control and struck her" instead of "I struck her with my car." In the first statement something associated with me, "my car," is the implied agent responsible for this action; in the second, "I," the actor, am the responsible agent. Someone says, "The thoughts that come to my mind are . . ." instead of "I think . . . ," thus implying that only a part of him, "his thoughts," should be held responsible for what he is to say. A more straightforward example of overspecificity is "His hands touched her hair" instead of "He touched her hair."

In all these cases, a part of the person speaking (his hand, his thoughts) or something that belongs to or is associated with the speaker (his car) is the ostensible actor and the responsible agent in a situation. Thus, we can infer that the speaker does not feel very comfortable about a statement he is going to make, since he is unwilling to assume full responsibility. Indeed, an entire set of nonimmediate statements can be analyzed directly in terms of the desire to minimize responsibility.

Responsibility

As he brings his date back home, a young man says, "I would like to see you again," instead of the less conditional "I want to see you again." In this case, he probably uses the less immediate conditional form because he does not want to seem too forward with a girl he has taken out for the first time or lay himself on the line to be rejected. In other words, he has trouble expressing his enthusiasm about the girl, not because he does not like her, but because there are social sanctions against it or because of the possiblity of being turned down.

Usually, the conditional is used when the speaker does not like what he is going to say. *Note:* "You'd think they would do something to improve the quality of service here" instead of "I think they ought to improve the quality of service here." Of course, this example involves at least two kinds of nonimmediacy. One is the use of "you" instead of "I," and the other is the use of the conditional. Here the speaker is trying to avoid seeming domineering or authoritarian to his addressee. Alternatively, the addressee in this case may be connected with the management of the place being criticized, and the speaker may be uncomfortable about being directly critical. Whatever the reason for making such conditional statements, it is obvious that the speaker is trying to imply a lack of familiarity and a weaker relationship with the object being discussed.

When an author sends his manuscript to a publisher and receives the following kind of initial response, he has some reason to wonder whether his manuscript will be accepted. "The manuscript seems very interesting and apparently does a very good job of portraying youth in our society. Our readers are now giving your manuscript a closer look, and I will be getting in touch with you about it." The words "seems" and "apparently" may indicate that the editor has some reserve about the manuscript. In this case, even though the editor is making a number of positive statements, the author probably should not take the letter as an enthusiastic reception of his manuscript.

In a similar minimizing of responsibility, a speaker makes no direct reference to himself: "It is evident that . . . ," "It is obvious that . . . ," or "Most people realize that she's an intolerable bitch." The implication here is that others are responsible for the view being expressed and that the speaker merely shares that view. This device is likely to be used by a speaker who does not wish to be held answerable for what he is going to say and is especially concerned about possible disagreement from his listener. By protecting himself from rebuff in this way, he hints at the quality of his relationship with the listener: They are not likely to agree on this and perhaps many other matters. Experimental findings have consistently shown that people tend to dislike others who hold different opinions and attitudes, that is, those they would disagree with frequently. So in this instance, the implication of expected disagreement of the listener is indicative of negative feelings toward him.

Of course, another way to avoid responsibility for what we say is to qualify our statements. Common forms are "I feel . . . ," "I think . . . ," "It seems to me . . . ," or "It is possible that she's pregnant." With such qualification, the speaker shows his reluctance to make the particular statement as a matter of established fact and again highlights his awareness of possible disagreement from his listeners. This device is also used in gossip. By prefacing a scandalous thought with "I think . . ." or "They say . . . ," the speaker technically avoids responsibility for the truth or falsehood of his statement, yet he still gets the pleasure of saying it.

In some situations, the nonimmediacy and associated negative feeling of the speaker is evident in statements that very obviously seek to minimize his responsibility. A girl who is asked for a date by someone whom she does not like says, "I have to go with someone else," instead of the more straightforward "I prefer (or want) to go with someone else." The nonimmediacy in "I have to" reflects her difficulty in being frank with him.

In departing from a friend's house, we could use the more immediate forms "I am leaving now" or "I want to leave now" instead of nonimmediate forms such as "I should leave now," "I have to leave now," or "I really should leave now." The second set of statements implies that we are leaving, not because we want to, but because of some extraneous circumstances that force us to do so. In other words, something other than our own desires is responsible for the fact that we must leave. This kind of nonimmediacy is used if the relationship with the listener is more formal, less straightforward, and generally one in which feelings cannot be clearly and directly expressed without fear of hurting others.

People tend to attribute responsibility to some external agent in their statement for departing, especially because the act of departure increases nonimmediacy. If we leave a party at 11:00 P.M. instead of 2:00 A.M. or if we are first rather than last to leave, this departure time indicates something about how much we are enjoying the party. So, when we do leave at a time that we think is too early and might lead the host to think we did not enjoy the party (which is actually the case), a statement such as "We've got to get back" helps to save face for the host and provides an easy out for the guest.

When a couple is going to get married, and they tell their friends, "We have to get married," it doesn't take much psychological training for friends to wonder about possible reservations and negative feelings of the engaged couple toward the marriage. But when someone says, "I can't come because I have to see a friend off at the airport," the negative affect is less likely to be detected without knowledge of speech immediacy. We know that he could have said, "I can't come because I am going to see a friend off at the airport."

Another way in which responsibility for an action or statement is minimized is through the use of the passive rather than the active form. I could say, "The results of my experiments have led me to this conclusion" instead of "I conclude this from my experiments." I would be more likely to use the passive form if I were not quite sure about the results or how they should be interpreted. The use of the passive form in this case implies that anybody else, just like myself, could have been led to the same conclusion, and that I should not be held responsible for making the particular interpretation. However, if I were to use the active form, I would not provide myself with this "out."

You may be able to think of some of your friends or acquaintances who are generally prone to using the passive form when they talk about certain topics. This should give you a clue about their sense of helplessness and consequent negative feelings when these topics are mentioned. Alternatively, if an individual resorts to the passive form more than most others, this could be a sign of his general unwillingness to assume responsibility for his actions.

Examples so far in this section show how avoiding responsibility is generally indicative of negative feelings about the contents of one's communication. There are other times, however, when the sharing of responsibility with the listener, a form of *mutuality,* can be informative about the relation between speaker and listener. *Note:* "Remember what we decided about the office?" instead of "Remember what I suggested about the office?" In the first case, the decision is a mutual one involving the speaker and the listener, whereas in the second the decision is a unilateral one. It involves the speaker alone and implies his separation from the listener, at least in terms of their contribution to this activity.

When such expressions occur frequently in a relationship, they can serve as clues about how two people, who are closely involved in either a social or working relationship, feel toward each other. The statements implying mutuality are likely to arise in more positive relationships, since they indicate a more intense involvement of the pair in the activity in which they are engaged. Let us say that two people are having lunch and a third person joins them. At this point, one of the two says, "John and I have been discussing your project" instead of "I have been telling John about your project." Either one of these two statements could be quite legitimate in the situation, but the former implies equality of status between John and the speaker and a more intimate feeling.

This concept allows us to interpret "I was dancing with her" or "She was dancing with me" differently from "We were dancing." The first statement implies that she really was not participating much, possibly because she does not like speaker. The second statement implies that the speaker does not like her or that he does not want to let his listener know that he likes her. The last statement shows no reservation about dancing with this particular person or the act of mentioning it to someone else.

Guarded Expressions of Liking

So far most of our discussion has focused on how nonimmediacy reflects negative feelings. On some occasions, a more nonimmediate statement is used because the speaker feels uncomfortable about saying what he wants to say to his listener. This idea can be turned to one's advantage. In a number of social situations, it may seem too forward to make strong statements of liking or interest to a stranger or a casual acquaintance, but a more nonimmediate statement of liking would be socially acceptable.

A man sees an interesting girl in the hallway of the office building where he works and wishes to get to know her. The first chance he gets, he says, "That's a nice dress you have on." In this instance, the less immediate remark ("I like you" would be immediate) serves as an indirect way of conveying his liking. The nonimmediacy of the remark reflects his uneasiness, not because he dislikes her, but because he feels uncomfortable about this initial contact with a stranger.

Other examples: "I heard that you have a marvelous wine cellar" or "Someone told me that you grow prize-winning camellias." The speaker desires to somehow compliment his listener but feels that he cannot do so in a very direct and obvious way. So he selects something related to the listener to compliment, because the more indirect statement involving greater nonimmediacy happens to be more socially appropriate. The non-immediacy of his statement still shows that the speaker feels uncomfortable in the situation, which is indeed why this kind of statement is more acceptable in formal relationships or contacts with a stranger.

Relations of Verbal and Nonverbal Immediacy

Our analyses of speech here . . . have been based on the same basic metaphor: People seek out and get involved with things they like and they try to minimize their relationship or, if possible, entirely avoid contact with things they dislike or fear. We have examined the many special devices that are available in speech to reflect a speaker's negative feelings. At this point, let us consider some analogues of these speech nonimmediacy forms in silent messages.

For example, the times at which various participants at major political negotiations arrive for a specific meeting can be important cues, provided the persons whose behaviors are under scrutiny have some prepared remarks for that session. Thus, if one of the participants comes with some prepared remarks of a hopeful quality, but makes his entrance late (relative to other sessions), this provides some grounds for questioning the sincerity of the remarks. His delay shows a reluctance to make those remarks. On the other hand, if he delivers some prepared negative remarks, his delay would constitute a positive sign and show his reluctance to seem antagonistic. In either case, the delay can also be a function of the importance of the remarks (he was busy up to the last minute preparing them) or a variety of other factors. This is of course true, but suppose we make these observations repeatedly over a large number of instances, say weekly meetings. In this case, the extraneous and unsystematic effect of some of these factors (for example, he was delayed in traffic) is washed out in the averaging process, and the underlying attitudes tend to become evident from the nonverbal or the verbal behavior of the participants. This is exactly what is done in any experiment where such ideas are tested. We do not rely on a single incident to make a judgment, so most of our experiments employ large numbers of subjects to test the immediacy ideas.

In a somewhat different context, Freud's discussion of forgetting provides another point of similarity between verbal and nonverbal forms of nonimmediacy. The verbal analogues of forgetting are the speech errors and other obstructions that delay the expression of an idea. As in the case of forgetting, such phenomena make it possible for the speaker or the actor to put off or avoid saying something that is unpleasant. Freud did not interpret forgetting or slips specifically in terms of immediacy. Nevertheless, his analyses always implied that the unconscious conflicts which led to these errors or even more serious symptoms were motivated by negative feelings. In the case of forgetting, the negative feelings were toward the forgotten object. Thus, when we forget to mail a letter we have written, this helps delay contact with the intended receiver of the letter and shows reservations of the writer about the contents of his letter or toward the person who would receive it.

I have frequently and painfully been reminded of the validity of this idea when I have belatedly come across an unpleasant chore which I had forgotten to get done on time. It seems much easier to forget an unpleasnt or time-consuming chore than a pleasant one.

Keep a tally of all the things you forget, listing the pleasant ones separately from the unpleasant ones. You will probably find that the unpleasant ones far outnumber the pleasant ones. Close examination of such a list can provide valuable insights into some feelings that you are not so willing to recognize in yourself.

After hearing a lecture on immediacy, a student asked if the immediacy concept could help explain why her boy friend was invariably about half an hour late for their dates. She said that this was very annoying for her but that otherwise the relationship was perfect. I suggested that this was a way for him to express some negative feelings that he was otherwise unable to convey. As we discussed her problem, it.became apparent that he had a great deal of trouble refusing her requests. It also became apparent that he was especially late to their dates when these also involved her parents, so that on such occasions his tardiness was especially embarrassing to her. She concluded that most of the time she had gotten her way in the relationship. The possibility of marriage, which was also her idea initially, was highlighted by those evenings spent with her parents and accounted for his greater tardiness when the parents were involved. Considering his inability to refuse her requests, the boy was resisting in the only way he knew how—on the most important issue that would affect the rest of his life. . . .

Part Five

Nonverbal Communication

We can tell by our own experiences in oral communication that "meaning" is conveyed by more than words. When people talk we are also aware of their voices, facial expressions and bodily movements—their nonverbal behavior.

"Communication Without Words" by Albert Mehrabian provides us with a brief general account of nonverbal communication. He raises several basic questions: What does language communicate? What does nonverbal behavior communicate? How do they reinforce or contradict each other?

Not only does nonverbal behavior "speak," but *time, color,* and *space* speak as well. Suppose you had an important job interview at 3:30 and did not show up until 4:30—or perhaps you did not show up at all. Or suppose you were thirty minutes early for the appointment. What a variety of "meanings" those several actions might have.

Don Fabun points out, for example, that even the color of the room in which you hold the interview may affect "a specific response pattern."[1] He observes:

> The prevailing color in an environment may have important effects on the kind of communication that takes place there. In general, it is felt that the 'warm' colors— yellow, orange, red—stimulate creativity and make most people feel more 'outgoing' and responsive to others. 'Cool' colors—blue, green, grey—have a tendency to encourage meditation and deliberate thought processes. . . .[2]

Moreover, the spatial relations in the room "communicate." Does the employer sit behind the desk at some distance from his prospective employee? Do they both sit on chairs away from the desk? Do they leave the office for a different atmosphere altogether?

The world of smell, even in what Joost Meerloo terms "our soulless deodorized" society,[3] communicates meanings—the salt sea spray of our coastlines, the pine forests of our mountains, the antiseptic smell of a hospital or prison. In the Speech Department mail room no coffee aroma early in the morning tells us that one of the secretaries is late or ill. And, one student recently recalled the smell of sheets hung out in the sun to dry as the smell that most reminds her of "home."

Of course, the language of time, color, space, and smell are as culture-bound as our own verbal communications.

The last article in this section, by Randall Harrison, can be thought of as an elaboration of the brief introductory article. In "Nonverbal Communications: Explorations into Time, Space, Action and Object," Professor Harrison discusses the various forms nonverbal communication may take. Then, he focuses specifically on *communicator goals* and the ways in which nonverbal communication may help or hinder us in reaching these goals: Selection, Comprehension, Acceptance, Recall, Use. This part of the article is directed toward helping the communicator expand his repertoire of nonverbal alternatives and help him "better predict which alternative will get the desired result." Further, this article encourages us, as does this whole section, to become more aware of the nonverbal "meanings" we send and receive.

Notes

1. "The Silent Languages," in Fabun, *Communications: The Transfer of Meaning* (New York: Macmillan Company, 1968), p. 22.
2. Ibid.
3. "A World of Smells," in Meerlo, *Unobtrusive Communication: Essays in Psycholinguistics* (Assen, Netherlands: Van Gorcum Ltd., 1964), pp. 166-69.

COMMUNICATION WITHOUT WORDS

ALBERT MEHRABIAN

Suppose you are sitting in my office listening to me describe some research I have done on communication. I tell you that feelings are communicated less by the words a person uses than by certain nonverbal means—that, for example, the verbal part of a spoken message has considerably less effect on whether a listener feels liked or disliked than a speaker's facial expression or tone of voice.

So far so good. But suppose I add, "In fact, we've worked out a formula that shows exactly how much each of these components contributes to the effect of the message as a whole. It goes like this: Total Impact = .07 verbal + .38 vocal + .55 facial."

What would you say to *that*? Perhaps you would smile good-naturedly and say, with some feeling, "Baloney!" Or perhaps you would frown and remark acidly, "Isn't science grand." My own response to the first answer would probably be to smile back: the facial part of your message, at least, was positive (55 per cent of the total). The second answer might make me uncomfortable: Only the verbal part was positive (seven per cent).

The point here is not only that my reactions would lend credence to the formula but that most listeners would have mixed feelings about my statement. People like to see science march on, but they tend to resent its intrusion into an "art" like the communication of feelings, just as they find analytical and quantitative approaches to the study of personality cold, mechanistic, and unacceptable.

The psychologist himself is sometimes plagued by the feeling that he is trying to put a rainbow into a bottle. Fascinated by a complicated and emotionally rich human situation, he begins to study it, only to find in the course of his research that he has destroyed part of the mystique that originally intrigued and involved him. But despite a certain nostalgia for earlier, more intuitive approaches, one must acknowledge that concrete experimental data have added a great deal to our understanding of how feelings are communicated. In fact, as I hope to show, analytical and intuitive findings do not so much conflict as complement each other.

It is indeed difficult to know what another person really feels. He says one thing and does another; he seems to mean something but we have an uneasy feeling it isn't true. The early psychoanalysts, facing this problem of inconsistencies and ambiguities in a person's communications, attempted to resolve it through the concepts of the conscious and the unconscious. They assumed that contradictory messages meant a conflict between superficial, deceitful, or erroneous feelings on the one hand and true attitudes and feelings on the other. Their role, then, was to help the client separate the wheat from the chaff.

The question was, how could this be done? Some analysts insisted that inferring the client's unconscious wishes was a completely intuitive process. Others thought that some nonverbal behavior, such as posture, position, and movement, could be used in a more objective way to discover the client's feelings. A favorite technique of Frieda Fromm-Reichmann, for example, was to imitate a client's posture herself in order to obtain some feeling for what he was experiencing.

Thus began the gradual shift away from the idea that communication is primarily verbal, and that the verbal message includes distortions or ambiguities due to unobservable motives that only experts can discover.

Language, though, can be used to communicate almost anything. By comparison, nonverbal behavior is very limited in range. Usually, it is used to communicate feelings, likings, and preferences, and it customarily reinforces or contradicts the feelings that are communicated verbally. Less often, it adds a new dimension of sorts to a verbal message, as when a salesman describes his product to a client and simultaneously conveys, nonverbally, the impression that he likes the client.

A great many forms of nonverbal behavior can communicate feelings: touching, facial expression, tone of voice, spatial distance from the addressee, relaxation of posture, rate of speech, number of errors in speech. Some of these are generally recognized as informative. Untrained adults and children easily infer that they are liked or disliked from certain facial expressions, from whether (and how) someone touches them, and from a speaker's tone of voice. Other behavior, such as posture, has a more subtle effect. A listener may sense how someone feels about him from the way the person sits while talking to him, but he may have trouble identifying precisely what his impression comes from.

Correct intuitive judgments of the feelings or attitudes of others are especially difficult when different degrees of feeling, or contradictory kinds of feeling, are expressed simultaneously through different forms of behavior. As I have pointed out, there is a distinction between verbal and vocal information (vocal information being what is lost when speech is written down—intonation, tone, stress, length and frequency of pauses, and so on), and the two kinds of information do not always communicate the same feeling. This distinction, which has been recognized for some time, has shed new light on certain types of communication. Sarcasm, for example, can be defined as a message in which the information transmitted vocally contradicts the information transmitted verbally. Usually the verbal information is positive and the vocal is negative, as in "Isn't science grand."

Through the use of an electronic filter, it is possible to measure the degree of liking communicated vocally. What the filter does is eliminate the higher frequencies of recorded speech, so that words are unintelligible but most vocal qualities remain. (For women's speech, we eliminate frequencies higher than about 200 cycles per second; for men, frequencies over about 100 cycles per second.) When people are asked to judge the degree of liking conveyed by the filtered speech, they perform the task rather easily and with a significant amount of agreement.

This method allows us to find out, in a given message, just how inconsistent the information communicated in words and the information communicated vocally really are. We ask one group to judge the amount of liking conveyed by a transcription of what was said, the verbal part of the message. A second group judges the vocal component, and a third group judges the impact of the complete recorded message. In one study of this sort we found that, when the verbal and vocal components of a message agree (both positive or both negative), the message as a whole is judged a little more positive or a little more negative than either component by itself. But when vocal information contradicts verbal, vocal wins out. If someone calls you "honey" in a nasty tone of voice, you are likely to feel disliked; it is also possible to say "I hate you" in a way that conveys exactly the opposite feeling.

Besides the verbal and vocal characteristics of speech, there are other, more subtle, signals of meaning in a spoken message. For example, everyone makes mistakes when he talks—unnecessary repetitions, stutterings, the omission of parts of words incomplete sentences, "ums" and "ahs." In a number of studies of speech errors, George Mahl of Yale University has found that errors become more frequent as the speaker's discomfort or anxiety increases. It might be interesting to apply this index in an attempt to detect deceit (though on some occasions it might be risky: Confidence men are notoriously smooth talkers).

Timing is also highly informative. How long does a speaker allow silent periods to last, and how long does he wait before he answers his partner? How long do his utterances tend to be? How often does he interrupt his partner, or wait an inappropriately long time before speaking? Joseph Matarazzo and his colleagues at the University of Oregon have found that each of these speech habits is stable from person to person, and each tells something about the speaker's personality and about his feelings toward and status in relation to his partner.

Utterance duration, for example, is a very stable quality in a person's speech; about 30 seconds long on the average. But when someone talks to a partner whose status is higher than his own, the more the high-status person nods his head the longer the speaker's utterances become. If the high-status person changes his own customary speech pattern toward longer or shorter utterances, the lower-status person will change his own speech in the same direction. If the high-status person often interrupts the speaker, or creates long silences, the speaker is likely to become quite uncomfortable. These are things that can be observed outside the laboratory as well as under experimental conditions. If you have an employee who makes you uneasy and seems not to respect you, watch him the next time you talk to him—perhaps he is failing to follow the customary low-status pattern.

Immediacy or directness is another good source of information about feelings. We use more distant forms of communication when the act of communicating is undesirable or uncomfortable. For example, some people would rather transmit discontent with an employee's work through a third party than do it themselves, and some find it easier to commnuciate negative feelings in writing than by telephone or face to face.

Distance can show a negative attitude toward the message itself, as well as toward the act of delivering it. Certain forms of speech are more distant than others, and they show fewer positive feelings for the subject referred to. A speaker might say "Those people need help," which is more distant than "These people need help," which is in turn even more distant than "These people need our help." Or he might say "Sam and I have been having dinner," which has less immediacy than "Sam and I are having dinner."

Facial expression, touching, gestures, self-manipulation (such as scratching), changes in body position, and head movements—all these express a person's positive and negative attitudes, both at the moment and in general, and many reflect status relationships as well. Movements of the limbs and head, for example, not only indicate one's attitude toward a specific set of circumstances but relate to how dominant, and how anxious, one generally tends to be in social situations. Gross changes in body position, such as shifting in the chair, may show negative feelings toward the person one is talking to. They may also be cues: "It's your turn to talk," or "I'm about to get out of here, so finish what you're saying."

Posture is used to indicate both liking and status. The more a person leans toward his addressee, the more positively he feels about him. Relaxation of posture is a good indicator of both attitude and status, and one that we have been able to measure quite precisely. Three categories have been established for relaxation in a seated position: least relaxation is indicated by muscular tension in the hands and rigidity of posture; moderate relaxation is indicated by a forward lean of about 20 degrees and a sideways lean of less than 10 degrees, a curved back, and, for women, an open arm position; and extreme relaxation is indicated by a reclining angle greater than 20 degrees and a sideways lean greater than 10 degrees.

Our findings suggest that a speaker relaxes either very little or a great deal when he dislikes the person he is talking to, and to a moderate degree when he likes his companion. It seems that extreme tension occurs with threatening addresses, and extreme relaxation with nonthreatening, disliked addressees. In particular, men tend to become tense when talking to other men whom they dislike; on the other hand, women talking to men *or* women and men talking to women show dislike through extreme relaxation. As for status, people relax most with a low-status addressee, second-most with a peer, and least with someone of higher status than their own. Body orientation also shows status: in both sexes, it is least direct toward women with low status and most direct toward disliked men of high status. In part, body orientation seems to be determined by whether one regards one's partner as threatening.

The more you like a person, the more time you are likely to spend looking into his eyes as you talk to him. Standing close to your partner and facing him directly (which makes eye contact easier) also indicate positive feelings. And you are likely to stand or sit closer to your peers than you do to addressees whose status is either lower or higher than yours.

What I have said so far has been based on research studies performed, for the most part, with college students from the middle and upper-middle classes. One interesting question about communication, however, concerns young children from lower socioeconomic levels. Are these children, as some have suggested, more responsive to implicit channels of communication than middle- and upper-class children are?

Morton Wiener and his colleagues at Clark University had a group of middle- and lower-class children play learning games in which the reward for learning was praise. The child's responsiveness to the verbal and vocal parts of the praise-reward was measured by how much he learned. Praise came in two forms: the objective words "right" and "correct," and the more affective or evaluative words, "good" and "fine." All four words were spoken sometimes in a positive tone of voice and sometimes neutrally.

Positive intonation proved to have a dramatic effect on the learning rate of the lower-class group. They learned much faster when the vocal part of the message was positive than when it was neutral. Positive intonation affected the middle-class group as well, but not nearly as much.

If children of lower socioeconomic groups are more responsive to facial expression, posture, and touch as well as to vocal communication, that fact could have interesting applications to elementary education. For example, teachers could be explicitly trained to be aware of, and to use, the forms of praise (nonverbal or verbal) that would be likely to have the greatest effect on their particular students.

Another application of experimental data on communication is to the interpretation and treatment of schizophrenia. The literature on schizophrenia has for some time emphasized that parents of schizophrenic children give off contradictory signals simultaneously. Perhaps the parent tells the child in words that he loves him, but his posture conveys a negative attitude. According to the "double-bind" theory of schizophrenia, the child who perceives simultaneous contradictory feelings in his parent does not know how to react: should he respond to the positive part of the message, or to the negative? If he is frequently placed in this paralyzing situation, he may learn to respond with contradictory communications of his own. The boy who sends a birthday card to his mother and signs it "Napoleon" says that he likes his mother and yet denies that he is the one who likes her.

In an attempt to determine whether parents of disturbed children really do emit more inconsistent messages about their feelings than other parents do, my colleagues and I have compared what these parents communicate verbally and vocally with what they show through posture. We interviewed parents of moderately and quite severely disturbed children, in the presence of the child, about the child's problem. The interview was video-recorded without the parents' knowledge, so that we could analyze their behavior later on. Our measurements supplied both the amount of inconsistency between the parents' verbal-vocal and postural communications, and the total amount of liking that the parents communicated.

According to the double-bind theory, the parents of the more disturbed children should have behaved more inconsistently than the parents of the less disturbed children. This was not confirmed: there was no significant difference between the two groups. However, the *total amount* of positive feeling communicated by parents of the more disturbed children was less than that communicated by the other group.

This suggests that (1) negative communications toward disturbed children occur because the child is a problem and therefore elicits them, or (2) the negative attitude precedes the child's disturbance. It may also be that both factors operate together, in a vicious circle.

If so, one way to break the cycle is for the therapist to create situations in which the parent can have better feelings toward the child. A more positive attitude from the parent may make the child more responsive to his directives, and the spiral may begin to move up instead of down. In our own work with disturbed children, this kind of procedure has been used to good effect.

If one puts one's mind to it, one can think of a great many other applications for the findings I have described, though not all of them concern serious problems. Politicians, for example, are careful to maintain eye contact with the television camera when they speak, but they are not always careful about how they sit when they debate another candidate of, presumably, equal status.

Public relations men might find a use for some of the subtler signals of feeling. So might Don Juans. And so might ordinary people, who could try watching other people's signals and changing their own, for fun at a party or in a spirit of experimentation at home. I trust that does not strike you as a cold, manipulative suggestion, indicating dislike for the human race. I assure you that, if you had more than a transcription of words to judge from (seven per cent of total message), it would not.

NONVERBAL COMMUNICATION: EXPLORATIONS INTO TIME, SPACE, ACTION, AND OBJECT

RANDALL HARRISON

Many verbal expressions point to the importance of nonverbal communication. We say, for instance, "actions speak louder than words," or "one picture is worth a thousand words."

In spite of these familiar clichés, nonverbal communication remains an underdeveloped area of study. It sprawls like a huge, mysterious continent, intriguing but impenetrable. The photographer, the artist, the motion picture and TV man, all draw on its riches. Yet these practitioners frequently fear to explore too far, lest they destroy its magic spell.

The behavioral scientist, fearless in the face of magic, now forages into the nonverbal more and more. But often the game he pursues is of only incidental interest to the communicator. He does return, however, spinning fascinating tales about the tangled jungles of meaning, the submerged swamps of unconscious symbolism, and the rich but unmarked wilderness of communication potential.

Is it possible to bring order to this mysterious region? Is it possible to point out some trails to the communicator who wishes to find a short-cut to his goal and to share in the riches this area promises?

Let us try. The maps are still crude, not unlike those used by Magellan when he set out to explore the world. But some work has been done; previous adventurers have given us some guidance.

Even before we unfurl the maps of the early explorers, however, let us try a small excursion into the nonverbal, a test-run to see how well equipped you are for the journey ahead. Look at Figure 1. What is going on here?

Look first at the verbal level. Both men are saying the word "right." Are they both saying it in the same way? No? In how many ways do their "rights" differ?

Most people will note that the man on the left, Mr. *A,* is asking a question; his voice will rise while Mr. *B*'s will not. Which "right" is louder? Most people would say Mr. *B*'s. Why? Because it's bigger? Why should bigness be equated to loudness?

Look next at the nonverbal level. Various people project different stories into this simple scene. The differences will tell quite a bit about your personality. But equally important, most people from your culture will come to certain common conclusions. Do you, for instance, have a meaning for a handshake? Not all cultures do.

Now let's look at some of the subtler visual cues in Figure 1. Who is more powerful? More aggressive? How do you know that? Who is more trustworthy? More honest? What

From *Dimensions in Communication: Readings,* second edition, by James Campbell and Hal Hepler. Copyright © 1970 by Wadsworth Publishing Company, Inc., Belmont, California 94002. Reprinted by permission of the publisher and Randall Harrison.

Figure 1

makes you think so? Who is more competent? More intelligent? Who is more friendly? If this is a business transaction, who is going to come out ahead?

With your hand or a sheet of paper, cover the lower left corner of the picture until you cannot see Mr. *A*'s left hand. Does the picture without that corner have the same meaning as with it? Why?

What has been going on here? What have you learned from this simple experiment?

At least three lessons might be drawn:

1. A good deal of nonverbal communication goes on around us.
2. This nonverbal communication is important; we make decisions based on it.
3. Frequently, nonverbal communication is at a low awareness level; we may not realize that we are sending or receiving.

Do you agree with these points? Let's recheck the evidence.

In this particular picture, relatively little information is transmitted in the verbal band; a great deal is transmitted in the nonverbal band. The proportion of information in each band varies, of course, with the communication situation. A textbook may include little nonverbal communication, while a sports event, a ballet, or a silent motion picture may be highly nonverbal. Interestingly enough, it has been estimated that in face-to-face communication no more than 35 percent of the social meaning is carried in the verbal messages.

What kinds of decisions have you made based on nonverbal cues? If you found differences in power, trustworthiness, and competence, you made some quite important decisions. Research indicates that these may be some of the key dimensions of source credibility, which in turn is believed to be a vital element of persuasiveness. In short, whether you are persuaded or not may rest on nonverbal cues.

Equally important, you may have a hard time putting your finger on what these cues are. What, for instance, communicates "power"? A jutting jaw? A straight-shouldered posture? Down-turned eyebrows? A straight arm instead of a curved arm in a handshake? What communicates low intelligence? A large nose and close-set eyes? A small forehead? An upper lip that protrudes beyond the lower lip?

If this were a real-life situation, Mr. *A* and Mr. *B* would probably be quite unaware of the nonverbal messages they are sending. If you were a receiver of those messages, you probably would be unaware that you were receiving and using them. Unless we stop the action and force ourselves to think about it, we are not likely to attend to many of the specific cues that lead to our feelings or hunches about a person or a situation.

With the lessons from this trial-run in mind, let us now unroll the mappings of the nonverbal made by previous explorers.

Previous Mappings of the Nonverbal

Any area of potential knowledge can be mapped in several ways, just as we can draw a variety of maps of the United States. We could have a political map that showed only state boundaries and major cities. We could have a highway map, a weather map, a map showing altitude above sea level, and so on.

Maps of intellectual areas are useful in much the way maps of physical regions are useful. They help the intellectual traveler identify major divisions and points of key interest. They help him see differences and similarities between various regions. They keep him from getting lost; from thinking he's in one area when he's actually in another. Finally, and especially important for progress, they allow other investigators to follow the path of the original mapper, expanding and improving his work.

The intellectual explorer makes a map that is useful to him. In charting the nonverbal, different boundaries have seemed useful to different investigators. Some of those who use the term "nonverbal" are likely to include everything except the spoken and written word. The meaning of the term would then encompass, for these users of it, messages obtained by touch and smell. Thus, the use of perfume might be considered nonverbal communication.

Even this distinction is not as clear-cut as it might seem, however. Some writers observe that the written and spoken word are not completely exempted from the nonverbal world. When we choose large type instead of small type, italics instead of regular, Old English type instead of modern, we are making communication decisions that might be considered nonverbal. The size of the words in Figure 1 might be considered nonverbal. Similarly, there are certain aspects of speech such as intonation, rhythm, and speech which seem to lie on the fringes of traditional linguistic mappings.

Some explorers prefer to draw the boundary around visual communication instead of nonverbal communication. This would cut off perfumery at one end and clearly include the selection and layout of type in printing at the other end. Perhaps one of the oldest ways to cut up this area is to speak of audio-visual communication. This includes the spoken word but tends to exclude the printed word.

Two of the most active explorers within the nonverbal boundaries have been Jurgen Ruesch and Weldon Kees. Ruesch is a professor of psychiatry at the University of California School of Medicine while Kees is a poet, critic, and film producer.

In their book, *Nonverbal Communication,* they divide the world of nonverbal into three parts: sign language, action language, and object language.

Sign language is in use when a gesture, such as the hitchhiker's thumbing, replaces words, numbers, or punctuation. The individual makes the gesture for the purpose of communicating.

Action language includes all bodily movements that communicate, but are not primarily meant to communicate. For instance, a young man wolfing down his food communicates something about his hunger, and perhaps about his upbringing. He does not eat that way primarily to communicate, however; he eats that way to satisfy his hunger quickly. Nevertheless, his actions are messages available for decoding by any observer.

Object language includes the display of material things, including the human body and its clothing. For Ruesch and Kees, object language includes both the intentional and unintentional. Some objects, for instance an engagement ring or a display model, are meant to communicate. Other objects, such as the furniture in a room, may be made and arranged for some utilitarian purpose, but may also communicate much about the person who lives there.

Ruesch and Kees suggest that one way to draw the boundary between verbal and nonverbal is to apply the concepts of analogic and digital codification. Recent work with computers has stimulated thinking about the coding, transmission, storage, and manipulation of information. Essentially, there are two types of computers, the digital and the analogic. In the analogic code, some similarity exists between the code element and the aspect of the world being represented. Examples would be pictures, maps, and model trains. Digital codes, such as numbers and letters, tend on the other hand to be sharply different from the things represented. For the practicing communicator, each of these codes has certain advantages in transmitting information. Ruesch and Kees point particularly to the way the two codes complement each other in spatial and temporal characteristics.

Edward Hall, in his book *The Silent Language,* marks space and time as two special areas of nonverbal communication worth studying in their own right. As Hall puts it, "time talks" and "space speaks." In the American culture, for instance, punctuality communicates respect while tardiness is an insult. (It says, "I don't think you're important; your time's not worth much.") In some other cultures, however, to arrive exactly on time is an insult. (It says, "You are such an unimportant fellow that you can arrange your affairs very easily; you really have nothing else to do.") Rather, an appropriate amount of tardiness is expected.

Similarly, the use of space can communicate. In our culture, when we talk to another person we stand about an arm's length apart. If you see two individuals standing closer, you are likely to conclude they are lovers or that they are plotting a conspiracy. You can demonstrate this to yourself quite easily. The next time you are chatting with someone, slowly move in. You'll find they will quite unconsciously withdraw to maintain the right distance. In some cultures, the accepted interpersonal distance is smaller. When people from different countries interact, you may find misunderstandings arise because they cannot find a distance that is mutually comfortable. As someone advances on you, you may feel, "He's pushy and overbearing," or "He's falling all over me." On the other hand, if someone withdraws, you may feel, "He's avoiding me; he's trying to hide something," or, "He doesn't like me."

While time and space are two important areas of communication for Hall, he would go on to codify all of what he calls the "primary message systems." Hall, an anthropologist, sees culture as communication, and he would apply to culture the approaches that have been so successful in descriptive linguistics. Spoken language is analyzed in terms of phonemes, morphemes, and syntax. Hall suggests that culture might be examined in somewhat comparable categories that he calls isolates, sets, and patterns.

Perhaps the most ambitious attempt at mapping part of the nonverbal area can be found in "kinesics," the study of communication through bodily movements. Ray L. Birdwhistell is the founder of this research.[1] Drawing on the mapping methods of linguistics, Birdwhistell developed a notational system that enabled him to make very precise, second-by-second recordings of bodily movements. In analyzing his data, he speaks of the kine and the kinemorph, concepts similar to the phone and the morpheme in linguistics.

Birdwhistell finds that, in the gestural language, very small shifts may make a big difference. He discovered, for instance, that in raising the eyebrows perhaps 23 different positions are seen as having separate meaning. Interestingly enough, from his early studies, it appears that men can produce these different positions at will more easily than women can.

Birdwhistell also finds that the eye area and the hand are particularly important for communication in our culture. Among the Japanese, the German, and the Bombay Indians, these areas seem less important.

Kinesics has opened the possibility of examining the relationship between communication bands. Birdwhistell notes that television announcers can sometimes be seen contradicting in gesture what they are saying in words. When this happens to an announcer, or an actor, it is frequently amusing, but this type of interband conflict in other communication situations can lead to tragedy.

Recently Birdwhistell has been working with psychiatrists exploring the origins of mental disturbances such as schizophrenia. One hypothesis is that schizophrenia arises when an individual has been placed constantly in what Gregory Bateson calls "the double bind." This means the person gets two conflicting orders at the same time; he cannot obey one without disobeying the other. Birdwhistell's work indicates that one or both of these conflicting orders may flow in through the nonverbal band.

While kinesics is perhaps the best mapped area of nonverbal communication so far, other areas are getting increasing attention. At Michigan State University, we have recently focused on the pictorial code. Much, of course, has been written in this area by artists, designers, and experts in aesthetics, but so far the maps do not agree very well. Different people going into this area see different things as being important.

We have begun by breaking down the code, using such categories as the pict, the pictoform, the pictomorph, the pictophrase, and so on. In Figure 2 are six simple face pictomorphs.

Figure 2

Do you have a meaning for each expression? What are your meanings? What cues are you using to arrive at these meanings?

These simple figures give us a chance to demonstrate one more aspect of nonverbal communication. Let's imagine that each of these little fellows is saying, "That's great!" Is there any difference when *A* says it and when *D* says it?

Any message can be broken down into two parts: the content and the instructions on how to interpret that content. The source is likely to communicate his own evaluation of the content, his interest, his excitement, his intentions. Implicitly or explicitly, he tells the receiver how to react to the content. This part has been called meta-communication. The nonverbal band can carry content or instructions, but it seems to have a particularly important role in meta-communication. It allows the instructions to arrive at the same time as the content and, as in the above case, it tells us whether the message is sincere or sarcastic.

Looking to the future, we can expect more and better mappings of nonverbal areas. We can already see, however, that at least four major areas are important; time, space, action, and object. These are related to each other as shown in Figure 3.

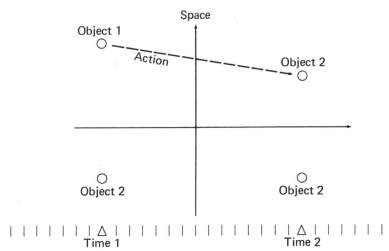

Figure 3

Time and space provide the major dimensions. Actions occur in time and objects occur in space. Actions and objects are related since actions occur through the movements of objects. In Figure 3, object 1 moves closer to object 2, from time 1 to time 2. The dotted line represents action.

Finally, we need to note that we can represent time, space, action, and object at various levels of abstraction. If you are object 1 and a friend is object 2, we have an event in real life. If you and your friend wish to tell me about this event and perform it again, we have a reenactment. This might be live, or we might do it in a motion picture. If you wish to show me what happened in a photograph or a drawing we have a portrayal. (Figure 3 is a diagrammatic sketch, or one kind of a portrayal.) Finally, you may wish to tell me about the event only in words, or even in numbers. Here we have a description.

You will note that as we moved from event to reenactment portrayal to description, we moved from analogic to digital coding. As we move each step, we lose some aspects of the original event, but we also gain some communication advantages. I cannot put you and your friend in this book; I *can* put Figure 3 in.

Now then! Studying a map is all well and good, but that alone does not get a traveler to his destination. The practical communicator has a right to ask: How does this help me get where I want to be? First, we need to make sure he knows where he wants to be.

Communicator Goals

The competent communicator usually wants certain things to happen to the information he sends out. He may want selection, comprehension, acceptance, recall, and use. These are his communication goals. Often he wants all these goals. Sometimes, he places more emphasis on one than on the others. If he is in entertainment, he may stress selection. If he is in education, he may point toward comprehension and recall. If he is interested in persuasion, he may concentrate on acceptance.

Each of these goals has subgoals. Selection, for instance, may involve attention and interest. The communicator wants his message selected over competing messages, and within the message he wants certain information attended to more than other information. He wants continued selection, or attention.

Comprehension includes meaning and understanding. The communicator wants some meaning response elicited, and he hopes it is a shared meaning, i.e., that there is understanding.

Acceptance includes belief and attitude. In other words, is the information true, and is it good for me? Finally, most communicators hope that the information they send out will be recalled and used at the appropriate time.

Given this array of goals, what routes are most likely to lead there? How can nonverbal communication help or hinder?

Selection

Selection is likely to increase as the perceived rewards of a message increase and the perceived costs go down. Nonverbal techniques are frequently used to boost rewards and slice costs. Time, space, object, and action all play a part in determining what will be selected. Similarly, the abstracting process that goes on in analogical codification can play a role. Let's see how this works.

The communicator can frequently control the timing of his message. Where he can, he will try to have the message land on target when the audience is most likely to select it, when the rewards are highest and the costs lowest. To help this process along, he may provide lead time; he may give his audience advance warning that a message is coming. If an audience is expecting a message at a given time, punctuality becomes an issue. A late message—whether a term paper, a business report, or a press release—is likely to have undesirable consequences for the communicator. Tardiness is likely to communicate, in our culture, low regard for the audience and for the message. Selection can sometimes be increased, of course, by communications off schedule. Delay may build anticipation and suspense. A call at "odd hours," late at night or early in the morning, may suggest urgency and importance. If the message is not worth the anticipation and urgency, however, the communicator may get initial selection but cut his chances of being accepted, or ever selected again.

Within a message, the communicator also makes decisions about timing. Pacing of information and message elements may make the difference between an exciting and a boring communiqué, between interest and disinterest. Similarly, duration of a message may influence selection. As the length increases, cost goes up and selection may drop.

Here the communicator may have to choose between selection and some other goal such as comprehension. Fortunately, using the nonverbal band can sometimes increase both selection and comprehension. A multiband presentation may provide redundancy that will bring the audience to the desired comprehension level faster. In other words, a ten-minute motion picture might do the job of a twenty-minute speech.

The multiband presentation may eliminate competing messages even where it does not introduce redundancy. The man listening to an after-dinner speech may be watching the pretty waitress; the man watching a film has this opportunity removed. (He may, of course, find other pursuits, such as dozing.)

The communicator seeks monochronism, which is a fancy way of saying "one thing at a time." He wants his audience's full attention, and in interpersonal communciation, he usually feels complimented when he gets it. He's likely to feel that his message is going to get the attention it deserves when the man behind the desk calls his secretary on the intercom and says, "I'll accept no calls, Miss Smith, we don't want to be disturbed."

Finally, multiband presentations provide a channel for meta-communication. As one band provides information, another band provides instructions for interpretation: "This is important, this is rewarding, this is for you." The simultaneous transmission of information and instructions seems more likely to hold attention than a message that alternates content and comment.

Within the visual band, space and object play a vital role in selection. One frequent way to boost selection is to increase size. As size increases, the object, whether headline type or motion picture image, becomes more easy to see; effort drops and selection should increase.

But beyond a certain point, an increase in size can no longer reduce effort, although it may increase rewards. The oversized object has a novelty value that may be rewarding in itself. Similarly, the oversmall object may be selected for its novelty.

Just as the communicator wants monochronism, or isolation in time, he may want isolation in space. The liberal use of white space may make a printed message stand out, while a spacious office may be the fitting setting for an important man.

Considering people as objects that may be arranged in space, the communicator may wish to give attention to the placement of his audience. A conference where everyone faces the speaker's platform suggests one kind of information flow, while a circular seating arrangement around a conference table suggests another. The effective communicator may also prearrange his own selection of messages. He may place over-communicators in the silent corners up front in a classroom, or at his elbows at a conference table, where they can be overlooked. He may place some more reticent communicator in a hot spot where he will be encouraged to speak.

Similarly, many men give attention to the seating arrangement in their offices. At one time, the executive communicated to the visitor only from behind his mammoth desk. Today, coffee tables and easy chairs are becoming an increasingly common feature of executive decor.

Finally, selection may be influenced by the type of codification used. Traditionally, cartoons and photographs are more popular in readership studies than printed material. This may be because of their novelty. It may be because they promise more reward for less effort.

For example, the use of pictures is believed to increase the popularity of the total publication. There are many examples, however, of a cartoon or photo being so popular that it reduced the attention given to surrounding printed material.

In general, it might seem that people like to be eye-witnesses at real events. As we move from reenactment, to portrayal, and thence to description, selection should drop off. Frequently, however, as the communicator re-codes an event he condenses and sharpens it, so that unimportant elements are dropped and pertinent elements are pointed up. The skillful communicator is ever seeking the proper level of code, one that gives him all he needs and yet eliminates the extraneous.

Comprehension

Selection is the first step in comprehension; the message that is not attended to cannot be understood. Comprehension may, however, also influence selection. Both that which is completely understood and that which cannot be understood are likely to be bypassed.

Timing is important in comprehension since a pace that is either too fast or too slow will lose the audience. Modern teaching programs offer an excellent example of a way of placing the control of pacing in the hands of the audience; the students progress only when they have comprehended.

In other communication situations, the communicator will have to devise other ways of checking his audience's comprehension. In speaking to an individual or a group, the communicator may increase his effectiveness by being a good receiver of nonverbal messages. While one man is speaking, it is impolite for another to interrupt verbally, but the receiver is very likely to be sending nonverbal messages in the form of perplexed frowns, nods of agreement, smiles of understanding, and so on.

It is frequently assumed that comprehension can be increased by moving from a digital to an analogic code. If we wish someone to understand an event, a reenactment may provide more complete information than a three-dimensional model. The model, in turn, may allow certain kinds of comparisons that could not be gleaned from a photograph. And the photograph or drawing may offer information not easily available in a written description.

This assumes that we want the receiver to understand the complete event. Frequently, however, the communicator wishes to point up some principle within the event, or some relationship among the number of events. Here, it is again important to move to the best level of codification for the abstraction desired. "Best" is defined, of course, in terms of the receiver.

Analogic codes tend to be more expensive to prepare and use. Thus, the communicator may need to balance the level of comprehension he'll settle for against the cost of reaching this level.

Acceptance

In courtrooms, we rule out hearsay evidence; we want only eye-witnesses. We also say, "Seeing is believing." If the communicator is concerned about being believed, he may try moving his receiver closer to the event by live demonstration, by newsreel, or by photograph. He may also invoke expert testimony from unimpeachable sources.

The receiver can evaluate any piece of information in terms of its fidelity and its authenticity. Fidelity is based on completeness; how much of the original event do I have here to look at? Authenticity relates to validity, and takes into account the amount of tampering or restructuring that may have taken place.

In general, films and photographs appear to have more fidelity and authenticity than verbal messages. We know, however, that films and photographs can deceive in many ways. First of all, the scene can be staged; it may not be a real event. Here the receiver may use nonverbal cues to decide on authenticity. The sharp, slick photograph, while having high fidelity, may be rejected as unauthentic. Meanwhile, the blurred, low fidelity picture may have the candid or newsreel quality that stamps it with authenticity.

Even when the event has not been staged, distortions can creep into a picture. The public has become aware in recent years of the composite photograph in which pictures of two individuals, taken separately, are rephotographed into one print so it appears that the two are friendly. Through retouching and a variety of photographic techniques, authenticity may be reduced.

Still photographs, even when they have not been tampered with, may lead to false impressions. For example, a rare event recorded in a photograph may be taken as the typical. Thus, anti-American propaganda may use actual photographs of violence and crime with the implication that this is the everyday norm. Similarly, a picture taken many years ago may be mistakenly assumed to represent conditions today.

With motion pictures, of course, editing can rearrange events so that totally different impressions are left with the viewer. By manipulating time, causal relationships can be made to emerge. Most commercial films are not shot in sequence. Rather, similar scenes are shot at the same time and then rearranged into the desired order in editing.

In interpersonal communication, nonverbal cues are frequently monitored to determine the authenticity of verbal statements. Partly this is because the sender may not realize he is sending nonverbal messages, and he might not be able to stop even if he knew. Thus, the blush or the frown is likely to be taken as more reliable than accompanying verbal reassurances.

Belief, as we have used the term, is only one step in acceptance. The communicator may want his audience not only to say, "That's true," but in addition, "I like it that way," or "I agree with you."

Much has been written about belief and attitude change, but let us take just two simple notions about attitude change and see how nonverbal communication fits in. One method we might call "sugar-coating." The other we can call, "I'm-your-buddy." Both are based on the theory that the attitude toward the information in a message may improve if the receiver, in the first case, likes the message treatment and, in the second case, likes the guy who sent it.

"Sugar-coating" can be done in purely verbal messages, but frequently the nonverbal band is brought into play. Color, pictures, cartoons, three dimensions, even music can be used. While these treatment devices can make a message more appetizing, they are not without danger. Sometimes the content gets lost in the sugar and the audience eats the coating but not the pill.

In the "I'm-your-buddy" approach, steps are taken to build up the source, his friendliness, his expertise, his power—all the qualities that make him a person you'd want to agree with. Many nonverbal cues contribute to these impressions, such as a man's dress, his letterhead, his office, his facial expressions, and so on. In less personal communication situations, inferences may be made about the source on the basis of the quality of his message treatment, whether, for instance, he uses high-grade or low-grade paper, multi-color or single color, pictures or type only, motion pictures or film strips.

Here again the more expensive is not necessarily the best. The natty congressman who drives around Washington in a limousine may switch to folksy clothes and an old jalopy when he tours his district talking to voters. Similarly, a lavish promotional piece put out by a government agency or a charitable organization can backfire. The receivers may resent the group's spending money on the publication instead of on its task; funds may be cut instead of increased.

Recall

Once you've gotten information into your receiver's head, how do you get it out again? How do you increase the chances that he will recall pertinent information at the appropriate time? Information is likely to be recalled if it is distinctive and if it is organized in such a way that it is available. For distinctiveness, we emphasize cue clarity. For organization, we look at cue association.

The verbal cue "d-o-g" is distinctively different from the cue "c-o-w." The two words both have three letters and a common middle letter. But the difference in the first and the last letters make it easy for us to discriminate between them.

If we move to a more analogic codification of the same two objects, whether in picture, model, or actual animal, we will find a great many more differences. The size, shape, and such physical features as horns, teeth, and tails, distinguish one animal from the other. Greater cue clarity exists.

While nonverbal codes are often used to increase cue clarity, they can also be used to build cue association so that an individual can more easily pull the right response out of his reservoir of knowledge. We learn verbal chains of association when we memorize a rhyme such as, "Columbus sailed the ocean blue . . ." This may be the most efficient way to remember the digital response, "1492." If, however, we want to remember the path of the voyage, a visual map may be more helpful than a verbal description or a numerical notation of longitudes and latitudes.

Space is perhaps used most frequently among the nonverbal mnemonic devices. We arrange objects or cues into spatial patterns and recall individual elements by remembering what was located around them. Interestingly enough, people seem to differ in their ability to use visual mnemonic devices; they are more helpful to some than to others.

Efficiency of recall may increase if we pair verbal with nonverbal stimuli (that is, use multibands). In learning a foreign language, for instance, seeing an object while hearing its name is more effective than seeing the English word and then the foreign word. With multibands we have been able to pair stimulus and response more closely in time and thereby improve learning.

A variety of nonverbal cues can be used to change the learning curve. If for instance, you memorize ten items in sequence, you will find a gentle U-curve of recall. You will remember the first and last items best, the middle items least. But if you make the fifth item distinctive in some way, you will find an upswing in your memory curve at that point. To make the fifth item distinctive, change its color, add a sound, introduce a picture, or provide some other convenient nonverbal cue. A string around your finger is one type of nonverbal reminder. There are obviously many other nonverbal techniques that can aid recall.

Use

The final test of communication effectiveness is whether the receiver uses the information he has obtained. In most academic settings, the first use of information is in a test. A student wants to be able to make verbal responses to verbal questions.

In many communication situations, however, the communicator wants more than a verbal response; he seeks some overt action. If you want a man to fly an airplane, you are not satisfied if he can only tell you how it's done. This may be a first step, but the real test is in getting the plane off the ground and back safely. In other words, as you move to seeking nonverbal responses, you may want to move to the nonverbal stimuli that will trigger those responses in the actual use situation.

In interpersonal communication, whether a person uses his information or not may depend on the group sanctions and expectations that he observes. Frequently these sanctions and expectations are communicated nonverbally. For example, an individual may see a wide variety of behavior on television. He has this information and presumably could use it. If he starts to use it, however, and it is not approved by his group, he will get nonverbal messages telling him so. His friends will look startled, they'll frown, glare, and possibly add specific verbal communications if he persists in his behavior.

A Final Word

In what we have said, we have implied that you can be more effective if you harness the nonverbal into your communication strategy. A final word needs to be said about communication efficiency—the price you are willing to pay for effectiveness.

Sometimes nonverbal communication is more expensive than verbal communication. This cost arises from three sources. It may come from the intrinsic costliness of nonverbal materials. It may come from a lack of knowledge about alternatives. It may come from poor planning. Many kinds of nonverbal communication are costly because they require expensive materials and the time and talent of skilled creators. A publication with pictures is likely to cost more than one without. A motion picture is more expensive to produce than a pamphlet.

However, not all nonverbal techniques are expensive. Some cost very little; some indeed are worth the price of many words. The proper timing of a message or an effective seating arrangement at a conference may cost only a little thought on the part of the communicator.

As you become aware of nonverbal techniques and increase your skill in their use, they take less effort, and in this sense are less costly. As you work, your repertoire of alternatives expands and you are also better able to predict which alternative will get the desired result.

Perhaps the greatest stumbling block in the path of the unskilled communicator, however, results from poor planning. Usually, he does not allow early enough for the incorporation of nonverbal communication into his strategy. Early incorporation is important for two reasons. Certain kinds of nonverbal materials take more lead time to produce than verbal materials. Even more important, however, the nonverbal dimensions can play a vital part in shaping the verbal dimensions of the message. The two should work together, each drawing on its strengths to complement the other and multiply the total impact. All too often, the verbal component is decided upon first. The nonverbal elements are attached last, and they never quite mesh; they detract as much as they add.

Since so much nonverbal communication flows at a low level of awareness, both for the source and the receiver, the alert communicator may want to build into his message framework checkpoints when he can stop and think about the nonverbal effectiveness of his communication.

Note

1. Ray L. Birdwhistell, "Background to Kinesics," *ETC.: A Review of General Semantics,* Vol. 13 (1955), pp. 10-18.

Part Six

Freedom of Speech and Ethical Considerations

In a climate where the right to speak from a public platform is denied to governmental officials, presidential candidates, Jerry Rubin, Angela Davis, General William Westmoreland and the Young Americans for Freedom; and in a climate where those denials take place in the form of reversing invitations, shouting down, pelting with objects, physical confrontations, surely it is time to raise serious questions about the rights and responsibilities of speaker-listeners. *Are* there limits to free speech? *Can* we deny any person the right to speak, however repugnant his views may be to us, without implicitly denying *ourselves* the right to speak? *How* shall we be "heard"; that is, through what forms of communication shall we speak? *Why* should we be heard? *If* we are to be heard, then, are we constrained by any responsibilities, legal or ethical?

In the articles that follow, we present a barrage of ideas relating to freedom of speech and ethical considerations.

We have only to pick up a daily newspaper or turn on the TV news to be aware of the variety of "tactics employed by contemporary protest groups—by the Vietnam war dissenters, the civil rights movement, or students demanding a greater share in campus decision-making." We might *expect,* of course, that those who oppose the views of these groups might be expected to "divert a portion of their hostility toward the methods used" by these groups. But, as Franklyn Haiman suggests in his article "The Rhetoric of the Streets," we should pause to think when "one finds those who profess neutrality or friendship toward the goals of the dissenters also expressing doubt about the methods." He undertakes a serious assessment of the three broad areas of criticism leveled at certain methods of protest. First, "insofar as the contemporary rhetoric of the streets violates the law it produces a climate of anarchy from which, in the end, no one can gain." Second, Haiman points to "those aspects of the new rhetoric, admittedly legal and appropriate under some circumstances, but alleged to violate the proposition that, in an orderly society, there must be prescribed and proscribed times, places, and manners for protest." Thus, he notes that often "... the new rhetoric exceeds the bounds of rational discourse ...; that the new rhetoric is 'persuasion' by a strategy of power and coercion rather than by reason and democratic decision-making." This he terms the "most difficult and profound" from the view of the rhetorical critic.

Professor Haiman examines the strengths and weaknesses of those who espouse one or all of the three critical postures discussed. He then challenges us all to avoid unexamined premises concerning the rhetoric of the street and to work together "to help create the conditions under which the achievement of [a high] standard [of public discussion] becomes a possibility." We will *not* do that by "condemning out of hand the contemporary rhetoric of the streets," nor by embracing it unthinkingly.

In "The Rhetoric of Confrontation," Robert Scott and Donald Smith discuss confrontation in the sense more specific than "the face-to-face coming together of spokesmen for disparate views." Rather, they discuss radical and revolutionary confrontation. They, as Professor Haiman did earlier, attempt to explore some of the basic premises of confrontation. First, they ask: "From what *roots* does the impulse to confront spring?" Here, they discuss two essential concepts: "radical division" and "the rite of the kill."

In their consideration of "radical division" they explore the conflict between the "haves" and the "have-nots" in terms of those "have-nots" who as they "confront established power do not seek to share" but to "supplant." Here, the "have-nots" are seen to argue: "The process of supplanting will be violent for it is born of a violent system."

In their consideration of "the rite of the kill," Professors Scott and Smith point to the have-nots' line of argument: "The enemy is obvious, and it is he who has set the scene upon which the actors must play out the roles determined by . . . cleavage and exploitation. The situation shrieks kill or be killed."

After examining two of the essential lines of arguments of the revolutionary have-nots, the authors examine confrontation both as a totalistic strategy and as a nontotalistic tactic.

We sometimes hear so much of "free speech" movements that we tend to forget that freedom of speech has long been a central concern of Western society. Walter Lippmann traces the urge for freedom of speech back to the Socratic dialogues. Although, in contemporary society the modern mass media have accentuated the problem, an essential fact remains:

> . . . freedom to speak can never be maintained by *objecting to interference with* the liberty of the press, of printing, of broadcasting, of the screen. It can be maintained only by *promoting debate.* (Italics mine.)[1]

Freedom of speech is, thus, viewed as "the means to a confrontation of opinion."[2] Implicit in such a definition is an *obligation*—"The obligation to subject [any] utterance to criticism and debate."[3]

Lippmann points out that what many people "most ardently desire is to suppress those who disagree with them, and therefore, stand in the way of the realization of their desires."[4] Thus, regardless of *who* the suppressor of ideas is, "when genuine debate is lacking, freedom of speech does not work. . . ."[5]

Now that we have examined the freedom to speak, let us raise again one of the questions posed earlier in this introductory section: If we are to be heard then are we constrained by any *ethical responsibilities*? The article that ends this section of the text would answer "Yes."

We are all aware of speakers who use whatever means they can to sell a product they know to be essentially worthless or even harmful, speakers who make promises they have no intention of keeping, and speakers who refuse to assume responsibility for what they say. We may have become *so* used to them that we rather cynically believe they are more the "rule" than the exception.

There have been striking instances of irresponsible speeches by public persons. Some have far-reaching implications, such as Joe McCarthy's: ". . . I have here in my hand a list of two hundred and five that were know to the Secretary of State as being members of the Communist Party and who nevertheless are still working and shaping the policy of the

State Department."[6] Few sentences have wreaked such havoc in our century despite the fact that McCarthy, when asked for a copy of that speech at Wheeling, West Virginia, could not find one, and despite the fact that McCarthy *himself* within two weeks reduced the number to 57 and then to 18.

Some have less far-reaching impact, but enormous immediate impact as this story in the *New York Times* illustrates:

> San Francisco, July 15—Senator Peter H. Dominick of Colorado said today that he was only spoofing when he read to the Republican convention last night an alleged quotation from the *New York Times* of 1765.
>
> The Senator was asked about a reference because there was no *New York Times* in 1765. The present newspaper was founded in 1851. Several earlier versions had existed briefly, starting in 1813. "I know that," Mr. Dominick said. "There were no daily newspapers in 1765." The mention last night left some delegates and television watchers with the impression that the Senator was reading a passage from a newspaper article published in 1765.
>
> He was speaking in opposition to the proposed platform amendment to condemn extremists.
>
> "The *New York Times* worried editorially about the extremism of Patrick Henry in 1765," Mr. Dominick said. Then he read what purported to be a quotation from that day criticizing Henry.
>
> Presumably the passage was supplied to the Senator by Tom Stagg, Jr., a delegate from Shrevesport, La. Mr. Stagg was a member of the Platform Committee and had opposed an extremist amendment there on the ground that it might have covered Patrick Henry in his day.
>
> Mr. Dominick declined to identify the source of the alleged quoted passage today. He said he was doing further research to be certain where it originated.[7]

One of the questions you may want to ask is whether excellence of a speech is always to be determined by its immediate effect. Aren't means and ends also important?

Karl Wallace, in "An Ethical Basis of Communication," suggests that ethical standards are related to both means and ends. Although Professor Wallace addresses "teachers of communication," the questions he raises are equally appropriate to speakers and critics.

He suggests four broad ethical guidelines which "are grounded in the public character of public utterance in a free society." They are:

1. The speaker "must reveal that he knows his subject, that he understands the implications and issues relevant to the particular time and occasion, that he is aware of essential and trustworthy opinions and facts, that he is dealing with a many-sided, rather than one-sided, state of affairs."

2. The speaker "who respects the democratic way of life must select and present fact and opinion *fairly.*"

3. The speaker "who believes in the ultimate values of democracy will invariably reveal the sources of his information and opinion."

4. The speaker, in a democratic society, "will acknowledge and will respect diversity of argument and opinion."

From these guidelines he extrapolates four "moralities": "the duty of search and inquiry; allegiance to accuracy, fairness, and justice in the selection and treatment of ideas and arguments; the willingness to submit private motivations to public scrutiny; and the toleration of dissent. . . ." These can serve, then, as the basis for developing an "ethic of communication in a free society."

Notes

1. Walter Lippman, *Essays in the Public Philosophy* (Boston: Little, Brown, and Co., 1955), pp. 129-30.
2. Ibid., p. 127.
3. Ibid.
4. Ibid., p. 130.
5. Ibid., p. 129.
6. For a fuller account of McCarthy's handling of this statement, see Richard H. Rovere, *Senator Joe McCarthy* (Cleveland: World Publishing Company, 1959), pp. 125-34.
7. *New York Times* (July 16, 1964).

THE RHETORIC OF THE STREETS:
SOME LEGAL AND ETHICAL CONSIDERATIONS

FRANKLYN S. HAIMAN

One hears considerable criticism these days of the tactics employed by contemporary protest groups—by the Vietnam war dissenters, the civil rights movement, or students demanding a greater share in campus decision-making. Many such challenges come from those in our society, presumably in a majority, who oppose some or all of the views of these protest groups and who might be expected to divert a portion of their hostility toward the methods used rather than the goals sought.

But when one finds those who profess neutrality or friendship toward the goals of the dissenters also expressing doubt about the methods they employ, it is time to attempt a serious assessment of the situation. For, indeed, many objective observers of the contemporary "rhetoric" of the streets do have misgivings about its propriety and even its legality. The term "rhetoric" as used here is put in quotation marks because only by the broadest of definition do some of the activities to be discussed fall into what has traditionally been called the province of rhetoric. If rhetoric means only verbal communication, we are clearly dealing here with matters outside that boundary. If, however, we take Aristotle's phrase to mean literally "*all* the available means of persuasion," then we do have here a problem in rhetorical criticism.

Regardless of terminology, our society today is confronted with a wide range of activities unfamiliar to those accustomed to thinking of protest in terms of a Faneuil Hall rally or a Bughouse Square soapbox orator. With respect to the Vietnam war we have witnessed everything from vigils, sit-ins at draft boards, and picket signs accusing the President of murder, to the burning of draft cards and self-immolation. On campuses across the country we have seen mass rallies doused by the hoses of firemen, sit-ins at administration buildings, and boycotts or threatened boycotts of classes.

The civil rights movement has generated perhaps the widest range of new forms. Invented to protest racial discrimination by restaurants, the sit-in has been extended to churches, libraries, real estate offices, and boards of education. The mass rally, an old form in itself, has been expanded to new locations and new dimensions—before the

Franklyn Haiman, "The Rhetoric of the Streets: Some Legal and Ethical Considerations," *Quarterly Journal of Speech* (April 1967), pp. 99-114. By permission of the Speech Communication Association and the author.

jailhouse, in the middle of the street, or through the center of the nation's capitol city. Slogans and folk-songs have assumed a new importance. Picketing, another older form, has also gone to new locations—before pavilions at the World's Fair or into a Chicago residential area to protest in front of the mayor's home. Mass marches through hostile territory—like Selma, Alabama, or all-white neighborhoods of Chicago—have attracted national attention. Going limp when arrested, obstructing the flow of traffic, and lying down in front of bulldozers on school construction sites have probably been the most extreme of the new forms—short, of course, of those employed in Harlem, Rochester, Cleveland, and Watts.

In attempting to review the major lines of criticism directed at this new array of rhetorical expressions, one finds that he can group them into three broad areas. The first line of criticism asserts that insofar as the contemporary rhetoric of the streets violates the law it produces a climate of anarchy from which, in the end, no one can gain. It is argued that to engage in the obstruction of traffic or to trespass on the property of others because one believes that his cause is good is to take the law into one's own hands and to create a society in which everyone's rights are threatened. The wanton looting and shooting which have erupted in some of our cities are alleged to be evidence of the ultimate end to which all of this leads. It is said that civil disobedience, even for the highest of motives, cannot be condoned in a society where legal channels—courts, legislatures, and the public forum—are available for the expression of grievances. One cannot condone civil disobedience for the "good guys" without allowing it for the "bad guys"; for who is to distinguish good motives from evil ones? Justice must be impartial and even-handed.

A second category of criticism is directed at those aspects of the new rhetoric, admittedly legal and even appropriate under some circumstances, but alleged to violate the proposition that, in an orderly society, there must be prescribed and proscribed times, places, and manners for protest. Critics point out that two of the leading spokesmen for the libertarian view regarding freedom of speech, philosopher Alexander Meiklejohn and Supreme Court Justice Hugo Black, have themselves supported this principle,[1] and that much of the current rhetoric of the streets exceeds the bounds of permissible time, place, and manner.

More specifically, they argue that protest is not justified if it constitutes an invasion of the privacy of others.[2] A prime example often cited is the series of marches of August, 1965, led by Negro comedian Dick Gregory to and around the home of Mayor Richard Daley in Chicago's Bridgeport section, an area of modest middle-class homes. Critics have condemned this and all other instances of picketing or parading in residential areas on the ground that "a man's home is his castle" and that such an intrusion was an invasion of the mayor's privacy, as well as that of his family and neighbors. Professor Alfred Kamin of Loyola University Law School in Chicago, makes an impressively documented presentation of the legal arguments for this point of view which he summarizes: "The thesis of this article is simple. . . . In the constitutional value scale, the quiet enjoyment and privacy of residential premises—even of the privately owned homes of public officials— merits a higher priority than freedom of speech."[3] Kamin draws support for his thesis primarily from court decisions in the area of labor-management disputes, which appear to reject any right of workers to carry their grievances to the doorsteps of their employers' homes, and from the substantial number of states (nine, to be exact) which have enacted statutory bans on residential picketing.

A slightly different rationale for objecting to the time, place, or manner of expressing deviant views was that used by Federal District Judge Samuel Perry in an injunction handed down in Chicago in Spetember, 1966. Judge Perry enjoined the American Nazi

Party and its leader, George Lincoln Rockwell, from demonstrating within one-half mile of any Jewish house of worship on any Jewish holy day, if clothed in Nazi garb or displaying Nazi symbols. He argued that such demonstrations would constitute an interference with the exercise of religious freedom by Jews attending their synagogues—a right which, unlike that of privacy, is explicitly recognized by the First Amendment.

Protests have also been challenged on the grounds that, under certain circumstances, they may place an undue strain upon the community's resources or may conflict with other community interests. One of the most current and significant illustrations of this rationale, found in an injunction issued by the Circuit Court of Cook County, Illinois, in August, 1966, limited the scope of marches then being conducted by the Chicago Freedom Movement under the leadership of Martin Luther King. This injunction, still in force, is of the utmost interest to the development of the law regarding freedom of speech, for it is a carefully drawn and relatively qualified ban which could well stand up on appeal to higher courts. It does not enjoin the marches entirely, but provides only that there shall not be more than one such march in Chicago per day, that only one neighborhood at a time may be the target, that no more than 500 persons may march, and that marches shall be confined to daylight times other than the rush hours. The basic justification of these limitations, argued before the Court on behalf of Chicago Police Superintendent O. W. Wilson, was that the police department could not simultaneously discharge its obligation to protect the marchers from the activities of hostile counter-demonstrators and fulfill its responsibilities to protect the safety and welfare of the community. Wilson charged that, at the height of the marches, when hundreds of policemen were diverted to the protection of demonstrators, crime rates had risen in other areas of the city.[4] He also suggested that the morale of the police department suffered severely during this period and that the financial costs to the city were exorbitant. How much effort, critics ask, can a city government reasonably be expected to make to protect dissenters from counter-violence, especially when the majority of taxpayers and voters may share the attitudes of those counter-demonstrators?

Finally, the time, place, or manner issue is sometimes argued on the basis of an "innocent bystander" theory which says that protest is permissible only so long as it is confined so as to affect the legitimate targets of the protest but not to inconvenience others. Hence one might concede that the mayor, as a public official, is a fair target for protest even when he is at home, but that his family and neighbors, the "innocent bystanders," should not have to be subjected to the same harassment. Similarly, the man who cannot get to work on time because of the congestion caused by a march, or the student who cannot study because of the turmoil created by campus demonstrations or boycotts of classes, may assert that their rights as innocent bystanders should take precedence over the free speech claims of the protesters. An analogy is sometimes made here to the secondary boycott in labor-management relations—an activity which is regarded as impermissible because of its harmful effects on those who are only tangentially related to the disputes.

The third major category of criticism directed at the contemporary rhetoric of the streets concerns objections which may be the most difficult and profound from the point of view of the rhetorical critic. At the core of these objections is the proposition that the new rhetoric exceeds the bounds of rational discourse, which teachers of rhetoric value so highly and are dedicated to promote; that the new rhetoric is "persuasion" by a strategy of power and coercion rather than by reason and demoncratic decision-making. This line of thought has been expressed in at least two different ways.

In an article in this journal, Professor Leland Griffin coined the phrase "body rhetoric" to express the thesis that much of the new rhetoric is not persuasion at all, at least as rhetoricians are accustomed to defining that term, but instead constitutes the "holding of a gun at the head" of those to whom the protests are directed.[5] Pickets at a mayor's home or college students sitting in at an administration building are simply throwing their weight around, says the critic, until the authorities give them what they want. If the Chicago Freedom Movement marchers are only interested in communicating a message, then why (given mass media coverage) cannot the same point be made with 500 marchers in one neighborhood as with 5,000 marchers in six neighborhoods simultaneously? To such critics the intention of the marchers seems not to be simply to *communicate* grievances, but to throw the city into such chaos that it will be *forced* to meet their demands.

Even the greatest champions of free speech have expressed doubts about such demonstrations. Justice Hugo Black has said:

> The First and Fourteenth Amendments, I think, take away from government, state and federal, all power to restrict freedom of speech, press, and assembly *where people have a right to be for such purposes.* This does not mean, however, that these amendments also grant a constitutional right to engage in the conduct of picketing or patrolling, whether on publicly owned streets or on privately owned property.... Were the law otherwise, people on the streets, in their homes and anywhere else could be compelled to listen against their will to speakers they did not want to hear. Picketing, though it may be utilized to communicate ideas, is not speech, and therefore is not of itself protected by the First Amendment.[6]

A majority of the United States Supreme Court, speaking through Justice Arthur Goldberg in the same case, proclaimed: "We emphatically reject the notion . . . that the First and Fourteenth Amendments afford the same kind of freedom to those who would communicate ideas by conduct such as patrolling, marching, and picketing on streets and highways as these amendments afford to those who communicate ideas by pure speech."[7]

The second line of criticism related to the general issue of rationality of discourse raises the age-old question of the new rhetoric's resort to emotional appeals. The focus here is on the popularity among contemporary protest movements of sloganeering, folksinging, draft-card burning, and other modes of communication that appear designed to elicit signal responses.[8] Catchphrases such as "Black Power," picket signs reading "Hey, Hey, LBJ, How Many Kids Have You Killed Today?" the joining of hands and the singing of "We Shall Overcome," the speeches of Mario Savio, the folksongs of Joan Baez and Pete Seeger are all cited as evidence of this tendency.

This is the outline of a rather formidable brief challenging the contemporary rhetoric of the streets. The challenge has been posed in both legal and ethical terms, and it raises, in substance, two kinds of questions about the new rhetoric: (1) Is the particular activity in question protected, or should it be, by the First Amendment? and (2) Even if legal, is the activity ethical? Let us turn now to the case for the defense.

Regarding the question of disobedience, civil or otherwise, to the law, one must concede that such activity does have an undermining effect on established authority and tends toward an anarchic social climate. Justice must be administered without discrimination either for or against the dissenter; if he breaks the law he must be punished. Yet, having recognized this, I would note some important qualifications often overlooked.

Many who currently advocate and practice civil disobedience do not expect nor ask for exemption from punishment. They are keenly aware that a lawless society cannot survive, but they are willing to pay whatever penalties the civil law may exact in order to obey what they regard as a higher law, be it it the law of their religion or their conscience, which requires them to protest what they view as some injustice in their society. They seek no special privileges, but rather hope that their willingness to suffer penalties for their convictions may communicate a message to the consciences of others and thus pave the way for social change. One can admire the courage and sympathize with the goals of such persons and still recognize, as they do, that they must be punished for their actions. One might go even further to suggest that such civil disobedience merits support, though not exemption from punishment, so long as it does no physical harm to others. Sharper distinctions may need to be made, for example, between the *inconvenience* resulting from the tying up of traffic to a World's Fair and the *physical danger* of a Watts riot. Indeed, a riot is not *civil* disobedience at all, and rioters are usually an entirely different group of people from the kind who engage in conscientious disobedience.

Critics of civil disobedience also need to be reminded that some kinds of lawbreaking are, paradoxically, quite legal. Again, finer distinctions are needed. So-called civil disobedience, which involves the violation of a law believed by the protesters to be unconstitutional and later found by the courts to be unconstitutional, may be exempt from punishment. One may, under some circumstances, with both legal and moral justification, disobey a local or state law in order to obey a higher civil law, i.e., the United States Constitution. Granted, one cannot embark on such a course lightly; for it is the United States Supreme Court, not the individual citizen, that, in our system, must ultimately decide whether a law is or is not constitutional. But if one is willing to run the risk of losing that decision (thereby paying the penalty, of course), he is fully justified in such a violation.

Many Supreme Court decisions, particularly those involving the First Amendment, support this position. One landmark case, in 1938, reversed the conviction of a member of the Jehovah's Witnesses who had been arrested and fined for distributing religious literature in Griffin, Georgia, under a city ordinance which the Court found to be an unconstitutional infringement on the freedom of speech and press.[9] More recently, in 1965, a Baltimore, Maryland, theatre manager who had deliberately flaunted the state's movie censorship statute because he thought it unconstitutional and was arrested and convicted in the lower courts, saw his conviction overturned by the Supreme Court, which agreed that the law violated the First Amendment.[10] Then, of course, there have been the long line of sit-in cases from the South, some of which have been decided on narrower grounds than the First Amendment, and some of which have involved refusal to obey police orders rather than laws, but all of which have been norm-breaking activities that provoked sanctions at the local level which were later reversed by the United States Supreme Court.[11]

One cautionary note must be appended here. The Supreme Court has, on occasion, taken the attitude that if a citizen believes a law or local administrative rule to be unconstitutional he must exhaust all possible administrative and judicial remedies before proceeding to its violation.[12] This position has not been sufficiently elaborated to make clear precisely how much effort a citizen must make to seek legal remedies before resorting to disobedience. This appears to depend somewhat on the particular circumstances of the law and violation in question. But, despite these qualifications, it is clear that dissenters have no obligation to conform indefinitely to statutes and ordinances that conflict with the Constitution. If this be deleterious to established authority, then established authority had better be brought into conformity with the law.

But what of *un*civil disobedience? Can anything be said in defense of Watts and of angry voices in the streets which sometimes seem to be calling for violence? Certainly not within the framework of a democratic society, where only peaceful change can be accepted. But should we not be somewhat troubled by the awareness that, despite the destruction to property, despite the loss of lives, despite the backlash of public opinion, these outbreaks have precipitated significant reforms that previously had been notably slow in coming? It would seem that even the "rhetoric of the riot," mindless and indiscriminate as it may be, has its positive function in contemporary America. What moral can be drawn from this, short of abandoning the conviction that a civilized society is preferable to the law of the jungle? Perhaps simply that if the channels for peaceful protest and reform become so clogged that they appear to be (and, in fact, may be) inaccessible to some segments of the population, then the Jeffersonian doctrine that "the tree of liberty must be refreshed from time to time, with the blood of patriots and tyrants" may become more appropriate to the situation than more civilized rules of the game.

The problems associated with the time, place, and manner of protest must now be addressed together with the possibility that countervailing interests such as privacy, convenience, or the safety and welfare of the community may justify some curtailments of the rhetoric of the streets. One can hardly quarrel with the general thesis, supported by Meiklejohn and Black, that there is no constituitonal right to protest whenever, wherever, and however one chooses. There must be, as Professor Harry Kalven has so aptly put it, a "Robert's Rules of Order for use of the public forum of the streets," for it is an "unbeatable proposition that you cannot have two parades on the same corner at the same time."[13] The real questions in this area are not questions about the correctness of the *principle,* but rather about the reasonableness and equity of its *application* to particular conflict situations. We must look beneath the pat phrases such as "innocent bystander" and "invasion of privacy," or the surface reasonableness of the Chicago Freedom Movement injunction, to do some honest weighing of the competing interests at stake.

The "innocent bystander" theory is the first which requires closer scrutiny. As was indicated earlier, an analogy is often made here to the illegality of secondary boycotts in labor-management relations. But serious questions can be raised about the validity of applying this theory to political and social protest movements. The grievances involved in labor-management disputes are essentially grievances held by one private party, or group of private parties, against the actions of policies of another private party, whereas the grievances involved in most protest movements are directed to the body politic as a whole and are redressable only by public policy or action. Thus it is arguable that on issues such as civil rights and the Vietnam war there is no such thing as an innocent bystander. Every citizen who supports the status quo, either actively or by passive acquiescence, is a legitimate target for the communications of the dissenter.

Furthermore, an examination of particular cases may reveal important shortcomings in the innocent bystander theory. The marches to Mayor Daley's home in the summer of 1965 provide a good example. Just how "innocent" were the "bystanders" in this case, the neighbors? After all, the message being communciated by the demonstrators concerned racial discrimination, and it was no accident (in view of either the motivations or effects of the march) that the mayor happened to live in an all-white neighborhood of the city, which has, over the years, been known for its resistance to the "intrusion" of Negro homeowners from adjacent areas. Although Mayor Daley was ostensibly the primary target of communication, the protesters certainly perceived his neighbors as legitimate recipients of their message. How often, in other instances where the innocent bystander theory is invoked, may the circumstances be similar?

But some would hold that even the mayor, although admittedly not an innocent bystander, should have the right to a private life, free from the harassments of political and social turmoil. What of this right to privacy as an alleged countervailing interest to freedom of speech? What of Kamin's case for the banning of protest from all residential areas? What of the fact that even Zechariah Chafee, one of the most respected proponents of freedom of speech, has been troubled over matters related to this issue?[14]

One can hardly deny that allowing for the expression of dissent in residential areas does indeed impinge on other important rights and privileges. The question, I think, is what price a society is willing to pay to insure that the messages of minority groups are not screened out of the consciences of those to whom they are addressed. For once the principle is invoked that listeners may be granted some immunity from messages they think they would rather not hear, or which cause them annoyance, a Pandora's box of circumstances is opened in which the right of free speech could be effectively nullified. Also, difficult problems arise in defining a residential area. Would not a prohibition against demonstrations in such areas turn out to mean that those who can afford to live in neighborhoods zoned exclusively for single-family dwellings would be protected, while those who live on a street with a shopping area, a gas station, a real estate office, or a public building would have no more protection than if they resided in an office building in the heart of the downtown center?

Perhaps appropriately, the United States Supreme Court, at least at this point in its development of a theory of free speech, has been unwilling to weight the scales in the manner suggested by Chafee and Kamin. On the contrary, there are cases which make clear the Court's view that the right to privacy, emotionally appealing as it may be, must not be purchased at major cost to the First Amendment.

An early precedent in this area was provided in 1943, in a case involving a city ordinance which prohibited the door-to-door distribution of handbills. A member of the Jehovah's Witnesses was arrested, convicted, and fined for circulating a leaflet announcing a religious meeting. Although the prosecution argued, in justification of the ordinance, that this was an industrial town in which many men worked a night shift and slept during the day, the Supreme Court ruled that "door to door distribution of circulars is essential to the poorly financed causes of the little people."[15] The Court indicated that a householder may post a notice on his door that he does not wish his doorbell rung and may enforce such a wish through the laws of trespass, but it held that a blanket prohibition of door-to-door soliciting by the city is unconstitutional. This position was reaffirmed in 1951, by implication, when the Supreme Court *upheld* a municipal ordinance prohibiting door-to-door solicitation for commercial magazines *only* because of the commercial element involved.[16] Had the solicitation been for political or religious causes, the Court presumably would have reached a different conclusion.

To be sure, these cases have involved only single solicitors, and a different posture might be taken by the Supreme Court if a case involving large numbers of marchers in a residential area goes up on appeal. But perhaps offsetting the numbers factor will be the consideration that marchers do not ordinarily ring doorbells and seldom walk on private property. If they remain on the public sidewalks and streets, the possible issue of trespass cannot intrude, and the Court will have to deal simply with the clash between an alleged right of residential privacy and freedom of speech.

Closely related to the right-to-privacy and innocent-bystander arguments is the assertion that the contemporary rhetoric of the streets sometimes creates inconvenience for other persons. This claim need not detain us long. Dissent is always an inconvenience to those who like the status quo, sometimes maddeningly so. But, again, a Jeffersonian epigram may give perspective—reminding us that it is "timid men who prefer the calm of despotism to the turbulent sea of liberty." One is tempted to be skeptical about those who complain so loudly over the congestion or annoyance generated by a civil rights march, but who do not raise similar objections to the St. Patrick's Day parade or the Saturday afternoon football crowds. Or, as Harry Kalven puts it, in suggesting that the "equal protection" clause of the Constitution may have some bearing on this problem: "Everyone at some time or other loves a parade whatever its effect on traffic and other uses of public streets. Municipalities pressed by concern with the protest movement may be inhibited in any rush to flat nondiscriminatory prohibitions by the difficulty of distinguishing between the parades we like and others. Equal protection may, therefore, require freedom for the parades we hate."[17]

Much more serious than the inconvenience argument is the claim set forth in the Chicago Freedom Movement case that unless protest marches are restricted in size and scope, dangerous consequences, such as a rise in the crime rate, may ensue for the city. How many police, critics query, can the government reasonably be expected to divert to the maintenance of order at locations where dissenters choose to aggravate hostile audiences? Or, put in another form, how large a hostile audience can dissenters reasonably expect the police to contain? The answer I am inclined to give is "Everything it takes including, if necessary, calling out the National Guard."

How can such an extreme position be defended? Simply on the grounds that to take any *other* course of action is to issue an invitation to hostile audiences to veto the right of dissent whenever they desire to do so. Only by the firmest display of the government's intention to use all the power at its disposal to protect the constitutional rights of dissenters will hecklers be discouraged from taking the law into their own hands. To be sure, the temporary costs may seem astronomical, but they may be nothing compared to the costs that could be suffered in the long run through any other course. This principle was clear to our national government when it posted an army on the campus of the University of Mississippi to insure that one man, James Meredith, was granted his rights to enter and to remain at that institution. Its reverse was equally clear in Little Rock, Arkansas, when Governor Orval Faubus let it be known (either out of conviction or desire) that the state's police power could not cope with those who wished to block the entry of Negro children to Central High School.

One can agree with this principle and still take the position that limitations on the time, place, and manner of protest designed to make the task of the police more manageable, are legitimate so long as they do not interfere substantially with the right of protesters to communicate their messages. This, in essence, is the rationale for the limited kind of injunction issued against the Chicago Freedom Movement marches; and, as evidence of good faith, the police superintendent could point to the rather formidable effort his department had put forth to protect the marches which had already taken place and which had aroused hundreds of hostile counter-demonstrators to potential and actual violence. But, again, one must look more closely at the specific facts of the situation to determine just how reasonable such limitations are.

Is it reasonable, for example, to confine protest marches to daylight hours? From the police department's viewpoint it is much simpler to control the behavior of crowds in daylight than in the dark. From the viewpoint of marchers who have to work for a living during the day, and who can protest only after-hours, it appears to be an effective deprivation of the right to communicate their grievances (except on Sundays!).

Is it reasonable to limit marches to no more than 500 persons? From the police department's viewpoint, yes; for the same message can be communicated by 500 as by 5,000, and at much less strain to community resources. From the viewpoint of the marchers, as well as from the theory of Marshall McLuhan, the medium of 5,000 marchers does *not* communicate the same message as 500. Furthermore, what of the constitutional rights to free speech of the potential 501st marcher? Who is to decide which 500 gets to march and which group does not?

Is it reasonable to limit marches to one neighborhood of the city per day? From the police department's viewpoint, certainly; for with little difficulty enough police can be assigned to one area to insure the maintenance of peace and order. From the viewpoint of the marchers, however, such a limit assumes a degree of coordination and unanimity among the parties enjoined that is rather presumptuous. To tell Mr. Albert Raby that he and his associates cannot march on the northwest side of the city because the Reverend Martin Luther King and his friends are marching that day on the southeast side not only presumes a conspiracy of planning between the two, but, more important, raises important constitutional issues of equal protection of the law. If the injunction against the Chicago Freedom Movement remains on the books and becomes, as it well might, a national precedent, I believe that a significant erosion of the First Amendment will have occurred.

I next turn to Judge Perry's injunctions against the Nazis, and its thesis that to allow Mr. Rockwell and his dozen-or-so goons to parade in Nazi garb in front of Jewish synagogues is to interfere with the right of Jews to exercise their religious freedom. The issue was *not* that Rockwell would disrupt services by throwing rocks through the synagogue windows or by broadcasting from a sound truck on the street in front; it was *not* that his pickets would obstruct the free flow of pedestrians on their way to and from their house of worship; it was *not* that they would do anything but peacefully and quietly parade with hated symbols (which might provoke *others* to violence), and *this* is what was alleged would be such an interference with the exercise of religious freedom that it justified the denial of Rockwell's freedom of speech. When making people angry or offending their sensibilities becomes a basis for shutting off communication because they happen to be on their way to pray, one can only marvel at the rationalizations a society will invent to justify suppression of the deviant.

One final issue in the time, place, and manner category asks whether certain areas within the public domain can legitimately be declared off-limits from the rest of the public forum. The most frequently proposed site for such an exception is the courthouse, on the theory that the right to a fair trial, unencumbered by the pressures on judge and jury that might accrue from demonstrators gathered on the courthouse grounds, justifies carving this exception from the free speech realm. Indeed, laws are already on the books at all levels of government providing for just such an exception. But now the question is being raised as to whether other sites should be similarly exempt. The most recent case of importance, decided by the Supreme Court on November 14 of last year [1966], found a narrow majority taking the position that not only was a Tallahassee, Florida, jailhouse entitled to such exemption, but even suggesting that the state may declare other public property out of bounds to protest, so long as it does so on a nondiscriminatory basis.[18] The facts in this case were relatively simple, as described by Justice Black in the majority opinion:

> Disturbed and upset by the arrest of their schoolmates . . . a large number of Florida A. & M. students . . . decided to march down to the county jail. . . . A group of around 200 marched from the school and arrived at the jail singing and

clapping. They went directly to the jail door entrance where they were met by a deputy sheriff. . . . He asked them to move back, claiming they were blocking the entrance. . . . They moved back part of the way, where they stood or sat, singing, clapping and dancing, on the jail driveway and on an adjacent area upon the jail premises.

There is then some difference of opinion about what happened. The majority asserts that "even after their partial retreat, the demonstrators continued to block vehicular passage over this driveway up to the entrance of the jail." After being warned by the sheriff to leave or face arrest, and after refusing to depart, they were arrested, and later convicted for trespass. The minority opinion, written by Justice William O. Douglas asserts:

The evidence is uncontradicted that the petitioners' conduct did not upset the jailhouse routine; things went on as they normally would. None of the group entered the jail. Indeed, they moved back from the entrance as they were instructed. There was no shoving, no pushing, no disorder . . . the entrance to the jail was not blocked. . . . If there was congestion, the solution was a further request to move to lawns or parking areas, not complete rejection and arrest.

Although this disputed emphasis in the factual situation may have had some bearing on the Court's decision, the difference between majority and minority went to more fundamental matters. The majority, in effect, seemed to be returning partially to a theory of law that had been propounded in 1897, in a case involving the use of the Boston Commons as a public forum, but which appeared to have been a dead letter since the famous *Hague* v. *C.I.O.* decision in 1939. In 1897, the Court had taken the position that the government has the same power to regulate the use of public property as an individual owner has to regulate the use of his private property, and that the government of Boston was fully within its rights to control the use of the Commons as it saw fit.[19] But in 1939, Justice Owen Roberts, in announcing the *Hague* decision of the Court, had said in a much-quoted passage: "Wherever the title of streets and parks may rest, they have immemorially been held in trust for the use of the public and time out of mind, have been used for purposes of assembly, communicating thoughts between citizens, and discussing public questions. Such use of the streets and public places has from ancient times, been a part of the privileges, immunities, rights, and liberties of citizens."[20]

The *Hague* v. *C.I.O.* philosophy seemed to prevail in all cases bearing on this issue that went to the Supreme Court after 1939. As recently as 1963, reversing the conviction of 187 Negro students who had gathered for a demonstration on the state capitol grounds at Columbia, South Carolina, an eight to one majority had declared: "The circumstances in this case reflect an exercise of these basic constitutional rights in their most pristine and classic form. The petitioners felt aggrieved by laws of South Carolina. . . . They peaceably assembled at the site of the State Government and there peaceably expressed their grievances."[21]

But now, in the *Adderley* case, a majority of the Court says, as in 1897, "The State, no less than a private owner of property, has power to preserve the property under its control for the use to which it is lawfully dedicated." This statement is reconciled with the *Edwards* decision as follows: "In *Edwards*, the demonstrators went to the South Carolina Capitol grounds to protest. In this case they went to the jail. Traditionally, state capitol grounds are open to the public. Jails, built for security purposes are not." Here the majority seems to be taking a slightly modified Boston Common position. The state may decide which public areas are appropriate for speech and which are not, so long as the uses to which these areas are "traditionally" and "lawfully dedicated" are taken into account.

Justice Douglas, speaking for the minority, did not think the matter so simple: "The jailhouse, like an executive mansion, a legislative chamber, a courthouse, or the state-house itself . . . is one of the seats of government whether it be the Tower of London, the Bastille, or a small county jail. And when it houses political prisoners or those whom many think are unjustly held, it is an obvious center for protest." There are other complexities as well. What of the frequent situation at small county seats, for example, or towns and villages, where the legislative chamber, executive offices, courtroom, and jail are all housed in the same building? Are the surrounding sidewalks, driveways, and lawns to be off-limits or not?

There are even difficulties, as Professor Kalven has pointed out, with laws such as the simple prohibition of courthouse picketing, which was one of the issues in *Cox* v. *Louisiana* in 1965. There, Justice Goldberg had said for the Supreme Court: "There can be no question that a State has a legitimate interest in protecting its judicial system from the pressures which picketing near a courthouse might create." But Kalven asks of this ruling: "Would this same protest have been permissible if moved a few blocks away? Could one, for example, distribute leaflets highly critical of the Court near the court-house? Is there pressure and intimidation in the protest in front of the courthouse that ceases to be present when it is in front of the statehouse? Or is the principle that it is all right to intimidate legislatures but not courts?"[22]

I must admit to sharing some of the ambivalence which has apparently plagued the Supreme Court concerning this last question. Perhaps the right to a fair trial *is* under-mined by crowds on the courthouse steps, just as it may be undermined by an unfettered freedom of the press to publicize pretrial allegations of guilt. And perhaps some carefully drawn measures are needed to protect the conduct of a trial from such distortions. But when extensions of this line of thought lead to decisions such as the one that was made in *Adderley,* I am inclined to join with Justice Douglas' dissent:

> There may be some instances in which assemblies and petitions for redress of grievances are not consistent with other necessary purposes of public property. . . . No one, for example, would suggest that the Senate gallery is the proper place for a vociferous protest rally. . . . But this is quite different than saying that all public places are off-limits to people with grievances . . . by allowing these orderly and civilized protests against injustice to be suppressed, we only increase the forces of frustration which the conditions of second-class citizenship are generating amongst us.

The category of criticism of contemporary protest movements which asserts that their rhetoric exceeds the bounds of rational discourse must, finally, be addressed. The first charge here was that the "body rhetoric" employed is a *physically* coercive tactic which has little to do with the exercise of freedom of *speech*. To deal intelligently with this charge a distinction must be made between demonstrations which do *not* directly ob-struct the functioning of an institution or society and those which do physically interfere with a normal flow of activity. I have already dealt with the latter type of protest in discussing civil disobedience, and wish here to address the issue solely in the context of admittedly legal and peaceful uses of the protesters' bodies to "bear witness" to their cause.

The difficulty people have in focusing exclusively on that issue and keeping it from being blurred with the other is itself instructive; for so often the reaction that is generated by the mass physical bearing of witness creates situations that deteriorate into physical disruption. Thus a march which begins as a peaceful parade of 1,000 through the streets of Chicago soon turns into a potential race riot requiring the intervention of hundreds of policemen. But let us be clear, as so few people seem to be, about what has changed this peaceful parade into such a potentially dangerous activity that the mere threat to march is perceived as a coercive weapon. The change has been wrought *by the hostile audience* which, rather than contenting itself to stay at home and ignore the demonstrators, chooses to go out on the streets to confront them. There is nothing *inherently* coercive about one dissenter, or one hundred, or one thousand, walking peaceably down a street or gathering to sing in front of a building. Their activity is endowed with coercive potential only if others go forth to do battle with them, or feel too guilty and fearful to leave them alone.

The logic of this seems so compelling that it is difficult to understand why it is so seldom perceived. It was apparently not perceived in the summer of 1966 by the mayor and police superintendent of Chicago who repeatedly suggested, in their public pronouncements on television and in the press, that the marchers, although admittedly within their legal rights, were holding a gun at the head of the city and should, for the sake of the general welfare, cease and desist. To be sure, a few appeals were also made to the white residents of affected neighborhoods to stay at home and ignore the marchers, but the burden of guilt and the call for maximum restraint were placed squarely on the shoulders of the Freedom Movement. Only Roman Catholic Archbishop John P. Cody seemed to analyze the problem more clearly, but even he ended up with essentially the same appeal:

> In the past several weeks, civil rights groups have been conducting marches and demonstrations in all-white neighborhoods of our community. Their purpose has been to draw the attention of the citizenry to the plight of minority groups, many of whose members are financially capable of buying or renting better homes but impeded from so doing by what can only be called a conspiracy of fear, suspicion and bigotry.
>
> The right of such groups to march and demonstrate is in itself beyond question. . . . Those who seek to deny this right by either threats or violence are clearly in violation of the law and morally blameworthy.
>
> This being said, it now appears that a new dimension has been added to the marches and demonstrations in the Chicago area. Because of the shameful reaction of some to the exercise of a basic freedom of our land, representatives of government, the police, and many other responsible groups are convinced that if the marches and demonstrations continue in the manner in which they have been proceeding, the result will very likely be serious injury to many persons and perhaps even the loss of lives.
>
> In view of all this, it would seem that the leaders of the civil rights movement are themselves confronted by a serious moral obligation, namely that they prayerfully reconsider the methods now being employed to achieve their altogether just and laudable purposes. They have not been guilty of violence and lawlessness. Others have. But the action of these others are now a circumstance which they must take into account in assessing their activities.
>
> It is truly sad, indeed, deplorable, that citizens should ever have to be asked to suspend the exercise of their rights because of the evil-doing of others. However, in my opinion and in the opinion of many men of good will, such is the situation in which we now find ourselves.[23]

The United States Supreme Court, in its latest dealings with the "body rhetoric" issue in *Cox* v. *Louisiana,* has attempted, as we noted earlier, to fashion a distinction between "pure speech" and "conduct" such as patroling, picketing, or marching, which may be the *vehicle* for speech but is not, according to Justice Goldberg's majority opinion, entitled to so wide a range of constitutional protection as speech itself. This opinion may well return to haunt the Court as having enunciated a distinction impossible to defend and maintain. For as Justice John Harlan wrote in 1961, in a concurring opinion in a decision to overturn the sit-in convictions of a group of Negroes at a Southern lunch-counter: "Such a demonstration in the circumstances . . . is as much a part of the free trade in ideas . . . as is verbal expression more commonly thought of as speech. It, like speech, appeals to good sense and to the power of reason as applied through public discussion . . . just as much as, if not more than, a public oration delivered from a soap-box at a street corner. This Court has never limited the right to speak . . . to mere verbal expression."[24]

Harry Kalven, too, in one of his typically keen analyses, has suggested: "The Court's neat dichotomy of 'speech pure' and 'speech plus' will not work. For it leaves us without an intelligible rationale. For one thing the exercise of constitutional rights in their 'most pristine and classic form' in *Edwards* has become an exercise in 'speech plus'. . . . If it is oral, it is noise and may interrupt someone else; if it is written, it may be litter. Indeed this is why the leaflet cases were an appropriate model . . . the leaflets were not simply litter, they were litter with ideas."[25]

Having said all I have in defense of "body rhetoric," let me indicate an important qualification. One would have to be naive to believe that the leaders of contemporary protest groups are unaware of the power potential of their demonstrations (even if that power is conferred upon them by the fearful or hostile audience) or that they are unwilling to exploit such situations to their own advantage. Some have been quite frank about it. For example, Professor Griffin calls attention to Bayard Rustin's comments:

> We need to go into the streets all over the country and to make a mountain of creative social confusion until the power structure is altered. We need in every community a group of loving troublemakers, who will disrupt the ability of the government to operate until it finally turns its back on the Dixiecrats and embraces progress.[26]

I have little doubt that the leaders of the Chicago Freedom Movement hoped that their marches would so distress the key people in the city's power structure that they would be forced to the bargaining table—which, indeed, they were—prepared to make substantial concessions. Such tactics are certainly no part of rational discourse, although they may establish the preconditions for it.

Furthermore, one cannot deny that sloganeering, folksinging, and draft-card burning fall into a category of persuasion that hardly passes muster by the standards of rational discourse, which this author and many others who have written on the ethics of persuasion have proposed. This is not to suggest that these activities are *illegal,* which is quite another question. Here I would support, for example, the proposition taken by the American Civil Liberties Union that public draft-card burning is an act of symbolic communication entitled to the protections of the First Amendment.

But on what *ethical* basis can these strategies of physical and psychological manipulation, insofar as this may be what they are, be defended? Their only justification, in my view, if that the norms of the democratic process may be inapplicable to the situations in which these strategies are employed. To be more explicit:

When one person or a few people in a group or society possess all the guns, muscles, or money, and the others are relatively weak and helpless, optimum conditions do not exist for discussion, mutual influence, and democracy. Discussion in such circumstances occurs only at the sufferance of the powerful; and generous as these persons may sometimes be, they are not likely voluntarily to abdicate their power when vital interests are at stake. ... The most solid and enduring basis for democracy exists when the participants possess relative equality of power. Discussion is assured only when those desiring discussion—usually those who are dissatisfied with the present state of affairs—have sufficient power to make those in control of the situation listen to them.[27]

It is not easy to determine, in any given setting, the degree to which the democratic process, and hence the opportunities for reasoned discourse, are indeed available; and the situation may be perceived quite differently from various vantage points. Perhaps the best one can do is to avoid the blithe presumption that the channels of rational communication are open to any and all who wish to make use of them and attempt, instead, a careful assessment of the power structure of the situation. To whatever extent one finds an imbalance of power and a concomitant unwillingness on the part of the holders of power to engage in genuine dialogue, he may be less harsh in his judgment of those who seek to redress the balance through nonrational strategies of persuasion.

What I am suggesting here is not a lowering of the standards to be espoused for the ideal conduct of public discussion and debate. On the contrary, every effort should be made to help create the conditions under which the achievement of those standards becomes a possibility. But we will not attain those conditions by closing our eyes to the realities of the world about us and condemning out of hand the contemporary rhetoric of the streets.

Notes

1. When self-governing men demand freedom of speech they are not saying that every individual has an unalienable right to speak whenever, wherever, however he chooses. ... The common sense of any reasonable society would deny the existence of that unqualified right. No one, for example, may without consent of nurse or doctor, rise up in a sickroom to argue for his principles or his candidate." Alexander Meiklejohn, *Political Freedom* (New York, 1960), p. 25.

"Such an argument has as its major unarticulated premise the assumption that people who want to propagandize protests or views have a constitutional right to do so whenever and however and wherever they please. That concept of constitutional law was vigorously and forthrightly rejected in ... *Cox* v. *Louisiana*. ... We reject it again." Justice Hugo Black, speaking for a majority of the Supreme Court on November 14, 1966, in *Adderley* v. *Florida*.

2. Although the "right to privacy" is nowhere mentioned in the U.S. Constitution or Bill of Rights, it has gained increasing recognition by legal scholars and the courts as a privilege worthy of some constitutional protection. This development reached its high-water mark in 1965, when the Supreme Court invalidated Connecticut's ban on the dissemination of birth control information. In the majority opinion written by Justice William O. Douglas the Court relied upon a right of privacy which it found *implied* in the First, Third, Fourth, and Ninth Amendments, as the primary basis for striking down the Connecticut law. *Griswold* v. *Connecticut,* 381 US 479.

3. Alfred Kamin, "Residential Picketing and the First Amendment," *Northwestern University Law Review,* LXI (May-June 1966), 182.

4. Paragraph 24 of complaint in *Wilson* v. *King,* et al., Case No. 66 Ch 4938 in Chancery in Circuit Court of Cook County.

5. Leland Griffin, "The Rhetorical Structure of the 'New Left' Movement: Part I," *Quarterly Journal of Speech,* L (April 1964), 127.

6. *Cox* v. *Louisiana,* 379 US 536 (1965), 578.

7. Ibid., 555.

8. Alfred Kamin also puts picketing in this category: "The picket line elicits conditioned responses . . . a primitive and unsophisticated illustration of McLuhan's dictum, 'The medium is the message.' " "Residential Picketing," 198-199.

9. *Lovell* v. *Griffin,* 303 US 444.

10. *Freedman* v. *Maryland,* 380 US 51.

11. See *Garner* v. *Louisiana,* 368 US 157 (1961); *Shuttlesworth* v. *Birmingham,* 373 US 262 (1963); *Peterson* v. *Greenville,* 373 US 244 (1963); *Lombard* v. *Louisiana,* 373 US 267 (1963); *Barr* v. *City of Columbia,* 378 US 146 (1964); *Robinson* v. *Florida,* 378 US 153 (1964); *Griffin* v. *Maryland,* 378 US 130 (1964); *Bouie* v. *City of Columbia,* 378 US 347 (1964); *Bell* v. *Maryland,* 378 US 226 (1964); *Hamm* v. *City of Little Rock,* 379 US 306 (1964); *Brown* v. *Louisiana,* 383 US 131 (1966).

12. See *Poulos* v. *New Hampshire,* 345 US 395 (1953).

13. Harry Kalven, Jr., "The Concept of the Public Forum: *Cox* v. *Louisiana,*" *The Supreme Court Review,* 1965, pp. 25-26.

14. "Great as is the value of exposing citizens to the novel views, home is one place where a man ought to be able to shut himself up in his own ideas if he desires. . . . A doorbell cannot be disregarded like a handbill. It takes several minutes to ascertain the purpose of a propagandist and at least several more to get rid of him. . . . A man's house is his castle, and what is more important his wife's castle. A housewife may fairly claim some protection from being obliged to leave off bathing the baby and rush down to the door, only to be asked to listen to a sermon or a political speech. . . . Freedom of the home is as important as freedom of speech." Zechariah Chafee, *Free Speech in the United States* (Cambridge, 1948), pp. 406-7.

15. *Martin* v. *Struthers,* 319 US 141, 146.

16. *Brerard* v. *City of Alexandria,* 341 US 622.

17. "The Concept of the Public Forum," p. 30

18. *Adderley* v. *Florida.*

19. *Davis* v. *Massachusetts,* 167 US 43.

20. *Hague* v. *C.I.O.,* 307 US 496, 515.

21. *Edwards* v. *South Carolina,* 372 US 229.

22. "The Concept of the Public Forum," pp. 30-31.

23. From the statement of Archbishop John P. Cody, *Chicago Daily News,* August 10, 1966.

24. *Garner* v. *Louisiana,* 368 US 157, 201-2.

25. "The Concept of the Public Forum," p. 23.

26. Bayard Rustin, "The Meaning of the March on Washington," *Liberation,* VIII (October 1963), 13.

27. Dean C. Barnlund and Franklyn S. Haiman, *The Dynamics of Discussion* (Boston, 1960), p. 12.

THE RHETORIC OF CONFRONTATION

ROBERT L. SCOTT and DONALD K. SMITH

"Confront" is a simple enough verb meaning to stand or to come in front of. Like many simple words, however, it has been used in diverse contexts for varied purposes and has developed complex meanings. Among these the most interesting, and perhaps the strongest, is the sense of standing in front of as a barrier or a threat. This sense is especially apparent in the noun "confrontation."

Repeatedly in his book *Essays in the Public Philosophy,* Walter Lippmann uses the word "confrontation" in the sense of face-to-face coming together of spokesmen for disparate views. Confrontation, as he saw it then, was the guarantee of open communication and fruitful dissent. But Lippmann's book was copyrighted in 1955. Today, his phrase "because the purpose of the confrontation is to discern truth" sounds a bit archaic. If so, the remainder of his sentence, "there are rules of evidence and parliamentary procedure, there are codes of fair dealing and fair comment, by which a loyal man will consider himself bound when he exercises the right to publish opinion,"[1] seems absolutely irrelevant to the notion of "confrontation" as we live with it in marches, sit-ins, demonstrations, and discourse featuring disruption, obscenity, and threats.

Although certainly some use the word "confrontation" moderately, we shall be concerned here with the radical and revolutionary suggestion which the word carries more and more frequently. Even obviously moderate circumstances today gain some of the revolutionary overtones when the word is applied, as it might be for example, in announcing a church study group as the "confrontation of sacred and secular morality."

Acts of confrontation are currently at hand in such profusion that no one will lack evidence to prove or disprove the generalizations we make.[2]

Confrontation crackles menacingly from every issue in our country (Black Power and Student Power, as examples), hemisphere (Castroism, for example), and globe (Radical Nationalism everywhere). But primary to every confrontation in any setting, radical or moderate, is the impulse to confront. From what roots does that impulse spring?

Radical Division

Radical confrontation reflects a dramatic sense of division. The old language of the "haves" and the "have-nots" scarcely indicates the basis of the division, nor its depth. The old language evokes the history of staid, well-controlled concern on the part of those who have, for those who have not. It suggests that remedy can come from traditional means—the use of some part of the wealth and talent of those who have to ease the burden of those who have not, and perhaps open opportunities for some of them to enter the mainstream of traditional values and institutions. It recalls the missionary spirit of the voluntary associations of those who have—the legislative charity of the New Deal, the Fair Deal, the Welfare State, and the whole spectrum of international development missions.

Robert L. Scott and Donald K. Smith, "The Rhetoric of Confrontation," *Quarterly Journal of Speech* (February 1969), pp. 1-8. By permission of Speech Communication Association and the authors.

A benevolent tone characterizes the old rhetoric of social welfare. The tone assumes that all men seek and should increasingly have more of the available wealth, or education, or security, or culture, or opportunities. The values of those who "have" are celebrated as the goals to which all should aspire, and effective social policy becomes a series of acts to extend opportunity to share in those values. If those who have can provide for others more of their own prequisites—more of the right to vote, or to find employment, or to go to college, or to consume goods—then progress is assured.

Although the terms "have" and "have not" are still accurate enough descriptions of the conditions that divide people and groups, their evocation of a traditional past hides the depth and radical nature of current divisions. Those on the "have not" side of the division, or at least some of their theorists and leaders, no longer accept designation as an inert mass hoping to receive what they lack through action by the "haves." Neither do they accept any assumption that what they wish is membership in the institutions of those who have, or an opportunity to learn and join their value system. Rather the "have nots" picture themselves as radically divided from traditional society, questioning not simply the limitations of its benevolence but more fundamentally its purposes and modes of operation. Whether they experience deprivation as poverty, or lack of political power, or disaffection from traditional values, the "have not" leaders and theorists challenge existing institutions. This radical challenge, and its accompanying disposition toward confrontation, marks the vague attitudinal web that links revolutionaries in emerging nations to Black Power advocates in America or to students and intellectuals of the New Left. Three statements will illustrate the similar disposition of men who serve rather different causes in varied circumstances.

For Franz Fanon, Algerian revolutionary and author of *The Wretched of the Earth,* the symbol of deprivation is the term "colonisation," and the end of confrontation is "decolonisation": "In decolonisation there is therefore the need of a complete calling in question of the colonial situation. If we wish to describe it precisely, we might find it in the well-known words 'The last shall be first and the first last.' Decolonisation is the putting into practice of this statement. That is why, if we try to describe it, all decolonisation is successful."[3]

For Black Power advocate Stokely Carmichael, the enemy is white racism, which is to be confronted, not joined: "Our concern for black power addresses itself directly to this problem, the necessity to reclaim our history and our identity from the cultural terrorism and depredation of self-justifying white guilt. To do this we shall hve to struggle for the right to create our own terms through which to define ourselves and our relationship to society, and to have these terms recognized. This is the first necessity of a free people, and the first right that any oppressor must suspend."[4]

For students in the New Left, the enemy to be confronted is simply "the establishment," or often in the United States, "technocracy." As student Frederick Richman sees the division:

> The world in which the older generation grew up, and which the political systems support, is no longer one which youth can accept. In a world of rampaging technology, racial turmoil, and poverty, they see a President whose program is constituted largely of finishing touches to the New Deal, and a Congress unwilling to accept even that. In a time when personal freedom is of increasing concern, they see a republic operated by an immense bureaucratic structure, geared more to cold war adventures than to domestic needs, stifling individual initiative along with that of states and cities. Finally, they see a political system obsessed with stability and loyalty instead of with social justice.[5]

Those have-nots who confront established power do not seek to share; they demand to supplant.

They must demand to supplant for they live in a Manichean world. Fanon, who features the term, argues that the settler (we may translate "settler" into other words, e.g., racist, establishment, or power structure) is responsible for the situation in which he must now suffer: "The colonial world is a Manichean world."[6] Those who rule and take the fruit of the system as their due create an equation that identifies themselves with the force of good (order, civilization, progress) which struggles with evil (chaos, the primitive, retrogression). In such a circumstance, established authority often crusades to eliminate the vessels of evil by direct action; but often its leaders work benignly and energetically to transform the others into worthy copies of themselves. At best, the process of transformation is slow, during which time the mass of the others must be carefully held apart to keep them from contaminating the system. Only a few can cross the great gulf to be numbered among the good. Claiming to recognize the reality of this process, which is always masked under exalted labels, black radicals in America cry that the traditional goal of integration masks and preserves racism. In an analogous posture, Students for a Democratic Society picture their educational system as a vast machine to recruit servants for a traditional society, perpetuating all of the injustices of that society.

Whether the force of "good" works energetically and directly or indirectly and somewhat benignly, those without caste must strive to supplant such holders of power. Forced to accept a Manichean struggle, they must reverse the equation, not simply to gain food, land, power, or whatever, but to survive. Reversing the equation will deny the justice of the system that has dehumanized them.

The process of supplanting will be violent for it is born of a violent system. To complete the long quotation introduced from Fanon: "The naked truth of decolonisation evokes for us the searing bullets and blood-stained knives which emanate from it. For if the last shall be first, this will only come to pass after a murderous and decisive struggle between the two protagonists. That affirmed intention to place the last at the head of things . . .can only triumph if we use all means to turn the scale, including, of course, that of violence."[7]

As Eric Hoffer concludes in his study of mass movements, those who make revolutions are apt to see themselves as spoiled, degraded, and without hope as things exist. But they locate the genesis of their degradation in things, in others, in the world as it is organized around them.[8]

The Rite of the Kill

The enemy is obvious, and it is he who has set the scene upon which the actors must play out the roles determined by the cleavage of exploitation. The situation shrieks kill-or-be-killed. "From here on in, if we must die anyway, we will die fighting back and we will not die alone," Malcolm X wrote in his "Appeal to African Heads of State." "We intend to see that our racist oppressors also get a taste of death."[9]

Judgments like "the oppressor" cannot be made without concomitant judgments. If there are those who oppress, there are those who are oppressed. This much seems obvious, but beneath that surface is the accusation that those oppressed have been something less than men ought to be. If one stresses the cunning, tenacious brutality of the oppressor, he suggests that the oppressed has been less than wise, alert, and strong. If one feels the heritage of injustice, then he senses the ignominy of his patrimony. The blighted self must be killed in striking the enemy. By the act of overcoming his enemy, he who supplants demonstrates his own worthiness, effacing the mark, whatever it may be— immaturity, weakness, subhumanity—that his enemy has set upon his brow.

To satisfy the rite that destroys the evil self in the act of destroying the enemy that has made the self evil, the radical may work out the rite of kill symbolically.[10] Harassing, embarrassing, and disarming the enemy may suffice, especially if he is finally led to admit his impotence in the face of the superior will of the revolutionary. Symbolic destruction of some manifestation of evil is well illustrated by the outbursts on campuses across America directed toward Dow Chemical. As far as we know in every confrontation of authority centering around the presence on the campus of a recruiter from Dow Chemical, the demonstrators early announced their intention of paralyzing the process until the recruiter agrees on behalf of the company to contaminate the scene no further with his presence.

Michael Novak, a Stanford University professor, pictures student disruption as a tactic to remove the mask of respectability worn by the establishment and kept in place both by the centralized control of communication processes and the traditional canon of free speech.

> The balance of power in the formation of public opinion has been altered by the advent of television. The society of independent, rational individuals envisaged by John Stuart Mill does not exist. The fate of all is bound up with the interpretation of events given by the mass media, by the image projected, and by the political power which results. . . . In a society with respect for its political institutions, officials have only to act with decorum and energy in order to benefit by such respect and to have their views established as true until proven false. . . .
>
> What, then, does freedom of speech mean in a technological society? How can one defend oneself against McCarthyism on the one hand and official newspeak on the other? The solution of the students has been to violate the taboos of decorum and thus embrace Vice President Humphrey, the CIA, Dow Chemical, and other enemies in an ugly scene, hoping that the unpopularity of the radicals will rub off on those embraced. They want to make the heretofore bland and respectable wear that tag which most alarms American sensibilities: "controversial."[11]

Student Stephen Saltonstall of Yale University views coercive disruption as the obvious tactic by which "a small concentrated minority" group can bring society to heel and proposes use of this tactic by students to "destroy the university's capability to prop up our political institutions. By stalemating America's intellectual establishment," he continues, "we may be able to paralyze the political establishment as well." Saltonstall's specific recommendations are far-ranging: "A small, disciplined group of shock troops could pack classes, break up drills, and harass army professors. . . . Students could infiltrate the office staffs of the electronic accelerators and foreign policy institutes and hamper their efficiency. The introduction of a small quantity of LSD in only five or six government department coffee urns might be a highly effective tactic. Students should prevent their universities from being used as forums for government apologists. Public figures like Humphrey and McNamara, when they appear, should be subject to intimidation and humiliation."[12]

Some who confront the oppressive authority seek to transform its representatives as well as themselves, working to wipe out the Manichean world. Such a stance is typical of the strongly Christian representatives of the Civil Rights Movement in this country. But those who advocate killing the enemy or degrading him symbolically act out more simply and more directly the dynamics dictated by the sense of radical division.

Confrontation as a Totalistic Strategy

Part of the attraction of confrontation is the strong sense of success, so strong that it may be a can't-lose strategy. After all in the Christian text Fanon cites ironically, "The last *shall* be first." The last shall be first precisely because he is last. The feeling is that one has nowhere to go but up, that he has nothing to lose, that after having suffered being down so long, he deserves to move up. Aside from the innate logic of the situation, four reasons for success seem apparent. In them we can imagine the radical voice speaking.

a. *We are already dead.* In the world as it is, we do not count. We make no difference. We are not persons: "Baby, it don't mean shit if I burn in a rebellion, because my life ain't worth shit. Dig?"[13] There is no mistaking that idiom, nor the sense behind it. Some radicals take oaths, changing their names, considering themselves as dead, without families, until the revolution succeeds. It is difficult to cow a dead orphan.

b. *We can be reborn.* Having accepted the evaluation of what is, agreeing to be the most worthless of things, we can be reborn. We have nothing to hang on to. No old identity to stop us from identifying with a new world, no matter how horrifying the prospect may seem at the outset; and a new world will certainly be born of the fire we shall create. You, the enemy, on the other hand, must cling to what is, must seek to stamp out the flames, and at best can only end sorrowing at a world that cannot remain the same. Eventually you will be consumed.

c. *We have the stomach for the fight; you don't.* Having created the Manichean world, having degraded humanity, you are overwhelmed by guilt. The sense of guilt stops your hand, for what you would kill is the world you have made. Every blow you strike is suicide and you know it. At best, you can fight only delaying actions. We can strike to kill for the old world is not ours but one in which we are already dead, in which killing injures us not, but provides us with the chance of rebirth.

d. *We are united and understand.* We are united in a sense of a past dead and a present that is valuable only to turn into a future free of your degrading domination. We have accepted our past as past by willing our future. Since you must cling to the past, you have no future and cannot even understand.

Confrontation as a Nontotalistic Tactic

Radical and revolutionary confrontation worries and bleeds the enemy to death or it engulfs and annihilates him. The logic of the situation that calls it forth bids it be total. But undoubtedly confrontation is brought about by those who feel only division, not radical division. For these the forces of good and evil pop in and out of focus, now clearly perceived, now not; now identified with this manifestation of established power and now that. These radicals may stop short of revolution because they have motives that turn them into politicians who at some point will make practical moves rather than toss every possible compromise and accommodation into the flaming jaws that could destroy the old order.

Student activists in the New Left vacillate in their demands between calls for "destruction" of universities as they are now known and tactical discussions of ways of "getting into the system" to make it more responsive to student goals.[14]

Drift toward nontotalistic goals seems consistent with both the general affluence of this group and its position as a small minority in a large student population generally committed to establishment goals and values. It may also reflect a latent response to the embarrassment of affluent students, beneficiaries of the establishment, who claim the language and motivations of the truly deprived.[15]

Similarly, the perception of confrontation as a tactic for prying apart and thus remodeling the machines of established power seems evident in many adherents of the Black Power movement. In many ways, the power Stokely Carmichael and Charles V. Hamilton forecast in their book is quite conventional, drawing analogies from past, thoroughly American experiences.[16]

Finally, one should observe the possible use of confrontation as a tactic for achieving attention and an importance not readily attainable through decorum. In retiring temporarily from his task of writing a regular newspaper column, Howard K. Smith complained bitterly of a press which inflated Stokely Carmichael from a "nobody who . . . had achieved nothing and represented no one" into "a factor to be reckoned with."[17] But Carmichael knows, from bitter experience, the art of confrontation. Martin Luther King writes of meeting a group of small boys while touring Watts after the riot. "We won!" they shouted joyously. King says his group asked them, "How can you say you won when thirty-four Negroes are dead, your community is destroyed, and whites are using the riot as an excuse for inaction?" The reply was, "We won because we made them pay attention to us."[18]

Without doubt, for many the act of confrontation itself, the march, sit-in, or altercation with the police is enough. It is consummatory. Through it the radical acts out his drama of self-assertion and writes in smeary, wordless language all over the establishment, "We know you for what you are. And you know that we know." Justifying the sense of rightness and, perhaps, firing a sense of guilt in the order is the hopeful outcome of the many coy confrontations of some shy radicals.[19]

Confrontation and Rhetorical Theory

We have talked of the *rhetoric* of confrontation, not merely confrontation, because this action, as diverse as its manifestations may be, is inherently symbolic. The act carries a message. It dissolves the lines between marches, sit-ins, demonstrations, acts of physical violence, and aggressive discourse. In this way it informs us of the essential nature of discourse itself as human action.

The rhetoric of confrontation also poses new problems for rhetorical theory. Since the time of Aristotle, academic rhetorics have been for the most part instruments of established society, presupposing the "goods" of order, civility, reason, decorum, and civil or theocratic law. Challenges to the sufficiency of this theory and its presuppositions have been few, and largely proposed either by elusive theologians such as Kierkegaard or Buber, or by manifestly unsavory revolutionaries such as Hitler, whose degraded theories of discourse seemed to flow naturally from degraded values and paranoid ambitions.

But the contemporary rhetoric of confrontation is argued by theorists whose aspirations for a better world are not easily dismissed, and whose passion for action equals or exceeds their passion for theory. Even if the presuppositions of civility and rationality underlying the old rhetoric are sound, they can no longer be treated as self-evident.[20] A rhetorical theory suitable to our age must take into account the charge that civility and decorum serve as masks for the preservation of injustice, that they condemn the dispossessed to non-being, and that as transmitted in a technological society they become the instrumentalities of power for those who "have."

A broader base for rhetorical theory is also needed if only as a means of bringing up to date the traditional status of rhetoric as a theory of managing public symbolic transactions. The managerial advice implicit in current theories of debate and discussion scarcely contemplates the possibility that respectable people should confront disruption of reasonable or customary actions, obscenity, threats of violence, and the like. Yet the response mechanisms turned to by those whose presuppositions could not contemplate confrontation often seem to complete the action sought by those who confront, or to confirm their subjective sense of division from the establishment. The use of force to get students out of halls consecrated to university administration or out of holes dedicated to construction projects seems to confirm the radical analysis that the establishment serves itself rather than justice. In this sense, the confronter who prompts violence in the language or behavior of another has found his collaborator. "Show us how ugly you really are," he says, and the enemy with dogs and cattle prods, or police billies and mace, complies. How can administrators ignore the insurgency of those committed to jamming the machinery or whatever enterprise is supposed to be ongoing? Those who would confront have learned a brutal art, practiced sometimes awkwardly and sometimes skillfully, which demands response. But that art may provoke the response that confirms its presuppositions, gratifies the adherent of those presuppositions, and turns the power-enforced victory of the establishment into a symbolic victory for its opponents.

As specialists interested in communication, we who profess the field of rhetoric need to read the rhetoric of confrontation, seek understanding of its presuppositions, tactics, and purposes, and seek placement of its claim against a just accounting of the presuppositions and claims of our tradition. Often as we read and reflect we shall see only grotesque, childish posturings that vaguely act out the deeper drama rooted in radical division. But even so, we shall understand more, act more wisely, and teach more usefully if we open ourselves to the fundamental meaning of radical confrontation.

Notes

1. (New York, 1955), p. 128.
2. Readers will find our generalizations more or less in harmony with other discussions of radical rhetoric which have appeared in the *Quarterly Journal of Speech* recently, e.g., Parke G. Burgess, "The Rhetoric of Black Power: A Moral Demand?" LIV (April 1968), 122-33; Leland M. Griffin, "The Rhetorical Structure of the 'New Left' Movement: Part I," L (April 1964), 113-35; and Franklyn S. Haiman, "The Rhetoric of the Streets: Some Legal and Ethical Considerations," LIII (April 1967), 99-114.

These writers sense a corporate wholeness in the messages and methods of various men. An attempt to explain the combination of message and method which forms the wholeness gives rise in each case to a *rhetoric*. All these efforts seem to us impulses to examine the sufficiency of our traditional concepts in dealing with phenomena which are becoming characteristic of contemporary dissent. In seeing rhetoric as an amalgam of meaning and method, these writers break with a tradition that takes rhetoric to be amoral techniques of manipulating a message to fit various contexts.

Rhetoric has always been response-oriented, that is, the rationale of practical discourse, discourse designed to gain response for specific ends. But these writers see response differently. For them, the response of audiences is an integral part of the message-method that makes the rhetoric. Thus, rhetoric is shifted from a focus of reaction to one of interaction or transaction. (See especially Burgess, 132-33; Griffin, 121; and Haiman, 113.)

Although we believe we share the sense of *rhetoric* which permeates these essays, we claim to analyze a fundamental level of meaning which unlerlies them.

3. Tr. Constance Farrington (New York, 1963), p. 30.

4. "Toward Black Liberation," *Massachusetts Review*, VII (Autumn 1966), 639-40.

5. "The Disenfranchised Majority," *Students and Society*, report on a conference, Vol. 1, No. 1; an occasional paper published by the Center for the Study of Democratic Institutions (Santa Barbara, Calif., 1967), p. 4.

6. Fanon, p. 33. The book is replete with references to "Manicheanism."

7. Ibid., p. 30.

8. *The True Believer* (New York, 1951), pp. 19-20 and passim.

9. *Malcolm X Speaks*, ed. George Breitman (New York, 1966), p. 77.

10. See Fanon, p. 73.

11. "An End of Ideology?" *Commonweal*, LXXXVII (March 8, 1968), 681-82.

12. "Toward a Strategy of Disruption," from *Students and Society*, p. 29.

13. Quoted by Jack Newfield, "The Biggest Lab in the Nation," *Life*, LXIV (March 8, 1968), 87.

14. *Students and Society*. A full reading of the conference proceedings reveals clearly this split among the most vocal and militant of New Left students.

15. For an analysis of the structure and characteristics of the student left, see Richard E. Peterson, "The Student Left in American Higher Education," *Daedalus*, XCVII (Winter 1968), 293-317.

16. *Black Power: The Politics of Liberation in America* (New York, 1967), see especially Chapter 5.

17. "Great Age of Journalism Gone?" *Minneapolis Star*, February 19, 1968, p. 5B.

18. *Where Do We Go from Here: Chaos or Community?* (New York, 1967), p. 112.

19. See Norman Mailer, "The Steps of the Pentagon," *Harper's Magazine*, CCXXXXVI (March 1968), 47-142 [published in book form as *Armies of the Night* (New York, 1968)]. It may seem difficult to believe but Mailer, who calls himself a "right radical," fits our adjectives, coy and shy.

20. Herein lies a major problem for rhetorical theory. In a sense Haiman's essay (note 2) is a defense of these values accepting the responsibility implied by his analysis which shows a significant case made by the very existence of "A Rhetoric of the Streets" which demands a rebuttal. Burgess' essay (note 2) sees Black Power as a unique method of forcing conventional thought to take seriously its own criterion of rationality.

AN ETHICAL BASIS OF COMMUNICATION

KARL R. WALLACE

On a recent plane trip a friend of mine sat beside a citizen of Wisconsin. Inevitably the conversation came around to the junior senator from that state. Part of the dialogue went like this:

FRIEND: What do you think of Mr. McCarthy?

CITIZEN: Well, I happen to know him personally, and I just don't like him at all. And I don't like his investigating methods, either—his badgering people and twisting their words around and acting like he owned the whole Committee.

FRIEND: It's too bad you Wisconsin people don't have a chance of turning him out of office.

CITIZEN: What'd we want to do that for? He's doing a darn good job of blasting out those Communists. There ought to be more of it.

Karl R. Wallace, "An Ethical Basis of Communication," *Speech Teacher* (January 1955), pp. 1-9. By permission of Speech Communication Association and the author.

FRIEND: If there were an election tomorrow, would you vote for McCarthy?
CITIZEN: Yes, I would.

The conversation points up the age-old problem of judging the right and wrong of human conduct. There is a similar difficulty when we come to judge the right and wrong of communication. The problem is essentially this: Does the end warrant our using any means which seem likely to achieve it? Is the public speaker or debater who believes his purpose worthy justified in using any methods and techniques which he thinks would be successful? Is the play director, convinced that his educational objectives are right, free to select any play and employ any methods of interpretation and production which seem likely to be "effective"? Is the speech correctionist, profoundly motivated to help the child with deviant speech behavior, free to adopt any techniques which seem workable?

This is an ethical problem. It is time that teachers of communication confronted it squarely. The signs of warning are about us. One of the more prominent signs is implicit in the widespread growth of research in communication, as may be seen in the serious study of polling techniques designed to measure the effectiveness of persuasive methods, the new interest of political scientists and bureaucrats in methods of propaganda, the progress made by linguists and psychologists in applying scientific methods to the analysis of language behavior. The facts and data thus compiled are of course valuable; nevertheless, it is somewhat disquieting to observe that such research is centered overwhelmingly on processes, operations, mechanisms, and techniques. There seems to be little, if any, prevailing interest in the *character* of the communicator or in the quality of the communicative product. Some parent groups, of course, have shown concern over the character of radio and television programs and over the comic books, but their activities have been largely sporadic and spotty. We are fascinated—often hypnotized—by what happens, how it happens, and why it happens, but we seem to be utterly unexcited by the question: *Ought* it to happen thus? What would be *better*?

There is room to mention here but one other sign of our apathy toward the ethics of communication. We can read it from our own behavior as teachers of speech. As we start out a new class in speech, or as we confront the thoughtful student who wonders if his praiseworthy purpose allows him to give his audience what it wants, we have been known to speak like this: "Remember, in this class we are studying and applying methods and techniques of speaking. Communication is a skill, a tool, and because it is a tool we are not directly concerned with who uses it and what he says. These are matters which the individual speaker must decide for himself. The main business of this course is to help you to become an effective speaker, a successful speaker. After all, the art of speaking is like the art of reasoning, or like mathematics and science, in that morality lies outside them; it is not *of* them; it is not *in* them." This kind of professional position, this disinterested attitude, this kind of easy reasoning, is leading many persons to look anew at the ethics of both the teacher and his student. Communication is in danger of being regarded as merely an art of personal success and prestige and of being forgotten as the indispensable art of social persuasion.

I

Any professional field which has reached maturity is ever-alive to its ethics. Law, medicine, engineering, and journalism have their codes of ethics. The profession of teaching, too, has its code of behavior. The field of speech shows some evidence of recapturing the maturity and stability it once enjoyed, under the name of *rhetoric,* in the educational systems of centuries past. Is it not time for the teacher of the arts of speech to face up to his special commitments? We must confront questions like these: Is there an ethic of communication? Specifically, is there an ethic of *oral* communication, a morality of rhetoric? I believe that there are ethical standards which should control any situation in which speaker and writer endeavor to inform and to influence others. I shall try to indicate where we find these standards and what they are like.

In the first place, ethical standards of communication should place emphasis upon the means used to secure the end, rather than upon achieving the end itself. A political speaker may win the vote, or a competitor in a speech contest may win the prize, but it is far more important that his means and methods, the character of his skill, and, indeed, the quality of his entire product, should conform to standards formulated by competent judges and critics of speech-making. Let us discover why.

If we give much weight to the immediate success of a speech, we encourage temptation. To glorify the end is to invite the use of any means which will work. The end can be used, for example, to sanction distortion and suppression of materials and arguments. We need here only to mention that there are still popular books on speech-making which some-times offer shocking advice. A recent manual advises the speaker that he may, if neces-sary, remodel a pet quotation to fill the bill, for, after all, no one will know the differ-ence! Such advice is on a par with the shoddy ethics of the debate coach who exclaims, "If my boys misquote, it's up to their opponents to spot it." The end, moreover, can be readily called upon to justify the misleading manoeuvres, the innuendos, and the short-cut tricks of the propagandists. The advertiser, in his zeal to sell, is constantly tempted to promise more than he can deliver. In brief, to exalt the end is often to be indifferent about means. As a result, we gradually undermine confidence in communication and, indeed, in all human relations; and with confidence gone, nothing is left but distrust and suspicion.

If we give first prize to the speaker who wins his goal, we not only unnecessarily tempt the honest and sincere man; we undermine the character of the communicator. We associate with "success" such values as popular prestige and personal ambition. We thus give a premium to the man with a compulsive drive, to him who must win at any cost; and we handicap the man who places the welfare of others above his personal gain. We give the advantage to Senator McCarthy; we hand a disadvantage to Secretary Stevens. John Morley, one of the best English critics of public address in the nineteenth century, has clearly described the risk which the popular persuader incurs when he measures his utterance by its immediate effect. To do so may undermine

> a man's moral self-possession. . . . Effect becomes the decisive consideration instead
> of truth; a good meeting grows into a final object in life; the end of existence is a
> paradise of loud and prolonged cheering; and character is gradually destroyed by
> the [parasite of] vanity.[1]

Finally, the worst evil which follows from an indifference to means is that we make easy the intent of the dishonest, insincere speaker. It is easy to assert high-sounding purposes; it is difficult for the listener to assess the sincerity of these assertions. In short, as Mahatma Gandhi often told us, "Evil means, even for a good end, produce evil results."

There is a better ethic than that which justifies the means by the end. It is an ethic which respects the means more than the end. It governs both the selection and the presentation of materials. Above all, the ethic measures the quality of the communicative product in terms of the communicator, rather than according to its immediate effect upon the audience. Some 2300 years ago Aristotle suggested the standard:

> [The function of speech-making] is not simply to succeed in persuading, but rather to discover the means of coming as near such success as the circumstances of each particular case allow. In this it resembles all other arts. For example, it is not the function of medicine simply to make a man quite healthy, but to put him as far as may be on the road to health; it is possible to give excellent treatment even to those who can never enjoy sound health.[2]

What does such a standard suggest? It implies, first, that a speaker does the best job he can under the circumstances; and doing his best job means that he has education, training, and competence in the art of communication. In the second place, the comparison of the speaker with the physician and with other arts implies that the standards of communication are determined by those who best know the art, that is, by the teachers and critics of communication. Finally, the passage suggests that since immediate success is not always possible, anyway, the end or purpose of a speech operates principally as a guide or direction. Purpose serves to give organization and shape to the speech, the discussion, or the play; it aids in the choice of means, but it should not dominate the moral values of either the product or the speaker.

It seems clear that the ethical standards of communication should be set by persons who know communication best, and that the standards or code they formulate will express their judgment as to what means are good, what means are bad. If the standards were clearly stated and widely understood, they could be freely used by expert and layman alike to measure the character of any case of communication.

II

Where does one look for such standards? They are derived from the function of an art. The function of any art takes its ultimate meaning from what it tries to accomplish in its social setting. What, for example, does a speaker do not only for himself, but also for society, the community?

Although there are many sides to society, its indispensable side is political. Indeed, when society behaves politically it has the technical name, *state*. And the state is simply another name for an association of men. Because it is the largest, most inclusive association we know of, its values and ends are reflected in nearly everything that its citizens do. They are reflected particularly in education and in the arts and sciences. The influence of the political society is stated in this passage from the *Ethics* of Aristotle:

> If ... there is some end of the things we do, which we desire for its own sake ... clearly this must be the good and the chief good. ... If so, we must try, in outline at least, to determine what it is, and of which of the sciences or capacities it is the object. It would seem to belong to the most authoritative art and that which is most truly the master art. And politics appears to be of this nature; in a state, and which each class of citizens should learn and up to what point they should learn them; and we see even the most highly esteemed of capacities to fall under this, e.g., strategy, economics, rhetoric; now, since politics uses the rest of the sciences,

and since, again, it legislates as to what we are to do and what we are to abstain from, the end of this science must include those of the others, so that this end must be the good for man.[3]

The passage demands that we recognize two basic facts. First, the political society aims to help its citizens to secure whatever they consider to be the good life. Indeed, the dominant tone of a political group is set by its ethical values. Thus Communism, e.g., has one set of values, democracy a quite different set. Second, the arts and sciences serve the ideals of the political society. Indeed, they share the same ethical values and goals. The art of rhetoric—and all the arts of communication—thus embraces the ethical part of politics. This point Aristotle states flatly in his book on rhetoric, and for this reason in his system of communication he incorporates materials which he borrows directly from the fields of political science and ethical science. For example, in discussing the materials of political oratory, he talks of the good, of happiness, of virtue, and of the general welfare. He even advises the political speaker to study ways of political life in different kinds of society. In discussing the speaking of the law courts, he treats of justice and equity. Thus, the instrumental art, rhetoric, shares the controlling ideas of the master art, politics. Hence, communication inevitably must stand for and must reflect the same ethical values as the political society of which it is a part. It is clear, furthermore, that this principle is as true today as it was in Aristotle's time. Although government and politics are much more complex than they were in the days of ancienct Greece, the modern political scientist acknowledges that the foundations of the state are laid in ethics.

Is it not becoming clear, therefore, that we look for the ethical basis of communication in the ideals of our own political society? That society, for all its manifest defects, is still a free and democratic society. If we can clearly state the essential values of democracy, we can then suggest an ethic of communication and the ethics of the teacher of speech.

III

A free and democratic society, first of all, is built on the notion that the individual has dignity and worth. Our society holds that government exists to uphold and preserve the worth and dignity of each and every person. A totalitarian society, on the other hand, holds that the individual lives for the state. In a democracy people are supreme and wield the ultimate power. In totalitarianism the state is almighty and is the final source of all power. The difference is crucial; it is as sharply different as black and white, as tyranny and freedom. The phrase, "dignity and worth of the individual" leads to a state of mind best described by the old-fashioned word, *respect.* Each man respects his fellow man. This fact has led some students of political science to describe a democratic society as a "commonwealth of mutual deference."

Respect for the individual leads us to a second basic belief: a profound faith in equality of opportunity. We believe that a man can best reach his greatest maturity if he has the chance. If we can say with Wordsworth that the child is father of the man, we believe that the child must have the opportunity to become the best possible father of the best posssible man. We believe, furthermore, that so far as we are able, every child must be given the *same* chance. Out of such beliefs we have developed the all-important notion of *fairness.* Like the rules of any game, the laws of the political game must be as fair as we can possibly make them.

We hold a third belief that has become one of the great hallmarks of a democratic society. It is the belief in freedom. Difficult as it may be to define freedom, we know well enough that each individual must be given as wide a field to roam in as he wishes. The word also means that if a person in his roaming prevents another man from ranging widely, he must so modify his behavior as to give his fellow a similar opportunity. He can do what he wants to do, so long as he does not hinder another from exercising a like range of choice and of action. So freedom always implies restraint. A person can behave as he wishes in his own home so long as he does not become a nuisance to his neighbors; he can drive his car where and how he wishes so long as he does not endanger others; he can compete as he may desire in business, in sports, in speech contests, so long as he respects the rules.

In a free democratic society, individuals acting in concert and with deliberation make their own restraints. The restraints are called *legislation* or *laws.* They are policies or guides of conduct. Indeed, they are no different in their origin and effect from the rules of family life or the regulations of a school. Furthermore, individuals through their government set up agencies to which they delegate power for administering the laws, and they create courts charged with the responsibility of enforcing the restraints. Lincoln showed deep wisdom in saying that our political society was of us, by us, and for us. In our democratic society, moreover, we insist that the laws bear equally upon everyone. In effect we say to our legislators and judges: "You must do your best to make laws which will be fair to everybody, and you must enforce the laws in the spirit of fairness and justice."

A free and democractic society rests upon a fourth deep and abiding belief. It is a conviction closely linked to the idea that each individual must have the opportunity of growing and developing the limits of his ability. The conviction is that every person is capable of understanding the nature of democracy: its goals, its values, its procedures and processes. This belief assumes that persons can acquire the knowledge necessary to form opinions and decisions and to test them by means of discussion and action. As a result of this conviction, a democracy demands that knowledge be made available to all, rather than to the few; it requires that the sources and channels of communication be wide and diverse, rather than limited and one-sided. It cannot tolerate restriction and distortion. Consequently, it must cherish and protect certain special freedoms: freedom of speech, freedom of press, and freedom of assembly. Without these freedoms democracy is meaningless: the life of a free society depends upon them.

· Is it not evident that each person participates in a political society? that he reflects its values and uses its procedures? In his role as communicator, whether he be playwright or play producer, public reader or public speaker, he must also reveal his political character. What he says and his method of saying it reveals his choices, and the choices a man makes are always an index to his character. Theoretically, of course, a man need not speak at all; or he can choose to speak only to himself, or to refuse to discuss matters of public interest. But if he chooses to speak, he reveals his political soul.

IV

What, then, are the ethics of the teacher of speech? They are grounded in the public character of public utterance in a free society.

First, a communicator in a free society must recognize that during the moments of his utterance he is the sole source of argument and information. His hearers know this fact, and they defer to him. He in turn must defer to them. Accordingly, his speech must reveal that he knows his subject, that he understands the implications and issues relevant to the particular time and occasion, that he is aware of essential and trustworthy opinions and facts, that he is dealing with a many-sided, rather than a one-sided, state of affairs. Although the speaker might find it difficult to know when he has met such standards, he can always direct a test question to himself: Can I answer squarely, without evasion, any relevant question that a hearer might ask? If he can answer *yes* in all honesty, he has met the standard of knowledge. In the learning situation, the teacher of speech has an obligation to teach the art of inquiry and investigation, to inculcate respect for scope and depth of fact and opinion—in a word, to help build the *habit of search.* The teacher has this duty because a free society demands that communication be informative and that knowledge be shared.

How can the teacher help his students develop the habit of searching widely for both fact and opinion? There is no simple answer, of course. Many teachers, both in high school and in college, are well aware of this duty and have developed their own methods of teaching the art of inquiry. But we shall not hurt ourselves if we periodically confront these questions: Am I keeping up with information and opinion on problems that are currently discussed, so that my chances are better, rather than worse, of being a good guide and critic of what my students know or do not know? Am I making sufficient use of discussion methods, in both the classroom and private conference, to stimulate interest and inquiry? Am I habitually encouraging the classroom audience, upon hearing a student speak, to discuss the adequacy of the speaker's knowledge and the trustworthiness of his materials?

Second, the communicator who respects the democratic way of life must select and present fact and opinion *fairly.* One of his great tasks is to help preserve a kind of equality of opportunity among ideas. He must therefore be *accurate* in reporting fact and opinion; he must *respect* accuracy. Moreover, he must not intentionally warp and distort ideas. Nor must he suppress and conceal material which his audience would need in justly evaluating his argument. He must, furthermore, avoid the short-cut methods of the propagandist. He cannot make one word guilty by loosely associating it with another guilty word. He cannot indulge in the tricks of emotion, cannot juggle with reason, at the expense of sound argument. In helping himself meet the standards of justice, a communicator can always quiz himself: In the selection and presentation of my materials, am I giving my audience the *opportunity* of making fair judgments? The speaker who can answer *yes* understands what is involved in the sharing of information and opinion. He knows that he has had a special opportunity to observe, to learn, to evaluate, which most of his hearers may not have had. He knows, accordingly, that one of his jobs as a communicator is to help his hearers compensate for the lack of special opportunity. He realizes that he cannot possibly give them the same chance he has had, but he can give them the best chance that time and occasion will allow. Speaker and hearer, writer and reader, cannot have had the same experience, but they can feel that they have had. In the classroom, accordingly, the teacher of speech must inculcate what I shall call the *habit of justice.* The habit is based on respect for truth and accuracy and respect for fair dealing. Neither can be disassociated from communication in a free society. The teacher of speech must stand for truth and justice in communication because the health and welfare of a free society depend upon the integrity of the communicator.

Third, the communicator who believes in the ultimate values of democracy will invariably reveal the sources of his information and opinion. As Al Smith said, a public figure must keep the record straight. A speaker before any audience is by that fact a public person, and he is no exception to the rule. A communicator, moreover, will help his hearers to weigh any special bias, prejudice, and private motivations which are inherent in source materials. He knows that argument and fact are unacceptable if their springs are contaminated. As an investigator preparing for his speech, he has had the opportunity of discovering whether private motives, such as those of self-interest, personal prestige, and personal profit, have merely imparted a special flavor to the source or have made it dangerous to drink. Such information he should share with his hearers. And if he is not already a public character well-known to his audience, he should be willing to reveal frankly his own motivations. The critical question which he poses to himself is this: Have I concealed information about either my source materials or my own motives which, if revealed, would damage my case? The communciator who can answer *no* is in the tradition of public integrity.

In the high school and the college, the teacher of speech must devise methods and techniques which will form the *habit of preferring public to private motivations.* Public communication is responsible communication; it remembers who said what under what circumstances and for what reasons. In this respect it is utterly unlike gossip and rumor which, if not malicious, we may tolerate as idle talk for idle pleasure.

How can the teacher of speech help his young communicators toward habits of fairness, justice, and public accountability? I do not wish to preach here. Let him who is without blemish cast the first stone. Nevertheless, we shall do well occasionally to examine ourselves as objectively as we can and to conduct the inquisition mercilessly. We may ask: In all my relationships with my students, am I as fair as I can be? Do I keep clear the differences between opinion and fact, and do I distinguish between my opinion and somebody else's? When I express an opinion, do I explain its basis, or do I take a short-cut and let the opinion rest on my own authority and prestige? Do I respond to questions frankly, without evasion? Am I withholding information, as "not being good for young persons," especially under the circumstances? What kind of censor am I?

Sometimes teachers effectively employ examples of what not to do. For a ready source of illustrations of unfair tactics in public address, the speeches and press releases of Senator McCarthy offer a rich hunting ground. One could start his collection of negative examples by reading Professor Barnet Baskerville's article, "Joe McCarthy: Brief-Case Demagogue," in the September number of *Today's Speech.*[4] Baskerville cites one careful study whose author checked McCarthy's initial charges of Communism in the State Department with the ascertainable facts. The investigator, Professor Hart of Duke University, examining only the charges as presented up to the fall of 1951, found that McCarthy's "assertions had been radically at variance with the facts in fifty specific instances."[5] Another examination of two 1952 campaign speeches reveals them as *"a most amazing demonstration of studied inaccuracy."*[6] McCarthy's nationally televised address which attacked Adlai Stevenson (the speech making use of documents from a Massachusetts barn) yields "no less than eighteen 'false statements or distortions' in the text which McCarthy described as having 'complete, unchallengeable documentation.' "[7] Baskerville comments on the Senator's documents, often raised aloft for all to see, "The deceit lies in the significant omissions, and in unwarranted inferences drawn from impressive but often completely irrelevant documents."[8] The article could well be the beginning of a case study in personal and public integrity.

Fourth, a communicator in a democratic society will acknowledge and will respect diversity of argument and opinion. His selection of issues, his analysis of the situation, the style of his address will reflect the attitudes which signify admission, concession, and compromise. Nevertheless, his communication will not sacrifice principle to compromise, and he will prefer facing conflict to accepting appeasement. For such a communicator, the test question will ever be this: Can I freely admit the force of opposing evidence and argument and still advocate a position which represents my convictions? The great duty of the teacher of speech is to devise ways and means and to maintain a climate which will favor the *habit of respect for dissent.* Can he teach what it means to hold convictions without loss of integrity and at the same time respect the convictions of others? The teacher who can do so is not merely skillful; he is a true representative of the free society.

It is these four "moralities": the duty of search and inquiry, allegiance to accuracy, fairness, and justice in the selection and treatment of ideas and arguments, the willingness to submit private motivations to public scrutiny, and the toleration of dissent—which provide the ethic of communication in a free society.

In view of these moralities, as teachers of speech we can no longer tell even the most elementary student of our discipline that speech skills and techniques, like tools, are divorced from ethical values. We can no longer say that how he uses his art is his own private affair. But we need not be content with an ethic which is external to communication. We need not rely solely upon the familiar, classic positions: "You'd better be good, or your audience may find out"; or "A good man skilled in speaking will in the long run be more effective than a bad man skilled in speaking." As I have tried to indicate, communication carries its ethics within itself. Public address of any kind is inseparable from the values which permeate a free and democratic community. A speaker is in a deep and true sense a representative of his constitution which defines his way of life, and therefore defines in part the social goals and methods of his rhetoric. His frame of political reference is not that of an aristocracy, an oligarchy, a monarchy, or a tyranny. In a word, there are ethical guides in the very act of communicating; and it seems to me that the guides are the same for all communicators, no matter whether they speak as politicians, statesmen, businessmen, or professional men.

Notes

1. *The Life of Richard Cobden,* 2 vols. (London, 1908), I, 223.
2. *Rhetoric* 1355b 9-14. Trans. W. Rhys Roberts, in *The Works of Aristotle Translated into English under the Editorship of W. D. Ross,* XI, (Oxford, 1924).
3. *Nicomachean Ethics,* 1094a 17-1094b 7. Trans. W. D. Ross, in *The Works of Aristotle Translated into English under the Editorship of W. D. Ross,* IX (Oxford, 1925).
4. II (September 1954), 8-15.
5. Ibid., II, 5.
6. Ibid.
7. Ibid., II, 13.
8. Ibid.

Part Seven

Rhetorical Criticism

The act of criticism is useful for two reasons: (1) It helps us to better understand what we read and hear, and (2) it may help us to be better speaker-writers as we become more aware of *what* happens in discourse and come to speculate more fully on *why* it happens.

What do we mean when we call someone a "critic"? What kinds of questions does the critic seek to answer? These are two of the essential questions raised by Professor Lawrence Rosenfield in his article, "The Anatomy of Critical Discourse."

After defining criticism as "a special form of reason-giving discourse" he points to those features of critical discourse that differentiate it from the general range of assertive discourse. Then, he examines the array of methodological approaches open to the critic.

Most of the focus on this section is on the *practice* of criticism. In the examples that follow, we observe a variety of critical approaches. These approaches are by no means the only approaches to these speeches. They are meant to encourage you to try your own hand at criticizing these and other rhetorical discourses.

To illustrate the possibility and value of looking at the same rhetorical act through a variety of perspectives or "perceptual screens," several critics take a look at the same speech. First, Professor Karlyn Campbell approaches Spiro Agnew's first major speech on the media by inquiring into the evidence and arguments he uses as he goes about the task of analyzing the power of the mass media. Then, Professor Hermann Stelzner looks at the same speech as a socio-cultural document.

Next, two student critics, Marie Rosenwasser and Edward Murphy, look at George Wallace's "Second Inaugural Address" in different but complementary ways. And then, this author takes yet another look at the Wallace Inaugural by following some of the suggestions of Hugh Duncan in his book *Symbols in Society.*

Critics may find their point of departure for analyses and evaluations from many sources. In the critical pieces on Wallace, this author begins by referring to the work of sociologist-rhetorical theorist Hugh Duncan; Ms. Rosenwasser uses historian Richard Hofstadter's concept of the "paranoid style"; and Mr. Murphy explores Wallace's speech using the principles of satire as a basis for his approach. Thus, one begins by trying out a particular *method of approaching communicative acts,* one by exemplifying the description of a particular *style of discourse,* and one by considering a particular *genre of discourse.*

Many of the other articles in this text can be used as the point of departure for a criticism of the speeches of Wallace, Agnew, and others: the Rokeach article for the basis of a *value analysis* or the Nichols article for a *constituents approach* to rhetorical acts.

The two speakers whom we have chosen to include in this section, Spiro Agnew and George Wallace, are two of the speakers students in our criticism class want to look at.

They generate controversy and often critics of their speaking also generate controversy. Such controversy may provoke useful questions: What *is* the critic's task? To describe? To analyze? To interpret? To evaluate? *How* may he go about that task? To what extent is the critic (as well as the speaker being criticized) a *persuader*?

THE ANATOMY OF CRITICAL DISCOURSE

LAWRENCE W. ROSENFIELD

The recent ferment in rhetorical criticism generated by Professor Black's provocative *Rhetorical Criticism: A Study in Method* challenges critics to formulate more carefully their goals and methods. The attempt to raise critical procedures from an *ad hoc* status to something more systematic is not new,[1] but, at least among rhetorical critics, it seems today to hold a place of special interest.

The discussion of some of the logical features of criticism contained in this essay responds to the call for a more formal understanding of the critical act. It is an effort to abstract the implicit assumptions of those whom we would clearly want to call critics, to consider the ways in which it would make sense for an ordinary but responsible user of the English language to talk about the behavior of critics and about their products (criticism).

It is the contention of this essay that criticism is most sensibly conceived of as a special form of reason-giving discourse. The nature of reason-giving in criticism becomes intelligible if we treat four particular questions concerning criticism: (1) What do we commonly mean when we call someone a "critic"? (2) What features of criticism distinguish it from other intellectual endeavors? (3) What kinds of questions does criticism seek to answer? (4) By what modalities (formulae) are reasons produced in criticism? Answers to these four questions, and hence support for the central assertion, constitute the bulk of this study.[2] Let us begin by raising the first question and asking of whom we are talking when we speak of "the critic."

Whenever the word "critic" comes up in conversation, a variety of images is liable to come to mind. Some think of the book reviewer or the drama critic for a newspaper. Others, who equate "critic" with "carper," are reminded of a sour, negative individual who cannot be pleased. Still others (particularly if they are conversant with too many master's theses in public address) may imagine that "the speech critic" is a kind of reporter of public address in history.[3] Clearly, common usage has made the term so vague as to be practically meaningless. Is it possible to restrict the meaning of "critic" by adopting semantic boundaries which enable us to distinguish the legitimate critics from those for whom the label represents simply encomium (or invective)? To do so we would need to ascertain what actions we may ordinarily expect of one who is fulfilling the office of critic. If we investigate what I have chosen to call the "critical posture," or the stance habitually assumed by one who is fulfilling the logical requirements of critic, we can

Lawrence Rosenfield, "The Anatomy of Critical Discourse," *Speech Monographs* (March 1968), pp. 50-69. By permission of Speech Communication Association and the author.

reach some consensus as to the behavior of the critic; we will then be in a better position to understand "criticism" itself. In order to clarify what is meant here, it may be helpful to draw a rough comparison between events discussed by critics and those events we commonly call "athletic." We shall discover that in the main the critical posture resembles the "spectator" half of an agent-spectator dichotomy.[4]

First of all, it is easy enough to understand that some sporting events are not only played but are observed as well—by individuals we call "spectators." And it is common that these spectators, if they are genuine fans, do more than simply purchase a ticket of admission so that they may sit in proximity to the athletic activity. They will also devote a certain time and effort to contemplating and discussing the events they observe. That is to say, the role of the spectator often entails reflection and communication about the athletic events. For instance, the baseball fan may attend winter Hot Stove meetings where particular plays will be recalled and mulled over; likewise, the Monday Morning Quarterbacks derive a certain satisfaction from assembling to debunk the maneuvers executed in recent football games.

The same quality of spectatorship seems to be common among those whom we might call fans of aesthetic events, whether their particular "sport" be painting or public communication.[5] One characteristic of the rhetorical critic, then, is his interest in observing and discussing instances of rhetorical discourse, be they speeches, essays, or advertisements, from the vantage of the spectator.

Another characteristic which critics share with at least some sports fans is that both show an appreciation for the execution of the event or object.[6] The involvement of some fans is limited to being loyal followers of a favorite team; they are mainly concerned to share in the exaltation of the home team's victories. For such "part-time" fans, the outcome of a contest is of paramount interest. True enthusiasts, however, seldom gather merely to report the results of games; they do not confine their comments to the immediate, utilitiarian aspects of athletic events. Such fans derive satisfaction from watching a film replay of a game whose final score they already know, a satisfaction we may label as appreciation. This appreciation, whether in the fan or the critic, is not inherently related to enthusiasm or suspense over outcome.

A third similarity between the posture of the critic and that of the athletic fan is that heightened appreciation (and hence increased satisfaction or pleasure) accompanies increased knowledge of the events or objects observed. The football fan who knows more than the formal rules of the game (e.g., understands the tactics of blocking assignments and the relative merits of the T-formation and the single wing) derives a satisfaction from second-guessing the coach which the less informed "rooter for the home team" misses. In other words, consciousness of artistic principles contributes to appreciation.

A final commonality follows from the notion of heightened appreciation. Some spectators, because of especially fine training or acute sensitivity, attain the status of "experts." In the athletic sphere such persons are often hired to act as sportscasters and sportswriters, and in the aesthetic realm they may be called upon to act as "critics" in giving reviews of books, plays, and the like. However, their titles do not derive from the fact that they are appointed or paid to perform these tasks. Rather, it is because of their competence that they are asked to assume the critic's office. An expert can be an amateur and still be a fine sports analyst or critic. What matters is exceptional understanding. Accordingly, "critical posture" refers to *the capacity a person has to act as an expert commentator,* and the critic, if he is nothing else, must be one who is capable of fulfilling this role.

Simple *capacity* to render commentary is not yet criticism. The expert-spectator who relishes the events he observes but does not relate his appreciation to others is not a critic. Criticism is therefore the special variety of discourse which results when a person who has adopted a critical posture makes assertions, i.e., statements by an expert about "the way things are."[7] How then may we distinguish critical discourse from the general range of assertive discourse?

One procedure would be to examine several instances of discourse which we would definitely wish to call criticism and seek to discover its typical features. I refer the reader to two short essays dealing with the speech delivered by General Douglas MacArthur to a joint session of Congress (and through direct broadcast, to the nation) on April 19, 1951. The first essay is by journalist Richard Rovere, the second by Herbert Wichelns, a professor of speech.[8] Let them represent clear cases of discourse we would ordinarily consider rhetorical criticism. What characteristics make them intuitively admissible as criticism?

Richard H. Rovere

As a literary critic and political observer, I view the speech solely from the literary and political points of view. I am not qualified to criticize oratory or elocution.

As a piece of composition, the speech seemed to me a good deal but not a great deal better than the general run of public prose in the United States today. MacArthur has eloquence of a kind, but it strikes me as a rather coarse eloquence. He never shades his meanings, never introduces a note of humor, never gives the feeling that he is one man, only one, addressing himself to other men. His language is never flat and bloodless; neither is it flabby and loose-jointed, as so much writing of this sort is. But to me there is rather a fetid air about it. It does not leave me with the impression that a cool and candid mind has been at work on difficult matters of universal concern. Instead, it leaves me with the impression that a closed and in a sense a rather frantic mind has been at work to the end of making an appeal to history—not neglecting to use any of the rulebook hints on how to do it. I think not of history but of second-rate historian as I read the speech.

Form and content are, if not inseparable, very closely related. Politically, MacArthur's speech seemed extremely weak to me. This is not, I think, because I am opposed to his politics; I believe he could have made out a much stronger case for himself. But he never came to grips with the issues. For example, he wanted to have it that he was being persecuted for "entertaining" his particular views. This, of course, is rubbish. He got into trouble not for the political and military views he entertained (no doubt he was right in saying they were entertained by many of his colleagues) but for seeking to usurp the diplomatic function. He never sought to answer the objections to his position that rest on political and economic facts recognized by both sides; that if we followed him, we would be abandoned by several allies; that if Russia invaded Europe, which he has admitted might be an early consequence of his policy, the industrial balance would favor the Communist world; that, like it or not, American power does have its limitations. MacArthur's policy may be sounder than Truman's. But the contention cannot be sustained without facing these stubborn facts about the world today. MacArthur, in his speech, never faced them.

Herbert A. Wichelns

Demosthenes had the problem too; how much to spell out, how formal and explicit to make his proposals. At times Demosthenes judged it best not to "make a motion" but merely to offer comment and advice at large. MacArthur made a similar choice. In the main he chose not to debate, in the sense of formulating proposals and defending them in full. Instead he indicated the heads for debate, leaving no doubt as to the direction of his policy. Definite proposals were few, and sharply limited to Formosa and Korea. Supporting reasons were very sparingly given, and sometimes confined to bare assertions (as on the extent of China's present military commitment and Russia's probable course). But the call for a harder and more aggressive policy is plain from the beginning ("no greater expression of defeatism"). The chief support for that policy is neither logical argument nor emotional appeal, but the self-portrait of the speaker as conveyed by the speech.

It is an arresting portrait. Certain colors are of course mandatory. The speaker respects Congress and the power of this nation for good in the world. He is free from partisanship or personal rancor. He sympathizes with the South Koreans and with his embattled troops. He prefers victory to appeasement. He seeks only his country's good. He hates war, has long hated it. If these strokes are conventional, they take little time, except for the last, on which the speaker feels he must defend himself.

More subtle characterizing strokes are found in the "brief insight into the surrounding area" which forms a good half of the speech. Here the General swiftly surveys the nature of the revolution in Asia, the island-frontier concept and Formosa's place in the island-chain, the imperialistic character of the Chinese communities, the regeneration of Japan under his auspices, the outlook for the Philippines, and the present government of Formosa. All this before reaching Korea. Most of these passages have no argumentative force. But all together they set up for us the image of a leader of global vision, comprehending in his gaze nations, races, continents. The tone is firmest on Japan ("I know of no nation more serene, orderly and industrious"), least sure on the Philippines, but always positive.

Rarely indeed have the American people heard a speech so strong in the tone of personal authority. "While I was not consulted . . . that decision . . . proved a sound one." "Their last words to me"—it is the Korean people with whom the General has been talking. "My soldiers." The conduct of "your fighting sons" receives a sentence. A paragraph follows on the General's labors and anxieties on their behalf. The pace at which the thought moves, too, is proconsular; this is no fireside chat. Illustration and amplification are sparingly used; the consciously simple vocabulary of the home-grown politician is rejected. The housewife who "understood every word" was mistaken; she missed on epicenter and recrudescence and some others. But having by the fanfare been jarred into full attention, she understood quite well both the main proposition of the speech—a harder policy—and the main support offered—the picture of a masterful man of unique experience and global outlook, wearing authority as to the manner born.

One feature these comments display, which is often noted as an essential of critical discourse, is that both contain verdicts (sometimes called judgments or evaluations). Not all assertive discourse contains appraisal as criticism does. Scientific reports, for instance, display an exploratory impulse rather than an evaluative one.[9] Nor is this to say that critical essays must reach a settled and final verdict, for clearly Wichelns is at pains to avoid assessing MacArthur's speech as good or bad. But criticism does eventuate in, or at least has as an ultimate objective, assessment. Professor Black has put it most succinctly:

> At the culmination of the critical process is the evaluation of the discourse or of its author; a comprehensive judgment which, in the best of criticism, is the fruit of patient exegesis. . . . Even the purely technical objective of understanding how a discourse works carries the assumption that it does *work*, and that assumption is an assessment. Similarly, to understand *why* a thing has failed is at least to suspect that it *has* failed, and that suspicion is an assessment. There is, then, no criticism without appraisal; there is no "neutral" criticism. One critic's judgment may be absolute and dogmatic, another's tentative and barely commital; but however faint the judicial element in criticism may become, it abides.[10]

If Black is correct, we ought seldom to find a critic engaged in description of a rhetorical event for its own sake; and if we do, we ought perhaps proceed most cautiously in determining whether to label the product "criticism."[11]

Clearly our two samples of criticism meet the criterion of making assessments. Rovere is explicit:

> . . . the speech seemed . . . a good deal but not a great deal better than the general run of public prose . . . there is a rather fetid air about it. . . . Politically [the] speech seemed extremely weak. . . .

Wichelns' appraisal is more complex. Avoiding any "good-bad" evaluation, he invites us to accept his verdict on how the speech was executed (i.e., what made it work as it did). In Wichelns' judgment the speech called for a harder policy and this call was supported by the speaker's self-portrait. Both Rovere and Wichelns present us with settled, though not necessarily final or definitive, assertions as to the character and/or worth of the speech; their critical comments betray momentary terminations (benchmarks) in their thought processes, terminations which are expressed in the form of verdicts.

Once we grant that the assertive discourse of criticism strives for appraisal, we should concurrently examine the "reasons" offered to justify the verdicts. The bulk of both critical essays consists of reasons justifying the judgments. Notice, for example, Wichelns' assertion that MacArthur's main form of proof was his own self-portrait. It is supported by three contentions: that it was an arresting portrait, employing both "mandatory colors" and "subtle . . . strokes"; that the speech otherwise is lacking in argument and abounding in assertion; and that the speech was couched in the language of personal authority. From these Wichelns is enabled to conclude that the speech offered "the picture of a masterful man of unique and global outlook" as support for MacArthur's claims.

Dealing as we are with evaluative discourse, it is only natural to speculate further about the relationship linking verdicts and reasons. Imagine for instance the following situation: a friend says, "I read the novel *Tom Jones* last week." You treat this statement as a factual report. But were your friend to co-append, "It struck me as a rather shallow book," there is an immediate change in conditions. You may then decide to treat the combined statements as criticism, with the second sentence serving as an appraisal and the first now transformed from a report into part of the justification for the judgment. Furthermore, it would be extremely odd if your friend were to utter the second statement and at the same time deny having ever read the novel, having had any contact with anyone who had read it, or having had access to any critical comments about it. Obviously, we expect a critical verdict to be in some way conditional upon the reasons offered in its support. We are not yet in a position to see why reasons are expected or to determine how they function as support, but that they do so function to make criticism a reason giving activity is evident.[12]

A valuable first step in grasping the logical structure underlying this conditional relation of reasons-and-verdict is to realize that criticism is an exercise in forensic reasoning. The critic's commentary is analogous to that of the trial lawyer who bases claims as to the proper verdict in a case on his interpretation of the facts in the light of some legal code. What tactics are open to the legal advocate? He may in some circumstances accept a set of legal standards (canons or laws) and apply them rigorously to the facts in the case. He may on the other hand feel that the laws as they are commonly interpreted hurt his case. In that event he could propose a new interpretation of the laws which does more justice to the position he is defending; or if his mind functions after the fashion of an Erskine, he could seek to "make law" by questioning the established norms and attempting either to amend them or to substitute a code of his own choosing as the standard of evaluation. Again, some circumstances may be such that the counsel will accept a verdict contrary to his position but then go on to try to mitigate the thrust of the verdict by showing how special factors in the case deserve attention. Or perhaps there is a conflict in the legal code such as a contradiction between two laws. In the case of such an overlap, the advocate may argue for the priority of one law over another. In each of these instances the essential forensic tactic is to measure facts or observations against a code or canon.

A similar juxtapositioning of observations and normative standards constitutes the essence of critical activity:

> The code may be the law of the land, the theory of probabilities, the standards of historical research, the *canons of artistic excellence* [my italics], or their own standards for distinguishing truth from error. Whoever judges in these ways, then, needs two distinct kinds of knowledge: (1) knowledge about the facts or events he is to judge and (2) knowledge about the standards against which he is to measure the facts or events.[13]

We may thus expect that reasons offered in critical discourse will lay claim to being the product of a "measurement" (comparison of data observed and norm). This does not mean that the verdict need follow inevitably from the comparison, only that it will claim such a juxtapositioning as a warrant for its own worth.

If the notion of forensic reasoning as the foundation of critical strategy is plausible, we have further grounds for rejecting some evaluations which are offered as specimens of criticism. Though tradition recognizes as "movie reviews" the placement of stars next to film titles in newspapers (four stars equivalent to "excellent," one star meaning "terrible"), we need not accept such markings as criticism (or if we do, as more than decapitated criticism). Again, what should one make of an argument which runs, "I feel that MacArthur's speech was unsatisfactory because the General once insulted me"? Such a remark is ordinarily disturbing. In part this is because the comment does not fulfill forensic requirements: the reason offered, although it explains why the commentator holds the position he does, is not admissible as a justification for the verdict. In this case the norm (such as it is) violates the critical posture, and there is in addition a failure to juxtapose the norm to facts about the speech.

Observe how Wichelns illustrates the forensic pattern. He opens his essay by distinguishing between speeches which offer advice and those which join a debate. He thereby establishes the norm. He then spends the remainder of his first paragraph drawing attention to those facts about the speech which place it in the category of speeches of advice. In his next paragraph Wichelns formulates the principle that some remarks are mandatory on this kind of occasion—and then observes the extent to which MacArthur met those demands. In his third paragraph the critic implies that some rhetorical tactics reveal a proconsular image and then presents facts which enable him to ascribe such an image to MacArthur. The forensic pattern is evident throughout Wichelns' essay.

But the notion of forensic reasoning highlights one curious feature of criticism: although both norms and observations are logically essential, they need not be expressed separately. This aspect of criticism is illustrated in the dialogue concerning *Tom Jones.* When your friend justifies his evaluation of the novel with "I read the novel last week," where is the standard of judgment? Clearly, if it exists at all it is only implicit. One might suspect that your friend really meant, "I read the novel, and it did not measure up to my taste in novels," but that would only be speculation. Or take Rovere as a case in point. True, he announces at the outset that his standards will be "literary" and "political" ones. But then he goes on to call MacArthur's eloquence "coarse" and to say that MacArthur's language is neither "flat and bloodless" nor "flabby and loose-jointed." Are these observations or verdicts? And what are Rovere's standards for eloquence? Apparently, Rovere demands that the reader accept the existence and the excellence of the norms on faith. The norms do not appear in the criticism, though they are presupposed by Rovere's comments.

This fusion of otherwise distinct components is not an accident of composition. When Rovere condemns MacArthur's prose for its unshaded meanings, its lack of humor, its fetid language, is he hypothesizing that "the occurrence of these three elements results in coarse eloquence" after the fashion of the experimental scientists? Or is he calling to attention these particular observable features which, in these particular rhetorical circumstances, lend an air of coarseness to this particular speech? Rovere is obviously affirming his possession of standards of eloquence; but the application of the standards to a particular aesthetic event is, as we shall discover when we treat the modalities of analysis, far more complex than the measurement of the length of a metal pipe. In aesthetic judgments the standards often defy expression as general propositions for any but the most gross (and hence, trivial) features. And the standards applied are bound to the particulars of the single event because the events are too diverse and complicated to be comprehended by universal precepts. Such is the case of Rovere seeking to illuminate the coarseness of MacArthur's prose. He would be unable to provide general rubrics for what makes prose coarse because too many factors enter in; but he is able to account for the "coarse eloquence" in this case, and he does so.[14]

To answer what features of criticism distinguish it from other types of reason-giving discourse, we have so far maintained that the term "criticism" is most sensibly reserved for that assertive discourse produced by expert-spectators whose judgments as to the execution of (in this case) rhetorical phenomena are supported by forensic arguments. We may now consider the two remaining questions posed at the beginning of this essay. Let us for present purposes exclude from attention questions concerning the goals of rhetorical criticism or the origin and validity of rhetorical canons, interesting as these questions may be. In this essay we shall take for granted that the rhetorical critic possesses certain *a priori* objectives; he engages in the critical act for the sake of some preestablished end(s) which need not be specified here. We shall also presume that if called upon to do so, the critic could vindicate by means extrinsic to the realm of criticism (e.g., by metaphysical justification of some sort) his adoption of whatever rhetorical concepts he employs in his criticism.[15] Our interest is not in why he acts and believes as he does, but in how he exploits the critical opportunities available to him.

We are consequently obliged to examine the array of methodological options open to the rhetorical critic. At least two method-related questions invariably confront the critic in the exercise of his office: 1) what shall be the major focus of his critical analysis (what data will he find primarily relevant)? 2) what sorts of measurements or readings shall he take on the rhetorical transactions under investigation (in what fashion shall he transpose and describe the data he chooses to fix upon)? How he elects to answer these questions will in part influence both the nature and function of the critical reasons produced. Let us first address ourselves to the alternative foci open to the critic of "public address."

If we schematize an instance of public communication encountered by the critic, we intuitively recognize four gross variables: the source(s) or creator(s) of the message, the message itself, the context or environment in which the message is received (including both the receivers and the social "landscape" which spawns the message), and the critic himself (who, especially in the study of public address of the past, is in a sense a unique receiver). For the sake of convenience, let us lable the variables "S" (source), "M" (message), "E" (environment), and "C" (critic). Obviously, in a total interpretation of the communicative act all four variables are relevant. But equally obvious from past critical practice, such all-encompassing analysis will be rare if not impossible for the single critic. Perhaps the two most thoroughly examined messages in the English language are Shakespeare's *Hamlet* and Lincoln's *Gettysburg Address;* the very fact that criticism of these two is not yet exhausted attests to the impracticality of completely enveloping one verbal act with another. We are therefore forced to recognize that critics will have to concentrate on some permutation of the four variables as a means of making their critical tasks manageable.

For the rhetorical critic the one indispensable factor is M, the message. Exclusive concern for S, the source, is the biographer's business; study of E, the environment, is the historian's; studies relating speakers to audience apart from the substance of the message (as in explorations of the role of status or leadership in public affairs) are performed mainly by sociologists. The rhetorical critic sees the entire communicative transaction as somehow "suspended" from the language of the message under examination. For the rhetorical critic the verbal utterance constitutes a kind of linguistic architecture which supports and gives form to the total rhetorical act. In this belief the critic differs from the historian and sociologist, who may choose to treat the verbal factors as mere artifacts of the event. The rhetorical critic not only fastens his observation to M; he does so in the conviction that the message is fundamental to an appreciation of the entire event.[16]

The critic therefore occupies himself with some combination of variables which focus on the message: S-M, M-E, M-C, S-M-E, S-M-C, or M-E-C. These are combinations which constitute genuine critical options. It is not the critic's task to inspect these variables in isolation; neither is it sufficient for him to report that they all converged in a particular instance of public discourse.

Consider first the nature of the M-C focus, which represents an unashamedly introspectionist stance. This focus seeks to gauge the critic's personal response to the aesthetic object.[17] The critic who directs his attention to the M-C relationship will conceive of himself as a kind of sensitive instrument, and his analysis will be comprised primarily of reports of his own reactions to the work apart from any impact the work may have had on any particular "public." In this vein, Anatole France remarked that the good critic:

. . is he who relates the adventures of his soul among masterpieces. . . . The truth is
that one never gets out of oneself.[18]

Rovere's commentary suggests that he adopted a focus such as the one described by
France.

The M-C orientation grounds its validation on the premise that communication is essentially a unique event, a private transaction between message and receiver which can never
be known to a third party. The critic is simply one more receiver of the message, albeit
more sensitive than the typical, untrained receiver. If one accepts the notion that critical
interpretation is so uniquely personal, it then follows that no interpretation can expect to
be more than a justification of the critic's own state of mind as he responds to the
aesthetic object.

And if communication is inherently a private matter, then one's faith in the critic's
explication and overall taste constitutes at least as important a means of support for the
verdicts offered as do the critic's stated reasons for his evaluation. Hence, in the case of
Rovere, we need to trust his sensitivity as much as we need to be persuaded by his
analysis of the prose. It is even possible to imagine that the primary function served by
reasons submitted by an observer with the M-C focus is to demonstrate to a reader the
observer's competence as a critic, to "exhibit his credentials," to make authoritative
judgments.[19] Such a conception of M-C analysis may account for the propensity of
prominent critics to set forth lists of their favorite books, or of the best plays or speeches
of all time. Having achieved eminence, they need no longer justify their selections, but are
able to telescope or even abort their arguments in favor of short explications of why a
particular book, play, or novel pleased them personally.

The next three foci are related to each other in their denial of an introspectionist
critical stance and their advocacy of greater detachment. The S-M focus concentrates on
understanding discourse as an expression of its creator. Most often the critic attempts to
trace out the creative process by which the speaker externalized and structured the
feelings, thoughts, and experiences contained within himself. The relation of source to
message has prompted two general schools of criticism. One (which actually concentrates
on the S $\Rightarrow$ M relationship) seeks to account for the rhetor's behavior as a function of the
factors which influenced him: his education, the books he read, the persons who inspired
him, and the like.[20] The other variation of the S-M focus, S $\Leftarrow$ M, is best typified by
neo-Freudian critics who treat the aesthetic event as symptomatic of the artist's personal
life and psychodynamics. The critic, in other words, acts as a kind of lay psychoanalyst,
using the message as a key to understanding and evaluating the creator of the message.[21]

The M-E focus also incorporates two divergent streams of critical practice. In the one
instance (M $\Leftarrow$ E), "environment" is interpreted broadly (as by historians and literary
critics) to encompass the age and the civilization in which the message originated. This
historian of ideas attempts to set the historical background in which particular works or
clusters of works were produced, showing how the messages are themselves a reflection of
their era. This emphasis finds its rationale in the assumption that to the extent that an
aesthetic event can be considered typical of its age it will provide valuable insight into the
intellectual and social trends of that age.[22] Another direction which critics with an M-E
focus have chosen to follow, one which has gained its widest acceptance among critics
with a bent toward social science, interprets "environment" in a more prescribed sense,
referring to the specific audience which the message had. These critics consider the
"functional" relationship which existed between the discourse and its receivers. They

seek to determine how the receivers used the messages presented to them as stimuli. The assumption underlying the functional (M⇒E) approach to the M-E relationship is that, whatever the speaker's intention, the auditor attends to a speech in a manner which fulfills his own personal needs. An old man may attend a July 4th celebration, not prepared to be persuaded or inspired to increased patriotism, but simply because the ceremonial oratory reminds him of the speeches he heard on similar occasions in his youth. Similarly, the daily newspaper may function for some readers as a means by which they maintain an intimate contact with their favorite celebrities. For such readers, news of a Hollywood scandal is as welcome as a letter from home. In cases such as these, the M-E critic might concern himself with determining expectations of the audience as well as the extent to which those expectations were fulfilled by the discourse.[23]

Although it is possible for a rhetorical critic to employ any of the three foci so far mentioned, the bulk of traditional speech criticisms has not explored dyadic relationships but the triadic formulations of S-M-E. Essentially, this "pragmatic" orientation treats the message as an effort at persuasion and ventures to assess the artistic skill of the speaker in achieving his persuasive goals with his audience.[24] The extensive use of the S-M-E framework can be justified if we accept the notion that public address is, literally, discourse addressed to a public by a speaker who is carrying on public business by his act of communication. Because the critic takes for granted the Janus-like quality of public address, revealing simultaneously the communicator and the social environment to which he seeks to adapt himself, the S-M-E critic emphasizes in his study the mediating nature of the message in moving (or failing to move) the audience toward the speaker's vision of how the demands of occasion ought to be met and resolved.[25]

The three foci—S-M, M-E and S-M-E—comprise a set because they share one quality which distinguishes them from the introspectionist reports of the M-C focus. This shared quality is a stress on objective, verifiable, critical statements. By placing the spectator outside the critical equation, each method attempts to make of criticism a dispassionate report of what actually "is," a judicious, unbiased account of properties which inhere in the communicative event itself. In so doing they imply that the critic should strive to produce an analysis of the essential nature of the phenomenon apart from any idiosyncracies in his personal responses.[26]

None of the three "impersonal" approaches so far mentioned can serve the ends of the introspectionist, and hence, none of the three kinds encourages critical reasons employed mainly to establish the critic's own credentials as a sensitive observer. Instead, the critic who strives for a dispassionate and reliable report of the rhetorical act will find that the reasons he gives in support of his verdicts function primarily to call to the attention of others those characteristics of the original communication which merit their further contemplation. The method is similar to that of the football announcer who uses an instant replay camera. A team scores a touchdown, and seconds later the television commentator says, "As we play back the scoring play, notice the excellent footwork of the man with the ball." The listener-viewer is thus primed to observe for himself a feature of the event which the expert-commentator feels merits attention. The same ostensive function applies to the selection of reasons by the impersonal, rhetorical critic; his reasons do not report, nor do they simply support a conclusion—they call on the reader to observe for himself.

The last two foci available to the critic, S-M-C and M-E-C, reject the cleavage between introspection and impersonal functions of critical discourse. Justification for these two foci stems from the recognition of contemporary science that the very act of observation alters the event observed and so distorts the information one is able to obtain about the event. The distortions can never be overcome by more precise observations or measurements, but can only be acknowledged by specifying a degree of uncertainty and looseness in one's formulations.

As applied to the critical act, such a position holds that criticism is inevitably the product of the critic's encounter with the rhetorical event, that the locus of criticism is neither critic nor ontic event but the critic's intrusion upon the event. Such an intrusion may not directly influence the agents involved in the communication; we may wish to admit, for instance, that as he prepared his first inaugural address Thomas Jefferson probably did not significantly alter his behavior in conscious anticipation of twentieth-century rhetorical critics. But neither should we misconstrue the dilemma faced by the critic who would do more than resurrect the data of the past. His problem is less one of succumbing to personal bias than it is of taking and formulating precise measurements on the event under investigation.[27] Our final two foci suit the critic who has reconciled himself to the inevitable impossibility of making meticulously accurate statements about the events he observes, who wishes instead the maximum fidelity possible within the limits imposed on him by the nature of perception and critical language. His framework for observation indexes neither the event *in vacuo* nor his own response to the event, but the relation which joins him to the rhetorical act.

The critic who adopts the S-M-C focus assumes that a speech will no more exist "out there" in some ontic world than does a symphony reside "in" a musical score or a drama "in" a manuscript.[28] Instead, he believes that we can discern an artistic intention in a work of art; and the aesthetic experience, be it to speech or symphony, is the experiencing and articulation of that artistic intention. Artistic intention is understood as the peculiar way in which the elements of the message cohere in the movement of confrontation with the observer-critic.

There are objective clues in the messages as to the meaning which will be actualized by the interaction of observer and thing observed. It becomes the critic's task to investigate that cooperation of elements and ratios in the message which gives rise to the artistic meaning-as-experienced. In other words, speaker, speech, and observer momentarily coalesce as the elements of the rhetorical event unite to move toward some terminal condition. The critic's objective is to explicate that condition and the communication factors which contribute to or retard the transaction. The critic seeks to determine the nature of the demands made by the rhetorical event upon the beholder of the event. He is of course obligated to be alert to his own predilections as an instrument of observation, but his attention is focused outward upon artistic intention rather than inward as with introspection.[29]

The source enters into this equation because it is posited that the artist's intention(s) in creating the message may provide a key to understanding the artistic intention embodied in the message. The critic assumes that the speaker, by virtue of his close connection with the message, is something of an authority on the event; that is, the speaker often possesses special knowledge about the speech which adds depth to the critic's own interpretation. Hence a comparison of artist's intentions with artistic intentions may prove a valuable aid in centering interest on the decisive qualities of the work of art.

Consider, for example, John Kennedy's television address to the nation on the Cuban missile crisis in 1962: we might regard the policy enunciated on that occasion as rhetorically inappropriate. However, if we knew that Kennedy was privy to secret information indicating that the Russians would withdraw their missiles if we took a strong line, this knowledge would help clarify the forceful posture Kennedy chose to adopt and possibly alter our critical assessment of the artistic intention evidenced in the discourse. We might now see the message as primarily a warning to Russia rather than as a report to the nation.

Notice that the S-M-C focus does not obligate the critic to accept the artist's personal conception of his creation; the purpose of uncovering Kennedy's purpose in speaking is not to whitewash Kennedy but to understand the parameters within which his verbal behavior operated. We might still find that Kennedy chose an inappropriate rhetorical strategy. Or we might conclude that Kennedy was himself not fully aware of the real significance of the discourse he produced. Our search does not necessarily tell us anything about the ultimate character of the message for the artist's intentions are ancillary to our primary concern, which is artistic intention.[30] We seek to discover the speaker's point of view; the symptoms of artistic and intellectual choice thereby revealed may lend depth to our apprehension of the design of the message.

Like its S-M-C counterpart, M-E-C rests on a conception of the critical act as an encounter. And it also recognizes the importance of artistic intention, of the demands made by the work upon the recipient of the message. The primary distinction between the two frameworks is the emphasis that the M-E-C focus places on the rhetorical event as an act, a performance which is only fully consummated in that instant when message is apprehended by receiver. Just as a play is not theatre until it is being performed for an audience, so the rhetorical artifact (such as a speech manuscript) becomes discourse only when it is experienced in a public "arena" or forum.[31] The rhetorical critic therefore necessarily fastens his attention not on the moment of creation but upon the moment of reception, realizing all the while that by his intrusion he is mutilating the confrontation of message and audience.

One consequence of this shift in emphasis is that the M-E-C critic is less concerned with the speaker's influence on the message than is the S-M-C critic. As the French symbolist Paul Valéry has contended:

> There is no true meaning to a text—no author's authority. Whatever he may have wanted to say, he has written what he has written. Once published, a text is like an apparatus that anyone may use as he will and according to his ability: It is not certain that the one who constructed it can use it better than another.[32]

Although there are important differences between symbolist literary criticism and the traits of M-E-C rhetorical analysis, they are in this respect similar.

Whereas the S-M-C focus concentrates on the aesthetic demands of the event upon *an* auditor (the potential interpretation which any sensitive recipient might make), M-E-C considers the aesthetic demands made by the event upon *the* auditors (the likely meaning of the message for a given public). To illustrate, the S-M-C critic would seek to assess the enduring worth of medieval morality plays, taking account of their original cast as inculcators of religious faith; the M-E-C critic, on the other hand, would distinguish between the meaning of a morality play for its original audience and its meaning (perhaps totally different) for a typical contemporary auditor. Constrained thus by context, the M-E-C critical focus is more particularlized, with the critic acting as a kind of surrogate for the audience he projects into the communicative event.[33]

Nor is the M-E-C frame simply a variation of the more objective message-environment focus. M-E analysis offers a predominantly historical interpretation of "how it was" when the public confronted the speech. The M-E critic seeks to understand the nature of the transaction as it in fact originally occurred. He may even go so far as to evaluate the speech using the rhetorical norms of the period and society in which the speech was delivered. He has a tendency to work back from the context to the message as he engages in assessment.

In contrast, an historistic interpretation might be more appropriate to an M-E-C focus. The M-E-C critic would try to go beyond understanding the message *as* the original participants understood it and attempt also to understand it *better than* they did.[34] He would seek to determine "how it would have to be" if one were to derive the fullest significance implicit in the rhetorical event. It is likely that an observer with an M-E-C orientation would follow a course of action in which he first analyzed the message, then projected from his analysis a description of the public for whom the message would be most appealing, and finally compared the bulk of the actual audience with his composite ideal auditor.

It is suggestive for us to bear in mind that both frames originate in the physicist's efforts to accommodate his formulations to the inherent uncertainty of the cosmos. We might therefore expect S-M-C and M-E-C critics to be somewhat more heedful of the limitations of their investigations and less inclined to construct a brief for a particular interpretation. They might be somewhat more prone to employ their reasons as part of a calculation of the validity of particular rhetorical concepts. Their primary objective would then be to modify rhetorical theory to accommodate their clinical observations rather than to establish their own credibility or assist readers to derive increased satisfaction from the rhetorical event under discussion. We would expect critics with this cast to be more tentative in their reason-giving, since their comments would operate less in an advocative capacity and more as a special kind of scientific discourse. Such a critic might very well take the view that if his reasons are sound those to whom he reports will *probably* attach greater value to his judgments. He would therefore seek to determine the strength of his reasons.[35]

Let us conclude consideration of alternative critical foci by reminding ourselves that the focus adopted by the critic determines what kind of questions he will find most interesting. Insofar as the critic chooses to relate the rhetorical event to its creator he will ask: How did the message come to be? Is it symptomatic of the speaker? What are the capacities of the rhetor as an artist? How does the man shape the message? The critic who regards the message as the initial stimulus in his formula will aks himself a complementary set of questions: How does the message reflect its context? What evidence is there that the message as created was appropriate to the climate in which it was employed? How did the message serve to influence its environment? How and why does my experience with this message differ from the likely experiences of other recipients? These are all legitimate questions for a critic to ask; but his decision as to which shall occupy his attention will be at least partially influenced by the focus he has chosen to adopt.

Although many more problems pertaining to the logic of rhetorical criticism remain, this essay will treat only one more topic, the procedures available to the critic for relating norm and observation. This topic is essential since reason-giving has been shown to be the fundamental aspect of the logic of critical discourse.

We can imagine judgments which do not entail even the possibility of supporting reasons, but we ordinarily treat such evaluations as capricious remarks when uttered by critics. The manner in which a critic relates fact and criterion is of some moment if we hope to understand the character of his reason-giving. For our purposes, the term "modality" will refer to any characteristic manner (or formula) for joining observations and norms so as to produce justificatory reasons in criticism. The term's meaning is thus roughly comparable to the sense of "function" as used in calculus.[36] To explain this special use of "modality" it is necessary to begin with a clarification of the term "juxtapose."

Earlier in this essay the critic was compared to the lawyer pleading a case. It was then suggested that a critic's primary task is to formulate justificatory bases for his verdicts by "juxtaposing" descriptions and norms. The term "juxtapose" is purposely vague, and it must be understood in light of John Dewey's observation that criticism:

> . . . is judgment engaged in discriminating among values. It is taking thought as to what is better and worse in any field at any time, with some consciousness of *why* the better is better and *why* the worse is worse.[37]

Now determination of better-and-worse may take several forms. One might "grade" a speech according to various criteria or rank it with respect to other speeches and along designated scales, or he might simply classify it by type as part of a general act of recognizing features (when one labels a speech "epideictic," what he in fact does is provide a shorthand notation of several qualities we expect to find in epideictic oratory).[38]

Whatever the informative pattern evident in criticism, we expect that two related features of the critical act will remain constant. The critic will first have alternative speeches in mind as he approaches the object of study. Better-and-worse implies better-or-worse-than something else. To say that Adlai Stevenson was a great speaker suggests that the critic can discriminate between the speeches of Stevenson and those of some not-so-great speakers. To find fault with Lyndon Johnson's style suggests that the critic has in mind alternative stylistic tactics which Johnson might employ to improve his style.

The second implication to be drawn from Dewey's comment is that the alternative(s) the critic has in mind will take the form of particular speeches or aspects of speeches. To illustrate: suppose we feel that "good" speeches generally require transitions between main points. Should we find a speech lacking transitions is it perforce a "bad" speech? Obviously not. Some speeches do not need transitions. Hence, the rubric "good speeches have transitions" is merely a guiding principle which serves to canalize critical observations; it is a reminder to consider the possibilities of an alternative speech containing transitions. To judge a discourse deficient in its use of transitions we need to have in mind how the addition of transitions might improve the speech; we must have an alternative image of a speech which is better, in particular ways, than the one we are observing. The "juxtaposition" called for in criticism is not straightforward application of rules to events in the manner by which we measure the length of an object against a yardstick. There is instead an oblique, two-step process by which the critic either generates or selects an appropriate alternative discourse and then compares that specific alternative to the discourse under analysis. The two modalities we shall consider represent general procedures for so joining observations and rhetorical norms.

A model modality is employed when the critic starts by generating some sort of paradigm which he will use as a basis of comparison. Laymen commonly speak of models in reference to airplanes, toy houses, or sets of blueprints. They tend to associate the term with miniatures, objects and/or plans drawn to scale.[39] However, the more appropriate sense of "model" in criticism is one which roughly corresponds to "prototype" or to "exemplar of a kind." Drawing on his rhetorical theory, the critic generates a model representing his conception of what would have constituted the ideal speech for the situation. He then compares his archetype with the speech which was actually delivered in order to determine the degree and the nature of the disparity between paradigm and actual speech. The comparison precipitates a kind of diagnosis; if the model conforms to the critic's rhetorical theory (as we must assume it does if it is to be regarded as a paradigm), then disparity between the norm-discourse and the actual one should provide some insight into both the aesthetic excellence and the rhetorical weaknesses evident in the discourse being inspected.

This notion of the norm as a model presupposes that the critic can himself create a prototype which is neither a stock image ("the speech for all occasions") nor yet a capricious whim. His model must be one which in its essentials conforms to his rhetorical theory. As we noted earlier, no rhetorical theory is so detailed that it can account for every aspect of every speech except in general outline. The well-wrought model requires a sensitive creator who can use his theory as a point of departure in developing in his imagination the model uniquely suited to assess a particular message. The search for an explanation for the extent and character of deviation from the paradigm model will then constitute the invention of critical reasons.

Both Rovere and Wichelns illustrate the model modality of reason-giving. Rovere contrasts MacArthur's speech by means of a treatment of issues demanded by the controversy; on that basis he decides MacArthur's effort is inappropriate to the occasion. Wichelns, too, seems to reason from an implicit prototype insofar as he comments on attributes present and lacking, manadatory and optional in MacArthur's prose. If Wichelns is unwilling to discuss the appropriateness of MacArthur's tone of authority (and his silence on this score is revealing), he is at least willing to address himself to MacArthur's skill in executing the tactic; and such comments, responsibly made, entail a theoretical conception of how public image is conveyed in a speech.

The essential feature of the second tactic of comparison, the analog modality, is that the norm employed is some actual discourse and not a theoretically derived prototype. Imagine the behavior of a critic who wished to characterize the rhetoric of Fidel Castro on those occasions when Castro justifies his failure to hold popular elections. The critic might use his rhetorical theory to generate a model of what would be appropriate for Castro to say; he might, on the other hand, be reminded of the rhetoric of another revolutionary in similar circumstances, say Cromwell dissolving Parliament. In the latter case, the critic might choose to juxtapose Castro's discourse to Cromwell's. His norm would no longer be paradigmatic, for he would have no *a priori* grounds for judging either Castro or Cromwell the more worthy rhetorician.

In lieu of such assessments, the critic would use Cromwell's speeches for topological purposes, much as he would a road map. Cromwell's discourse would serve to focus and guide the critic in his interpretation of Castro. Critical judgments would thus assume the form of statements of more-or-less or better-and-worse respecting particular qualities evident in the discourses. Perhaps Cromwell is more likely to engage in personal invective while Castro is more discursive in justifying his policies.

An illustration of the analog modality is found in Professor Laura Crowell's criticism of the speaking of John Pym, the English Parliamentarian. Crowell is contending that a distinctive feature of Pym's address is his interpretation of new events within the context of already-accepted materials and attitudes:

> To people whose world was changing from medievalism to modernism under their feet, the words of a man who consistently saw events in larger context and who had details ready at hand on Biblical, philosophical, legal, financial, and parliamentary matters were extremely comforting. A cocksure age is ready for persuasion to new proposals, easily abandoning the present, not fearing the leap. But a skeptical age, such as Pym's asks a persuasion that keeps its hold upon the present even while raising questions; it needs to feel the security of the past even while rising to meet new problems.[40]

The contrast between the debate of Pym's time and contemporary debate over, say, social welfare enables the critic in this case to highlight a quality in Pym's discourse which might not be readily evident were one to attempt to conceive the ideal rhetorical strategy for Pym solely on the basis of a rhetorical theory.

The analog relation of two particulars without direct recourse to a set of precepts entails a special role for rhetorical theory in the interpretative act. In the model modality the critic's norm is generated and constrained by theoretical precepts. In the analog situation rhetorical theory constitutes a shorthand account of those rhetorical categories which are typically helpful to the act of comparison. In the latter instance the critic is less concerned with creating a prototype than he is with "characterizing" an actual discourse.[41]

The analogical modality opens realms of critical analysis which have been for the most part neglected by rhetorical critics. Let us imagine that a critic, having assessed Castro in the light of the rhetorically similar Cromwell, decides to compare him with some apparently unrelated speaker, such as William Faulkner accepting the Nobel Prize for literature. There is no logical reason why such a comparison would be fruitless, yet it is clear that such a juxtaposing would yield results quite different from the comparison of Castro and Cromwell. Theroretically, the possibilities of analysis are infinite. Why not compare messages across cultures (say inaugural addresses of Presidents and coronation speeches of Kings), or across genres (John Adams the speaker and John Adams the writer of diaries)? Why not juxtapose various rhetorical forms, such as Ingersoll's witty ripostes at the Lotus Club and the cryptic visions of a religious mystic? Or why not contrast totally different rhetorical objects (Burke to the electors of Bristol and Martin Luther King to a college audience)?

The model modality finds its optimal use in confirming or qualifying rhetorical theory, where the analog modality, because of its factorial character, provides a point of departure which enables the critic to derive new categories and precepts from his investigation. The model-based critic is asking whether the rhetorician met certain criteria which were established by a given rhetorical system; the analog critic compares and contrasts, searching out theoretical explanations to accommodate his discoveries. In both instances theory assists the critic in his task and is in turn refined by the act of criticism. But it is clear that slatternly reliance on rhetorical canons to perform critical tests is futile in either modality. Even where the canons suggest no obvious fault in a particular discourse, it is always possible that the astute critic could imagine a better speech or pamphlet, it is always possible that a felicitous comparison might expose qualities beyond the scope of the rhetorical theory at hand.[42]

Conclusion

This essay began by asserting that criticism is distinguished as a form of discourse by its peculiar reason-giving qualities. The ensuing discussion of this assertion holds two implications for speech scholars. The first is the suggestion, implicit in our analysis of the terms "critic" and "criticism," that rhetorical criticism does not operate *in vacuo.* Speech criticism can be best understood within the broader context afforded by a general conception of criticism's logical features. It has been argued that among the formal aspects which unite speech criticism with other varieties of critical discourse is the expert-spectator posture assumed by all critics. Another feature common to all criticism and setting it apart from the bulk of public discourse is its reliance upon forensic reasons-in-support-of-verdicts as its primary method for advancing contentions.

The second implication derives from our consideration of critical foci and modalities: it is possible to discern a finite set of relatively clear-cut methodological options open to the critic. There is, in other words, a system of alternatives inherent in critical endeavor; criticism is not the "blooming, buzzing confusion" it may at times seem. Thus, for example, conceiving of the critical act as encompassing the four gross components of the communicative event enables us to specify in at least loose terms the kind of questions to which a given critic has addressed himself. Indeed, the recognition that various critics will give primary emphasis to particular combinations of S, M, E and C helps us to understand (although not necessarily to resolve) controversies which pit critics of one focus against those of another. We are at least aware that the issue in the debate is often not so much the validity of the critics' arguments or the acuity of their observations as it is the importance each school attaches to particular relationships among the four communicative variables.

We have also considered the two fundamental modalities open to the critic as he relates his artistic criteria to the rhetorical event. We have seen that the common conception of the critic as one directly applying his cannons in the manner of a measure applied to an object is overly simplified. The relation of criteria to object is oblique, entailing the critic's own conception of what the rhetorical work might have been. And this need for a one-to-one comparison again reminds us that the critic's selection from among the methodological options available will influence the character of his discourse.

Criticism, in sum, reveals itself to be a peculiarly open-ended frustrating, but not incomprehensible endeavor. If the general condition of the critical act is diversity of substantive and methodological options, there are still reasonable limits to the range of those options. In the final analysis it is perhaps this vast complexity of opportunity that makes understanding the formal facets of critical method tenuous and difficult, yet at the same time renders understanding virtually indispensable to the student of criticism.

Notes

1. Cf. L. H. Levy, *Psychological Interpretation* (New York, 1963), p. 30; R. McKeon, "The Philosophic Bases of Art and Criticism," *Critics and Criticism, Ancient and Modern,* ed. R. S. Crane (Chicago, 1952), pp. 147-75; L. Thonssen and A. C. Baird, *Speech Criticism* (New York, 1948).

2. The reader should beware of confusing the remarks made in this essay about the nature of criticism with handbook directions on how to do criticism or with empirical descriptions of how criticism is done. The aim here is simply to offer a typology which suggests the characteristic formal relationships normally encountered by critics.

3. Cf. E. G. Bormann, *Theory and Research in the Communicative Arts* (New York, 1965), pp. 227-38, for a discussion of the confusion which often arises between the role of historian and that of critic.

4. Cf. N. Smart, "Sense and Reference in Aesthetics," *British Journal of Aesthetics,* III (October 1963), 363-66; L. W. Beck, "Agent, Actor, Spectator and Critic," *Monist,* XLIX (April 1965), 167-182; D. Van de Vate, Jr., "Disagreement as a Dramatic Event," *Monist,* XLIX (April 1965), 248-61.

5. Nothing esoteric is meant by "aesthetic." I intend only to convey the notion that the logical conditions mentioned here apply to the full range of interests open to the critic: dramatic productions, musical performances, traditional "fine art," as well as to orations and political dialogues. "Aesthetics" is derived from the Greek *aisthetikos* (of sense perception), and I use the term to suggest that the phenomena which provoke discussion by spectators are of the order which manifest themselves to the perceptions.

6. The notion of execution should not be confused with the idea of intent. The football pass may have ·been an accident and still have been well executed. "Skill in execution" is not synonymous with "doing what the creator intended." Cf. M. Eshleman, "Aesthetic Experience, the Aesthetic Object and Criticism," *Monist,* L (April 1966), 281-91.

7. This places literary and rhetorical critics in the peculiar position of producing verbal objects as comment on other verbal objects (e.g., novels, plays, speeches, etc.), so that both types of critic are in fact engaged in producing discourse about discourse. Cf. A. Hillbruner, "Criticism as Persuasion," *Southern Speech Journal,* XXXVIII (Summer 1963), 260-67; E. Black, "Moral Values and Rhetorical Criticism," lecture delivered at University of Wisconsin, July 12, 1965; Thonssen and Baird, pp. 13-14.

8.· Both essays are drawn from F. W. Haberman, "General MacArthur's Speech: A Symposium of Critical Comment," *Quarterly Journal of Speech,* XXXVII (October 1951), 321-31. They are reprinted in C. C. Arnold, D. Ehninger, and J. C. Gerber, *The Speaker's Resource Book* (Chicago, 1961), pp. 283-86. Cf. also P. Wylie, "Medievalism and the MacArthurian Legend," *Quarterly Journal of Speech,* XXXVII (December 1951), 473-78; P. R. Beall, "Viper-Crusher Turns Dragon-Slayer," ibid., XXXVIII (February 1952), 51-56; K. R. Wallace, "On the Criticism of the MacArthur Speech," ibid, XXXIX (February 1953), 69-74; M. H. Nichols, *Rhetoric and Criticism* (Baton Rouge, La., 1963), pp. 68-9.

9. Bormann, pp. 227-29; E. Black, *Rhetorical Criticism: A Study in Method* (New York, 1965), p. 4.

10. Black, "Moral Values. . . ." Cf. Hillbruner, pp. 264-66; P. W. Taylor, *Normative Discourse* (Englewood Cliffs, N.J., 1961), p. 52; W. Righter, *Logic and Criticism* (New York, 1963), pp. vii-3; Bormann, p. 229; J. Holloway, "Symposium: Distinctive Features of Arguments Used in Criticism of the Arts," *Proceedings of the Aristotelian Society* (supplement), XXIII (1949), 173.

11. A. Isenberg, "Critical Communication," *Philosophical Review,* LVIII (April 1949), 331. See also the following articles in *Monist,* L (April 1966): M. Scriven, "The Objectivity of Aesthetic Evaluation," 159-87; H. Osborne, "Reasons and Description in Criticism," 204-12; H. Morris-Jones, "The Logic of Criticism," 213-21; P. Wilson, "The Need to Justify," 267-80.

12. Let us momentarily disregard a related problem, whether one's verdicts must follow inevitably from one's reasons, as in a valid syllogism, or whether there is some looser connection between the evaluations and the justificatory reasons, perhaps a relation of appropriateness instead of one of the correctness. What matters here is that both components are inseparable parts of the critic's assertions, no matter what their bearing on each other. Cf. Righter, pp. 78-84; M. Weitz, "Reasons in Criticism," *Journal of Aesthetics and Art Criticism,* XX (Summer 1962), 427-37; B. C. Heyl, "The Critic's Reasons," ibid., XVI (Winter 1957), 169-79.

13. J. F. Wilson and C. C. Arnold, *Public Speaking as a Liberal Art* (Boston, 1964), p. 87. Cf. Weitz; Isenberg, pp. 330-35; Taylor, pp. 9-14.

14. Righter, p. 22.

15. Cf. Taylor, pp. 128-38; McKeon, pp. 489-90; K. Burke, *A Grammar of Motives* (New York, 1945), p. 472; E. Olson, "The Poetic Method in Aristotle: Its Powers and Limitations," *Aristotle's Poetics and English Literature,* ed. E. Olson (Chicago, 1965), pp. 187-91.

16. Cf. T. Clevenger, Jr., "Research Opportunities in Speech," *Introduction to the Field of Speech,* ed. R. F. Reid (Chicago, 1965), pp. 222-24.

17. Cf. Heyl, p. 170; R. Wellek and A. Warren, *The Theory of Literature* (New York, 1949); W. Embler, "The Language of Criticism," *ETC.,* XXII (September 1965), 261-77. This cryptic account is obviously not the entire story. The critic is not privileged simply to report his pleasure and/or pain on confronting the discourse. He is in some manner obligated to explain how and why the work justifies his particular response. It is also important to note that contemporary literary critics who claim to focus entirely on the work itself are in fact often employing the M-C paradigm; their failure to recognize the implications of their critical orientation results occasionally in rather odd exigeses.

18. Anatole France, "The Literary Life," *The Book of Modern Criticism,* trans. and ed. L. Lewisohn (New York, 1919), pp. 1-3. Cf. I. A. Richards, *Principles of Literary Criticism* (New York, 1925), pp. 5-24.

19. Embler, p. 265; M. Beardsley, *Aesthetics: Problems in the Philosophy of Criticism* (New York, 1958), pp. 129-34.

20. Cf. M. H. Abrams, *The Mirror and the Lamp: Romantic Tradition* (New York, 1953), pp. 21-25; J. Thorp, "The Aesthetics of Textual Criticism," *PMLA,* LXXX (December 1965), 465-82; L. D. Reid, "Gladstone's Training as a Speaker," *Quarterly Journal of Speech,* XL (December 1954), 373-80; L. Crocker, "The Rhetorical Training of Henry Ward Beecher," *Quarterly Journal of Speech,* XIX (February 1933), 18-24.

21. Cf. H. D. Duncan, *Communication and Social Order* (New York, 1962), pp. 3-16; M. Maloney, "Clarence Darrow," in *A History of Criticism of American Public Address,* III, ed. M. K. Hochmuth, (New York, 1955), 262-312; H. M. Ruitenbeek, ed., *Psychoanalysis and Literature* (New York, 1964); N. Kiell, ed., *Psychological Studies of Famous Americans* (New York, 1964); W. S. Scott, *Five Approaches of Literary Criticism* (New York, 1962), pp. 69-73; R. L. Bushman, "On the Uses of Psychology: Conflict and Conciliation in Benjamin Franklin," *History and Theory,* V (No. 3, 1966), 225-40.

22. For example, V. L. Parrington, *Main Currents in American Thought* (New York, 1927), 3 vols.; R. T. Oliver, *History of Public Address in America* (Boston, 1965); M. Meyers, *The Jacksonian Persuasion* (New York, 1960); A. O. Lovejoy, *The Great Chain of Being* (Cambridge, Mass., 1936); D. M. Chalmers, *The Social and Political Ideas of the Muckrakers* (New York, 1964); G. Orwell, "Boys' Weeklies," in *A Collection of Essays by George Orwell* (Garden City, N.Y., 1954), pp. 284-313; Scott, pp. 123-26.

23. Cf. Heyl, p. 169; D. Katz, "The Functional Approach to the Study of Attitudes," *Public Opinion Quarterly,* XXIV (Summer 1960), 163-204; J. K. Galbraith, *Economics and the Art of Controversy* (New York, 1955), pp. 3-31; L. W. Lichty, "The Real McCoys and It's (*sic*) Audience: A Functional Analysis," *Journal of Broadcasting,* IX (Spring 1965), 157-65; B. DeMott, "The Anatomy of Playboy," *Commentary,* XXIV (August 1962), 111-19.

24. Abrams, pp. 16-21; W. N. Brigance, "What Is a Successful Speech?" *Quarterly Journal of Speech Education,* XI (April 1925), 272-77; Black, *Rhetorical Criticism,* pp. 36-58; Thonssen and Baird, pp. 448-61.

25. D. C. Bryant, "Rhetoric: Its Scope and Function," *Quarterly Journal of Speech,* XXXIX (December 1953), 401-24.

26. B. Harrison, "Some Uses of 'Good' in Criticism," *Mind,* LXIX (April 1960), 206; A. H. Hanney, "Symposium: Distinctive Features of Arguments Used in Criticism of the Arts," p. 169.

27. A. G. Van Melsen, *The Philosophy of Nature* (New York, 1953), p. 226; L. Brillouin, *Science and Information Theory* (New York, 1962), p. 232; F. C. Frick, "Some Perceptual Problems from the Point of View of Information Theory," *Psychology: A Study of a Science,* II (New York 1959), 77; J. Rothstein, "Information and Organization as the Language of the Operational Viewpoint," *Philosophy of Science,* XXIX (October 1962), 406-11; J. Ruesch, "The Observer and the Observed: Human Communication Theory," *Toward a United Theory of Human Behavior,* ed. R. R. Grinker (New York, 1956), pp. 36-54; M. Bunge, *Causality: The Place of the Causal Principles in Modern Science* (New York, 1963), pp. 348-49; P. Frank, *Philosophy of Science* (Englewood Cliffs, N.J., 1957), pp. 207-31; A. Moles, *Information Theory and Esthetic Perception* (London, 1958).

28. Cf. A. G. Pleydell-Pearce, "On the Limits and Use of 'Aesthetic Criteria,'" *Philosophical Quarterly,* IX (January 1959), 29-30.

29. Cf. E. Berne, *Transactional Analysis in Psychotherapy* (New York, 1961); Ch. Perelman and L. Olbrechts-Tyteca, "Act and Person in Argument," *Philosophy, Rhetoric and Argumentation,* eds. M. Natanson and H. W. Johnstone, Jr. (University Park, Pa., 1965), pp. 102-25.

30. Cf. R. Kuhns, "Criticism and the Problem of Intention," *Journal of Philosophy,* LVII (January 7, 1960), 5-23; S. Gendin, "The Artist's Intentions," *Journal of Aesthetics and Art Criticism,* XXIII (Winter 1964), 193-96; E. Roma III, "The Scope of the Intentional Fallacy," *Monist,* L (April 1966), 250-66.

31. M. O. Sillars, "Rhetoric as Act," *Quarterly Journal of Speech,* L (October 1964), 277-84; H. Arendt, *Between Past and Future* (Cleveland, 1963), pp. 143-72; S. K. Langer, *Problems of Art* (New York, 1957), pp. 1-58; S. C. Petter, *The Work of Art* (Bloomington, Ind., 1955); M. Natanson, "The Claims of Immediacy," in *Philosophy, Rhetoric and Argumentation,* eds. M. Natanson and H. W. Johnstone, Jr. (University Park, Pa., 1965), pp. 10-19; W. Sacksteder, "Elements of the Dramatic Model," *Diogenes,* LII (Winter 1965), 26-54; P. K. Tompkins, "Rhetorical Criticism: Wrong Medium?" *Central States Speech Journal,* XIII (Winter 1962), 90-95.

32. Paul Valery, *The Art of Poetry* (New York, 1958), p. 152.

33. The problem of a possible shift in meaning for morality plays is raised in F. J. Coleman, "A Phenomenology of Aesthetic Reasoning," *Journal of Aesthetics and Art Criticism,* XXV (Winter 1966), 197-203.

34. The distinction has been alluded to by R. L. Scott in his review of E. Black's "Rhetorical Criticism," *Quarterly Journal of Speech,* LI (October, 1965), p. 336. Scott suggests that one may go to extremes in appealing to the immediate audience as a decisive measure of rhetorical merit, that in such instances the critic may be more concerned with direct measures of audience response such as shift-of-option ballots than with the speech itself. An extremist M-E critic might indeed tend to fit such a description, but an M-E-C critic would be unlikely to find himself in such a posture.

35. E. H. Hutten, "Uncertainty and Information," *Scientia,* IC (No. 9-10, 1964), 199-206; J. J. Kupperman, "Reasons in Support of Evaluations of Works of Art," *Monist,* L (April 1966), 222-36; J. Rothstein, *Communication, Organization, and Science* (Indian Hills, Colo., 1958). The problem we face at this point in the discussion is that no clear instances of this critical stance are available as of this date.

36. Cf. R. P. Agnew, *Analytical Geometry and Calculus with Vectors* (New York, 1962), pp. 111-17.

37. Cited in M. K. Hochmuth, ed., *History and Criticism of American Public Address,* III (New York, 1955), 4.

38. Hanney, p. 170; Righter, pp. 64-69; Kupperman, pp. 229-33; Levy, p. 11.

39. M. Black, *Models and Metaphors* (Ithaca, N.Y., 1962), pp. 219-24.

40. L. Crowell, "The Speaking of John Pym, English Parliamentarian," *Speech Monographs,* XXXIII (June 1966), 100.

41. Levy, pp. 65-66.

42. In at least one instance the model-analog distinction breaks down and the modalities seem to fuse. That is where the critic relies on a touchstone as a standard of comparison. The touchstone, or "classic of its kind," at once represents an ideal and is at the same time an actual discourse which could conceivably be replaced in its role or prototype by some other discourse yet to be discovered. That the touchstone fulfills this dual role may explain its attraction for many critics as well as the rarity of its appearance as an effective critical tool. Cf. Wilson, pp. 272-76.

INTRODUCTION TO TWO CRITIQUES OF SPIRO AGNEW'S "ADDRESS CRITICIZING TELEVISION ON ITS COVERAGE OF THE NEWS"

At the beginning of the Presidential campaign of 1968, Spiro Agnew's name could hardly be termed "a household word." By May, 1970, he was perhaps the most sought after speaker in the country. According to the *Los Angeles Times* he averaged 50 requests a day to speak and he was the leading fund raiser for the Republican Party.[1] What has happened since Richard Nixon chose the former Maryland governor for his running mate is amply choronicled by the press, friendly and unfriendly. The news has been sprinkled with Agnewisms: "knee-jerk liberal," "nattering nabobs of negativism," "effete corps of impudent snobs," "radiclib," and the like. Some equally interesting polysyllabic creations peppered even his less-publicized efforts; e.g., "hapless hysterical hypochondriacs of history"[2] and "ennui of easy-chair existence."[3]

Mr. Agnew has taken on all comers—the members of Congress who suffer from "marble-hallitis,"[4] opposers to the Vietnam war ("the cacaphony of seditious drivel emanating from the best-publicized clowns in our society and their fans in the fourth estate"),[5] the "seaboard Media" and their "editorial doublethink,"[6] the United Nations (a "paper tiger"),[7] the Democrats (Hubert Humphrey's "lust for mediocrity"; Henry Jackson

"Meanys well"),[8] members of his own party (of Paul McCloskey: "Yesterday he sold his favorite painting—Benedict Arnold crossing the Delaware"),[9] and the American Medical Association (they use "apocalyptic rhetoric").[10]

Few major events took place without attracting Mr. Agnew's attention; for example:

> What happened at Attica proves once again that when the responsible voices of a society remain mute, the forces of violence and crime grow arrogant. One need only recall the era of Hitler's storm troopers to realize what can happen to the most civilized of societies when such a cloak of respectability is provided thugs and criminals.[11]

When events were less striking, the focus of his speeches was often more sweeping. In one speech the Vice-President targeted:

—the *Washington Post*
—the *New York Times* (particularly columnist Tom Wicker)
—Trotskyites
—Marxists
—"raving radicals" such as Senators Fulbright and Javits
—other unnamed congressional liberals who were likened to Neville Chamberlain.[12]

And in another speech about five months later, he targeted:

—Hubert Humphrey
—the Senate majority who rejected the SST
—unnamed revolutionary "social philosophers"
—the decline of "self-discipline" in high schools and colleges
—"give-away programs"
—the "liberal and radical left"
—the "insolence" of many sales clerks.

Mr. Agnew's rhetoric was not only used to "assail" but also to "endorse." On this occasion, Mr. Agnew spoke positively of:

—hard work
—aggressive competition
—sports
—vocational education
—the FBI and J. Edgar Hoover.[13]

From such rhetorical "jousts" the Vice-President emerged for some a White Knight[14] and for others an "intellectual sadist."[15] If the estimates were polar, they were representative of the polarizing effect much of Mr. Agnew's rhetoric seemed to have. But both friends and foes would likely agree with the *National Observer* when it noted: "The Vice-President has shown a mastery of invective that seems unmatched."[16]

The Agnew speech analyzed by two critics in this text elicited and continues to elicit considerable response both pro and con. In the four months immediately after the Des Moines speech criticizing TV's coverage of the news, Mr. Agnew reportedly received 149,000 letters and telegrams, only 10,000 of which disapproved of what he said.[17] "A sampling of radio and television stations throughout the country by the wire services showed that the callers supported Mr. Agnew by more than two to one."[18] *TV Guide* carried a variety of responses ranging from Eric Sevareid's "In Defense of TV News: An Interview"[19] to articles such as Edith Efron's "There *Is* a Network News Bias."[20] Magazines as diverse as *The American Legion Magazine*[21] and the *New Republic*[22] responded to the speech. Rhetorical critics came to write about it.[23]

Even if Mr. Agnew himself were not so controversial, prevailing attitudes toward TV and the other media make the subject discussed in this speech a crucial one to consider. Since 1959, TV has moved steadily ahead as the "people's choice" of media. Consider, for example, these questions and answers reported in a 1971 Roper Survey.[24]

1. "... where [do] you usually get most of your news about what's going on in the world today ... ?"

TV	60%
Newspapers	48%
Radio	23%
Magazines	5%
People	4%
TV only	31%
Newspapers only	21%
Both TV and newspapers	22%

2. "If you got conflicting or different reports of the same news story from radio, television, the magazines and the newspapers, which of the four versions would you be most inclined to believe ... ?"

TV	49%
Newspapers	20%
Radio	10%
Magazines	9%

Not only the potential power, but the concentration of power of the mass media is a subject for our concern. For example, in 1969, 75 million people watched the three network evening news shows. The Vice-President was not the only one to stir public attention. Federal Communications Commissioner, Nicholas Johnson, during 1969-1970, wrote widely of his concern over the potential power of media and of the ways viewers could mitigate some of it.[25]

Thus, whether one views Spiro Agnew as one who touches "the raw nerve of discontent and [articulates] the frustrations and fears ... of millions of Americans,"[26] as one who reflects the "politics of suburbia,"[27] or as one who has sunk lower than Joe McCarthy,[28] his speech criticizing TV coverage of the news is worth our attention both for what it does and for what it fails to do.

Notes

1. Jules Witcover, "Agnew: The Step-by-Step Creation of a Conservative," *Los Angeles Times* (May 10, 1970).

2. *Newsweek* (November 29, 1971), p. 27.

3. Address to the Middlesex Club, Boston (March 18, 1971). From a mimeographed copy supplied by the Vice President's office.

4. *Washington Post* (June 4, 1971).

5. *Washington Post* (May 14, 1972).

6. *Washington Post* (May 19, 1971).

7. *Boston Globe* (October 28, 1971).

8. *Los Angeles Times* (October 1, 1971); *Washington Post* (August 26, 1971).

9. *Newsweek* (November 29, 1971), p. 27.

10. *Washington Post* (November 29, 1971).

11. *Los Angeles Times* (September 17, 1971).

12. *Washington Post* (May 19, 1971).

13. *Washington Post* (October 1, 1971).

14. The title of a book by Jules Witcover is *White Knight: The Rise of Spiro Agnew* (New York: Random House, 1972).

15. In exceedingly strong language for the House floor, a member of Congress pinned this and other labels to the Vice-President. See the account in *Newsweek* (August 2, 1971), p. 16.

16. *National Observer* (July 12, 1971).

17. John Osborne, "Agnew's Effect," *New Republic* (February 28, 1970), p. 14.

18. Linda Charlton, "Agnew's Criticism of TV Is Backed by Most Callers," *New York Times* (November 16, 1969), p. 20.

19. *TV Guide* (March 14, 1970). See also Walter Cronkite, "What It's Like to Broadcast News," *Saturday Review* (December 1970), pp. 53-55.

20. *TV Guide* (February 28, 1970).

21. Robert B. Pitkin, "An Analysis of the News Media," *American Legion Magazine* (March 1970). Reprinted in Francis and Ludmila Voelker, eds. *Mass Media: Forces in Our Society* (New York: Harcourt, Brace, Jovanovich, 1972), pp. 282-84.

22. "Now Listen to This," *New Republic* (November 29, 1969), p. 9.

23. See, for example, L. Patrick Devlin, *Contemporary Political Discourse* (Belmont, Calif.: Wadsworth Publishing Company, 1971), pp. 47-52; Karlyn Kohrs Campbell, *Critiques of Contemporary Rhetoric* (Belmont, Calif.: Wadsworth Publishing Company, 1972), pp. 94-109.

24. From *An Extended View of Public Attitudes Toward Television and Other Mass Media 1959-1971.* Report by the Roper Organization, Inc.

25. For example, see "Now Listen to This," *New Republic* (November 29, 1969), p. 9; "Two Views on the Regulation of Television: We Need the Pastore Bill—No We Don't," *New Republic* (December 6, 1969), pp. 16-19; "What You Can Do to Improve TV," *Harper's* (February 1969), pp. 14ff.; "What Do We Do about Television?" *Saturday Review* (December 6, 1969), pp. 16-19; *How to Talk Back to Your Television Set* (Boston: Little, Brown and Company, 1970).

26. Haynes Johnson, "He Touches the Raw Nerve of Discontent," *Providence Sunday Journal* (April 5, 1970).

27. See Theodore Lippmann, *Spiro Agnew's America: The Vice President and the Politics of Suburbia* (New York: Norton and Company, 1972).

28. Gary Wills, in "Is Vice-President a New McCarthy?" *Washington Post* (June 28, 1971), wrote: "Joe McCarthy was no angel—but this has to be said of him: He was no Agnew either. He never sank that low."

Related Readings

Agnew, Spiro, T., "Another Challenge to the Television Industry," *TV Guide* (May 16, 1970), pp. 6-8, 10.

Alsop, Stewart, "The Secret of Spiro T.," *Newsweek* (September 28, 1970), p. 104.

"Analyses that Touched It All off (The)," *Broadcasting* (November 24, 1969), p. 50-52.

Buckley, William, "Agnew on TV," *National Review* (December 2, 1969), p. 1235.

Coyne, John R., Jr., *The Impudent Snobs: Agnew vs. the Intellectual Establishment* (New Rochelle, N.Y.: Arlington House, 1972).

Crawford, Kenneth, "Government and the Press," *Newsweek* (December 1, 1969), p. 33.

"Faces of Faceless Men (The)," *Newsweek* (November 24, 1969), p. 92.

Ferretti, Fred, "President of CBS Says Agnew Tries to Intimidate TV," *New York Times* (November 26, 1969), p. 1.

Friendly, Fred W., "Some Sober Second Thoughts on Vice President Agnew," *Saturday Review* (December 13, 1969), pp. 61-62ff.

Hennessy, Bernard, "Welcome, Spiro Agnew," *New Republic* (December 13, 1969), pp. 13-14.

Kenworthy, E. D., "Agnew Charges News Distortion in TV Networks," *New York Times* (November 14, 1969), p. 1.

Lucas, Jim G., *Agnew: Profile in Conflict* (New York: Charles Scribner's Sons, 1970).

McLaughlin, John, "Public Regulation and the News Media," *America* (December 13, 1969), p. 586.

Naughton, James M., "Agnew Between His Fiery Banquet Speeches Maintains a Low-Key Style," *New York Times* (June 22, 1970), p. 14.

"Response to Vice-President's Attack," *New York Times* (November 21, 1969), p. 22.

Reston, James, "Washington: Mr. Agnew and the Commentators," *New York Times* (November 21, 1969), p. 46.

Semple, Robert B., Jr., "Assent: Agnew Calls for Protest Against TV," *New York Times* (November 16, 1969), p. E1.

Shayon, Robert Lewis, "Those Substantial Licenses," *Saturday Review* (February 7, 1970), p. 39.

"Storm Over Agnew," *National Review* (December 16, 1969), p. 1220.

Tobin, Richard, "The Mirror of the News and Big Brother," *Saturday Review* (December 13, 1969), p. 59.

ADDRESS CRITICIZING TELEVISION ON ITS COVERAGE OF THE NEWS

SPIRO AGNEW

1   Tonight I want to discuss the importance of the television news medium to the American people. No nation depends more on the intelligent judgment of its citizens. No medium has a more profound influence over public opinion. Nowhere in our system are there fewer checks on vast power. So, nowhere should there be more conscientious responsibility exercised than by the news media. The question is are we demanding enough of our television news presentations? And are the men of this medium demanding enough of themselves?

2   Monday night a week ago, President Nixon delivered the most important address of his Administration, one of the most important of our decade. His subject was Vietnam. His hope was to rally the American people to see the conflict through to a lasting and just peace in the Pacific. For 32 minutes, he reasoned with a nation that has suffered almost a third of a million casualties in the longest war in its history.

3   When the President completed his address—an address, incidentally, that he spent weeks in the preparation of—his words and policies were subjected to instant analysis and querulous criticism. The audience of 70 million Americans gathered to hear the President of the United States was inherited by a small band of network commentators and self-appointed analysts, the majority of whom expressed in one way or another their hostility to what he had to say.

4   It was obvious that their minds were made up in advance. Those who recall the fumbling and groping that followed President Johnson's dramatic disclosure of his intention not to seek another term have seen these men in a genuine state of nonpreparedness. This was not it.

Speech text taken from *Congressional Record,* Vol. 115, Part 25, pp. 34257-59, with the acknowledgment of the Office of the Vice-President. Speech was given at Midwest Regional Republican Committee, Des Moines, Iowa, November 13, 1969.

5   One commentator twice contradicted the President's statement about the exchange of correspondence with Ho Chi Minh. Another challenged the President's abilities as a politician. A third asserted that the President was following a Pentagon line. Others, by the expression on their faces, the tone of their questions and the sarcasm of their responses made clear their sharp disapproval.

6   To guarantee in advance that the President's plea for national unity would be challenged, one network trotted out Averell Harriman for the occasion. Throughout the President's message, he waited in the wings. When the President concluded, Mr. Harriman recited perfectly. He attacked the Thieu Government as unrepresentative; he criticized the President's speech for various deficiencies; he twice issued a call to the Senate Foreign Relations Committee to debate Vietnam once again; he stated his belief that the Vietcong or North Vietnamese did not really want a military take-over of South Vietnam; and he told a little anecdote about a "very, very responsible" fellow he had met in the North Vietnamese delegation.

7   All in all, Mr. Harriman offered a broad range of gratuitous advice—challenging and contradicting the policies outlined by the President of the United States. Where the President had issued a call for unity, Mr. Harriman was encouraging the country not to listen to him.

8   A word about Mr. Harriman. For 10 months he was America's chief negotiator at the Paris peace talks—a period in which the United States swapped some of the greatest military concessions in the history of warfare for an enemy agreement on the shape of the bargaining table. Like Coleridge's Ancient Mariner, Mr. Harriman seems to be under some heavy compulsion to justify his failure to anyone who will listen. And the networks have shown themselves willing to give him all the air time he desires.

9   Now every American has a right to disagree with the President of the United States and to express publicly that disagreement. But the President of the United States has a right to communicate directly with the people who elected him, and the people of this country have the right to make up their own minds and form their own opinions about a Presidential address without having a President's words and thoughts characterized through the prejudices of hostile critics before they can even be digested.

10   When Winston Churchill rallied public opinion to stay the course against Hitler's Germany, he didn't have to contend with a gaggle of commentators raising doubts about whether he was reading public opinion right, or whether Britain had the stamina to see the year through. When President Kennedy rallied the nation in the Cuban missile crisis, his address to the people was not chewed over by a roundtable of critics who disparaged the course of action he'd asked America to follow.

11   The purpose of my remarks tonight is to focus your attention on this little group of men who not only enjoy a right of instant rebuttal to every Presidential address, but, more importantly, wield a free hand in selecting, presenting and interpreting the great issues in our nation.

12   First, let's define that power. At least 40 million Americans every night, it's estimated, watch the network news. Seven million of them view A.B.C., the remainder being divided between N.B.C. and C.B.S. According to Harris polls and other studies, for millions of Americans the networks are the sole source of national and world news. In Will Rogers's observation, what you knew was what you read in the newspaper. Today for growing millions of Americans, it's what they see and hear on their television sets.

13   Now how is this network news determined? A small group of men, numbering perhaps no more than a dozen anchormen, commentators and executive producers, settle upon the 20 minutes or so of film and commentary that's to reach the public. This selection is made from the 90 to 180 minutes that may be available. Their powers of choice are broad. They decide what 40 to 50 million Americans will learn of the day's events in the nation and in the world.

14   We cannot measure this power and influence by the traditional democratic standards, for these men can create national issues overnight. They can make or break by their coverage and commentary a moratorium on the war. They can elevate men from obscurity to national prominence within a week. They can reward some politicians with national exposure and ignore others.

15   For millions of Americans the network reporter who covers a continuing issue—like the ABM or civil rights—becomes, in effect, the presiding judge in a national trial by jury.

16   It must be recognized that the networks have made important contributions to the national knowledge—for news, documentaries and specials. They have often used their power constructively and creatively to awaken the public conscience to critical problems. The networks made hunger and black lung disease national issues overnight. The TV networks have done what no other medium could have done in terms of dramatizing the horrors of war. The networks have tackled our most difficult social problems with a directness and an immediacy that's the gift of their medium. They focus the nation's attention on its environmental abuses—on pollution in the Great Lakes and the threatened ecology of the Everglades.

17   But it was also the networks that elevated Stokely Carmichael and George Lincoln Rockwell from obscurity to national prominence.

18   Nor is their power confined to the substantive. A raised eyebrow, an inflection of the voice, a caustic remark dropped in the middle of a broadcast can raise doubt in a million minds about the veracity of a public official or the wisdom of a Government policy.

19   One Federal Communications Commissioner considers the power of the networks equal to that of local, state and federal governments all combined. Certainly it represents a concentration of power over American public opinion unknown in history.

20   Now what do Americans know of the men who wield this power? Of the men who produce and direct the network news, the nation knows practically nothing. Of the commentators, most Americans know little other than that they reflect an urbane and assured presence seemingly well-informed on every important matter.

21   We do know that to a man these commentators and producers live and work in the geographical and intellectual confines of Washington, D.C., of New York City, the latter of which James Reston terms the most unrepresentative community in the entire United States. Both communities bask in their own provincialism, their own parochialism. We can deduce that these men read the same newspapers. They draw their political and social views from the same sources. Worse, they talk constantly to one another, thereby providing artificial reinforcement to their shared viewpoints.

22   Do they allow their biases to influence the selection and presentation of the news? David Brinkley states objectivity is impossible to normal behavior. Rather, he says, we should strive for fairness.

23   Another anchorman on a network news show contends, and I quote: "You can't expunge all your private convictions just because you sit in a seat like this and a camera starts to stare at you. I think your program has to reflect what your basic feelings are. I'll plead guilty to that."

24   Less than a week before the 1968 election, this same commentator charged that President Nixon's campaign commitments were no more durable than campaign balloons. He claimed that, were it not for the fear of hostile reaction, Richard Nixon would be giving into, and I quote him exactly, "his natural instinct to smash the enemy with a club or go after him with a meat axe." Had this slander been made by one political candidate about another, it would have been dismissed by most commentators as a partisan attack. But this attack emanated from the privileged sanctuary of a network studio and therefore had the apparent dignity of an objective statement.

25   The American people would rightly not tolerate this concentration of power in Government. Is it not fair and relevant to question its concentration in the hands of a tiny, enclosed fraternity of privileged men elected by no one and enjoying a monopoly sanctioned and licensed by Government?

26   The views of the majority of this fraternity do not—and I repeat, not—represent the views of America. That is why such a great gulf existed between how the nation received the President's address and how the networks reviewed it. Not only did the country receive the President's address more warmly than the networks, but so also did the Congress of the United States. Yesterday, the President was notified that 300 individual Congressmen and 50 Senators of both parties had endorsed his efforts for peace.

27   As with other American institutions, perhaps it is time that the networks were made more responsive to the views of the nation and more responsible to the people they serve.

28   Now I want to make myself perfectly clear. I'm not asking for Government censorship or any other kind of censorship. I'm asking whether a form of censorship already exists when the news that 40 million Americans receive each night is determined by a handful of men responsible only to their corporate employers and is filtered through a handful of commentators who admit to their own set of biases.

29   The questions I'm raising here tonight should have been raised by others long ago. They should have been raised by those Americans who have traditionally considered the preservation of freedom of speech and freedom of the press their special provinces of responsibility. They should have been raised by those Americans who share the view of the late Justice Learned Hand that right conclusions are more likely to be gathered out of a multitude of tongues than through any kind of authoritative selection.

30   Advocates for the networks have claimed a First Amendment right to the same unlimited freedoms held by the great newspapers of America. But the situations are not identical. Where the *New York Times* reaches 800,000 people, N.B.C. reaches 20 times that number on its evening news. The average weekday circulation of the *Times* in October was 1,012,367; the average Sunday circulation was 1,523,558.

31   Nor can the tremendous impact of seeing television film and hearing commentary be compared with reading the printed page. A decade ago before the network news acquired such dominance over public opinion, Walter Lippmann spoke to the issue. He said there's an essential and radical difference between television and printing. The three or four competing television stations control virtually all that can be received over the air by ordinary television sets. But besides the mass circulation monthlies, out-of-town newspapers, and books. If a man doesn't like his newspaper, he can read another from out of town or wait for a weekly news magazine. It's not ideal, but it's infinitely better than the situation in television.

32   There if a man doesn't like what the networks are showing, all he can do is turn them off and listen to phonograph. Networks, he stated, which are few in number have a virtual monopoly of a whole media of communications. The newspapers of mass circulation have no monopoly on the medium of print.

33   Now a virtual monopoly of a whole medium of communication is not something that democratic people should blindly ignore. And we are not going to cut off our television sets and listen to the phonograph just because the airways belong to the networks. They don't. They belong to the people. As Justice Byron White wrote in his landmark opinion six months ago, it's the right of the viewers and listeners, not the right of the broadcasters, which is paramount.

34   Now it's argued that this power presents no danger in the hands of those who have used it responsibly. But, as to whether or not the networks have abused the power they enjoy, let's call as our first witness former Vice-President Humphrey and the city of Chicago. According to Theodore White, television's intercutting the film from the streets of Chicago with the current proceedings on the floor of the convention created the most striking and false political picture of 1968—the nomination of a man for the American Presidency by the brutality and violence of merciless police.

35   If we are to believe a recent report of the House of Representative Commerce Committee, then television's presentation of the violence in the streets worked an injustice on the reputation of the Chicago police. According to the committee findings, one network in particular presented, and I quote, "a one-sided picture which in large

measure exonerates the demonstrators and protestors. Film of provocations of police that was available never saw the light of day while the film of a police response which the protesters provoked was shown to millions."

36   Another network showed virtually the same scene of violence from three separate angles without making clear it was the same scene. And, while the full report is reticent in drawing conclusions it is not a document to inspire confidence in the fairness of the network news.

37   Our knowledge of the impact of network news on the national mind is far from complete, but some early returns are available. Again, we have enough information to raise serious questions about its effect on a democratic society. Several years ago Fred Friendly, one of the pioneers of network news, wrote that its missing ingredients were conviction, controversy and a point of view—the networks have compensated with a vengeance.

38   And in the networks' endless pursuit of controversy, we should ask: What is the end value—to enlighten or to profit? What is the end result—to inform or to confuse? How does the ongoing exploration for more action, more excitement, more drama serve our search for internal peace and stability?

39   Gresham's Law seems to be operating in the network news. Bad news drives out good news. The irrational is more controversial than the rational. Concurrence can no longer compete with dissent. One minute of Eldridge Cleaver is worth 10 minutes of Roy Wilkins. The labor crisis settled at the negotiating table is nothing compared to the confrontation that results in a strike—or better yet, violence along the picket lines.

40   Normality has become the nemesis of the network news. Now the upshot of all this controversy is that a narrow and distorted picture of America often emerges from the televised news. A single dramatic piece of the mosaic becomes in the minds of millions the entire picture. And the American who relies upon television for his news might conclude that the majority of Americans feel no regard for their country. That violence and lawlessness are the rule rather than the exception on the American campus.

41   We know that none of these conclusions is true. Perhaps the place to start looking for a credibility gap is not in the offices of the Government in Washington but in the studios of the networks in New York.

42   Television may have destroyed the old stereotypes but has it not created new ones in their places? What has this passionate pursuit of controversy done to the politics of progress through local compromise essential to the functioning of a democratic society?

43   The members of Congress or the Senate who follow their principles and philosophy quietly in a spirit of compromise are unknown to many Americans, while the loudest and most extreme dissenters on every issue are known to every man in the street. How many marches and demonstrations would we have if the marchers did not know that the ever-faithful TV cameras would be there to record their antics for the next news shows?

44   We've heard demands that Senators and Congressmen and judges make known all their financial connections so that the public will know who and what influences their decisions and their votes. Strong arguments can be made for that view. But when a single commentator or producer, night after night, determines for millions of people how much of each side of a great issue they are going to see and hear, should he not first disclose his personal views on the issue as well?

45   In this search for excitement and controversy, has more than equal time gone to the minority of Americans who specialize in attacking the United States—its institutions and its citizens?

46   Tonight I've raised questions. I've made no attempt to suggest the answers. The answers must come from the media men. They are challenged to turn their critical powers on themselves, to direct their energy, their talent and their conviction toward improving the quality and objectivity of news presentation. They are challenged to structure their own civic ethics to relate their great feeling with the great responsibilities they hold.

47   And the people of America are challenged, too, challenged to press for responsible news presentations. The people can let the networks know that they want their news straight and objective. The people can register their complaints on bias through mail to the networks and phone calls to local stations. This is one case where the people must defend themselves; where the citizen, not the Government, must be the reformer; where the consumer can be the most effective crusader.

48   By way of conclusion, let me say that every elected leader in the United States depends on these men of the media. Whether what I've said to you tonight will be heard and seen at all by the nation is not my decision, it's not your decision, it's their decision.

49   In tomorrow's edition of the *Des Moines Register,* you'll be able to read a news story detailing what I've said tonight. Editorial comment will be reserved for the editorial page where it belongs. Should not the same wall of separation exist between news and comment on the nation's networks?

50   Now, my friends, we'd never trust such power, as I've described, over public opinion in the hands of an elected Government. It's time we questioned it in the hands of a small and unelected elite. The great networks have dominated America's airwaves for decades. The people are entitled to a full accounting of their stewardship.

ADDRESS EXTENDING CRITICISM
OF THE NEWS COVERAGE TO THE PRESS

SPIRO T. AGNEW

1   Governor and Mrs. Brewer, Postmaster General and Mrs. Blount, Congressman Dickinson and the other distinguished members of the Alabama Legislature in the audience, officers, members of the board of directors and members of Alabama Chamber of Commerce and my Alabama friends all—I want to first express my very sincere appreciation to the people of Alabama for the very warm welcome which they have given to me and to my wife on our arrival here today.

2   And I particularly want to thank Governor Brewer for that very gracious and warm introduction. Governor Brewer and I never got to know each other as well as perhaps I would have liked because after he became Governor of this state, I didn't stay Governor much longer. But I want you to know one thing—that I did have a chance to serve with him and to be with him at a Southern Governors Conference, and I was tremendously impressed with the sincerity and the depth and the dedication of Governor Brewer, and I think the state of Alabama is very fortunate to have him.

3   As for the Postmaster General and his lovely wife, what can I say? He's taken us in Washington by storm, with his very perceptive feeling for people and his very warm concern about the problems of the country and, above all, his courage. Who else would dare to take on the monumental problems of reforming the postal division of the United States single-handed, other than Red Blount.

4   And to Red and Mary Kaye, also, a very, very warm thank you for opening your home to us and making us feel so welcome. I'm sorry we can't try that tennis court, but there just isn't time and the weather doesn't seem too conducive to that right now, anyhow.

5   I am really pleased that, included in the warmth of the welcome of the people of Alabama today was something that struck me as particularly significant and that was the fact that the young people at the airport were so enthusiastic. And it showed me beyond any doubt that young people, just as old people, refuse to be conformed and patterned into a specific mold and they have a right and a privilege and an obligation to think for themselves, and I'm glad to see how the young people of Alabama are thinking.

6   One week ago tonight I flew out to Des Moines, Iowa, and exercised my right to dissent. This is a great country—in this country every man is allowed freedom of speech, even the Vice President. Of course, there's been some criticism of what I said out there in Des Moines. Let me give you a sampling.

7   One Congressman charged me with, and I quote, "a creeping socialistic scheme against the free enterprise broadcast industry." Now this is the first time in my memory that anyone ever accused Ted Agnew of having socialist ideas.

From *Congressional Record,* Vol. 115, Part 26, pp. 35330-31. Speech given at the Chamber of Commerce, Montgomery, Alabama, November 20, 1969.

8   On Monday, largely because of that address, Mr. Humphrey charged the Nixon Administration with a "calculated attack" on the right of dissent and on the media today. Yet it's widely known that Mr. Humphrey himself believes deeply that the unfair coverage of the Democratic convention in Chicago, by the same media, contributed to his defeat in November. Now his wounds are apparently healed, and he's casting his lot with those who were questioning his own political courage a year ago. But let's leave Mr. Humphrey to his own conscience. America already has too many politicians who would rather switch than fight.

9   There were others that charged that my purpose in that Des Moines speech was to stifle dissent in this country. Nonsense. The expression of my views has produced enough rugged dissent in the last week to wear out a whole covey of commentators and columnists.

10   One critic charged that the speech was disgraceful, ignorant and base; that leads us as a nation, he said, into an ugly era of the most fearsome suppression and intimidation. One national commentator, whose name is known to everyone in this room, said: "I hesitate to get in the gutter with this guy." Another commentator charges that "it was one of the most sinister speeches that I've ever heard made by a public official."

11   The president of one network said that it was an unprecedented attempt to intimidate a news medium which depends for its existence upon government licenses. The president of another charged me with an appeal to prejudice, and said that it was evident that I would prefer the kind of television that would be subservient to whatever political group happened to be in authority at the time.

12   And they say I have a thin skin.

13   Here indeed are classic examples of overreaction. These attacks do not address themselves to the questions I raised. In fairness, others, the majority of the critics and commentators, did take up the main thrust of my address. And if the debate that they have engaged in continues, our goal will surely be reached, our goal which of course is a thorough self-examination by the networks of their own policies and perhaps prejudices. That was my objective then, and that's my objective now.

14   Now let me repeat to you the thrust of my remarks the other night and perhaps make some new points and raise a few new issues. I'm opposed to censorship of television, of the press in any form. I don't care whether censorship is imposed by government or whether it results from management in the choice and presentation of the news by a little fraternity having similar social and political views. I'm against, I repeat, I'm against media censorship in all forms.

15   But a broader spectrum of national opinion should be represented among the commentators in the network news. Men who can articulate other points of view should be brought forward and a high wall of separation should be raised between what is news and what is commentary. And the American people should be made aware of the trend toward the monopolization of the great public information vehicles and the concentration of more and more power in fewer and fewer hands.

16   Should a conglomerate be formed that tied together a shoe company with a shirt company, some voice will rise up righteously to say that this is a great danger to the economy and that the conglomerate ought to be broken up. But a single company, in the nation's capital, holds control of the largest newspaper in Washington, D.C., and one of the four major television stations, and an all-news radio station, and one of the three major national news magazines—all grinding out the same editorial line—and this is not a subject that you've seen debated on the editorial pages of the *Washington Post* or the *New York Times.*

17   For the purpose of clarity, before my thoughts are obliterated in the smoking typewriters of my friends in Washington and New York, let me emphasize that I'm not recommending the dismemberment of the Washington Post Company, I'm merely pointing out that the public should be aware that these four powerful voices hearken to the same master. I'm raising these questions so that the American people will become aware of—and think of the implications of—the growing monopoly that involves the voices of public opinion, on which we all depend for our knowledge and for the basis of our views.

18   When the *Washington Times-Herald* died in the nation's capital, that was a political tragedy; and when the *New York Journal-American,* the *New York World-Telegram* and *Sun,* the *New York Mirror* and the *New York Herald Tribune* all collapsed within this decade, that was a great, great political tragedy for the people of New York. The *New York Times* was a better newspaper when they were all alive than it is now that they are gone.

19   And what has happened in the City of New York has happened in other great cities of America. Many, many strong, independent voices have been stilled in this country in recent years. And lacking the vigor of competition, some of those who have survived have—let's face it—grown fat and irresponsible.

20   I offer an example: When 300 Congressmen and 59 Senators signed a letter endorsing the President's policy in Vietnam, it was news—and it was big news. Even the *Washington Post* and the *Baltimore Sun*—scarcely house organs for the Nixon Administration—placed it prominently in their front pages. Yet the next morning the *New York Times,* which considers itself America's paper of record, did not carry a word. Why? Why?

21   If a theology student in Iowa should get up at a PTA luncheon in Sioux City and attack the President's Vietnam policy, my guess is that you'd probably find it reported somewhere in the next morning's issue of the *New York Times.* But when 300 Congressmen endorse the President's Vietnam policy, the next morning it's apparently not considered news fit to print.

22   Just this Tuesday when the Pope, the spiritual leader of half a billion Roman Catholics, applauded the President's effort to end the war in Vietnam, and endorsed the way he was proceeding, that news was on page 11 of the *New York Times.* The same day a report about some burglars who broke into a souvenir shop at St. Peter's and stole $9,000 worth of stamps and currency—that story made page 3. How's that for news judgment?

23   A few weeks ago here in the South I expressed my views about street and campus demonstrations. Here's how the *New York Times* responded:

> He (that's me) lambasted the nation's youth in sweeping and ignorant generalizations, when it's clear to all perceptive observers that American youth today is far more imbued with idealism, a sense of service and a deep humanitarianism than any generation in recent history, including particularly Mr. Agnew's generation.

24   That's what the *New York Times* said. Now that seems a peculiar slur on a generation that brought America out of the great depression without resorting to the extremes of communism or fascism. That seems a strange thing to say about an entire generation that helped to provide greater material blessings and more personal freedom—out of that depression—for more people than any other nation in history. We have not finished the task by any means—but we are still on the job.

25   Just as millions of young Americans in this generation have shown valor and courage and heroism fighting the longest, and least popular, war in our history, so it was the young men of my generation who went ashore at Normandy under Eisenhower, and with MacArthur into the Philippines. Yes, my generation, like the current generation, made its own share of great mistakes and great blunders. Among other things, we put too much confidence in Stalin and not enough in Winston Churchill.

26   But, whatever freedom exists today in Western Europe and Japan exists because hundreds of thousands of young men of my generation are lying in graves in North Africa and France and Korea and a score of islands in the Western Pacific. This might not be considered enough of a sense of service or a deep humanitarianism for the perceptive critics who write editorials for the *New York Times,* but it's good enough for me. And I'm content to let history be the judge.

27   Now, let me talk briefly about the younger generation. I have not and I do not condemn this generation of young Americans. Like Edmund Burke, I wouldn't know how to draw up an indictment against a whole people. After all, they're our sons and daughters. They contain in their numbers many gifted, idealistic and courageous young men and women. But they also list in their numbers an arrogant few who march under the flags and portraits of dictators, who intimidate and harass university professors, who use gutter obscenities to shout down speakers with whom they disagree, who openly profess their belief in the efficacy of violence in a democratic society.

28   Oh, yes, the preceding generation had its own breed of losers and our generation dealt with them through our courts, our laws and our system. The challenge is now for the new generation to put its house in order.

29   Today, Dr. Sidney Hook writes of "storm troopers" on the campus; that "fanaticism seems to be in the saddle." Arnold Beichman writes of "young Jacobins" in our schools who "have cut down university administrators, forced curriculum changes, halted classes, closed campuses and sent a nationwide chill of fear all through the university establishment." Walter Laqueur writes in *Commentary* that "the cultural and political idiocies perpetuated with impunity in this permissive age have gone clearly beyond the borders of what is acceptable for any society, however liberally it may be constructed."

30   George Kennan has devoted a brief, cogent and alarming book to the inherent dangers of what's taking place in our society and in our universities. Irving Kristol writes that our "radical students find it possible to be genuinely heartsick at the injustice and brutalities of American society, at the same time they are blandly approving of injustice and brutality committed in the name of ' the revolution.' " Or, as they like to call it, "the movement."

31   Now those are not names drawn at random from the letterhead of the Agnew-for-Vice President committee. Those are men more eloquent and erudite than I, and they raise questions that I've tried to raise.

32   For we must remember that among this generation of Americans there are hundreds who have burned their draft cards and scores who have deserted to Canada and Sweden to sit out the war. To some Americans, a small minority, these are the true young men of conscience in the coming generation. Voices are and will continue to be raised in the Congress and beyond asking that amnesty—a favorite word—amnesty should be provided for these young and misguided American boys. And they will be coming home one day from Sweden and from Canada and from a small minority of our citizens they will get a hero's welcome.

33   They are not our heroes. Many of our heroes will not be coming home; some are coming back in hospital ships, without limbs or eyes, with scars they shall carry for the rest of their lives. Having witnessed firsthand the quiet courage of wives and parents receiving posthumously for their heroes Congressional Medals of Honor, how am I to react when people say, "Stop speaking out, Mr. Agnew, stop raising your voice"?

34   Should I remain silent while what these heroes have done is vilified by some as "a dirty, immoral war" and criticized by others as no more than a war brought on by the chauvinistic anti-communism of Presidents Kennedy, Johnson and Nixon? These young men made heavy sacrifices so that a developing people on the rim of Asia might have a chance for freedom that they obviously will not have if the ruthless men who rule in Hanoi should ever rule over Saigon. What's dirty or immoral about that?

35   One magazine this week said that I'll go down as the "great polarizer" in American politics. Yet, when that large group of young Americans marched up Pennsylvania Avenue and Constitution Avenue last week, they sought to polarize the American people against the President's policy in Vietnam. And that was their right. And so it is my right, and my duty, to stand up and speak out for the values in which I believe.

36   How can you ask the man in the street in this country to stand up for what he believes if his own elected leaders weasel and cringe? It's not an easy thing to wake up each morning to learn that some prominent man or some prominent institution has implied that you're a bigot or a racist or a fool. I'm not asking immunity from criticism. This is the lot of a man in politics; we wouldn't have it any other way in a democratic society.

37   But my political and journalistic adversaries sometimes seem to be asking something more—that I circumscribe my rhetorical freedom while they place no restriction on theirs. As President Kennedy observed in a far more serious situation: This is like offering an apple for an orchard.

38   We do not accept those terms for continuing the national dialogue. The day when the network commentators and even the gentlemen of the *New York Times* enjoyed a form of diplomatic immunity from comment and criticism of what they said is over. Yes, gentlemen, the day is passed.

39   Just as a politician's words—wise and foolish—are dutifully recorded by press and television to be thrown up at him at the appropriate time, so their words should be likewise recorded and likewise recalled. When they go beyond fair comment and criticism they will be called upon to defend their statements and their positions just as we must defend ours. And when their criticism becomes excessive or unjust, we shall invite them down from their ivory towers to enjoy the rough and tumble of public debate.

40   I don't seek to intimidate the press, or the networks or anyone else from speaking out. But the time for blind acceptance of their opinions is past. And the time for naïve belief in their neutrality is gone. As to the future, each of us could do worse than to take as his own the motto of William Lloyd Garrison who said, and I'm quoting: "I am in earnest. I will not equivocate. I will not excuse. I will not retreat a single inch. And I will be heard."

AN EXERCISE IN MANICHEAN RHETORIC

KARLYN KOHRS CAMPBELL

From a national nonentity when nominated, from the apparently insensitive bungler of the 1968 Presidential campaign, Spiro T. Agnew emerged as one of the most significant rhetorical forces and became perhaps the most formidable rhetorical weapon in the Administrative armory.[1] Agnew's fame as a speaker dated from an address he made in New Orleans on October 18, 1969, in which he characterized antiwar demonstrators as "an effete corps of impudent snobs," and increased with the "snobs and rotten apples" speech delivered at Harrisburg, Pennsylvania on October 30, 1969.[2] However, his national notoriety was, to a large extent, the product of live television coverage by all three networks of his address at Des Moines, Iowa, criticizing television news coverage. One week later at Montgomery, Alabama he amplified his criticism to include newspapers. On January 30, 1970 he said he was calling off his war on television broadcasters and then commented on how pleased he was to be in Baltimore when the *Sun* papers were on strike, even though the strike might cause a sanitation problem, because "you know how they get rid of the garbage—they print it."[3] Subsequent speeches,[4] letters to newspaper editors,[5] and a statement issued in response to press criticism[6] clearly indicated that

From *Critiques of Contemporary Rhetoric* by Karlyn Kohrs Campbell. Copyright © 1972 by Wadsworth Publishing Company, Inc. Reprinted by permission of Wadsworth Publishing Company, Inc. and the author.

Agnew was still deeply engaged in a struggle with the mass media over the quality and fairness of news coverage and the criticism of Administrative statements and policies.

This analysis focuses on the speeches at Des Moines and Montgomery and draws three conclusions: (1) Administrative actions directly contradict Agnew's apparent intention of questioning the concentration and monopolization of the power of the mass media over American public opinion; (2) the real intent of these speeches is to discredit and/or limit critical analysis and evaluation of Administrative statements and policies; and (3) the power of Agnew's rhetoric lies in his ability to conceal a partisan attack on persons who dissent from Administrative policy behind a superficial analysis of a real and serious problem and to hide the exploitation of the fears and resentments of his audiences behind techniques that appear to be objective, scholarly, and rational. Agnew's ultimate objective is to discredit critical analysis and the disparate opinions it may produce so that his audiences will come to believe that, at least as regards overt and public dissent, "no true intellectual, no truly knowledgeable person, would so despise democratic institutions."[7]

The concentration and power of the mass media is indeed a compelling and serious problem. One-quarter of all television stations are controlled by newspapers, and every commercial VHF television license in the top 10 United States markets is controlled by a network, a group owner, or a metropolitan newspaper chain. Over one-half of all television revenue regularly goes to the 15 network-owned stations in the top 25 television markets.[8] Moreover more Americans receive their public affairs information from television than from any other souce, and the 40 million nightly newswatchers *trust* television more than any other medium because they believe that its newsmen are impartial and nonpartisan and that the Federal Communications Commission effectively monitors television to keep its news treatment full, fair, and impartial. Agnew is accurate in saying that few men make the crucial decisions about television news coverage—probably somewhere between 75 and 100—and that these men of the networks plus another hundred or so wire service editors and officers[9] represent "a concentration of power over American public opinion unknown in history." However, the steadily increasing power of the media has been the subject of public criticism,[10] and Federal Communications Commissioner Nicholas Johnson in particular has been engaged in an extensive campaign to warn of the dangers and to inform citizens of the forms of recourse open to them.[11] Then why should a Republican Vice President select this issue and assume what appears to be an antiprivate power stance? At least in part the answer is that television networks and major newspapers are now clearly left of most political leaders in America.[12] The news media are in conflict with the Administration on many issues and constitute a powerful counterpersuasive force. In light of this rhetorical situation do Administrative statements and policies consistently reflect Agnew's purported concern for "the trend toward monopolization of the great public information vehicles and the concentration of more and more power over public opinion in fewer and fewer hands"? Strong evidence of inconsistency is provided by the Agnew's selection of certain media representatives as his targets and by the positions taken by the Administration on the Newspaper Preservation Act (S. 1520), the Pastore Bill (S. 2004), and the Federal Communications Commission *Policy Statement on Comparative Hearings Involving Regular Renewal Applications.*

At Montgomery, Agnew singled out the *Washington Post* for attack, a newspaper that exists in one of the three remaining large cities with more than one major newspaper under separate ownership.[13] He attacked the *Washington Post* ownership of WTOP-TV and radio but neglected to mention that there are four major television stations, three UHF stations, and 35 radio outlets in Washington, D.C.[14] He also failed to mention the obvious examples of news media concentration surrounding him as he spoke. The *Montgomery Advertiser* and the *Alabama Journal* are both owned by Multimedia, Inc. In Alabama, the Newhouse newspaper chain owns both dailies in Huntsville and Mobile, WAPI-TV, AM and FM radio stations in Birmingham, and CATV in Annison. Newhouse and another giant chain, Scripps-Howard, share ownership of the daily papers in Birmingham. In nearby areas Newhouse owns the dailies in New Orleans and Pascagoula, Missippi, and Scripps-Howard owns the papers and WMC-TV in Memphis.[15] Agnew also neglected to mention a major media conglomerate generally well disposed to the President's Vietnam policy.[16] Along with the Hearst Corporation these media conglomerates were active proponents of the Newspaper Preservation Act, a bill that repeals a Supreme Court decision and permits newspapers to violate certain antitrust laws, particularly profit pooling and price fixing. Ironically the *Washington Post* and the *New York Times,* the two newspapers Agnew singled out for criticism, are among the small number of newspapers that had the editorial courage to oppose this bill.[17] Agnew's failure to discuss this bill is itself somewhat unusual, considering his stated purpose. Even more unusual, however, is the history of Administrative behavior toward the bill. Initially the Justice Department testified against the bill before Congressional antitrust committees, and Richard McLaren, the Assistant Attorney General for Antitrust, stated that the bill would allow newspapers to share in the fruits of "an absolute monopoly." Subsequently, however, after Richard Berlin, president of the Hearst Corporation, made an apparently propitious visit to the White House, the Commerce Department unexpectedly endorsed the bill at a House antitrust committee hearing. Emanuel Cellar, chairman of the committee, said it was the first case in his 47 years in the House in which anyone except the Justice Department could speak for the White House on an antitrust bill. Later, aides to Nixon and Agnew, responding to questions about the bill, said that "the Administration supports it."[18] The President signed the bill into law on July 28, 1970.[19] Administrative action, in this case, seems directly contrary to Agnew's purported concern over newspaper monopolization.

A similarly contradictory situation existed in relation to the now-defunct Pastore bill, which would have protected and advanced concentration by making it virtually impossible for anyone to have a hearing to protest or compete with existing communications licensees at renewal time.[20] Robert Wells, the first broadcast station owner on the Federal Communications Commission since 1947, was on record as favoring the Pastore bill at the time of his appointment,[21] a fact indirectly indicating Administration support for the bill. This bill was allowed to die after it met with stiff and unexpected opposition from citizen groups.[22] However, the purpose of the bill has been realized in the *Policy Statement on Comparative Hearings Involving Regular Renewal Applications* of the Federal Communications Commission, which now includes the Nixon-appointed chairman, Dean Burch, and member, Robert Wells. The 1934 Communications Act provided for hearings in which incumbent and challenging applicants presented their conflicting claims; licenses were to be awarded to applicants who demonstrated their willingness to do the better job of programming, a procedure intended to promote competition and produce the best possible service. As a result of the *Policy Statement,* the question of better service can arise only at a second hearing held if and only if the incumbent has been unable to show that his programming has been "substantially attuned to meeting the needs and interest" of the area he serves.[23] Agnew remained silent on the Pastore bill and the FCC policy statement. Once again the Administration seems to be on the side of concentration rather than decentralization of the mass media. Clearly there appears to be a serious discrepancy between the stated intent of Agnew's speeches and Administrative policy.

What then is Agnew's real purpose? A good case can be made for the conclusion that Agnew's attacks on the media are patently partisan, designed to discredit hostile news sources and limit criticism of Administrative policy. At Des Moines, Agnew's major example in his attack on television news coverage was the medium's treatment of the President's Vietnam War speech of November 3, 1969. Agnew's attitude toward criticism is evident in his statement that the President "has a right to communicate directly with the people who elected him," and those people, in turn:

> . . . have the right to make up their own minds and form their own opinions about a Presidential address without having the President's words and thoughts character- ized through the prejudices of hostile critics before they can even be digested.

In short, Agnew implies that Presidential statements should be immune from prompt criticism before the immediate audience so that nothing will interfere with their persua- sive impact. To be precluded are the speculations, interpretations, and objections of commentators that slow the persuasive process and encourage considered judgments essential to policy making in a democratic society. Although he has rejected the idea of prompt criticism before the immediate audience, Agnew goes on to attack the quality of network commentary on four grounds: The analyses were "instant"; the criticisms were "querulous"; the commentators had made up their minds in advance; and the majority of commentators were hostile. Clearly the analyses were "instant" in the sense that they were made immediately after the speech. Frank Stanton, president of CBS, responded that commentators had had more than two hours advance notice on the speech itself and the advantage of weeks of informed speculation on the content of the speech.[24] How- ever, Agnew also argued the somewhat contradictory notion that their minds were made up in advance. This statement is true to the extent that they had advance notice of what was to be said or had speculated accurately about Presidential advocacy of the policy of Vietnamization. To demonstrate this point Agnew says:

> Those who recall the fumbling and groping that followed President Johnson's dramatic disclosure of his intention not to seek another term have seen these men in a genuine state of non-preparedness. This was not it.

If Stanton is correct, the commentators were and should have been prepared to analyze and evaluate the President's address. This was not the case with Johnson's speech, for the section in which Johnson said he would not run again was not released to the press prior to its delivery.[25] The two situations are significantly dissimilar.

Agnew supports his charges that the criticism was "querulous" and the critics hostile in his references to contradictions of "the President's statement about the exchange of correspondence with Ho Chi Minh" and to assertions "that the President was following a Pentagon line." He further maintains that facial expressions, gestures, and sarcasm by newsmen "made clear their sharp disapproval." He singles out Averell Harriman, former chief negotiator at Paris, as the paradigm of hostile network analysis. He says, sarcas- tically, that one network "trotted out" Harriman, who "waited in the wings" and then "recited perfectly." The "querulous" criticisms of Harriman were:

> He attacked the Thieu government as unrepresentative; . . . he twice issued a call to the Senate Foreign Relations Committee to debate Vietnam once again; he stated

his belief that the Vietcong or North Vietnamese did not really want a military take-over of South Vietnam; and he told a little anecdote about a "very, very responsible" fellow he had met in the North Vietnamese delegation.

True, these statements are in opposition to those of the President, but whether they are "nit-picking" is open to serious question. Harriman's chief sin is that of:

... challenging and contradicting the policies outlined by the President of the United States. Where the President had issued a call for unity, Mr. Harriman was encouraging the country not to listen to him.

If we accept Agnew's characterization,[26] Harriman is at fault simply because he is a critic—evaluating statements and policies in light of his experience, knowledge, and system of beliefs and then reaching a different conclusion from that of the President. The evil of his criticism is its call for dissent from the Presidential position and its lessening of the persuasive impact of the Presidential address. It is criticism as criticism, not the quality of the criticism, that is objectionable to Agnew.[27]

Agnew makes his final attack on network analysis: ". . . to a man these commentators and producers live and work in the geographical and intellectual confines of Washington, D.C., and New York City," communities that "bask in their own provincialism, their own parochialism." Consequently "the views of the majority of this fraternity do not—and I repeat, not—represent the views of America." Although many well-known newsmen come from small towns scattered throughout the United States,[28] whether the majority of newsmen accurately reflect the views of a majority of Americans is irrelevant. The important question is *what,* if anything, *should* the critic or commentator reflect? If Tom Wicker is right in his statement that "Agnew was really suggesting that television should serve Government's conception of the national interest and some consensus notion of 'the views of America,' "[29] there is a serious threat to free speech. Criticism and commentary are superfluous and indefensible if they mirror, simply and accurately, what is already known and believed. Critical statements that reflect and reinforce Administrative statements and policies will result in repression of the right to dissent, to question, and to evaluate—processes essential to any viable system of criticism. Finally, it should be noted that the Federal Communications Commission declared that the commentary following the President's speech was fair and impartial.[30]

The most significant issue is how effective Agnew's attacks on the media have been in limiting this form of criticism and commentary. Agnew boasted publicly that "somehow when I look around the tube from time to time, I feel that I've had a modicum of success here and there." Agnew has been said to feel, as do many others at the White House:

... that TV in particular treats him and the Administration generally with more care, that it carries more conservative and therefore friendly comment or non-comment on Administration pronouncements than it did before he opened up on it with his brutal reminders that it is a licensed business.[31]

Even commentators such as Eric Sevareid, who do not believe newsmen have consciously moderated their handling of Administrative and other news, concede that they are now forced to function in an atmosphere of public and official surveillance. Some affiliate stations have cancelled all post-Presidential address analyses, and a Washington, D.C., educational station cancelled a documentary critical of the Vietnam War.[32] Eric Sevareid has observed that perhaps discrediting the media could be one way for a government to protect itself from having its own credibility gap.[33] At several points Agnew seems to suggest that the problems of the Administration are caused by its critics: "Perhaps the place to start looking for a credibility gap is not in the offices of the government in Washington but in the studios of the networks in New York." Similarly he seems to place the blame for the problem of dissent on the media: "How many marches and demonstrations would we have if the marchers did not know that the ever-faithful TV cameras would be there to record their antics for the next news show?" The implication is that much dissent is exhibitionism rather than the outgrowth of legitimate grievances governments should confront and ameliorate.

Finally Presidential use of television subsequent to these speeches is notable. On February 1, 1970, Nixon made the unprecedented move of televising his veto of the educational appropriations bill, an act many commentators believe was the deciding factor in preventing a House override.[34] This veto message, despite its political implications, went undisputed because all three networks refused Democrats' requests for equal free time.[35] Nixon has used television more extensively than his predecessors. The political significance of unlimited access to the mass media and the power such access gives the Presidency have been the subject of hearings before the Senate communications subcommittee.[36]

Agnew's speeches have been eminently successful. They have effectively concealed a partisan attack upon the dissenting criticism of the "liberal" news media behind the real and serious problem of the increasing concentration and monopolization of news sources. The inconsistency between Agnew's statements and Administrative attitudes toward relevant legislation and FCC policy suggests that Agnew is primarily concerned with dissent by the news media and their criticism of Administrative statements and positions rather than with the power of the media. The danger is that:

> Mr. Agnew . . . seemed to be inviting not a thoughtful discussion of the very intricate problems of self-regulation but a partisan counterattack on broadcasters and the substitution of one small group of men whom the Vice President doesn't happen to like with another small group of men more hospitable to his own private vision of America.[37]

Regulation of the power of the media requires public discussion, but evidence indicates that Agnew has succeeded primarily in limiting the media in the amount and quality of criticism and analysis.

In response to considerable criticism of his speech making,[38] Agnew attempted to explain his theory of rhetoric and to justify his style and stratagems. Speaking before the International Association of Newspaper Publishers, he defined rhetoric as "the use of public discourse to persuade." He called for its "constructive use" to create "rational dissent" focused on an issue and open to debate, explaining that:

> . . . in the very act of encouraging peaceful argument, we automatically discourage violent protest. In agreeing to disagree, as reasonable people, we admit a unity of purpose.[39]

He has consistently called for presentation of "both sides" and defended his style by calling that of newsmen and extremist groups on the left "equally inflammatory."[40] Just prior to the speeches under consideration, Agnew justified his style, saying, "Outspokenness is the only way a Vice President can hope to get attention."[41] More recently, complaining that his bland speeches were poorly reported, he said:

So, in a desire to be heard, I have to throw them what people in American politics call a little red meat once in a while, and hope that in spite of the damaging context in which those remarks are often repeated, that other things that I think are very important will also appear.[42]

These bits of "red meat," "all packed into a trim two minutes that can be snipped out for TV, almost without having to review the tape,"[43] are an effective device for attracting media coverage. Despite this admittedly deliberate stratagem, Agnew has objected to criticism based on such excerpts, contending he had been "misrepresented and misunderstood."[44] Considering his strategy and the difficulty involved in obtaining complete texts, at least for the general public, this plea seems inappropriate. As other rhetorical critics have argued, political figures can and should be held responsible for the highly predictable excerpting of controversial statements by the mass media.[45]

Agnew makes a sharp distinction between the substance and the style of his speeches, attacking media criticism of his rhetoric on the grounds that it "dealt with how he was saying something instead of what he was saying. . . . Nowhere do they come to grips with the inherent veracity of what I've been saying."[46] Such a distinction is always dubious but particularly so in a case in which stylistic techniques are deliberately employed to attract popular attention. Consequently the final stage in this analysis examines Agnew's rhetorical stratagems to show that they are designed to *simulate* rational deliberation and preclude "the intelligent judgment of its citizens" on which he says this nation depends.

Agnew is, for the most part, the mouthpiece for an array of sophisticated ghost writers,[47] who consciously choose techniques used in his speeches. Gerald Johnson, former editorial writer for the *Baltimore Sun,* comments:

Persons who became familiar with the Vice President's syntax while he was a county executive, and then as the surprise Governor of Maryland, and who read his November 13 assault on the television news analysts, are convinced that Mr. Agnew has a new and better speech-writer. Never did such crisp and lucid English issue from the Towson courthouse or the Annapolis statehouse, during his tenure of those offices.[48]

However, there is little doubt that Agnew believes what he is saying. In reference to the Des Moines speech, Gerald Johnson wrote, "While the style of the speech was astonishingly improved, the content was entirely familiar. . . . His speeches may have been written by some other hand, but they express his sincere belief."[49]

The critical methodology of the following section is adapted from the noted Canadian literary critic, Northrop Frye, who makes a basic moral distinction between "genuine speech, . . . the expression of a genuine personality,"[50] and "bastard speech," the voice of what he calls the ego. He explains that:

. . . the ego has no interest in communication, but only in expression. . . . The ego is not the genuine individual, consequently it has nothing distinctive to express. It can express only the generic: food, sex, possessions, gossip, aggressiveness and resentments. Its natural affinity is for the ready-made phrase, the cliché, because it tends to address itself to the reflexes of its hearer, not to his intelligence or emotions.[51]

Frye describes the audience to which such speech is addressed and suggests an application of these concepts to political rhetoric:

> An aggregate of egos is a mob. A mob can only respond to reflex and cliché; it can only express itself, directly or through a spokesman, in reflex and cliché. A mob always implies some object of resentment, and political leaders who speak for the mob aspect of their society develop a special kind of tantrum style, a style constructed almost entirely out of unexamined clichés.[52]

Such characterization of Agnew's rhetoric may seem presumptuous to all but the most rabidly anti-Agnew primarily because he has refined this form of speech to conceal the nature of the rhetoric and maximize its effectiveness. His techniques include: (1) the use of Latinate and relatively esoteric language; (2) the use of literary or scholarly allusions; (3) the appearance of an attitude of fairness and objectivity; (4) the extensive use of specific examples and factual data in support of conclusions; and (5) the use of expert opinion, particularly from his opposition. These techniques suggest an argumentative rhetoric calling for rational deliberation, but they function instead to dignify and legitimize the invective of the speaker and the fears and resentments of his audience.

The terminology of Agnew's speeches is likely to challenge the well-educated individual, much less "the common man" he seems to be addressing. In his Des Moines speech, for example, he uses the words *querulous, gratuitous, disparaged, veracity, expunge,* and *nemesis.* At Montgomery he uses *efficacy, chauvinistic, vilified, erudite,* and *circumscribe.* Although these terms may not be so esoteric as to be unintelligible to the majority of Americans, many individuals would have difficulty defining them accurately. These terms serve two functions: They lend an aura of intellectualism to the speaker, and they serve to dignify the aggressive statements in which he uses them. Media criticism is not petty but *querulous;* Harriman's advice is not unrequested but *gratuitous;* newsmen do not belittle but *disparage,* and so on. In both speeches Agnew uses Latinate or esoteric terminology almost exclusively in extreme statements of praise or blame, whereas he uses simpler language in description or explanation. He makes a dignified appeal to the reflex and couches his invective in terminology that makes it appear less cliché, less directly angry and attacking. Yet despite their Latinate character these terms are clearly loaded and extreme.

Agnew uses allusions similarly. In the Des Moines speech he compares Averell Harriman to Coleridge's Ancient Mariner, as a man "under some heavy compulsion to justify his failure to anyone who will listen"; and without explaining the economic referent, he tells the audience that "Gresham's Law seems to be operating in the network news. Bad news drives out good news." At Montgomery, after citing an unfavorable *New York Times'* comment on his generation, Agnew says, "Like Edmund Burke, I wouldn't know how to draw up an indictment against a whole people." In each case he couches a personal or emotional attack in a form that gives it intellectual respectability.

Many statements in both speeches suggest his fairness and objectivity. In the Des Moines speech he gives credit to the media: "It must be recognized that the networks have made important contributions to the national knowledge." He asks, "Is it not fair and relevant to question . . . ?" as he does, and repeatedly states that he is "not asking for government censorship or any other kind of censorship. I'm asking whether a form of censorship already exists." His statement "Our knowledge of the impact of network news on the national mind is far from complete" and his insistence that he has only "raised questions" but made "no attempt to suggest the answers. The answers must come from the media men. . . . challenged to turn their critical powers on themselves" also imply objectivity. At Montgomery, after citing eight extreme examples of "critical overreaction" to his earlier speech, he says, "In fairness, others, the majority of critics and commentators, did take up the thrust of my address." He explains that his goal was only "a thorough self-examination by the networks of their own policies and perhaps prejudices." These and other statements create an aura of apparent impartiality. But the contradictions and omissions and the highly loaded language and examples with which he exploits the fears and resentments of his audience belie such objectivity. The network newsmen are a "small band of self-appointed analysts," a "gaggle" or "covey of commentators," "a tiny enclosed fraternity of privileged men," "a small and unelected elite" "responsible only to their corporate employers," who have "grown fat and irresponsible" and whom "the nation knows practically nothing." On an issue the newsman is "the presiding judge in a national trial by jury." The newsman's attacks have been protected because "they emanated from the privileged sanctuary of a network studio and therefore had the apparent dignity of an objective statement." These are the men who "elevated Stokely Carmichael and George Lincoln Rockwell from obscurity to national prominence," who say "one minute of Eldridge Cleaver is worth 10 minutes of Roy Wilkins" because they are engaged in an "endless" or "passionate pursuit of controversy." Such terms and illustrations are not designed to produce a fair or considered judgment. They are selected to induce an immediate, uncritical response.

Agnew's use of specific support materials creates the impression that he is knowledgeable about his subject. In his Des Moines speech he provides detailed instances of the criticism of Nixon's speech, data on the numbers of television viewers and polls indicating its impact. In his Montgomery speech he cites the *Washington Post* and delineates what it owns. He attacks the *New York Times* in terms of coverage of specific events. Agnew appears to have done thorough research and is prepared to present data to support his conclusions. Once again appearances are deceptive; the evidence he does *not* cite is significant. The evidence he does present is open to serious objection. He compares the situation of Nixon in relation to the Vietnam War with that of Winston Churchill during World War II and that of John Kennedy during the Cuban missile crisis to demonstrate that Nixon should be immune from dissenting criticism. He contrasts the critical preparedness of commentators on Nixon's speech with their shocked response to Johnson's announcement that he would not seek reelection in order to show that they had made up their minds in advance. Hypothetically, Agnew says, an attack on the President's Vietnam policy by a Sioux City, Iowa, theology student at a PTA meeting would have received *New York Times* coverage, whereas endorsement of that policy by 300 Congressmen did not.[53] These comparisons seems extremely dubious bases for the conclusions he draws. In addition he cites highly controversial statements of news commentators without any indication of the specific source; hence the typicality and significance of these statements are extremely difficult to judge in evaluating the quality of media commentary. Even a superficial examination indicates that the evidence provides a poor basis for the conclusions asserted.

Expert opinion, particularly from souces within the media, is employed in a similar fashion. In the Des Moines address Agnew cites James Reston on the unrepresentative character of New York City, David Brinkley on the impossibility of objectivity in normal behavior, and Walter Lippmann on the essential and radical differences between print and television. He claims that Supreme Court Justices argue for greater variety in points of view in news commentary and hold paramount the rights of viewers and listeners, not that of broadcasters. In his Montgomery address he cites statements by Sidney Hook, Arnold Beichman, Walter Laqueur, George Kennan, and Irving Kristol without providing any of their credentials. He merely adds: "Those are men more eloquent and erudite than I, and they raise questions that I've tried to raise." And, in a final and magnificent gesture, he has the temerity to conclude a speech in the deep South with a quotation from abolitionist William Lloyd Garrison: "I am in earnest. I will not equivocate. I will not excuse. I will not retreat a single inch. And I will be heard." In apparently the best traditions of argumentation Agnew has used expert opinion, even from opposing sources, to establish his case. However, the citation from Hook permits Agnew to call student demonstrators "storm troopers" among whom "fanaticism seems to be in the saddle"; the citation from Beichman permits him to call them "young Jacobins" who have "sent a nationwide chill of fear all through the university establishment." George Laqueur permits him to state that dissenters "have gone clearly beyond the borders of what is acceptable for any society," and Irving Kristol becomes the means for saying that "radical students . . . are blandly approving of injustice and brutality committed in the name of 'the revolution.' " These citations from experts do not provide insight into the problem of dissent but instead become the means to introduce highly loaded language, even invective, into the address under the guise of authoritative evidence. Agnew's arguments are clichés directed toward the reflexes, but the means are carefully designed to legitimize the fears and beliefs of the audience and dignify the most vicious attacks on the dissenters.

Agnew's numerous references to himself even more directly support the charge that this rhetoric is the voice of the ego. At the end of the Des Moines speech, despite the fact that it was being carried live on all three television networks, Agnew says: "Whether what I've said to you tonight will be heard and seen at all by the nation is not my decision; it's not your decision; it's their decision." In his Montgomery address he says that a week ago "I . . . exercised my right to dissent" and then cites eight negative reactions, each of which becomes the basis for self-defense or an attack on the critic. The comments Agnew selects make him appear as a fearless white knight fighting against overwhelming odds. He asks: "Should I remain silent while what these heroes have done is vilified by some as 'a dirty, immoral war'?" and:

> How can you ask the man in the street in this country to stand up for what he believes if his own elected leaders weasel and cringe? It's not an easy thing to wake up each morning to learn that some prominent man or some prominent institution has implied that you're a bigot or a racist or a fool.

The tone of these remarks fits Frye's notion of the voice of the ego as a monologue primarily concerned with self-expression and self-justification. The tone is petty, shrill, and defensive, and such rhetoric is at the farthest extreme from "genuine speech," which, wherever spoken, "creates a community."[54] "Positive" or not, the "polarization" is evident.[55]

The contradictions between these speeches and Administrative policy and the omission of relevant data and supporting materials substantiates the charge that this is "bastard speech." John McLaughlin, in summarizing Agnew's basic rhetorical choice, points out that the Vice President "failed to call for reform through legislative or judicial process. Instead he politicized the issues by focusing on those media personalities—individual and collective—who in his view have been failing to meet standards of fairness." Mr. McLaughlin continues by suggesting the sorts of reform Agnew might have advocated.[56] Instead of such advocacy, Agnew's attacks have been personal, political, and emotional, a rhetorical stance that seems to fulfill Northrop Frye's criteria.

Interestingly even sympathetic commentators have noted what Frye terms the "tantrum style" of such rhetoric. Brock Brower, for example, describes the typical

Agnew speech as a "good old-fashioned parental talking-to," with the crux of the speech contained in "the tongue-lashing" and characterized by "nil politics, total moralization, big words, high-thoughts and a rabbit-punch ending."[57] No one can doubt that Agnew is angry, even furious, over questions of dissent from and criticism of Administrative policies and statements or that he sees his war with the press as a personal vendetta.[58]

The power of Agnew's rhetoric lies in his ability to conceal his exploitation of the resentments, fears, and hostilities of his audience behind the facade of a serious and real problem—in this case the power of the mass media and the quality of media news coverage. His power also derives from his ability to dignify and legitimize the use of clichés, invective, and highly personal attacks with Latinate language, literary allusions, specific data, citations from experts, and an appearance of objectivity. The danger of such rhetoric in a democracy, which does in fact rely heavily "on the intelligent judgment of its citizens," should be stifling dissent and criticism. The threat posed is even clearer when these discourses are contrasted with "genuine speech." Unlike Agnew's rhetoric, genuine speech, "is the voice of the genuine individual reminding us of our genuine selves, and of our role as members of a society" and "is heard whenever a speaker is honestly struggling to express what his society, as a society, is trying to be and do."[59] Such rhetoric is unique, rather than cliché, giving the peculiar and private insight of an individual into the problems of our society. It calls on each person to transcend the known, the believed, and the familiar to find new ways of viewing and solving problems. Genuine rhetoric is inevitably the rhetoric of dissent and criticism, and Agnew's speeches are not merely "bastard speech" but are attempts to stifle "genuine speech." That intention is unmistakable in Agnew's own words:

> There are people in our society who should be separated and discarded. . . . Not in a callous way, but they should be separated as far as any idea that their opinion shall have any effect on the course we follow.[60]

Notes

1. As of January 1970, Agnew had received 149,000 letters and telegrams in less than four months, and all but 10,000 of them approved of him and of what he had been saying (John Osborne, "Agnew's Effect," *New Republic,* 162 [February 28, 1970], p. 14). A Gallup Poll of late May 1970 reported that 49 percent of those questioned had a favorable impression of Agnew (*Los Angeles Times,* 21 June 1970, p. E1). He is the most sought-after public speaker in the land, averaging 50 requests per day, and the Republican Party's leading fund raiser (Jules Witcover, "Agnew: The Step-by-Step Creation of a Conservative," *Los Angeles Times,* 10 May 1970, p. G1).

2. John Osborne, "Spiro Agnew's Mission," *New Republic,* 161 (November 15, 1969), pp. 17-18.

3. "Agnew Calls Off TV War, Attacks Press," *Los Angeles Times,* 31 January 1970, p. I3.

4. Press reports of his speeches at Atlanta (Kenneth Reich, "Won't Be Quiet Until Leftists Are—Agnew," *Los Angeles Times,* 22 February 1970, p. A16), at Houston (Nicholas C. Chriss, "Not Muzzled by Nixon, Agnew Says as He Raps Press Again," *Los Angeles Times,* 15 May 1970, p. 1), at Los Angeles (Carl Greenberg, "News Media Fail to Treat President Fairly, Agnew Says," *Los Angeles Times,* 9 June 1970, p. 122), at Washington, D.C. (Don Irwin, "Some Media Slanting Reports on War—Agnew," *Los Angeles Times,* 16 June 1970, p. I5), at Cleveland ("Agnew Assails Critics Who 'Couldn't End or Win' War," *Los Angeles Times,* 21 June 1970, p. 1), and at Denver ("Don't Hobble Nixon, Agnew Tells Critics," *Los Angeles Times,* 25 June 1970, p. I20) document his ongoing rhetorical war with the media and critics of the Administration.

5. Excerpts from his letters to the *Washington Post* and the *New York Times* may be found in "Agnew Hits 2 Papers for Speech Criticism," *Los Angeles Times,* 24 June 1970, p. I5.

6. "Agnew Strikes Back at Latest Criticism," *Los Angeles Times,* 5 July 1970, p. A9.

7. "Snobs and Rotten Apples," *New Republic,* 161 (November 15, 1969), p. 18.

8. John McLaughlin, "Public Regulation and the News Media," *America,* 121 (December 13, 1969), p. 586.

9. Bernard Hennessy, "Welcome, Spiro Agnew," *New Republic,* 161 (December 13, 1969), pp. 13-14.

10. See, for example, Robert Montgomery, *Open Letter from a Television Viewer* (New York: James H. Heineman, 1968).

11. See, for example, *How to Talk Back to Your Television Set* (Boston: Little, Brown and Company, 1970); "Now Listen to This," *New Republic,* 161 (November 29, 1969), p. 9; "Two Views on the Regulation of Television: We Need the Pastore Bill—No We Don't," *New Republic,* 161 (December 6, 1969), pp. 16-19; "What Do We Do about Television?" *Saturday Review,* 53 (July 11, 1970), pp. 14ff; "What You Can Do to Improve TV," *Harper's,* 238 (February 1969), pp. 14ff.

12. Tom Wicker, "Place Where All America Was Radicalized," *New York Times Magazine,* 24 August 1969, p. 95.

13. Morton Mintz, "Spiro Agnew's Candles," *New Republic,* 162 (January 17, 1970), p. 14.

14. "Response to Vice President's Attack," *New York Times,* 21 November 1969, p. 22.

15. Mintz, "Spiro Agnew's Candles," pp. 13-14.

16. "He neglected to mention, however, the New York News Co., with its interlocking ownership of WPIX-TV (New York), WGN-TV (Chicago), KDAL-TV (Duluth), KWGH-TV (Denver), WICC (Bridgeport, Conn.), and the *Chicago Tribune*—media that have been generally well disposed to the President's Viet Nam policy." (McLaughlin, "Public Regulations and the News Media," p. 587.)

17. Mintz, "Spiro Agnew's Candles," p. 14.

18. Ibid.

19. *Los Angeles Times,* 29 July 1970, p. 2.

20. "Pastore's Pet," *New Republic,* 161 (October 25, 1969), pp. 10-11.

21. "Dubious Appointments," *Nation,* 209 (October 6, 1969), p. 333.

22. Robert Lewis Shayon, "Those Substantial Licenses," *Saturday Review,* 53 (February 7, 1970), p. 39.

23. Ibid., p. 38. The United States Court of Appeals has declared this policy to be "contrary to law." See "Court Rules FCC License Policy Illegal," *Los Angeles Times,* 13 June 1971, p. A3.

24. Fred Ferretti, "President of C.B.S. Says Agnew Tries to Intimidate TV," *New York Times,* 26 November 1969, p. 1.

25. "Lyndon Johnson's renunciation of a second term as President dumbfounded all but a score of relatives and top aides. . . . It was not included in the advance text." *Time,* 91 (April 12, 1969), p. 22.

26. Rather a different picture is given from reading some of Harriman's statements. See E. W. Kenworthy, "Agnew Charges News Distortion in TV Networks," *New York Times,* 14 November 1969, p. 1.

27. Despite what Agnew characterized as hostile and inappropriate criticism, a Gallup Poll reported that 77 percent of those interviewed who had heard the President's speech supported the policies that he advocated, *Los Angeles Times,* 5 November 1969, p. I25.

28. James Reston, "Are You an Agnewistic?" *New York Times,* 23 November 1969, p. E12.

29. "Dr. Agnew's Patent Medicine," *New York Times,* 16 November 1969, p. E13. See also Fred W. Friendly, "Some Sober Second Thoughts on Vice President Agnew," *Saturday Review,* 52 (December 13, 1969), pp. 61ff.

30. The FCC made this declaration after its chairman, Dean Burch, called upon network news presidents for transcripts, an act more threatening than it appears, as the White House already had complete tape recordings of every word spoken on each network about the President's address collected by the Army Signal Corps detail assigned to the White House Communications Branch. CBS news reported that members of the Presidential staff made at least 20 calls to television stations on the night of November 3 to check on editorial comment ["Now Listen to This," *New Republic,* 161 (November 29, 1969), p. 9].

31. John Osborne, "Agnew's Effect," *New Republic,* 162 (February 28, 1970), p. 14.

32. Ibid., pp. 14-15.

33. Ibid., p. 15.

34. Rowland Evans and Robert Novak, "How TV Aided the Veto," *Los Angeles Times,* 2 February 1970, p. I19.

35. "Veto Answer Time Denied by Networks," *Los Angeles Times,* 31 January 1970, p. I3.

36. "Presidential Access to TV" *Los Angeles Times,* 5 August 1970, p. 15.

37. Robert B. Semple, Jr., "Assent: Agnew Calls for Protest Against TV," *New York Times,* 16 November 1969, p. E1.

38. See, for example, Jules Witcover, "Hickel, Mentioning Agnew, Hits Administration Policy on Youth," *Los Angeles Times,* 7 May 1970, p. 1; Kenneth Reich, "Agnew Plays It Cool in Georgia Dedication," *Los Angeles Times,* 10 May 1970, p. A14; "Finch Says Agnew Fed Unrest; Later Denies Quotation," *Los Angeles Times,* 10 May 1970, p. 1; Don Irwin, "New Disputes Flares Over Agnew Speeches," *Los Angeles Times,* 15 May 1970, p. I5; "Muskie Raps Agnew on Approach to Youth," *Los Angeles Times,* 25 May 1970, p. I7; "Agnew Talks Blamed in Student Alienation," *Los Angeles Times,* 24 June 1970, p. I16; "Agnew Words Wound Nation," *Los Angeles Times,* 24 June 1970, p. I16; "Agnew Elicits Radical Acts, Fulbright Says," *Los Angeles Times,* 6 July 1970, p. I22; John A. Averill, "Harriman Links Agnew Attacks to Nazi Tactics," *Los Angeles Times,* 9 July 1970, p. I4.

39. Irwin, "Some Media Slanting . . ."

40. Reich, "Won't Be Quiet . . .": Chriss, "Not Muzzled by Nixon . . ."

41. "Agnew Finds a Role," *Newsweek,* 73 (November 17, 1969), p. 40

42. John Osborne, "Agnew and the Red Meat," *New Republic,* 163 (July 25, 1970), p. 12.

43. Brock Brower, "Don't Get Agnew Wrong," *Life,* 68 (May 8, 1970), p. 66B.

44. Osborne, "Agnew and the Red Meat," p. 11.

45. Robert L. Scott and Wayne Brockriede, *The Rhetoric of Black Power* (New York: Harper & Row, 1969), pp. 78-81.

46. "Agnew Gives Defense of His Style," *Los Angeles Times,* 1 July 1970, p. I6.

47. "The Vice President's speeches, when they do not spring from his own pen (he wrote the New Orleans speech himself), are largely the work of a petite, auburn-haired former public-relations woman named Cynthia Rosenwald . . ." ("Agnew Finds a Role," p. 41), "Nixon's speech writers prize and acknowledge their assignments to draft Agnew speeches. Patrick Buchanan deplores reports that he has written some of the more abrasive ones, not because the reports are false, but because Agnew resents any indication that he is a mouthpiece for others and the stories might impair a working relationship that Buchanan and his colleagues have come to value" (Osborne, "Agnew's Effect," p. 13). In addition to his New Orleans speech, the speeches Agnew has authored, at least for the most part, include those delivered at Harrisburg, Pennsylvania; Atlanta, Georgia; and Minneapolis, Minnesota, although "Agnew admits to outside drafts on such important positional diatribes as that boomed at the TV networks last November 13" (Bower, "Don't Get Agnew Wrong," p. 66B).

48. Gerald W. Johnson, "The Old Agnew We Knew," *New Republic,* 161 (November 29, 1969), p. 13.

49. Ibid.

50. Northrop Frye, *The Well-Tempered Critic* (Bloomington: Indiana University Press, 1963), p. 41.

51. Ibid., pp. 41-42.

52. Ibid., p. 43.

53. "Mr. Agnew is again mistaken when he says that *The Times* did not 'carry a word' on the story about the Congressmen and Senators signing a letter endorsing the President's policy in Vietnam. *The New York Times* printed the story. Unfortunately, it failed to make the edition that reached Washington but was carried in a later edition of *The Times.* Moreoever, *The Times* has given considerable attention to that story as it developed. . . . In the paper of November 13, there was the story to which the Vice President referred. In the paper of November 14, President Nixon's visit to the House and Senate to convey his appreciation to those who supported his Vietnam policy was the lead story. That story again reported the fact that more than 300 Congressmen and 59 Senators had signed the resolution" ("Response to Vice President's Attack: Mr. Sulzberger's Reply").

54. Frye, 41. See also Richard B. Gregg, "The Ego-Function of the Rhetoric of Protest," *Philosophy and Rhetoric,* 4 (Spring 1971), pp. 71-91.

55. "Snobs and Rotten Apples," p. 18.

56. McLaughlin, "Public Regulation and the News Media," pp. 587-88.

57. Brower, "Don't Get Agnew Wrong," p. 66B.

58. Agnew is still deeply resentful of press treatment of him during the 1968 campaign and during his terms as governor of Maryland (Ibid., pp. 66, 72).

59. Frye, pp. 44-45.

60. Osborne, "Agnew and the Red Meat," p. 12.

AGNEW PACKAGES A MEDIA HAPPENING FOR MIDDLE AMERICA: "A HOT SUBJECT IN A COLD FRAME"[1]

HERMANN G. STELZNER

Avant-garde artists and playwrights created the first happenings and though the genre is ill-defined, most of the events termed "happenings" are a mix of the following characteristics: (1) The event is brief and is marked by chance, spontaneity, and surprise; further it lacks structure, having no clearly defined beginning, middle, and end. Although the maker of a happening may organize and even rehearse sections of the event, generally he is guided by "root directions" and his primary concern is to keep the whole "shaking right."[2] (2) The event occurs in a place or context in which the maker and the participants are commingled; the latter are often acted upon physically. (3) The event emphasizes spectacle and sound, often to the disregard of the word. (4) The event takes place and disappears; impermanence characterizes it; thus the meaning of the event is in the present tense. (5) Though the "best" of happenings "have a decided impact . . . one feels 'here is something important,' they appear to go nowhere and do not make any particular literary point."[3]

Susan Sontag explains that avant-garde happenings are a contemporary way of "destroying conventional meanings, and creating . . . new meanings through radical juxtaposition."[4] She concludes that art that places radical juxtaposition at its center "is obviously animated by aggression, aggression toward the presumed conventionality of its audience and, above all, aggression toward the medium itself."[5]

Because avant-garde happenings usually take place in the larger cities of this country, New York, Chicago, Los Angeles, and San Francisco, relatively few citizens have actually participated in them. But the difficult to define term has become a contemporary idiom, referring to the presence of some of the characteristics of avant-garde happenings, though the degree and the intensity of the mix may vary markedly. More importantly, the contemporary idiom refers to the spirit and flavor of an event that is a reflection of the participants' attitudes, pointing ultimately to a collective state of mind.[6]

Calling Agnew's address in Des Moines a "Media Happening for Middle America" is not to argue for a point-by-point correspondence between it and an avant-garde event. It is to apply a sociocultural term, a contemporary idiom, to a nationally televised event that features a maker, a presentation, and an audience. The term is potentially heuristic because it provides a general perspective and basic characteristics. However, it must be kept in mind that Agnew's happening for Middle America develops from its juxtaposition to television, the "newest" of the mass media. Agnew carefully chooses examples and illustrations having a radical flair from television presentations, thus portraying both the medium and its men as avant-garde. For example, he concludes that the views of news broadcasters are quite unconventional: "The views of this fraternity do not—and I repeat, not—represent the views of America."[7] The juxtaposition of minority versus majority views foreshadows a more serious problem, the radical juxtaposition of minority versus majority cultural values that has lead to the weakening and even loss of the conventional: "Television may have destroyed the old stereotypes, but has it not created new ones in

This piece was originally prepared for this volume. © 1972 by Hermann G. Stelzner. For permission to reprint contact the author, University of Massachusetts, Amherst 01002.

their places?" Agnew's judgment about the materials and the effects of the medium closely parallels Sontag's observation about the ultimate function of all avant-garde happenings.

The first half of the title of this essay both frames the event and posits a perspective on it. The second half, "A Hot Subject in a Cold Frame," centers on Agnew's matter and manner. The matter or "what" of Agnew's happening is the television medium which is a controversial, i.e., hot, subject. Although Agnew attacks the medium severely, he, unlike the avant-garde and the medium, is not bent upon destruction. Much of his sharp criticism he advances and justifies in the name of restoration, a term not only central to his argument but central to the manner of his happening as well. The "Cold Frame" refers to Agnew's manner or "how"; that is, to rhetorical choices and arrangements that make matter both significant and negotiable. The interaction of matter and manner, the hot and the cold, keeps Agnew's rhetorical happening "shaking right" in the situation.

On November 13, 1969 Spiro T. Agnew arrived in Des Moines, Iowa, to address the Midwest Regional Republican Committee. That Des Moines, Iowa, is radically different from Washington, D.C., and New York City (the latter described by James Reston, a *New York Times* commentator, as the "most unrepresentative community in the United States") is self-evident. That an audience of dedicated Republicans would gather to honor and to attend to a fellow Republican is equally self-evident. But this particular speaker is more than a Republican. He is the Vice President . . . and more. His advance notices suggest that he will speak about matters that concern this audience in a manner the listeners are likely to appreciate. The primary relationship between speaker and listeners is a political one, but it transcends that, bordering on the spiritual as well.

Yet Agnew, Vice President, Republican, politician, begins and ends his presentation in a low key, seeking to function in a decidedly nonpolitical manner: "Tonight I want to discuss the importance of the television news medium to the American people." And "Tonight I've raised questions. I've made no attempt to suggest answers." The constant and consistent effort to divorce himself from his professional status leaves Agnew reporting a role rather than being one.[8] But the discrepancy between the numerous statements of neutrality and objectivity and the ordering of other statements in the rhetorical design results in a radical juxtaposition between the role professed and the role implemented, or in rhetorical terms between regard for the word and disregard for it.

However, the decision to report a role rather than be one is perfectly consistent with the subject of the address, the medium of television. History records that the relationship between men of government and men of the mass media is sensitive and fragile. A public clash between them is likely to polarize not only the participants but the citizenry as well. "I'm not asking for Government censorship or any other kind of censorship. I'm asking whether a form of censorship *already* (italics added) exists. . . ." Reporting what began in the historical past and thus standing above or outside the immediate present is one way of removing himself from the discussion, despite the recency of many of his examples and the fact that his major illustration, the medium's treatment of an address by President Nixon about Vietnam, occurred only "Monday night a week ago." Thus the current examples only bring the historical issue up to date. But within that context Agnew also applies the term "censorship" to practices of private organizations which is to reverse the usual social and political meaning of the term. In a variety of ways Agnew places the hot, controversial subject of the medium within a cold frame: a form that detaches and provokes reflection, a juxtaposition of matter and manner. Constantly counterbalancing emotional materials with those that promote distance and impartiality, he imposes a certain discipline on himself and his audience, thereby postponing easy gratification. To the extent that Agnew's overall, rhetorical design invites reflection, even if of a low order, his appeals to feelings are through the route of the intelligence. The listener, constantly made aware of the cold frame and its stress upon detachment, cannot but help have his retarded intellectual and emotional responses strengthened and intensified.

Despite his intense analysis and severe criticism of the medium, Agnew remains personally aloof. He offers no meaningful program, nor is he willing to lead.[9] He leaves the medium to look into itself—"The answers must come from the media men"—and citizens to look after themselves—"The people are challenged to press for responsible news presentations." So sensitive is he to the charge of bias that Agnew carefully avoids inviting citizens to lodge their complaints with the government, excluding even the Federal Communications Commission, the agency directly responsible to the people for the performance of the medium. Of course, Agnew's suggestions are consistent with both the meanings of the traditional maxims of a democracy and the contemporary idiom, "participatory democracy."

Many institutions in this country, including television, should be improved. The proposition is not often seriously questioned. But if the shortcomings of the medium are as serious as Agnew maintained, one approach to the problem would have been to call for an inquiry either by an agency of the government or by some private citizen's group. But such a call would have weakened Agnew's stance, that of reporting a role. He would have had to be what he is, Vice President, Republican, and politician.[10] A quite different speech would have been necessary, but it would have been impossible to avoid tarnishing another traditional maxim, that of the separation of the press and the state. Committed by his role not to involve himself and/or his Administration directly with reform, Agnew is left with a "case where the people must defend themselves; where the citizen, not the Government, must be the reformer; where the consumer can be the most effective crusader," and the choice of "crusader" suggests Agnew's awareness of the odds against the achievement of meaningful reform by unaided people who are perhaps not as aware of the broader implications of the suggestion.

Although Agnew obviously has the attention of large numbers of concerned conservative listeners—the address was televised to the nation—it is not fantasy to argue that if the situation were serious large numbers of equally concerned liberal citizens might welcome a call for responsible inquiry and ultimately perhaps even action. Agnew says that his discussion is important "to the American people." The radical juxtaposition of Agnew's description and analysis of severe shortcomings in the medium contrasts sharply with his "it's out of my hands" solution. It is a sign that Agnew's involvement with the medium is a matter of style and not one of commitment. The juxtaposition constitutes an assault upon the listeners who are asked to expend time and energy on a matter that they cannot by themselves solve, and ironically the juxtaposition is also an assault upon the government itself; its representative believes that a serious problem affects all citizens, but neither the representative nor the government will openly commit its resources to the resolution of the problem.

Lacking a concrete and meaningful program for the improvement of the medium (roughly equivalent to being without a literary point), Agnew can only offer a simple and impractical suggestion. Concerned but unorganized citizens, a kind of verbally disciplined but structurally dissipated crowd, should operate outside the system and do their own thing—"register their complaints . . . through mail . . . and phone calls . . ." to the networks and the local stations.

Now it is Agnew who uses the medium as a vehicle much like those agitators who performed actions and enunciated values contrary to those welcomed by a majority of citizens. In Agnew's view it was the medium that was partially responsible for creating troublesome surpises for both the citizens and the government. He now prepares troublesome surprises for the medium which he supports with quick, crisp, and intense emotionally-laden examples that are spaced out in his development, thus performing a repetitive and reinforcing function: ". . . The networks . . . elevated Stokely Carmichael and George Lincoln Rockwell from obscurity to national prominence." "How many marches and demonstrations would we have if the marchers did not know that the ever-faithful cameras would be there to record their antics. . . ." ". . . Has more than equal time gone to the minority of Americans who specialize in attacking the United States—its institutions and its citizens?" The medium creates "heroes," and Agnew, too, uses it to fashion instant celebrities, now.

Of course, Agnew's unorganized and unstructured people happening cannot be televised. So the mail and the telephone, alternative media also subject to varying degrees of governmental supervision, are utilized. The irony is self-evident, but its mocking tone is not. Thus despite his announcements that he will not do to the medium as the medium has done to the President (for example, compare paragraphs 1, 2, and 29 with 3, 4, 5, and 6), Agnew invites the people to do to the medium what the medium has done to both the government and to them—create immediate, if temporary, trouble which obviously must be confronted and dealt with at some cost.[11] Had Agnew called for a reasoned programmatic approach to the medium, it would undoubtedly have taken time and weakened seriously the stress on the present tense—the *now*—so central to the entire address and especially to the horns of the dilemma, a variant radical juxtaposition, which Agnew creates for the medium. If enough people respond and there is a reciprocal and positive response by the medium, then the issue might, but only might, be considered closed. If enough people respond, but the medium does not, then the government at least has a legitimate collective concern as the basis for involvement. If too few people respond, thus leaving the medium free not to respond, the threat of government involvement nonetheless remains.[12] Juxtaposing Agnew's veiled threat, camouflaged by the connotations of a people's crusade to his calls for more objectivity and openness in the medium, also results in a shift in his posture—from that of reporting a role to that of being a role.

Thus far this discussion has offered only a general sketch of the interaction between matter and manner and it remains now to consider how additional dimensions of the interaction develop and give thrust to Agnew's presentation. The first clues to meaning and tone usually arise from a detection of principal contrasts, and Agnew's early statements are harbingers of his purpose and attitudes.

Agnew's first paragraph illustrates well how the tone of objective, analytical inquiry is established and furthered. The first sentence is declarative and the "I want to discuss" phrase indicates both his purpose and his approach. A position is taken and fixed. Two interrogative sentences conclude the paragraph. Unlike declarative sentences that anchor positions, questions open them. Thus Agnew's first sentence and final two questions function together to establish a manner that is altogether consistent with the enormity and significance of their matter, given an additional importance by the second question which mounts above the first.

Between these sentences Agnew offers four judgments that many listeners would not contest; the judgments function as facts. But Agnew's judgments could have been stated affirmatively. For example: This nation, more than any other, depends on the intelligent judgment of its citizens. This medium has the most profound influence over public opinion. Instead Agnew affirms by negation: "No nation," "No medium," "Nowhere," "So, nowhere." The emphasis on the repetitive noes foreshadows and even directs the answer that Agnew expects to the questions the listeners have not yet heard. In short, there is a radical juxtaposition between the professed intention of the syntax and diction of the first and final two sentences and the negative emphasis of the no, no, no, no, chantlike cheer.

The cheer is supported by additional constituents of the design. The four "no" statements are declarative, categorical, and parallel. Although they do not make a formal syllogism, heard cumulatively they suggest the appearance of one, and the "so" in the final statement strengthens and rounds out the appearance. "Syllogisms" having negative "premises" yield negative conclusions. Thus the "formal pattern" of the four "no" statements demands a negative answer to the other formal patterns, the interrogative questions, that supposedly are to open the discussion.

The negative thrust of the introductory remarks interacting with the positive political attitudes of the immediate listeners makes it literally impossible to sustain objectivity about Agnew's first example, the President's speech about the war in Vietnam, the divisive social and political issue of the moment. The example is important and Agnew devotes much time to it. But he also reveals much about his ultimate purpose by his placement of it in the development. He centers on the medium's immediate, negative reaction to the President's speech, his sign that "minds were made up in advance." The polarization of the country on the Vietnam issue is not only important in itself; it is coupled to the response of the medium to the President's address. Together they become the primary justification for the enlargement of the discussion to "men who ... more importantly, wield a free hand in selecting, presenting and interpreting the great issues in our nation."

To the partisan audience, Agnew's discussion of the circumstances surrounding the President's speech would not be beyond belief. But the extension and expansion of them to the great issues of the society is a transformation of the size and the magnitude of Agnew's matter and had Agnew proceeded directly to develop his enlarged observation he would have risked overdrawing it. A listener might suspect that he was manipulating his data for purely political ends; further, a listener might feel that he had heard too much. To avoid overdrawing his enlarged observation, Agnew momentarily steps away from it, an act of diminution, to generally describe the power and influence of the networks (paragraphs 12-15) and to acknowledge the positive contributions of the networks (paragraph 16). The resulting reduction of scope and tone provides proportion to the discussion, keeping it within the realm of belief.

Agnew's placement, a dimension of manner, of his acknowledgment, his matter, is an indication of its significance. Often a speaker who intends to explore a controversial social problem begins his discussion by acknowledging the positive contributions of the parties involved, suggesting thereby his good will, his awareness, and his concern. Not Agnew. Not until his discussion of the medium's treatment of the President is concluded does he acknowledge that "the networks have made important contributions to the national knowledge." The placement diminishes the significance of the contributions. But given the negative focus of Agnew's introductory remarks, paragraph 16 cannot follow paragraph 1. The two clash; the movement is disrupted; and more important, the listeners' immediate expectations are detoured, not fulfilled.

Agnew aims to deflate network contributions. His acknowledgment is not personal; the passive voice introduces it. Not "I recognize," or even "We recognize," but "It must be recognized that. . . ." Obviously Agnew is aware that the average listener knows that the networks had highlighted "national issues" and "difficult social problems." But one of the special strengths of television is that it features people doing something; action is central to its presentations. Agnew's many observations and his own appearance on national television indicate that he understands this well. Yet his laudatory remarks carefully enumerate issues and specify networks, substituting the former for specific television programs and the latter for the individual men who used "their power constructively and creatively" to "awaken the public conscience." Neither specific programs nor individual men are applauded; issues efface the former and the latter remain faceless behind the networks. Agnew's recognition of television's accomplishments does, of course, provide a measure of objectivity to his discussion. But the very distant and impersonal acknowledgment that is a movement away from the medium constitutes at the same time a movement toward his own interpretation.

When he is critical, Agnew specifies. To summarize his less than emphatic acknowledgment of network contributions, he offers a single honed negative: "But it was also the networks that elevated Stokely Carmichael and George Lincoln Rockwell from obscurity to national prominence." Personalities, not issues, anchor the political spectrum and energize the observation. The response to Averell Harriman is specific and less than gracious. Although individual network commentators who disagreed with the President are unnamed, enough detail is offered so that listeners could attach it to a personality and please themselves by their recognition of the specific. Here, as elsewhere, Agnew warns the people about *distinctive* personalities.

It is significant that Agnew's critical remarks often parallel one another. Obviously such remarks cannot be clustered in a given place in the development, but need to be spaced out to achieve a repetition or doubling. Thus a disciplined tension controls the criticisms, and the similarities of their forms aids in the anticipation and recognition of them.

It has already been observed that although Agnew recognizes "important" network "contributions" (paragraph 16), he immediately counters the acknowledgment with a single honed negative (paragraph 17). Similarly in paragraph 44 Agnew recognizes that "strong arguments" can be made for public disclosure by civil servants of "all their financial connection . . . ," and it would be equally helpful if the "personal views" of network commentators were disclosed. Why? The question is answered by another (paragraph 45): ". . . Has more than equal time gone to the minority of Americans who specialize in attacking the United States—its institutions and its citizens?" The positive-negative relationship of paragraphs 16 and 17 is repeated in paragraphs 44, the positive, and 45, the negative, except that 45 is a question, whereas 17 is declarative. Yet paragraph 17 prepares the listener for paragraph 45. It suggests to him how he should respond to the open, interrogative form that demands to be filled in. Paragraph 45 could have been cast into a declarative form. But such a form would not have allowed the listeners to participate as fully in the happening.

The spaced out repetition of parallel forms is apparent elsewhere. The problems that Agnew discusses obviously exist in time and if they are to be dealt with someone must begin at some point or place. Often considerations of time and place are discussed together. Agnew believes that his analysis supports action *now* (paragraph 27): "As with other American institutions, perhaps it is time that the networks were made more

responsive to the views of the nation and more responsible to the people they serve."
Following some further discussion of social responsibility, he concludes (paragraph 41):
"Perhaps the place to start looking for a credibility gap is not in the offices of the
Government in Washington but in the studios of the networks in New York." Both
illustrations are introduced with "perhaps," the adverb expressing the cold, unemotional
caution of the intellectual. The similarity of the forms is again helpful to the recognition
of the thoughts, but the distance between time and place spaces out the listeners' emotional development as well. These sentences might have been joined in Agnew's development. Little harm would have been done to their meaning, but the listeners' emotional
responses would have been intensified in one place:

> As with other American institutions, perhaps it is time that the networks were
> made more responsive to the views of the nation and more responsible to the
> people they serve. Perhaps the place to start looking for a credibility gap is not in
> the offices of the Government in Washington but in the studios of the networks in
> New York.

Parallel interrogatives, concentrated within space, pattern the topical analysis of the
networks (paragraphs 13-23). "Now how is this network news determined?" No
persons are mentioned, but "a small group of men" exercises power. "Now what do
Americans know of the men who wield this power?" James Reston's observation illumi-
nates dimensions of their geographic proximity and by extension their social and political
cohesiveness. "Do they allow their biases to influence the selection and presentation of
the news?" David Brinkley is the named observer. The question centers on attitudes, and
given the similarities of function and location expressed within the parallel forms, the
similarity of attitudes follows. Although the formal interrogatives suggest the opening of
the discussion, the parallel forms demand that the answer to question three follow the
form, and thus the substance, of the first two questions. A listener would have to be
unusually tough-minded to resist closing question three contrary to the expectations of
the matter and the manner of questions one and two.
    If the few examples above illustrate both Agnew's efforts to direct and listeners' abil-
ities to receive, it does not mean that his "formless observations" are without merit in
keeping the situation "shaking right." When he is less directive he weakens his commitment even as he enlists listeners in the working out of ideas. Their experiences commingle
with Agnew's statements, moving in and around them. For example, his very general "do
your own thing" proposal for reform, a leaderless people's crusade, is ultimately absolutely formless. Unless the people are led and become cohesive, the suggestion cannot be
fashioned into a movement; impermanence will characterize whatever results from
Agnew's suggestion. But he is not concerned with such details. Of course, the idea has
strength because of the connotations that result from its juxtaposition to the closed and
controlled medium that is, Agnew suggests, accountable to no one. His idea is impractical,
but has emotional impact. It involves, rather than rejects, people: it is nonpolitical, rather
than political; it is open, not closed; it suggests action, not inaction. However Agnew does
not hazard even a guess about its effectiveness, unless, of course, all righteous crusades are
ultimately effective. Still many may get some satisfaction from the proposed "trip" to
restore values cloaked in the name of legitimate social action.
    Agnew's discussion of the medium's treatment of the President's address (paragraphs
1-10) is quite specific. Although he stresses his objectivity, he clearly has a vested interest
in the matter. Anticipating the charge of bias, he attempts to weaken it. He did not invent

the issue. It "should have been raised by others long ago," an observation that fore-shadows an approach to the subject from yet another angle, that of history.

The discussion of history (paragraphs 29-39) is limited to the recent past to preserve the tone of immediacy, the *now*. Because Justice Learned Hand and the First Amendment introduce the discussion, a listener might expect to hear a legal interpretation or a historical overview. Neither emerges. Furthermore, there are no clear indications to the listener of what to expect. In swift order Walter Lippmann says there is an "essential and radical difference between television and printing," Justice Byron White writes a "land-mark opinion" that judges listener and viewer rights to be "paramount." Vice President Hubert Humphrey is called "as our first witness," but the journalist, Theodore White, witnesses. A "recent report" of the Commerce Committee of the House of Representatives is referred to. Fred Friendly, "one of the pioneers of network news," has the last word, though no listener could have determined that Agnew was about to conclude his history.

The disjointed and fragmented review of a variety of materials adds up only if the listener makes it, although he is offered by direction by Gresham's Law, given meaning by the juxtaposition of Eldridge Cleaver and Roy Wilkins. At this point Agnew's description resembles a collage with a montage-like movement. A listener cannot be informed in any meaningful way by the scurrying prose of this loosely arranged collection of eclectic materials. He is made aware of breadth and scope, but if it is to have meaning, he must provide it. And he is probably not unduly bothered by the disjointed review of recent history. After all, it has much in common with the loose topical form of a television news broadcast or variety and talk shows. Or indeed, a happening!

Contributing to Agnew's media happening for middle America is language woven throughout the address to buttress his matter and manner. His descriptive and evaluative terms generally have a quality and tone that contrasts markedly with the direct, gutterlike Anglo-Saxon expressions that many listeners associated with avant-garde radicals. On the level of simple description and explanation he uses terms that are familiar and acceptable to those with his point of view: "trotted out," "recited perfectly," "privileged sanc-tuary," "artificial reinforcement," "enclosed fraternity." On the level of personal attack, he uses terms that are less familiar: "gratuitous," "disparaged," "veracity," "expunge," "mosaic," "nemesis." The latter choices especially further support the cold frame of the entire address, elevating and intellectualizing Agnew's discussion of the hot, controversial subject.

Part of Agnew's appeal to audiences is explained by his ability to choose and order language. Prior to his appearance in Des Moines, he had achieved a minor reputation as a maker of phrases. One of his writers has suggested that his phrases were "slightly tongue-in-cheek. You can't use 'nattering nabobs of negativism' with enormous seriousness." The "exaggerated hyperbole or alliteration" was intended "to be humorous."[13]

In the Des Moines speech there is no singularly striking phrase like "nattering nabobs of negativism." But there are lines that sustain Agnew's reputation for phrase-making, and his reputation creates a degree of suspense. Listener expectations need to be satisfied.

The on-the-lookout listener probably expects such lines to appear late; they often function as climaxes. Four of the more exaggerated lines fit the pattern and their close proximity tends to cluster them. Three of the four are quite similar: (1) "Normality has become the nemesis of the network news." (2) "A single dramatic piece of the mosaic becomes in the minds of millions the entire picture." (3) "And the American who relies upon television for his news might conclude that the majority of Americans feel no regard for their country."

This cluster of alliterations has a function in the overall design beyond merely satisfying listeners' expectations. In these statements, nasal continuants dominate. They are relatively continuous and unchanging, stable and ongoing; they hum. They are Agnew's surrogates in sound for the normality the networks find a nemesis. The sustained, low-volume, soft and muted background sound is in direct juxtaposition to Agnew's thought —that the networks present the exception, violence and lawlessness, as the rule.

The fourth line, stronger than the first three, thereby structuring a climax to the alliterative cluster, is embedded in a different context. Within the formal frame of an interrogative that seemingly opens the discussion, Agnew wonders if the established procedures of politics, "through local compromise," have not been weakened: "What has this passionate pursuit of controversy done to the politics of progress through local compromise essential to the functioning of a democratic society?" Plosives, not continuants, are now alliterated. Agnew's repetitive "p's" dance, pop, and gyrate round in his question much like radicals through a police picket line. The plosives, surrogates in sound for radical action, are juxtaposed to the traditional idea of local compromise and literally and figuratively overwhelm it. But unlike the actions they mimic, Agnew's plosives are happily not explosive.

The alliterative cluster, a contrived sound set, moves from muted nasal continuants to expressive plosives and foreshadows Agnew's conclusion which is structured to parallel the cluster's development: "The members of Congress or the Senate who follow their principles and philosophy quietly in a spirit of compromise are unknown to many Americans, while the loudest and most extreme dissenters on every issue are known to every man in the street." And for the first time in the entire address Agnew brings together within a single declarative sentence two antithetical groups, representative of so many references in his text, but juxtaposing them so that radical dissent, supported by the medium, dominates and overpowers. And the alliteration contributes significantly to the development of the juxtaposition.

Although this analysis has centered on relationships between matter and manner within the text, Agnew's "happening" is further supported by some events surrounding his appearance in Des Moines. The Midwest Regional Conference, scheduled to begin on Friday, November 14, 1969, had not invited Agnew to address it. His Thursday evening, November 13, 1969, appearance "was scheduled as a special item" at a "hastily scheduled opening session," set in motion on Tuesday, November 11, 1969, when "vice presidential aides wangled the invitation." They " 'caught us entirely by surprise,' " admitted the conference chairman, who was obviously pleased by the prospect of Agnew's visit. "Great," he said.[14]

Because Agnew was scheduled as a "special," it is unlikely that the participants in the conference knew in advance the subject of his address. Agnew flew from Washington to Iowa on Thursday and about the time his plane landed in Des Moines, his Washington office released copies of his text. The networks were alerted to a Hobson's choice. If they televised, they became the vehicle for criticism of themselves. If they did not, they handed to Agnew a potentially potent up-to-the-minute *now* illustration that could easily have been woven into his prepared text. Apparently the networks were surprised by Agnew's subject, but his staff knew that he had long considered addressing himself to the mass media. Some had cautioned him against it, arguing "that the press is a big establishment, it's a no-win issue."[15] But the medium's response to President Nixon's November 3, 1969 speech and its preparations for the scheduled mid-November anti-Vietnam war demonstration in Washington, apparently convinced Agnew that the time was appropriate. Having made the decision to prepare an address, an appropriate place had to be found for its delivery.

If the immediate audience was pleased by Agnew's surprise appearance, the presence of unexpected television equipment and personnel must have provoked suspense. And the national audience, too, must have been mildly curious about shifts in programming. Ordinarily a Vice President does not merit thirty minutes of time on national television. Pointedly, but light-heartedly, Agnew refers in his introduction to the planned improvisation: "I think it's obvious from the cameras here that I didn't come to discuss the ban on cyclamates or DDT."[16] And at the end of his address he remarks: "Whether what I've said to you tonight will be heard and seen at all by the nation is not my decision; it's not your decision; it's their decision." Agnew says nothing about his actions to insure both his presence and that of the medium. It all just happened.

Within a week of his appearance in Des Moines, Agnew spoke in Montgomery, Alabama, shifting his focus to the press, but maintaining the relationships between matter and manner of the Des Moines speech. Agnew's conflict with the mass media waxed and waned over time, but by the summer of 1972 the public controversy between him and the media seemingly ceased. At least he told a convention of newspaper editors on July 22, 1972 that "bygone conflicts between state and press" were resolved.[17]

Agnew's address in Des Moines, a "happening" on the medium about the medium, achieved its goal, the arousal of public opinion. But the public, aroused in the name of social stability, was used for political ends. A "happening" is an intense and often emotional experience. Yet the complicated problem of the proper relationship between the men of government and the men of the medium, both ultimately committed to serve the entire citizenry, cannot be unraveled in the context of partisan "happenings." The problem demands and deserves a context of less heat and more light, the antithesis of a "happening" stressing juxtapositions, and thus requires relationships between matter and manner that are quite different from those found in Agnew's address.

Notes

1. Susan Sontag, *Against Interpretation* (New York, 1966), p. 180. Sontag's phrase describes relationships between "the material and the form" in drama and film, but it is an apt description for discursive prose as well.

2. Allan Kaprow, " 'Happenings' in the New York Scene," *Art News* (May 1961), p. 59. The five characteristics are drawn from Kaprow's essay, pp. 36-62.

3. Ibid., p. 39.

4. Sontag, p. 269.

5. Ibid.

6. *The Reader's Guide to Periodical Literature* indexes "Happenings," subdivided into "art" and "theater." In the *New York Times Index* they appear under "Multimedia." The term appears frequently in a variety of contexts, suggesting some or all of the five characteristics above. For example, Wayne C. Booth writes that "a rhetoric of the new communions" is needed. "Such a work would attempt a sympathetic treatment of what is happening in an age of 'happenings' that 'blow your mind,' of transformations through drugs or other routes to mystical vision, of total political transformations that claim to slough off, like old and ugly skin, the old life and bring in a new millenium of peace and light." Wayne C. Booth, "The Scope of Rhetoric Today: A Polemical Excursion," in Lloyd F. Bitzer and Edwin Black, eds., *The Prospect of Rhetoric* (New York, 1971), p. 104. Kingman Brewster, Jr., President of Yale, writes in "The Decade of Short Cuts": "Another campus characteristic running from the mid-sixties into the turn of the decade was the glorification of the 'happening.' " *New York Times,* October 5, 1972, p. 47. Gerald R. Miller writes of a national conference on speech communication: "The proceedings . . . summarize a scholarly happening that sought to

impose greater coordination and sharper focus, and as such, no matter how imperfect, they warrant examination by students of human communication." Gerald R. Miller, "Readings in Communication Theory: Suggestions and an Occasional Caveat," *Today's Speech,* 19 (Winter 1971), 10. The term obviously appears in advertisements. For example, the Campus Crusade for Christ ran an ad for a television show entitled "EXPLO 72." The ad's headline announced "An Historic Happening . . . 100,000 Young People Can Change the World." *New York Times,* August 4, 1972, p. 62. The first line of an ad for the 1972 "U.S. Open Tennis Championships" in Forest Hills, N.Y. read "It's an Every Day Happening." *New York Times,* August 27, 1972, Sec. 5, p. 3. The first line of an ad for a Kentucky Bluegrass read, "Before Adelphi, successful lawn grasses just 'happened.' " *New York Times,* August 27, 1972, Sec. 2, p. 28.

7. The text of Agnew's address used in this analysis appears in Karlyn Kohrs Campbell, *Critiques of Contemporary Rhetoric* (Belmont, Calif., 1972), pp. 79-87. The paragraphs in the text are numbered, and my references to numbered paragraphs are to those in Campbell. Agnew's address also appears here on pp. 253-259.

8. Sontag, p. 184, discusses the notion in film and theater, but it is applicable to a rhetorical situation as well.

9. Arthur Schlesinger, Jr., "The Amazing Success Story of 'Spiro Who?' " *New York Times Magazine,* July 26, 1970, p. 5, writes: "It is cultural politics, and not public policy, which is the Vice President's bag. He has emerged as hero or villain, not in the battle of programs but in the battle of life styles." A happening is an event that is consistent with a battle of life styles.

10. On April 13, 1970 Agnew returned to Des Moines to address a Republican Statewide Fund-Raising Dinner and referred to his address about the medium. His neutrality and objectivity were discarded as he referred to that presentation in militaristic images: "Five months to the day have passed since I visited Des Moines to present a few thoughts about the network news. It is a pleasure to be back—I enjoy visiting famous battlefields, especially when the outcome of the conflict was decisive and served a useful purpose." *Collected Speeches of Spiro Agnew* (New York, 1971), p. 116.

11. "Before the Vice President was off the air, the network switchboards began to light up. When all the phone calls, telegrams, and letters were in and counted (over 150,000 for the three networks), the tally was two to one in favor of Agnew. . . . Stations across the country got the same instantaneous reaction with calls backed up far into the night." Marvin Barrett, ed., *Survey of Broadcast Journalism 1969-1970* (New York, 1970), p. 32.

12. Eric Sevareid, news analyst for CBS in Washington, in "Candor Toward the Press" puts a slightly different emphasis on Agnew's speech tying it to the immediate political problem of a credibility gap which, he believes, the Admininstration sought to avoid. Agnew's speech was but one act in the effort: "What better way to avoid or postpone your own credibility gap than to impugn in advance the credibility of those who report and interpret your actions." *New York Times,* January 21, 1971, p. 35.

13. Jules Witcover, *White Knight: The Rise of Spiro Agnew* (New York, 1972), p. 363.

14. The details above are drawn from the Des Moines, Iowa *Register,* November 14, 1969, pp. 1, 12.

15. Witcover, p. 316.

16. The text in Campbell, *Critiques of Contemporary Rhetoric,* does not include Agnew's informal, extemporaneous, introductory remarks. They appear in an audio transcript of the address in L. Patrick Devlin, *Contemporary Political Speaking* (Belmont, Calif., 1971), p. 41.

17. *New York Times,* August 13, 1972, Sec. 4, p. 3.

INTRODUCTION TO THREE CRITIQUES
OF GEORGE WALLACE'S "SECOND INAUGURAL ADDRESS"

Mid-1971 headlines proclaimed: "Loyal Fans Cheer Wallace in Toledo"[1] and "1,000 Cheer Wallace at New York Dinner."[2] By November the *Los Angeles Times* observed: "George Corley Wallace runs for President again and maybe he ought to."[3] These were but signs of things to come. By May, 1972, Governor Wallace had run strong primary races in Indiana and Pennsylvania; he had won the primaries in Florida and Michigan. Indeed, his twin victories in Michigan and Maryland on the same day were labeled by the liberal as well as conservative press "stunning victories."[4]

By May 27, an article in the *Boston Globe,* "People's Choice . . . A Dilemma," by David Wilson pointed out that the Wallace strength was indeed highly visible.[5] Of the 19 state primaries to that date, the popular vote total stood at:

Wallace	3,383,028
Humphrey	2,548,292
McGovern	2,269,216

If, as the *Washington Post* observed, "rival national leaders assumed that Wallace's intuitive political skills would lose their flavor and his base of support would gradually fade away, they must have been disappointed."[6]

The *Monitor* described the 1972 Wallace bid for the Presidency in this way:

[Wallace is] the 'littleman's' St. George once again taking out after all those big, bad dragons—the Washington bureaucracy, the Eastern establishment press, the filthy rich with their big tax loopholes, the foundations which received tax exemptions, the boobs in the federal government who gave all that money to other countries and who let Peking into the U.N., those leaders who got us into that 'no-win' war, and on and on.[7]

They may also just have pinpointed an essential aspect of Wallacism, defining it as "basically a stubbornness, a not-wanting-to-be pushed around, an 'independent' streak shared by many Americans."[8]

It is clear, in retrospect, that Wallace *had* his impact on the primary campaigns of 1972. How fully he made good his threat, "I'm Gonna Shake Their Eyeteeth Out"—only more time will tell.[9] But the now long period of time over which George Corley Wallace has claimed the national attention makes it difficult to "dismiss him merely as a racist, egomaniac or spoiler."[10] For like it or not, he does appear to many as a "straight-talking unintimidated [spokesman] for grievances they feel the 'powers that be' are ignoring."[11] If, on the other hand, he is to be viewed as a "medicine man," then the critic would do well to ask, "Of *what* is his medicine made?"[12]

On January 18, 1971, George Wallace read aloud a passage from the well-known poem by Robert Frost, "Stopping by Woods on a Snowy Evening": ". . . if there are those who wonder why I stand here today . . . let me answer them through the words of a great poet when he wrote:

'But I have promises to keep,
And miles to go before I sleep,
And miles to go before I sleep.' "[13]

Almost one year before that, George Wallace had candidly announced he would "use the [Alabama] Statehouse as a platform from which to make another . . . try at the Presidency in 1972."[14] Thus, the "promises" alluded to at the close of his "Second Inaugural Address" were to have national as well as state implications.

Notes

1. *Akron* (Ohio) *Beacon Journal* (June 27, 1971).
2. *Washington Post* (September 26, 1971).
3. *Los Angeles Times* (November 19, 1971).
4. *New Republic* (May 27, 1972), p. 17.
5. *Boston Globe* (May 27, 1972).
6. *Washington Post* (August 30, 1971).
7. *Christian Science Monitor* (February 1, 1972).
8. *Christian Science Monitor* (January 14, 1972).
9. *Newsweek* (February 7, 1972), p. 80.
10. *Los Angeles Times* (November 19, 1971).
11. *Christian Science Monitor* (December 15, 1971).
12. Kenneth Burke, *The Philosophy of Literary Form,* rev. ed. (New York: Vintage Books, Inc., 1957), p. 164.
13. George Wallace, "Second Inaugural Address." From a mimeographed text supplied by Governor Wallace's office.
14. *Newsweek* (March 9, 1970), p. 20.

SECOND INAUGURAL ADDRESS

GEORGE C. WALLACE

Fellow Alabamians:

Honoring us today with their presence are the wives, mothers and families of our prisoners of war and of those men missing in action in Southeast Asia. Will these families please stand:

(Leads applause)

I know that the people of Alabama, and those present with us here today, join me in praying that you will soon be united once again with your loved ones.

(Continues the acknowledgment of honored guests and begins speech)

My Fellow Alabamians:

1   Today, I am both honored and humbled to stand before you and in your presence and that of our Almighty Creator to take the solemn oath of office as your governor. I am honored that you allow me once again to serve you as your governor. I am truly humbled by the trust and responsibility you have entrusted to me as we continue along the paths we have so long trod together.

Text supplied by Governor Wallace's Office. Permission to reprint by George C. Wallace. Speech given January 18, 1971.

2   While many are with us here today, there are many more who cannot honor us with their presence for they are busy in the fields and factories of our state earning through honest toil a livelihood for their families, while creating and producing those material goods upon which the wealth and economy of this state so largely depends.

3   These are the honest, hard working, God fearing, freedom loving men and women of our state who through the sweat of their brow, the toil of their bodies and the strength and courage of their convictions form the muscle, bone and sinew of that great and good land that we know as Alabama.

4   To you I say that we are conscious of your pride, your courage, your fierce independence and your deep devotion to those principles that make Alabama the great and glorious state that it is and I hope, and dare to believe, that you are here with us in spirit today—may God bless you as we salute you from afar.

5   We are grateful that you permitted us to take part in the advances attained during our previous periods of service. We point with humility, but with justifiable pride, to our unwavering support of education, highlighted by tremendous increase in appropriations for operations and capital outlay—a system of trade schools and junior colleges situated throughout the state that are both admired and envied by all our sister states—record breaking progress in industrial expansion and development—an unprecedented highway construction program—the health and hope that was provided the less fortunate and the mentally ill and retarded.

6   In all that we did, our sole purpose was to provide a better life for all our people— with your help we believe that this was accomplished.

7   Yet much remains to be done—together we must press on toward a more productive and more responsive state government designed to meet the needs of the people we serve—all of whom must feel that they have a voice in their destiny and fate.

8   This can only be accomplished in an atmosphere of freedom from unwarranted, unwise and unwanted intrusion and oppression by the Federal Government—a man must be free and unfettered by federal encroachments in his employment—his home—his community—his domestic institutions, including his schools and in his associations with his fellow man.

9   Each individual citizen is an important link in the chain of government. No individual should be above or below the law, for ours is a government of laws. But a law, simply because it is a law, is not necessarily a good law. However, our system provides for means and methods of change. The mob destroying a bank, school or business is not the American way for change. Violence is never the result of reason, but blind passion. Violence is dangerous because it is regressive and destructive. Violence must cease, for it breeds more violence.

10   We should return to basic principles, and these basic principles are plain and self-evident, and were set out in our Consitution, and especially our Bill of Rights. While we are on the subject of rights, with every right there is a corresponding duty. No duty is

more important than the duty of an individual citizen to voice his opinion, make his thoughts heard in a peaceful manner, and stand up for what he believes in.

11   All of us know and realize we cannot have justice without law and order, nor law and order without justice. Justice, among and for the people, is a primary duty of government for we all know that our government was created to help—not destroy. Too often the power of government is used to ride roughshod over the individual's rights rather than to preserve the individual's rights. No government is administered according to the objective and intent of the founding fathers and all lovers of liberty, unless it is administered for the weak, the poor and the humble as well as for the powerful. Government must be a friend of the people—not a tyrant.

12   Congress should rescue our schools from the wilful acts of malicious men. Our schools are being destroyed because the South and other sections of the country who believe in government by law and not by bureaucrats, failed to unite against despotic tyranny of a Federal Government—a government that looks upon the people not as people, but as so many units of votes to be gained by pleasing certain selfish politicians and sociologists at the expense of the children of America, both Black and White.

13   Even a basic and fundamental principle such as "freedom of choice" has been denied the parents and children of the South and certain other sections of the nation by the Federal Government. Today, the school children of the South and many parts of the nation are mere pawns in the hands of powerful politicians who, for sociological reasons, seek to destroy local self-government and deny the people a choice as to how their own children should be educated. What is the answer?
   The answer is: "People Power."

14   What is people power? People power is the strong voice and political action of the people expressed within the law.

15   The people of the South and those who think like the South, represent the majority viewpoint within our constitutional democracy, but they are not organized and do not speak with a loud voice. Until the day arrives when the voice of the people of the South and those who think like us is, within the law, thrust into the face of the bureaucrats, only then can the "people's power" express itself legally and ethically and get results. Rome fell and countless other civilizations have ceased to exist, not always from outside sources, but from weakness within. Too long, oh, too long, has the voice of the people been silenced by their own disruptive government—by governmental bribery in quasi-governmental handouts such as H.E.W. and others that exist in America today! An aroused people can save this nation from those evil forces who seek our destruction. The choice is yours. The hour is growing late!

16   If the descendants of those who founded this nation, together with those who came here one and two generations ago fleeing despotic government, will wake up and realize the importance of each individual standing up now for what one thinks and believes in, then, and then only, will the politicians answer the voice of the people. Remember! It is the people who create the politicians and it is the politicians who administer the government (bad or good government) and without a mass movement of the people, the present trends of despotic and centralized government can and will destroy America.

17   We in Alabama still cherish our independence and stand firm in our belief that we should be allowed to chart our own destiny.

18   We are proud of the youth of Alabama and thrill with them as they prepare to participate in the democratic processes of government—we welcome, seek and solicit their aid, assistance and encouragement.

19   We have sought to manifest our faith in our youth by selecting for major roles in our administration young men and women of vigor and imagination who understand the aims and desires of the fine young people of our state. We will rely heavily of them.

20   Yes, we are proud of the young people of Alabama and our purpose will be to develop their abilities, to protect them during their formative years, and to involve them in the operation of government at all levels.

21   Being concerned for the future of our young people, we are mindful of a frightening evil now stalking this land, preying on young and old alike, but wreaking particular havoc on the young. I refer to the illegal traffic in drugs and to drug abuse. This is something that must be stopped—forcefully, fully and immediately. To this end I commit myself and all the forces at my command, and I especially call upon the fine youth of Alabama to join me in this effort.

22   We will not cease until the drug peddlers, pushers and their slimy companions are driven from our midst.

23   As we reaffirm our commitments of the past campaign, we again pledge our best efforts towards reducing the daily cost of living for all Alabamians, especially the working men and women of our state and their families. We will work to reduce utility rates and basic insurance costs. We will examine and evaluate our structure of state government and we will streamline and modernize where necessary in the interest of economy and efficiency.

24   We renew our vow to work toward more adequate medical services for all our people, for this medical attention presently is beyond the economic reach of many. They simply cannot afford proper medical care even if they are fortunate enough to find a doctor. Any Alabamian who is sick enough to need a doctor or a hospital bed should be able to get one, regardless of financial condition or where they happen to live.

25   We will work toward a voluntary health insurance program which will put adequate medical attention within the financial reach of every family in Alabama. We will build and staff the necessary facilities to educate enough doctors, nurses and allied medical technicians to properly care for our sick, whether they live on a farm on in the heart of a city.

26   We will continue our struggle for equalization of the tax burden so that our working men and women of average and low income will not continue to bear a disproportionate share of the tax load. We must revamp and revise a system which allows multibillion dollar foundations, of at least questionable purposes, and multimillionaire property holders to escape taxation while the low and middle level wage-earner pays and pays and pays. We have raised this issue before and will raise it again, again and again until we are afforded some relief—only then will I be silent—and I believe you would have it this way.

27   Alabamians and Americans generally have had their fill of excessive and ill apportioned taxation and we propose to join in the fight to right these conditions. I issue a call to my fellow governors, to the members of Congress and to all Americans to join in this effort to the end that the average Alabamian and American be saved from tax destruction.

28   We allude again to the political power of the people, "People Power," if you will.

29   Let me remind you that any government that ignores the rights of individuals will not long endure, nor will a government that offers no redress from exorbitant and unjustly apportioned taxation. No government that rides roughshod over the mind and body of its youth can be representative of the people under the law.

30   However, the place to get the desired change is within the law and not by destruction of the system. The street is not a proper place to change America, but the ballot box through "People Power"—this is the method and forum. Every American can participate in government by voicing his or her thoughts within the law at every level of government.

31   And we must have faith and pride in ourselves as individuals, in our communities—in our state—our region and our nation—we must remember that we and those who bore us stand among the greatest patriots of all times—men and women who then and who today continue to resist in the face of oppressions from external sources and whose perseverance and desire for freedom and self-expression is exceeded by none under these Heavens.

32   To borrow from the words of a renowned author—"To have common glories in the past; a common wish in the present; to have done great things together; to wish to do greater; these are the essential conditions that make up a people."

33   One hundred years ago, the spirit of the South became passive as this spirit was subdued by violent means—yet remained undimmed. For the flame of our passion burned within us as an arc of our covenant—a covenant of our heritage of liberty under law with no surrender to those who would destroy us.

34   Today, twin evils face the American people. Communism on one hand and an illegal abuse of federal governmental power on the other. Either, if not curtailed, will destroy us. What can you do? You are more powerful than you think, provided you make yourself heard—for the politician will listen—but if you remain silent, there is nothing for the politician to hear but the yelping from those who seek to destroy us. We must not be a silent majority, but an alert, active voice within the law. Then we can help our state and our Nation.

35   This administration is not going to be one of favoritism to any special interest, individual or friend. It will be a people's administration with the goal that honesty is the best and only policy. Special priviledge has no place in government. Too long in Alabama's history have certain greedy interests blocked needed progress. Nearly every advance in humanity's long march toward human betterment and progress of the many has been delayed by the willful few. Greed has no place in the creed on government. A government that helps the few and injures the many is not good government. My administration may not achieve all its goals, try as we may, but rest assured, should corruption raise its filthy head, it will be promptly dealt with regardless from whence it comes.

36   I am old enough to know that the people are tired of promises and demand action. I am young enough to be an active governor. Our action will move Alabama forward on all fronts.

37   Today, the government is too costly and taxes are a constant burden to the people. Any waste on the people's money is a crime against the people. Government has become stagnated with its burdensome bigness. The Federal Government has too long thrust its sometimes greedy hands into the pockets of the people. If the Federal Government continues to dominate education, it could result in control over the minds of our children—leading, by natural tendency, to control over the body, thus destroying the freedom of all of us. You have a right to expect an Alabama moving forward on all fronts—better Alabama schools—health facilities—human welfare—antipollution, etc. For we hold the temporary power of government—hold it in trust for the people under the law.

38   The people have the right to know what goes on its state government. We are going to operate with an "open door-open book" policy. Our state government is for all—so let us join together, for Alabama belongs to all of us—Black and White, young and old, rich and poor alike.

39   And if there be those who wonder why I stand here today—curious as to what force and inspiration brings me to this point in our state's history, let me answer them through the words of a great poet, Robert Frost, who, perhaps, captured my feeling better than I could express when he wrote:

But I have promises to keep,
And miles to go before I sleep,
And miles to go before I sleep.

With God's help I will make you a good Governor!

THE MONEYCHANGERS MUST BE DRIVEN FROM THE TEMPLE: AN ANALYSIS OF GEORGE WALLACE'S SECOND INAUGURAL ADDRESS

JANE BLANKENSHIP

George Wallace announced in March, 1970, that he would, indeed, run a second time for the governorship of Alabama. That office had propelled him into national limelight when he held it from 1963-1697. Perhaps it would, again, serve as a useful launching pad for yet another bid for the Presidency.

In the state's Democratic primary he ran against the incumbent Albert Brewer, successor to Governor Lurleen Wallace, who had died of cancer. Brewer ran a campaign that defied conventional Alabama politics: "I'm convinced that the overwhelming majority of people in this state are tired of all this furor over race and are ready to get their state going."[1]

Wallace ran a populist campaign, denouncing the banks and utilities, the big newspapers, the rich on Wall Street, and those who "drink tea at the country club with their little finger stubbed straight up, and never do a thing for the people."[2] Denunciation was to be a useful tactic, for a deep air of general pessimism prevailed. For example, in answer to the question, "Had the U.S. changed for the worse over the past decade?", 46% agreed that it *had* changed and that the change had been for the worse. Thirteen percent held that no change had occurred. And only 36% felt that the change had been for the better.[3]

Concern was not limited to past fact but to future fact as well. Fifty-eight percent forecast that the U.S. is likely to change for the worse over the next decade. Fourteen percent predicted no change. And, only 19% felt that the future change was likely to be for the good.[4] *Newsweek*'s issue on "The Troubled American" vividly chronicles the depth and scope of the pessimism.[5] Along with many other Americans, Wallace's "folks," as he affectionately called them, were worried.[6] Whether the "demons" were bureaucrats, pseudointellectuals, college professors, guideline writers, anarchists, federal judges, the news media, militants, rioters, communists, activists, so-called liberals, people with long hair, the Kerner Commission, theoreticians who look down their ivory-tower noses at the common folk, public officials with briefcases, or someone else—there were *many* and they were perceived as insidious.

On the one hand the folks were "sick and tired" of the Establishment's apparent disregard for them, and on the other, they were concerned about permissiveness in general, student unrest, forced integration in the schools, and the breakdown of law and order. They were caught up in the middle of "the left wing media, Harvard disarmers, foundation limousine liberals, fat-cat labor leaders," and politicians who either did not see the danger from these groups or who, worse still, appeared to cultivate them.[7] The "folk's" best survival technique was to form a coalition of the disaffected and the discontented. The coalition needed a leader who would be irreverent, antiestablishment, sassy, feisty, and a gutsy campaigner who could do battle with all comers.

The Alabama air was full of charges during the primary. Brewer, accused of homosexuality, and his wife of alcoholism, charged that "this [was] the dirtiest campaign I've ever observed in Alabama."[8] At one point, a whisper campaign spread word that Brewer refused to give Wallace a state police bodyguard and thereby left him "exposed to . . . dope fiends and Communists. . . ."[9]

The racist overtones of the campaign were clear. For example, an ad run in several newspapers showed a blond four-year-old girl sitting on a beach surrounded by seven grinning black boys. "This could be Alabama four years from now! Do you want it?"[10] And, one radio spot intoned: "Suppose your wife is driving home at 11 o'clock at night. She is stopped by a highway patrolman. He turns out to be black. Think about it. . . ."[11]

Brewer was defeated by 32,000 votes in a run-off election. Wallace was to be a shoo-in against his Republican opponent.

I.

In *Symbols in Society,* Hugh Duncan writes that the form of any act consists of:

> . . . the stage (situation or environment) on which the act takes place, the kind of act it is (its social function), and the roles involved in the action, the ways in which communication occurs within the act, and the kind of social order which is invoked as the purpose of the act.[12]

I will treat briefly the "stage" on which the act, George Wallace's "Second Inaugural Address," takes place, and point to the particular social functions the act appears to have. Mainly, however, I will be concerned with *who* is involved in such an act.

First, it is clear that the Inaugural (in fact, most inaugurals) occur in a place more august and more hallowed than ordinary places, worthy of *formal* ceremonies. The particular place chosen by or for George Wallace (because of "tradition") holds especial value—not just because of what *it* represents (i.e., "stateliness," "seat of government") but because the people who *gather there* in person or by proxy (wives, mothers and families represent POWs or MIAs, Alabamians present also represent "those who are busy in the fields and factories")—*bring to it* value.

The absent are yet present:

> —the families of POWs are there to represent a great loss, great hope. They have come to be among the national *symbols* surrounding the war in Vietnam; that is, they represent more than themselves but stand also as one of the most enduring and poignant reminders of the war in Vietnam. They represent, then, a *national* loss.
>
> —the "present" absence of "honest, hardworking, God fearing, freedom loving. . . . (3) They, Wallace reminds us, are there in "spirit." (4)

Not only do the absent bring honor to the Inaugural scene, but the speech is delivered in the presence of the Almighty Creator and those who have attended the ceremony. They are "valuable" not only because they are intrinsically worthwhile as human beings, but also because they are an "important link in the chain of government." (9) They, too, "represent" more than themselves.

This is a place, moreover, where certain *kinds* of acts take place; a place to:

> reaffirm our commitments (23)
> renew vows (24)
> continue struggles (26)
> face evils (34)

remember men and women "whose perseverance and desire for freedom . . . is exceeded by none under these Heavens" (31)
to recall the "covenant of our heritage." (33)

It is indeed a holy place.

Yet all is not well. We learn that "The Federal Government has too long thrust its . . . greedy hands into the pockets of the people." (37) (Taxation without representation has after all been an important American theme since Revolutionary times.) But Wallace reminds us that the greed takes not one but many forms—bureaucrats, dope peddlers, sociologists, and the like. Such greed, of course, must be "promptly dealt with regardless from whence it comes." (35) Temples, even secular ones, are not to be debased by the presence of moneychangers whatever their guise.

Finally, this is no ordinary place because it is endowed by a "force and inspiration" that brings George Wallace himself there. (39) In most places promises are *made;* here in *this* place, they are *kept.* In such a scene we may expect to see *certain kinds of acts* performed by *certain kinds of persons.*

Duncan discusses some eleven kinds of "content" that acts may have.[13] Among the eleven are several that relate directly to George Wallace's "Second Inaugural Address." The two "contents" perhaps are more directly related to this particular act are: (a) ". . . ruling, being ruled, and reaching common agreement as in political modes of action" and (b) ". . . defense, or the means ranging from force to the apologetics and propaganda we use to defend ourselves from enemies within and without the community."

First, an essential question of the speech is: "Who shall be 'ruled' and in what ways by whom?" "People power" tells the listener immediately where George Wallace stands on the question. (12) He is not impressed, nor will he be cowed down by "powerful" and/or "selfish" politicians (13, 12)

The next essential question, "*How* shall the people be ruled?" is answered with equal firmness. The people will govern themselves *through law.* "Law" appears 16 times (not counting variants such as "legally"). For example,

> . . . we hold the temporary power of government—hold it in trust for the people *under the law.* . . . (37)
> . . . our heritage of liberty *under law.* . . . (33)

or,

> Every American can participate in government by voicing his or her thoughts *within the law* . . . (30)
> We must not be a silent majority, but an alert, active voice *within the law.* (34)
> . . . Voice of the people of the South and those who think like us, *within the law* . . . (15)

Many of the basic tenets held by the people focus on the law:

> . . . no individual should be *above or below the law* . . . (9)
> . . . ours is a government *of laws.* (9)
> . . . government *by law* and not by bureaucrats . . . (12)
> . . . we cannot have justice *without law and order,* nor *law* and order without justice. (11)

Notice how the two "contents," ruling and defense, are both inextricably associated with "the law." The people will *govern themselves through law* and law, in turn, provides them their best *protection*. They will not submit to "mobs," the "evil now stalking this land," dope pushers and "their slimy companions," "Communism on the one hand and illegal abuse of federal government power on the other." (9, 21, 22, 34) These forces are bent on *"destroying"* schools (12), "preying" on young and old alike (21), "wreaking havoc" (21), riding "roughshod over the mind and body" of youth. (29) In a society beset on every side by dangers, *defense* must become a prime priority.

II.

Now, that we have asked what *kinds of acts* take place, we are ready to ask: *"Who participates in such acts and by whom are they led?"* Those who take part in "ruling" and in "defense" look to certain kinds of leaders. They both shape and are shaped by them. They look to leaders who: (1) possess certain characteristics; (2) recognize problems for what they are; and (3) speak in certain ways.

The leader of such people must, as George Wallace says he is, be

humble (1)
honored by the people (1)
grateful (1)
justifiably proud of his record (5)
unselfish ("sole purpose" is to "provide a better life" for his people) (6)
ready to press on against great odds (7ff)

Such a leader likes an atmosphere of freedom from federal government, dislikes violence (it is not the American way), advocates a return to basic principles. He is wise enough to know that one needs not just law and order, but law, order and justice. Further, he looks on people *as* people; he gets angry when "fundamental principles" are "denied"; he gets upset when children are considered "mere pawns." (13)

Such a leader can paraphrase great men, quote poetry and even philosophy; but through it all be a doer. He is, as Wallace says he is, "a man old enough to know that people are tired of promises and demand action." Yet he is "young enough to be an active governor." (36)

Perhaps most important, such a leader can see problems for what they are—problems. And he points them out:

—unwarranted, unwise and unwanted intrusion and oppression by the Federal government. Fettered by federal encroachments in employment, home, community, domestic institutions, including schools and "associations with his fellow man." (8)
—violence. It is not the American way for change and it represents "blind passion." (9)
—loss of "basic principles" which are "plain and self-evident" (10)
—government which "rides roughshod" over individual rights (29)
  Government has forgotten that it should be a "friend" not a "tyrant" (11)
—schools menaced by willful and malicious men doing things at "expense of children of Americans . . . both Black and White." (12) Children made "mere pawns." (13)
—governmental bribery in quasi-governmental handouts such as H.E.W. (15)

Lastly, such leaders talk in certain ways. They call a spade a spade. They are not afraid to call the enemy "slimy," "despotic," "malicious," (22, 12); to brand their services "handouts" (15)

But they are not afraid to be "eloquent," to say: ". . . the flame of our passion burned within us as an arc of our covenant . . . (33)" and ". . . the rights of individuals will not long endure . . . (29)" A purple passage or two is to be tolerated for such a touch may remind us that true royalty resides, after all, in the common man.

Who *appreciates* such leaders? From what kinds of people do such leaders emerge? They, are as detailed in the Inaugural:

honest (3)
hardworking (3)
God fearing (3)
freedom loving (3)

Such people possess:

pride (4)
courage (4)
fierce independence (4)
deep devotion to principles (4)

Together, the leader and the people who allow themselves to be led by him, constitute the "We" who must constantly struggle against a myriad of "Theys," for surely "We" are menaced by corruption and greed on every hand.

In the Inaugural there are at least two groups of "Theys." Group One consists of the general public, those who are harmless; they simply are not as enlightened as "We" are.

But it is Group Two who constitutes the real danger, for they are the insidious. "They" takes such forms as:

the mob (9)
the powerful who ride roughshod over individual rights (29)
certain unspecified willful and malicious men destroying schools; bureaucrats (12)
certain selfish politicians and sociologists (12)
powerful politicians with sociological reasons who look at children as pawns (13)

With sweat and conviction, "they" will be overcome. "We" the community guardians, the conscious of the community will prevail—essentially for two reasons: (1) We are the *people* and (2) we work within the *law*.

"We" will not be silenced; the "voice of the people" *will* be heard. But the people must be reminded of their power by their leaders: "*You* are more powerful than you think provided *you* make yourself heard—for the politician will listen . . ." (34)

If *you* do not speak up, *we* will be challenged: ". . . if you remain silent, then there is nothing for the politician to hear but the yelping from those who seek to destroy us." (34) So perhaps that explains why the "you" shifts to "we" and leader and followers become one again—they are threatened by a common menace.[14] Thus, *we* must not be a silent majority, but an alert, active voice within the law. (34)

Still if the leader is not careful—"we" may slip into "I": "For we [I] hold the temporary power of government—hold it in trust for the people under the law." (37) And, "we" may be just a bit jolted *not* to hear the Frost poem paraphrased to suit "people power":

> But we have promises to keep,
> And miles to go before we sleep,
> And miles to go before we sleep.

Notes

1. *Newsweek* (March 9, 1970), p. 20.
2. *Newsweek* (May 4, 1970), p. 108.
3. *Newsweek* (October 6, 1969), p. 36.
4. Ibid.
5. *Newsweek* (October 6, 1969).
6. *Newsweek* (September 16, 1968), pp. 25-28.
7. Kevin Phillips in the *Washington Post* (June 14, 1971).
8. *Newsweek* (June 15, 1970), p. 27.
9. Ibid.
10. Ibid.
11. Ibid.
12. Hugh Dalziel Duncan, *Symbols in Society* (New York: Oxford University Press, 1968), p. 16. Duncan is indebted, as he notes, to the work of Kenneth Burke for this model. See, particularly, Burke's *Grammar of Motives* and *Rhetoric of Motives*.
13. He says: "The *content* of an act exists in social interests as these are expressed in the basic institutions of society. Eleven such contents of social experience are distinguished. These are: (1) the family; (2) ruling, being ruled, and reaching common agreement, as in political modes of action; (3) economics or the provision of goods and services; (4) defense, or the means ranging from force to the apologetics and propaganda we use to defend ourselves from enemies within and without the community; (5) education, or the creation and transmission of culture; (6) sociability, or the purely social forms we use to court each other as superiors, inferiors, and equals; (7) play, games, entertainments and festivals, in which we learn to act together under rules, and in joy so that our social bonds will be strengthened in the euphoria of "togetherness"; (8) health and welfare; (9) religion; (10) art; and (11) science" (Duncan, p. 7).
14. Early in the speech there are these shifts from "I" to "We"; e.g., "In all that we did, our sole purpose was to provide a better life for all our people—with your help we believe that this was accomplished." (6)

EXPLOITING THE ABSOLUTES:
FEDERAL POWER VS. PEOPLE POWER

MARIE J. ROSENWASSER

An inaugural address is usually classified as ceremonial discourse, but George Wallace's 1971 "Second Inaugural" was not a *typical* ceremonial speech. Rather than devoting the entire speech to the traditional expression of appreciation to his supporters and announcement of his Administration's goals and proposals, Governor Wallace used the speech to accomplish at least three purposes beyond the one of accepting the oath of office. In his 1971 inaugural Wallace sought to: (1) warn his audience of an insidious enemy, (2) convince his immediate and unseen audiences that individual citizens *do* have the power to make government responsive, and (3) further establish himself as the right and most dedicated leader to fight the people's oppressor. To accomplish these purposes Governor Wallace used the archetypal strategy of opposing his absolute force of evil (the federal government's abuse of power) with the equally absolute force—his concept of good or "people power." The content of the speech is largely the development of this strategy, and Wallace's style serves to reinforce the strategy and allow him to accomplish his purposes, to the extent that any one speech can further a candidate's cause and election.

To aid in analyzing and evaluating Wallace's speech and style of expression, we look to historian Richard Hofstadter's description of what he calls the "paranoid style" in American politics. Explaining that his use of the word "paranoid" is unrelated to any clinical application of the term or any implication that the user of such a style is psychologically paranoid,[1] Hofstadter suggests that the speaker who uses the *exaggerated style of a crusader* operates as though "all ills can be traced to a single center and hence be eliminated by some kind of final act of victory over the evil source."[2] George Wallace speaks as though he views the world in this way. From this general description, Hofstadter identifies and illustrates several specific characteristics of the zealot's style, which to various degrees can be found in this and other speeches by Mr. Wallace. The characteristics identified as part of such a style include: visions of a conspiracy; a belief that the crusader is more aware of the impending danger and thus more qualified to lead the movement; creation of unrealistic goals and demands; imitation of the enemy's acts; indignation over the moral outrages attributed to the enemy; exploitation of those who break from the enemy's camp and join the renegade's cause; extensive demonstration of the "truth" of the charges; and, pleas to act now before it is too late.[3]

In the "Second Inaugural" George Wallace repeatedly cites federal usurpation of individual and state's rights and envisions "those who would destroy us" as conspirators against the common folk. These conspirators must be exposed, and it is Wallace's campaign that will accomplish this feat. Wallace builds himself as the most available man to lead the crusade, for he is a committed governor who recognizes the threat of left-wing liberals, the federal government, and "selfish politicians." His very general promises to decrease taxes and make them more equitable for all, as well as providing adequate medical care for everyone are just two examples of his movement's goals that stretch credulity. If the enemy is conspiratory, he must be "outconspired." Wallace uses "people

This piece was originally prepared for this volume. © 1972 Marie J. Rosenwasser. For permission to reprint contact the author, University of Massachusetts, Amherst 01002.

power" to overpower federal power and to creep up, vote by vote, on the conspirators. The "twin evils" of communism and the federal government have become moral affronts, for the reader will recall that the government rides "roughshod" over our minds and bodies!

There is little evidence of Wallace exploiting those who have seen the light and left the enemy's camp; although the special praise for youth illustrates the courting of potential renegades, and the remonstrances against the silent majority imply that he who stands up for what he believes is a member of Wallace's crusade. Unlike many other users of the same style, Wallace demonstrates the "truth" of his charges in general terms rather than specific cases and examples. The "truth" is supplied by the listeners as they hear general references to: intrusion into the operation of local schools, tax destruction, and threats to American traditions. There is no doubt, though, that Wallace exhibits the stylistic characteristic of calling for "action now"; for we are warned that "the hour is growing late."

This discussion of characteristics of the zealous crusader's style, with examples from the "Second Inaugural," serves as a frame of references for a more careful criticism of the speech. An analysis of Wallace's central strategy and style of expression helps us evaluate the validity and effectiveness of the candidate's world-view and his crusade.

Strategy

The dominant strategy of the speech is to put people power against federal power. Mr. Wallace first identifies the evil that must be irradicated—federal tyranny. He then urges the soldiers of his army to hope, rather than despair, that they can defeat this source of oppression. Pitting something called "people power" against what some would call one of its synonyms, "federal power," works for Wallace because the strategy allows his followers to express their frustrations at something so vague it can encompass all of their doubts and fears and so terrible that anyone who ignores the threat is less than a good citizen. The strategy simplifies a complex and potentially confusing explanation of "what has gone wrong in America." It names rather than analyzes; it inspires action rather than careful deliberation; it encourages ready and rapid agreement rather than contemplative and skeptical evaluation.

What are the ways in which the source of evil is identified and how does Wallace create for his audiences a conspiracy massive in its power and monstrous in its impact? As we said earlier, the major source of evil identified in the "Second Inaugural" is tyrannical and oppressive use of federal power; however, more specific sources of evil are also named. As illustrative of Wallace's treatment of the federal government as the general enemy, we are told that people can feel that they have a voice in their government only if there is an atmosphere of freedom from "unwarranted, unwise, and unwanted intrusion and oppression by the Federal Government." (8) The federal government is made even more villainous when it is described as "riding roughshod" over the individual's rights, and we are warned that the "present trends of despotic and centralized government" are going to destroy America. (11, 16) Perhaps the danger is most ominous when Wallace refers to the ambiguous threat of "oppressions from external sources" and the even more conspiratory villains as "those who would destroy us." (31, 33)

Should there be doubt about the danger imposed by excessive federal power, Governor Wallace cites "bureaucrats," "selfish politicians," and "sociologists" as more specific sources of evil. He cleverly objectifies rather than villifies[4]—after all, who likes bureaucracy, or selfishness, or those members of that already suspect academic world called "sociologists"? On the other hand, some of his audience could ask: What government, at any level, operates without bureaucracy? What human being, whether politician or not, is unselfish? What citizen, be he a member of "academia" or the "real world" does not play sociologist? Thus, it is not enough to identify bureaucrats and selfish politicians as enemies, especially when even more acceptable objects of evil are at hand. Consequently, Wallace condemns dope peddlers and drug abusers; he condemns violence as a means of change. In these two condemnations he is not unlike many Americans.

But if some members of his audiences remain unconvinced, they might become believers when Wallace explicitly names "communism on one hand and an illegal abuse of federal government power on the other" as today's "twin evils" that face the American people. (34) Clearly, Wallace creates for his audience the illusion of conspiring forces at work destroying our nation's traditional values and highest ideals. Over one-fourth of the paragraphs in the speech deal mainly with a discussion of abusive federal power as the people's greatest enemy, whether it is interfering with state systems of education or taxing excessively and unfairly. Yet, identification of the general and specific enemies in this speech is mild when compared with earlier addresses by Governor Wallace. In his July 4, 1964 speech on the Civil Rights Bill, Wallace identifies the members of the Supreme Court as "omnipotent black-robed despots" and calls the passers of the bill left-wing liberals who have "struck the assassin's knife in the back of liberty" and given a "black-jack" to the "federal force cult" which will allow those liberals to "try to force us back into bondage."[5] In a 1968 speech on Law Enforcement we find more evidence of a belief that there is a conspiracy abroad and that the people must act to expose it. Wallace says that the current demonstrations and militant protest are "national or international in origin, scope, planning, financing, and leadership."[6] His proof is the identification of "elitists" running our federal government and an assertion that the federal judicial system is infested with people who have lost contact with the real world and real people.[7]

What does the establishment of an evil that must be eliminated achieve for the speaker? It not only generates interest and provides an opportunity for venting hostilities and expressing vague feelings of dissatisfaction—it not only solidifies support by polarizing issues—it allows Wallace to prepare the audiences for his 1972 presidential campaign slogan, "Send them a message."[8] The "them" in 1972 was the federal government, the bureaucrats, the selfish politicians, the sociologists, the federal judiciaries, and the Supreme Court justices of 1971, 1968, and 1964. How more safely, yet more generally, can one identify an enemy than with the pronoun "them"?

If there is an absolute evil, the crusading politician who wants votes must identify the absolute good that can overcome the evil. In the "Second Inaugural," Wallace coins the phrase "people power" and then elaborates on this slogan until it becomes the absolute good—the only force capable of overcoming the ominous tyranny of a central government with growing despotic tendencies. In fact, Wallace balances the speech between discussion of the evil and discussion of the good; one-fourth of the 40 paragraphs[9] in the speech proper are devoted to explicitly telling the listeners that they do have the power to control their government, that they must act *now* rather than remaining part of the silent majority, and that it is their power that will restore to America her most sacred values and ideals. In addition to explaining and reiterating his theme of "people power," Wallace implies the slogan by spending the first several paragraphs of the speech praising the laborers who cannot attend the Inauguration; complimenting Alabamians for supporting and building fine schools, hospitals, and other public institutions; and praising the youth for their vigor and imagination. There is parallelism, then, in the way Wallace handles the source of evil and the way in which he handles the source of good; he is both direct and indirect; he is both general and specific, and he balances the speech between the two opposing forces.

Very generally Wallace urges the people to "press on together" because "each individual citizen is an important link in the chain of government." (7, 9) Thus every individual has the "duty . . . to voice his opinion, make his thoughts heard in a peaceful manner, and stand up for what he believes in." (10) These generalizations build in intensity as Wallace prepares the audience for introduction of his slogan and the explanation of what people power is. The definition of "people power" is remarkably similar to a definition of "democracy" found in history texts and political tracts or uttered so frequently in speeches throughout the history of our country.

After introducing his slogan, Wallace becomes somewhat more specific when he indicates *what* must be done and *when* it must be done. The people must "wake up and realize the importance of each individual standing up now for what one thinks and believes"; they must form a mass movement now, for "the hour is growing late." (16) More specifically, Alabamians and Americans who "think like the South" are called to join in this effort to save the average person from "tax destruction" and "federal intrusion." We also learn *how* and *where* this power must be exercised. The Governor tells us that every American can participate in government by voicing his or her thoughts within the law at every level of government and that the ballot box is the appropriate place to change America.

The discussion culminates when we are told that we are more powerful than we think and that if we remain silent only the "yelping" of that vague and sinister force ("those who would destroy us") will be heard. Wallace sympathizers cannot remain silent, passive, and inactive, for history has shown the South the price of passivity, inactivity, and silence.

How does the strategy of pitting evil against good function for the speaker? It allows Wallace to engage the audience in a conflict, and we attend to conflict and combat.[10] We cannot easily escape from a battle, so we are drawn into a speech which without this strategy would be only a typical campaign speech. Wallace's strategy allows his audiences to polarize *against* whatever they identify as the source of frustration in their public lives and *for* themselves and their own power. It allows his audiences to feel as though they are doing something just by listening intently, for it takes energy to listen to such a vigorous address. It allows the audiences to congratulate themselves in their wisdom, for here is a *Governor* finally *saying* what *they* have been *thinking* for a long time. It also gives Wallace a very practical way of gaining support not only for his state administration but also for his presidential campaign. While asking nothing specific of either the citizens of Alabama or her legislators, Wallace does ask them to "wake up" and cast a ballot. (But the people cannot cast a ballot for George Wallace in *1971;* their first chance is *1972.*)

This discussion of the dominant strategy of the speech has demonstrated Wallace's world-view to be one of opposing forces—good versus evil, little versus big, honesty versus deceit, the people versus the government. It has also demonstrated that Wallace is on a crusade to save *his image of America,* an America where there are no tendencies by the federal government to by tyrannical, abusive, and despotic, and an America where the people express themselves peacefully. We know more about what kind of America Mr. Wallace *does not want* than about what kind of America he *does want.* We can only infer from his general commitments to keep his administration honest and open, to reduce utility rates and basic insurance costs, to provide adequate medical services for all people, to equalize the tax burden, to fight drug abuse, and to streamline and modernize state

government that these are the features of an America he wants. If this list reads remarkably like any candidate's campaign brochure, recall that the purposes of the "Second
Inaugural" reach far beyond accepting the oath of office.

The final content of Wallace's strategy is to coalesce the people around his leadership.
He is capable of leading the people because he has identified the enemy, and, as we all
know, to identify the problem is half the battle. He is capable of leading because he has
faith in the people, and it is the people who elect politicians. He is capable of leading
because he is committed; he tells us that. He is capable of leading the people because he
recognizes the urgency of the problem and is ready to act now, for he has "promises to
keep and miles to go before he sleeps."

Style

Governor Wallace's characteristic method of expressing himself[11] is integrated with his
strategy. Three of his more typical and useful stylistic features include: (1) piling adjective on adjective or noun on noun in phrase patterns of three or four words in a series, (2)
using dynamic metaphors and intense vocabulary, and (3) matching his language with that
of his supporters.

Several purposes are accomplished by using series of words and phrases when one such
phrase would convey the same basic meaning. First, the pattern *magnifies* the evil or
emphasizes the importance of the act to be performed. Federal intrusion is not just
undesirable, it is "unwarranted, unwise, and unwanted." Drug abuse is not merely going
to be stopped; it is going to be stopped "forcefully, fully, and immediately." Wallace is
not just pleased with young voters participating in politics; we "welcome, seek and solicit
their aid, assistance, and encouragement." He has not only raised the tax issue once; he
has raised it "again, again, and again." Occasionally, Mr. Wallace combines a series of
three phrases or words with a series of four, and then the total effect is even more
noticeable.

> These are the *honest, hard working, God fearing, freedom loving* men and women
> of our state who through *the sweat of their brow, the toil of their bodies,* and *the
> strength and courage of their convictions* form the *muscle, bone,* and *sinew* of that
> great and good land. . . . (3; italics mine)

While the speaker's series of modifiers are repetitive and thus emphasize and reempha-
size the ideas, Wallace also uses this style of expression to list what is to be done. For
example, the individual citizen has a duty to: (1) "voice his opinion," (2) "make his
thoughts heard in a peaceful manner," and (3) "stand up for what he believes in."

Several additional effects are generated from Governor Wallace's use of this reiterative
pattern. The habit of piling on modifiers allows Wallace to *seem specific* and *appear to
develop* ideas while really repeating the idea already introduced. It also allows him to
praise magnaminously:

> To you I say that we are conscious of your pride, your courage, your fierce
> independence and your deep devotion to those principles. . . . (4)

The speech is made more rhythmical by Wallace's use of words in a series. For example,
say aloud: "unwarranted, unwise, and unwanted" or "forcefully, fully, and immediately."

Finally, this stylistic feature aids in the *recall of a feeling, not an idea.* Repetition that magnifies a simple statement does not challenge intellectual exercise; nor does it call for exercise of one's best logical skill. Instead it stimulates *psychological* activity.

Wallace's language intensity,[12] like the phrase patterns, stimulates psychological reaction. The speaker is intense both in the metaphors he chooses and in the adjectives and verbs he uses. Some of his more intense and imagistic metaphors are:

"pawns in the hands of powerful politicians"
"evil now stalking this land"
"preying on young and old alike"
"the government riding roughshod over the mind and body of its youth"

The image of the government as a roughrider simply but creatively reveals Wallace's belief that the people are being trampled by a wreckless force that moves so rapidly that we are being physically, intellectually, and psychologically destroyed without realizing it.

In addition to the metaphors, Wallace prefers strong terms that help dramatize his strategy of pitting absolutes against each other. One of his favorite and more forceful terms in the "Second Inaugural" is the word "destroy"; we are threatened with "tax destruction" and there are forces which would destroy us; hence we in turn must *destroy.* We must also unite against *"despotic tyranny"* of a federal government run by *"malicious* men" who commit *"willful* acts" against those who believe in government by law. The list of dynamic and intense words could continue, but the point is that whenever Wallace can use an active verb or a vivid, forceful modifier rather than a passive and mild word, he will.

A third characteristic of Governor Wallace's style is that it is plain, angry, and vague. In these respects, his style matches the style of many of his supporters. He speaks their language. If one examines some of the responses that people give to the question, Why do you support George Wallace?, he finds responses like these:

George Wallace is the only man that can put this country back where it belongs and give people back their rights.

I don't like what is happening to us. It is enough to make your backbone curl up.

I think we really need a change in this country, and get it back where it belongs.

I think the Supreme Court is taking over this country. I don't think they should.

The country is going backward. I think he will lead it forward.

He is the man who stands up and talks straight off the shoulder exactly the way things are. He doesn't beat around the bush like the majority of these other politicians do.[13]

Common to all of these statements is the overgeneralization about a mass of complex problems and a belief that "turning this country around" is the answer to all those problems. The language is as simplistic, bitter, and equivocal as Wallace's. Perhaps the best proof that Wallace's style is successful is this response from a voter in Florida, "Governor Wallace is the only man in politics that I have heard speak the truth. In the days of lies and deceit and hypicrisy, *I find refuge in this man's rhetoric.*"[14] (italics mine)

Conclusions

George Wallace's 1971 "Second Inaugural" is more of a campaign address than a typical promise to remain loyal to his Office. The speech is particularly interesting for it reveals the essence of Wallace's style and strategy as he approaches political issues and appeals for support. This criticism reveals that what Wallace says is not so unique; what makes the candidate and this speech special is his skillful development of a strategy that exaggerates and condemns and then offers a simplistic solution that will let us solve our problems. Because Governor Wallace can communicate his world-view so dynamically and because his world-view matches that of his supporters, Mr. Wallace and this address are successful.

We have seen that the central strategy in the "Second Inaugural" is to engage the audience in a conflict between good and evil. The strategy of identifying abusive use of federal power and coining "people power" as the force strong enough to slay the dragon allows Wallace to name and blame without developing specific arguments or proposals for really improving life in Alabama and America. Consisting of a series of sermonettes and campaign promises, the speech is balanced between discussion of the evil and indication of how the good can triumph. A surprising lack of attention is given to the immediate occasion and the specific programs Wallace will implement as the new Gorvernor, but, then, he has "miles to go before he sleeps."

The contribution of the speech lies in its inspirational quality which is created by stylistic support of the central, gripping strategy. The style reveals the essence of Wallace as rhetor and just may be the best explanation of why he gathers the number and diversity of supporters he does. Without his exaggerated style and extremist strategy, Wallace might not be seen as the "devil's advocate" by his opponents or the best presidential contender by his supporters. The style and strategy correlate to make the "Second Inaugural" a firm step in George Corley Wallace's steady march to the presidency as he heads his mass movement to "turn this country around."

Notes

1. Richard Hofstadter, "The Paranoid Style in American Politics," *The Paranoid Style in American Politics and Other Essays* (New York: Alfred A. Knopf, 1965), pp. 3-4.

2. Ibid., p. xii.

3. Ibid., pp. 29-39. The eight characteristics listed are this writer's summary; Professor Hofstadter provides several examples and full discussion of the distinguishing features of what he calls the "paranoid style." He further identifies this style with leaders of minority movements, used by speakers on both the political left and right.

4. In the literature "objectification" refers to naming a class, group, or institution as the guilty party of the foe to be opposed; "villification" refers to condemning and blaming a specific individual. The use of objectification lets the speaker cite general objects of displeasure, and the listeners can supply their specific connotations of the object and thus personalize their anger. Objectification has the advantage of condemning more lasting institutions or agencies while villification condemns a person who may be out of office in two years and thus a fruitless force to aid in polarization of the crusader's cause. For good discussions of these two and other strategies available to protesters see, for example: Arthur Smith, *The Rhetoric of Black Revolution* (Boston: Allyn and Bacon, 1969), pp. 25-42 and John Bowers and Donovan Ochs, *The Rhetoric of Agitation and Control* (Reading, Mass.: Addison-Wesley Publishing Company, Inc., 1971), pp. 16-56.

5. George C. Wallace, "The Civil Rights Bill: Fraud, Sham, and Hoax," delivered July 4, 1964, reprinted in Floyd W. Matson, ed., *Voices of Crisis* (New York: Odyssey Press, Inc., 1967), p. 179.

6. George C. Wallace, "Address on Law Enforcement," delivered to Fraternal Order of Police, Miami, Florida, August 29, 1967, reprinted in James C. McCroskey, *An Introduction to Rhetorical Communication* (Englewood Cliffs, N.J.: Prentice-Hall, Inc., 1968), p. 271.

7. Ibid., pp. 274-75.

8. The campaign slogan is mentioned as "carry back the message" and "the message you are going to send back to this nation" in George C. Wallace's "Speech at Birmingham, Alabama," delivered April 10, 1970, reprinted in L. Patrick Devlin, *Contemporary Political Speaking* (Belmont, California: Wadsworth Publishing Co., Inc., 1971), p. 86.

9. Of the 40 paragraphs, 27.5 percent deal with the source of evil; 27.5 percent deal directly with "people power" as the force capable of destroying federal intrusion and opporession; roughly one-fourth of the speech deals with praising Alabamians for their success in developing fine schools and public institutions, and the remaining fourth of the speech is spent of Wallace's commitments to his office and an explanation of why he is there.

10. In a 1969 article Professor Rosenfield suggested that what remained of Wallace's image in the minds of the viewers after they turned the television set off was "Most likely a tableau depicting George Wallace *combatively* (italics mine) arrayed against most respectable issues." Lawrence W. Rosenfield, "George Wallace Plays Rosemary's Baby," *Quarterly Journal of Speech* (February 1969), p. 44.

11. In the first chapter of her book on style, Professor Blankenship defines "style" as "one's characteristic way of using the English language"; it is in this sense that style is used in the following discussion. Jane Blankenship, *A Sense of Style* (Belmont: Dickenson Publishing Co., Inc., 1968), p. 11.

12. "Language intensity" refers to the degree of forcefulness of the utterance. Specifically, John Bowers' definition of language intensity as "the quality of language which indicates the degree to which the speaker's attitude toward a concept deviates from neutrality" is assumed here. John Waite Bowers, "Language Intensity, Social Introversion, and Attitude Change," *Speech Monographs* (November 1963), p. 345. See also, William J. McEwen and Bradley S. Greenberg, "The Effects of Message Intensity on Receiver Evaluations of Source, Message and Topic," *Journal of Communication* (December 1970), pp. 340-41.

13. *Wallace Labor Action,* a tabloid created and produced by Organized Labor Members for the Wallace Campaign, p. 2. Obtained from Wallace Campaign Headquarters, P.O. Box 1972, Birmingham, Alabama.

14. Ibid.

GEORGE WALLACE: POLITICAL SATIRIST

EDWARD MURPHY

American humor has long been characterized by outrageous and witty exaggeration. Authors since the days of Ben Franklin have taken liberties with reality in order to achieve comic effect. H. L. Mencken, for example, became famous for his overstatements. "No man," he once wrote, "is genuinely happy, married, who has to drink worse gin than he used to drink when he was single." Another master of hyperbole was Will Rogers who once sent his niece a picture postcard of Venus de Milo from Italy; on it he wrote: "See what'll happen to you if you don't stop biting your nails."[1]

It is not surprising that this penchant for hyperbole has carried over into other areas of American life, particularly into our political affairs where it is often equally outrageous but occasionally less witty. Most citizens will recall, for example, the dozens of times in recent years when the Vietnam war was "on the verge" of being won, the many "corners" that we turned (so many that South Vietnam seems like an infinitely-sided polygon), and the innumerable occasions upon which the "light at the end of the tunnel"

This piece was originally prepared for this volume. © 1972 Edward M. Murphy. For permission to reprint contact author of the piece directly, University of Massachusetts, Amherst 01002.

became visible to some Pentagon visionary. Indeed, it seems that the most significant outcome of the Indochina war has been the emergence of the military establishment as a rival to elected politicians in the dissemination of hyperbole.

Both elected politicians and candidates for elective office are still the disputed masters of *The Big Truth.*[2] In fact, our highest offices are likely to go to those politicians whose exaggerations are the grandest. The political career of Richard M. Nixon provides an interesting illustration. Nixon's successful senatorial campaign against Helen Gahagan Douglas in 1950 was characterized by exaggerations of the "commie-behind-every-tree" variety.[3] His famous 1952 "Checkers" speech set a pattern of hyperbole that persists into his presidential years. As a vice-presidential candidate, Nixon claimed that the disclosure of his financial background was "unprecedented in the history of American politics."[4] Twenty years later, as President, he offered, to the North Vietnamese, peace terms that were "the maximum of what any President of the United States could offer."[5] Nixon fathered the "New American Revolution"[6] and he spent "the week that changed the world" in China.[7] In attempting to make himself appear sublime, Nixon differs only in degree from other contemporary politicians who feel that they must expand on their exceedingly modest exploits. But there are a few people in political life who manage to go beyond simple exaggeration, who raise hyperbole to the status of an art, the art of satire.

Satire: Criticism Through Exaggeration

Satire, which is found in all time periods and in all cultures, is a curious mixture of exaggeration and restraint. Such a mixture can be easily seen in Jonathan Swift's *A Modest Proposal,* one of the most famous satires in the English language. Published in 1729, at a time when Ireland was undergoing one of its numerous famines, Swift's proposal was that Irish peasants should eat their babies. Writing in a moderate, even bland tone, Swift pointed out that this solution would halt the growth of an already over-crowded population, provide food for people who would otherwise starve to death, reduce the number of "papists," and generally contribute to a higher standard of living. *A Modest Proposal* is, in fact, a scathing indictment of British rule in Ireland. Swift could have presented his attack in a direct plea, but, by presenting his atrocious scheme with feigned reasonableness, he made moderation seem comic. He even went so far as to explain the details of the slaughter.

> A child will make two dishes at an entertainment for friends; and when the family dines alone, the fore or hind quarter will make a reasonable dish, and, seasoned with a little pepper and salt, will be very good boiled on the fourth day, especially in winter . . . .

> Those who are more thrifty (as I must confess the times require) may flay the carcase; the skin of which, artificially dressed, will make admirable gloves for ladies, and summer boots for fine gentlemen.[8]

These details are, of course, absurd, but by their very specificity they heighten the dramatic impact of Swift's criticism.

Swift's essay teaches us several things about satire. First, satire is always critical, and in this sense it is the most rhetorical of all the forms of literature. The practice, and the understanding, of satire presupposes a knowledge of rhetorical devices like irony and metaphor. More importantly, satirists have traditionally excelled at argumentation; they are, after all, trying to compel us to take some action, to recognize some vice, to correct some deficiency. To be successful, satire "must practice the art of persuasion and become proficient with the tools of that art." Rhetoric teaches those lessons.[9]

Secondly, satire distorts that which is familiar.

> All satire is exaggeration. It always intensifies or contrasts dramatically, or empha-
> sizes one thing at the expense of something else. But it does so more obviously than
> other literary forms and achieves humor because . . . by confusing the categories of
> actuality, exaggeration implies that these categories are ultimately unimportant. By
> distorting accepted values, exaggeration makes them seem ludicrous.[10]

This distortion, when vividly displayed, forms the heart of any satire. For example, Swift's eighteenth-century peers considered themselves to be men of reason but, by "rationally" proposing cannibalism, Swift showed them that their logic was inadequate to deal with the pressing human problems of the day. Their "reason," in its mercantile manifestation, had, in fact, created the horrible conditions of starvation in Ireland. Thus, "true satire implies the condemnation of society by reference to an ideal; the satirist is engaged in measuring the monstrous aberration from that ideal."[11] Exaggeration and hyperbole, by distorting the ideal, become the instruments of measurement.

George Wallace: Political Satirist

Contemporary political satire comes from several sources. First, and most obvious, are the professional critics like Art Buchwald, Russell Baker and Arthur Hoppe. These men produce, on an irregular basis, literature that we recognize as satire. Second is the entertainment industry where we find films like *Dr. Strangelove* and occasional satiric routines by television comedians. Finally we have the politicians themselves; this is a source that has gone largely unnoticed by the general public.

There are many funny people in politics today, but one should not get the impression that all of these people are satirists. Indeed, with the possible exception of Senator Roman Hruska,[12] there has not been a genuinely good satirist in Washington since Joe McCarthy died.[13] But there are at least two good satirist-politicians at large in the country today. These are, of course, George Wallace and Pat Paulsen.[14]

A comparison of the respective political careers of George Wallace and Pat Paulsen provides an insight into contemporary values and an important object lesson for any aspiring satirist-politicians: The public will sooner accept a politician turned comedian than a comedian turned politician. True, there are some surface differences between Wallace and Paulsen—one is a Democrat while the other is a Republican, and Wallace has lost three Presidential races while Paulsen has lost only two—but their comic styles are quite similar. Both employ outrageous hyperbole, clever grammatical construction, double meaning phrases, and a generally diffusive approach to political affairs.

Paulsen achieves his satiric effect by mimicking, and exaggerating, the normal style of political campaigning. On the stump in New Hampshire, Paulsen explained his program. He made promises:

> Let me make one thing perfectly clear to a nation sick of solutions: I bring the
> hope of promise. I promise to halt the bombing in Vietnam, end the war and secure
> a total victory on terms acceptable to both sides.

He identified his constituency:

> I represent all that is mediocre in this country and I'm proud of it for this is a
> country rich in mediocrity.

And he appealed to the higher planes of the national spirit:

> So hold your head up high, America, and look at the sky. Look at the lofty
> skyscrapers and the towering smokestacks and tell me this doesn't inspire a catch in
> your breath, a tear in your eye and a murmur in your heart.[15]

The very first paragraphs of George Wallace's inaugural address reveal direct similarities
to Paulsen's style. Wallace says that he is

> humbled to stand before you and in your presence . . . humbled by the trust . . .
> you have entrusted to me . . . . (1)

Just as Paulsen had done, Wallace insults his audience in a cleverly left-handed way by
saying that those "who cannot honor us with their presence" today are the people who
earn a living through "honest toil." (2) The obvious implication is that those who are
present do not earn a living through honest toil.

Wallace's bombastic description of the people of Alabama follows the time-honored
rules of satire by carrying the mean to its ridiculous conclusion.

> These are the honest, hard working, God fearing, freedom loving men and women
> of our state who through the sweat of their brow, the toil of their bodies and the
> strength and courage of their convictions form the muscle, bone and sinew of that
> great and good land that we know as Alabama. (3)

The governor contends that the system of trade schools and junior colleges in Alabama
is "admired and envied by all our sister states." (5) The system is indeed admired, at least
by the governors of other financially pressed states who are eager to learn how Alabama
manages to spend so little. Wallace's state habitually lags behind the others in aid to
education.[16]

Next, Wallace degenerates into a Paulsen-like incoherence with a discussion of legal
responsibilities and corresponding rights. The drift of Wallace's pronouncements seem to
be that we should obey repressive laws while continuing to stand up against the federal
government. Wallace ironically expands his discussion to include the rights of all Americans, "both black and white." (12) The white members of the Governor's audience would
surely smile at the recollection of the decidedly racist campaign that Wallace supporters
had just waged against Albert Brewer.[17] But a satirist can't make everybody laugh and,
for the black members of the audience, that recollection was distinctly unfunny.

George Wallace brings down the house with his puns ("among the greatest patriots of all
time" are "those who bore us"), his mixed metaphors ("the flame of our passion burned
within us as an arc of our covenant"), and his feeble mimicking of Agnewian rhetoric
("government has become stagnated with burdensome bigness").[18] (31, 33, 37)

Any satirist-politician as successful as George Wallace is certainly aware of the importance of comedy as an instrument for social change. Communication theorist Hugh
Duncan points out that "jokes serve as a resistance against authority and as an escape

from its pressure."[19] By poking fun at the federal bureaucrat-sociologist, Wallace resists the authority of the central government. But his satire is conservative as well as radical because he wishes to substitute a new authority, his own, for the one that he wants to displace. Satiric comedy begins by exposing authority but it must also end in some kind of authority.[20]

Wallace, like all satirists, needs a scapegoat. "Through the comic perspective we view the spectacle of the deceiver deceived and laugh at his punishment because he deserves it."[21] The scapegoat in Wallace's speech hardly need comment. He is the greedy, wilful, yelping, malicious, despotic, slimy, social planner who would rob us of our rights, suppress our liberty and push drugs on the side. Comedy, Duncan says, "treats incongruity as ignorance of proper social ends." And Wallace's scapegoat is as ignorant as they come.

> Comic incongruities arise as we confront one audience with what is meant for another, or as we let one audience 'overhear' what is supposed to be kept secret from it.[22]

Considering Wallace's prominence and the well-known likelihood that he would run for President again, it is certain that more than a few of the scapegoats were eavesdropping on his speech that day.[23]

Wallace, like Swift before him, proposes a method of dealing with the problem that borders on the farcical.[24] With a final ironic twist, Wallace calls for "people power," a movement designed to insure that the pie of public opinion is "thrust into the face of the Washington bureaucrat." (15)

Clearly, George Wallace is fed up with politics as usual in the United States. The common people must be freed "from unwarranted, unwise and unwanted intrusion and oppression by the federal government." (8) He recognizes that politics as usual is often constituted by politicians who do little more than flatter the electrorate and make undeliverable promises. Wallace has apparently decided that his brand of dissent will be satirical.

Notes

1. Leonard Feinberg, *Introduction to Satire* (Ames: Iowa State University Press, 1967), p. 106.

2. *The Big Truth,* an expansion of a simple, unimpressive truth, is not to be confused with *The Big Lie* used by Hitler et al., which is the expansion of a simple, unimpressive lie.

3. Robert Griffith, *The Politics of Fear* (New York: Hayden Book Company, Inc., 1971), p. 88.

4. The entire speech is reprinted in *U.S. News and World Report* (October 3, 1952), pp. 66-70.

5. *The New York Times* (May 9, 1972), p. 18.

6. *Newsweek* (February 1, 1971), p. 15.

7. *Newsweek (March 13, 1972), p. 18. Also, in his "Silent Majority" speech of November 3, 1969,* Mr. Nixon took "the unprecedented step of disclosing" some secret peace initiatives. See: *Vital Speeches* (November 15, 1969), p. 67. On June 3, 1970, Mr. Nixon said that his decision to invade Cambodia "was subjected to an unprecedented barrage of criticism." See *The New York Times,* (June 4, 1970).

8. "A Modest Proposal" appears in many anthologies, among them is *The Rhetoric of No,* R. Fabrizio, E. Karas, and R. Menmuir, eds., (New York: Holt, Rinehart and Winston, Inc., 1970), pp. 341-48. The "Proposal" is also treated by Gilbert Highet in *The Anatomy of Satire* (Princeton: Princeton University Press, 1962), pp. 57-61.

9. David Worcester, *The Art of Satire* (New York: Russell & Russell, 1960), pp. 8-9.

10. Feinberg, p. 105.

11. J. Middleton Murry, *The Problem of Style,* cited in Basil Willey, *The Eighteenth Century Background* (Boston: Beacon Press, 1961), p. 101. Willey discusses the intellectual climate that produced the great satires of Swift and others, pp. 100-9.

12. Roman Hruska, U.S. Senator from Nebraska, gained a measure of notoriety by defending the "mediocrity" of Supreme Court nominee G. Harrold Carswell.

13. A lot of people apparently thought that Joe McCarthy was serious, but an examination of his speeches reveals all the elements of great satire. In fact, McCarthy gained a status attained by few other satirists, he became a caricature of himself. One person who has recognized McCarthy for what he was is the hilarious William F. Buckley, Jr. Buckley has continued the tongue-in-cheek McCarthy tradition. See: *McCarthy and His Enemies* (Henry Regnery Co., 1954 and 1961). See also the confessions of the ingenuous McCarthy straightman, Roy Cohn, in his book, *McCarthy* (New American Library, 1968).

14. Political satirists come from all parts of the political spectrum. For example, Jerry Rubin recently told a Florida television audience that "ten thousand naked hippies" would descend on Miami Beach for the 1972 Democratic Convention. Hunter S. Thompson, "Fear and Loathing: The Banshee Screams in Florida," *Rolling Stone* (April 13, 1972), p. 6. Abbie Hoffman, while giving a speech on Boston Common, pointed to the obelisk-like John Hancock Building and said that it was, in fact, "a giant syringe."

15. James Conaway "Paulsen for President," *The New York Times Magazine* (March 5, 1972), p. 58.

16. According to the *1971 Standard Educational Almanac,* Alabama spends less per pupil on elementary and secondary education than any other state (table 83). In per capita expenditures for all educational purposes, Alabama ranked 45th (table 22).

17. See the introduction to the three critical essays on the Wallace speech for more information on the campaign.

18. Vice President Agnew has a well-known fondness for alliteration. For example, he referred to television news commentators as "the super-sensitive, self-annointed, supercilious electronic barons of opinion." This remark was delivered, appropriately enough, in Birmingham, Alabama, on October 28, 1970. For this and other examples of Agnewspeak, see *Collected Speeches of Spiro Agnew* (Audubon Books, 1971).

19. Hugh D. Duncan, *Communication and Social Order* (New York: Oxford University Press, 1968), p. 376.

20. Ibid., p. 390.

21. Ibid., p. 402.

22. Ibid., p. 407.

23. Paulsen recognizes and speaks to his concealed audience. Opening a speech in New Hampshire, he said:

Fellow scholars, members of the faculty, representatives of the F.B.I. and the C.I.A., state and local police. *(New York Times Magazine,* March 5, 1972, p. 58.)

24. Gilbert Highet explores the relationship between farce and satire in *The Anatomy of Satire,* pp. 154-55.